BESTSELLING
BOOK SERIES

Adopting a Pet For Dummies®

Cheat Sheet

SO-AAD-658

What to Find Out Before You Adopt

Ask a shelter worker or rescuer

- What is the pet's probable age, breed, and gender?

- What is the pet's past health history? Is the pet spayed or neutered? Has he had all his vaccinations? Has she had any training?

- Does the pet have any current health problems that you'll need to deal with?

- What is the pet's temperament like? Is he shy, aggressive, hand-tame? Is she afraid of anything in particular? Is he hyperactive or a real couch potato?

- What are the pet's grooming needs?

- Does the pet get along with other pets? What about kids?

- Is the pet housetrained, cage trained, or litter-box trained? If so, what kind of litter-box filler is used?

- What has the pet been eating?

- How many homes has the pet had already? How long has the pet been with the shelter or rescue group?

- Does the pet show any signs of abuse? Does he need any special care or considerations?

Signs of a Healthy Animal

- Bright, shiny eyes with no discharge.

- Cool moist nose (for mammals) with no discharge.

- Clean, shiny, soft coat with no mats, tangles, dirt, or signs of skin irritation like rashes, sores, or hair loss (for mammals).

- Tight shiny bright scales or feathers (for reptiles and birds).

- Moist, bright, clear skin with no flakes or sores (for amphibians).

- Active and interested in you. Cautiousness is okay, but cowering in fear or lunging aggressively can be signs of ill health and/or a bad temperament.

A Quick Check for Good Temperament

- **Approach the pet.** Does he want to interact with you? Pets with good temperaments are confident and curious.

- **Try to touch the pet.** Does she flee, shy away, or try to bite you? Pets with good temperaments are not shy or aggressive, although some animals naturally will be that way at first.

- **Try to hold the pet.** Does he snuggle in, explore you, or engage you in play? Or does he try desperately to escape? Tame pets don't mind handling. Mammals that consistently resist handling *may* have some temperament problems.

- **Remember not to make snap judgments.** Your adopted pet has been through a lot. Spend several visits together in a relaxed setting to get the best idea of temperament. Apparent shyness or aggressiveness on a first visit may not always be indicative of the pet's real temperament.

For Dummies: Bestselling Book Series for Beginners

Adopting a Pet For Dummies®

Cheat Sheet

Your Adopted Pet's Personal Record

Name	
Date of adoption	
Age when adopted	
Breed/species	
General health history	
Vaccinations	
Spay/neuter date	
Nutritional needs	
Specific care needs	
Special issues/problems, including date	
General notes	

Your Adopted Pet's Essential Phone Numbers

Shelter/rescue group	
Veterinarian(s)	
After-hours animal hospital	
ASPCA Poison Control Center	1-888-426-4435
Other important numbers	

Best Adopted Pet Resources

- Petfinder: www.petfinder.com
- Pets 911: www.pets911.com
- 1-800-Save-a-Pet: www.1-800-save-a-pet.com
- ASPCA: www.aspca.org
- Humane Society of the United States: www.hsus.org

For Dummies: Bestselling Book Series for Beginners

Adopting a Pet
FOR
DUMMIES®

Adopting a Pet

FOR
DUMMIES®

by Eve Adamson

Wiley Publishing, Inc.

Adopting a Pet For Dummies®

Published by
Wiley Publishing, Inc.
111 River St.
Hoboken, NJ 07030-5774
www.wiley.com

WILEY

About the Author

Eve Adamson is an award-winning pet writer and the author, coauthor, or contributor to more than 40 books including *Labrador Retrievers For Dummies* and *Dachshunds For Dummies*. She is a contributing editor for *Dog Fancy* magazine and writes frequently for many pet publications; among them are *Your Dog, Dogs USA, Puppies USA, Cat Fancy, Cats USA, Kittens USA, Veterinary Practice News,* and *Popular Pets,* including the issues on *Guinea Pigs, Rats,* and many issues on dog training and behavior. She writes the "Good Grooming" column for *AKC Family Dog* magazine and a breed profile column and a natural dog care column for *Pet Product News,* and she is a member of the Dog Writer's Association of America and the Cat Writer's Association of America.

Eve is an active supporter of the Iowa City/Coralville Animal Adoption Center, where she adopted her terrier, Sally, in 1999. She lives with her family in Iowa City, which includes partner Ben Minkler, sons Angus and Emmett, terriers Sally and Jack, a parakeet named Snugglebunny, a dwarf hamster named Mr. Hampy, and three little fish ceremoniously dubbed Little Fishies 1, 2, and 3. You can find out more about Eve and her most recent publications at her Web site, www.eveadamson.com.

Dedication

This book is dedicated to all the animals around the world tamed by humans but then left behind and to all the humans who stood up, stepped forward, and put their hearts on the line to give these animals a second chance at health and happiness. This book is also dedicated to Sally, my heart dog.

Author's Acknowledgments

Thank you to the many people who have helped this book come to fruition: Stacy Kennedy, who brought me this project in the first place with the confidence that it was the right book for me; Alissa Schwipps, for her amazingly perceptive editing skills; Lee Ann Chearney, my agent, who always looks out for my best interests no matter how much time she doesn't have; Jennifer Doll, DVM, who provided such wonderful comments and edits to this book from the vet's point of view; and to Ben for keeping children and dogs out of the office when I was absolutely under deadline and for being so patient about it all.

Thanks also to the Iowa City/Coralville Animal Adoption Center for providing so many helpful resources, and to the many experts out there — whose passions may be dogs, cats, guinea pigs, rats, rabbits, parrots, snakes, iguanas, or spiders — who not only have helped me with my specific questions but who also spend so much of their time and energy providing exceptionally valuable online information, forums, and resources for new pet owners, all for free. You provide adopted pets and their people with an invaluable service and have certainly saved many lives.

Publisher's Acknowledgments

We're proud of this book; please send us your comments through our Dummies online registration form located at www.dummies.com/register/.

Some of the people who helped bring this book to market include the following:

Acquisitions, Editorial, and Media Development

Senior Project Editor: Alissa Schwipps

Acquisitions Editor: Stacy Kennedy

Copy Editor: E. Neil Johnson

Technical Editor: Jennifer Doll, DVM

Senior Editorial Manager: Jennifer Ehrlich

Editorial Assistants: Hanna Scott, Nadine Bell

Cover Photos: ©Andrew Linscott/Alamy

Cartoons: Rich Tennant (www.the5thwave.com)

Composition Services

Project Coordinator: Ryan Steffen

Layout and Graphics: Joyce Haughey, Stephanie D. Jumper, Clint Lahnan, Barbara Moore, Barry Offringa, Heather Ryan, Erin Zeltner

Special Art: Lisa Reed, illustrations, and Todd Adamson, photographs

Proofreaders: Leeann Harney, Carl William Pierce, Charles Spencer, TECHBOOKS Production Services

Indexer: TECHBOOKS Production Services

Publishing and Editorial for Consumer Dummies

Diane Graves Steele, Vice President and Publisher, Consumer Dummies

Joyce Pepple, Acquisitions Director, Consumer Dummies

Kristin A. Cocks, Product Development Director, Consumer Dummies

Michael Spring, Vice President and Publisher, Travel

Kelly Regan, Editorial Director, Travel

Publishing for Technology Dummies

Andy Cummings, Vice President and Publisher, Dummies Technology/General User

Composition Services

Gerry Fahey, Vice President of Production Services

Debbie Stailey, Director of Composition Services

Contents at a Glance

Introduction 1

Part I: All About Pet Adoption 7
Chapter 1: Exploring the Pet Adoption Option................................9
Chapter 2: Seeking Shelter: Finding and Using Animal Shelters................23
Chapter 3: Rescue Me! All About Pet Rescue Groups................35

Part II: Welcoming a Dog into Your Life 49
Chapter 4: Choosing Your Dog................................51
Chapter 5: Helping Your Adopted Dog Make the Homecoming Transition 73
Chapter 6: Caring for Your Adopted Dog................................91
Chapter 7: Doggy Boot Camp: Basic Training and Behavior Management............109

Part III: Here Kitty Kitty: Rescuing a Cat 135
Chapter 8: Finding the Purrrfect Feline for You................................137
Chapter 9: Welcoming Home Your Adopted Cat................................151
Chapter 10: Kitty Care................................165
Chapter 11: You Really Can Train a Cat................................183

Part IV: Befriending a Little Critter 197
Chapter 12: Choosing Your Critter................................199
Chapter 13: Getting Ready for Your Critter................................213
Chapter 14: Taking Charge of Your Critter's Care................................221
Chapter 15: Critter Behavior and Training................................231

Part V: Bringing Home a Feathered Friend 245
Chapter 16: From Macaws to Budgies: Choosing Your Feathered Friend 247
Chapter 17: Creating a Bird-Friendly Home................................259
Chapter 18: Caring for Your Adopted Bird................................269
Chapter 19: Training Your Bird................................281

Part VI: Giving an Exotic a Second Chance 295
Chapter 20: Choosing a Creepy Crawler................................297
Chapter 21: Preparing for Your Exotic Pet................................307
Chapter 22: Exotic Care and Feeding................................317
Chapter 23: Snake Charming and Herp Handling: How to Train Your Exotic Pet 329

Part VII: The Part of Tens 339

Chapter 24: Ten Great Reasons to Spay or Neuter Your Adopted Pet.....................341
Chapter 25: Ten Favors You Can Do for Your Adopted Pet.......................................343
Chapter 26: Ten Ways to Support Your Local Shelter or Rescue Group 345

Index 347

Table of Contents

Introduction 1

About This Book 2
Conventions Used in This Book 3
What You're Not to Read 3
Foolish Assumptions 4
How This Book Is Organized 4
    Part I: All About Pet Adoption 4
    Part II: Welcoming a Dog into Your Life 5
    Part III: Here Kitty Kitty: Rescuing a Cat 5
    Part IV: Befriending a Little Critter 5
    Part V: Bringing Home a Feathered Friend 5
    Part VI: Giving an Exotic a Second Chance 5
    Part VII: The Part of Tens 6
Icons Used in This Book 6
Where to Go from Here 6

Part 1: All About Pet Adoption 7

Chapter 1: Exploring the Pet Adoption Option 9

Making Sure You're Ready to Be a Good Pet Parent 9
    Considering the time commitment 10
    Being mindful of housing restrictions 12
    Affording a pet 13
The Good Part: Adopted Pets = Love 14
Perfect Pet Profile Quiz: Find Out What Kind of Pet You Really Want 15
Beyond the Glamour: What It Means to Adopt 18
    A dog 18
    A cat 19
    A small mammal 19
    A birdie 20
    An exotic 21
Finding Your New Best Friend through Shelters,
   Humane Societies, and Rescues 21
    Uncovering the basics of animal shelters 22
    Demystifying the rescue group 22

Chapter 2: Seeking Shelter: Finding and Using Animal Shelters ... 23

Animal Shelters Explained 24
    Shelter pros 26
    Shelter cons 27

Finding a Great Shelter Near You 28
    Checking the Yellow Pages and Internet 28
    Rounding up recommendations 29
Walking through the Adoption Process...30
    Checking out the facility...30
    Looking at the pets...31
    Asking the right questions 32
    Avoiding second thoughts: The waiting period 33
Sealing the Deal 34

Chapter 3: Rescue Me! All About Pet Rescue Groups 35

Weighing the Pros and Cons of Adopting from a Rescue Group..............36
    Rescue group pros 36
    Rescue group cons 38
Scouting Out a Particular Rescue Group 38
    Asking around 39
    Surfing the Net 39
Surviving the Screening Process 40
    Making contact and checking references 41
    Answering questions, questions, and more questions..................42
    Preparing for a house visit 44
    Meeting the pets 45
Making a Commitment: Signing the Rescue Contract 47

Part II: Welcoming a Dog into Your Life 49

Chapter 4: Choosing Your Dog 51

Puppies Are Precious, but 51
    Pros and cons of adopting a puppy 52
    Pros and cons of adopting an adult dog..53
Deciding on a Male or Female..54
Identifying Signs of a Healthy Dog 55
    Bright eyes and bushy tails 55
    Skin-tastic 56
    Bringing up the rear 57
    The great big world: How the dog interacts 58
Temperament Testing...58
    Exploring the effects of breed temperament 59
    Understanding the basics of temperament...................................62
    Go-getters, chill-outers, and wait-and-seers 63
What Kind of Dog Is That? The Joy of Mixed Breeds...........................64
Adopting a Purebred Dog..66
    All about breed groups 67
    Good buddies: Companion dogs 67
    Imposing Guardian breeds 68
    Active Sporting breeds 69
    Born to run: Cold-hardy Northern breeds....................................70

Eye on the prize: Sighthounds 70
The nose knows: Scenthounds 71
Feisty Terrier breeds...71
Superfocused Herding breeds 72

**Chapter 5: Helping Your Adopted Dog
Make the Homecoming Transition** **73**
Preparing Your Pad 73
Puppy-proofing first (even for adult dogs) 74
Gathering doggy accoutrements 76
Welcoming Doggy Home...80
Dog, meet potty spot 80
Showing your dog to his den 81
Introducing your people...83
Introducing other pets...85
Downtime 88
Recognizing Adjustment Problems..89

Chapter 6: Caring for Your Adopted Dog **91**
Keeping Your Dog Healthy 92
First things first: Choosing a great vet...............................92
Giving your new friend a good once-over: The first exam 93
Noticing problems after you get home 97
Following up with an annual exam 99
Somebody's Hungry!..99
Choosing the right food for your dog 100
Addressing bad nutritional habits: What your dog
doesn't need to eat 101
Helping Fido's tummy transition 101
Deciding when to ring the dinner bell 102
Keeping an eye on your dog's waistline 102
Administering the body evaluation test 103
Correcting a weight problem 104
Good Grooming Matters...105
Grooming disguised as a checkup.....................................105
Brush, comb, trim, bathe, and polish 106

**Chapter 7: Doggy Boot Camp: Basic Training
and Behavior Management** **109**
Housetraining Made Easy...110
Beginning with the basics 110
Adding crate training 112
Adding schedule training 113
Dealing with mistakes 113
Teaching Good Doggy Manners...114
Off to school: Finding a training class 114
Socialization strategies..116
Teaching the building-block training cues 118

Breaking Adopted Dogs of Bad Habits 123
Managing Behavior Problems Common to Adopted Dogs.................125
  Lassie come home: Keeping your dog from running away 125
  Oh the noise, noise, noise, noise, noise:
    Curtailing excessive barking 126
  My dog is knocking me over: Teaching dogs
    to quit jumping up 127
  Didn't I have a couch here? Ending destructive chewing 127
  Ouch! Nipping that annoying nipping and biting 129
  But this is my dinner! Stopping your dog from begging..........129
  Where's the garden? Reclaiming your yard from a digger 130
Comeback Kid: Coping with Separation Anxiety 130
Who's the Boss? Managing Aggression 131
Managing the Mistreated Dog.......................................133
  Deciding whether you can handle a problem....................133
  Getting professional help 134

Part III: Here Kitty Kitty: Rescuing a Cat **135**

Chapter 8: Finding the Purrrfect Feline for You **137**
Deciding between a Kitten and a Cat...............................138
  Considering a kitten 138
  Acknowledging the advantages of an adult cat 139
  Boy cat or girl cat? 140
  What about feral and stray cats?.............................140
Recognizing Signs of a Healthy Cat................................141
  Silky coats and eyes like jewels 142
  Itchy kitty? Signs of parasites and skin/coat problems.......142
  The tail end 142
  Curiosity quotient: How your cat interacts 143
Temperament Testing...143
  Determining what traits suit your fancy.....................144
  Profiling kitty companions 144
  Asking the experts: Shelter workers
    provide the skinny on your kitty 145
Finding a Good Match: What to Expect
  from Different Breeds and Mixes 146
  Cats of undetermined origin: Mixed-breed cats 146
  Perfectly stunning Persians (and their relatives) 148
  Clever Siamese . . . both types!.............................149
  The all-American shorthairs 149
  Mellow Maine coons, America's native long-haired cat 150

Chapter 9: Welcoming Home Your Adopted Cat **151**
   Kitten-Proofing — Even For Adult Cats! 151
   Stocking Up on Supplies 153
      Gathering the basics 153
      Spoiling Fluffy with fancy supplies 157
   What to Expect When You Get Home 158
      Getting acclimated 158
      Meeting the family 159
      Meeting resident pets 160
      Run of the house 163
   Recognizing Adjustment Problems 164

Chapter 10: Kitty Care **165**
   Keeping Your Cat Healthy 165
      Choosing a great cat vet 166
      The first exam 166
      Remaining on the lookout for health problems 169
      Making time for an annual exam 172
   Chow Time! 173
      Choosing the right food for your cat .173
      Avoiding harmful foods 174
      Switching foods 175
      Deciding between free feeding and meal feeding 175
      Do you have a fat cat or a scrawny kitty? 176
   Helping Your Cat Practice Good Feline Hygiene 178
      Grooming disguised as a health-care checkup 178
      Brushing and combing basics 179
      Clipping nails down to size, not the quick 180
      Giving a cat a bath 181

Chapter 11: You Really Can Train a Cat **183**
   Not Going Outside the Box 184
      Kitty, meet litter 184
      Dealing with litter-box aversion 184
   Your Cat: Mighty Hunter 185
   Scratch Zone 186
   Foiling the Climbing Cat 188
   Attack Cat: Biting, Scratching, and Pouncing 189
   The Amazing Disappearing Kitty: Shyness and Hiding 191
   Harry Hou-Kitty: The Escape Artist Cat 192
   Cat Talk: When Your Cat Just Won't Be Quiet 193
   Cat on Cat: Sibling Rivalry and Other-Pet Issues 193
   Calming Kitten Chaos 194
   Finding a Feline Behaviorist 194
   Training Your Cat the Easy Way 195

Part IV: Befriending a Little Critter 197

Chapter 12: Choosing Your Critter 199

Considering a Little Critter 199
    Exploring the appeal of small-animal pets 200
    Deciding you and small critters aren't a fit 201
    Pairing kids with critters: Perfect pet or potential problem? 201
Finding the Critter That's Right for You 203
    Ferret facts 203
    Rabbit run-down 205
    Guinea-pig guide 205
    Rats rule 206
    Hamster and gerbil handbook 207
    Mouse manifesto 208
    Exotics: Chinchillas and hedgehogs 209
Save a Critter Today! Finding Adoptable Critters 210

Chapter 13: Getting Ready for Your Critter 213

Preparing Your Home for Critter Conditions 213
    Making your home critterproof 214
    Considering the free-roaming route 214
Stocking Crucial Critter Supplies 215
    Settling into a new enclosure 215
    Getting the supplies your pet needs 218
Helping Your New Critter Settle In 219
    Understand the limits of handling 219
    Give him space 219
    Supervise your children 220
    Know when to get help and when to back off 220

Chapter 14: Taking Charge of Your Critter's Care 221

Keeping Your Critter Healthy 221
    Finding a good critter vet 222
    Understanding potential health problems 223
    Keeping your critters from breeding! 225
    Knowing when to see a vet 226
Feeding Your Critter 227
Critter Grooming 229

Chapter 15: Critter Behavior and Training 231

Adopted Small Animal Issues 231
    Fixing what you can 232
    Managing what you can 234
    Accepting what you can't change 235
    Knowing when it's a physical problem 236

Understanding What Small Animals Can and Should Learn..................236
Litter-box training your ferret...237
Litter-box training your rabbit...238
Hand-taming pocket pets 239
Teaching small animals to come 241
Interpreting Your Small Animal's Sounds and Movements...................241
Understanding ferret sounds and behavior......................241
Hearing what your rabbit is saying...................................242
Figuring out your rat's behavior......................................243
Listening to your guinea pig..243
Checking out hamster, gerbil, and mouse behaviors 244

Part V: Bringing Home a Feathered Friend 245

Chapter 16: From Macaws to Budgies:
Choosing Your Feathered Friend 247
Understanding Your Adopted Bird 248
Knowing What Adopted Birds Need 249
Finding a Breed that Suits You 250
Choosing for health and temperament............................251
Go large: Macaws and cockatoos 252
Talking about Amazon parrots and African greys.............253
Conures, Quakers, toucans, and other medium-sized birds........254
What about doves?...255
Parakeets and cockatiels: Pros and cons 256

Chapter 17: Creating a Bird-Friendly Home .259
Getting Ready for a Bird in the House....................................259
Bird-proofing...259
To fly free or not to fly free?...261
The Best Bird Supplies 262
Cage considerations..262
Food for the birds..263
Perches 263
Bird stimulation: Toys and climbing devices....................264
Travel carrier or small travel cage..................................264
Cage cover..264
Perch cleaner..264
Cuttlebone...265
Nontoxic cage bedding..265
Spray bottle, grooming spray, or a bird bath...................265
Nail trimmers or cement perch 265
Bringing Home Birdie..265
Introducing your new bird to its new home 266
Getting to know the family 267
Child-bird relations 267
Other pets: The Tweety and Sylvester syndrome.............268

Chapter 18: Caring for Your Adopted Bird .269

Keeping Your Bird Healthy...269
Finding a good bird vet...270
The first vet visit 271
Common health problems in adopted birds................................272
Bird breeding: Why — and how — not to 274
Feeding Your Adopted Bird: A Mixed Bag..275
Giving your bird a balanced diet...275
Giving your bird the best and worst foods 276
Understanding the diets of specific species................................278
Knowing how often to feed your bird 279
Converting your bird to the proper diet 279
Grooming Your Bird 280

Chapter 19: Training Your Bird 281

Understanding Bird Behavior..281
Solving Bird Behavior Problems 282
The bird that won't adjust: Fear and anxiety.............................283
Noise solutions 285
Biting and aggression...286
Feather picking and chewing 287
Finding an Avian Behavior Consultant 288
Bird Bonding: Bringing Out Your Bird's Best 288
Bird Basic Training...289
Socializing with your bird...290
Hand-training 290
The step-up cue 291
Teaching your bird to behave on your shoulder 292
Cage-free manners...292
Mating Season and Avian Adolescence 293

Part VI: Giving an Exotic a Second Chance 295

Chapter 20: Choosing a Creepy Crawler .297

Determining Whether Exotic Herps and "Bugs" Are Right for You........298
Picking Your Exotic Pet 299
Constrictors: Pythons, boas, and other huggable snakes.............300
Small slitherers: Garter snakes, king snakes,
corn snakes, and other Colubrids 301
Green iguanas 301
Turtle time..302
Other reptiles of the tropics and the deserts 303
The slime factor: Frogs, salamanders, and newts 304

Shell chic: All about hermit crabs 305

Bugs: Tarantulas and beyond 305

Seeking Out Secondhand Snakes, Lizards, and Spiders 306

Chapter 21: Preparing for Your Exotic Pet 307

Herp-Proofing Your Home 307

Exotic Equipment and Supplies..309

Exotic enclosures 309

Light, heat, bedding, and water..311

Exotic supply list 313

Exotic Homecoming: What to Expect 314

Traveling with your exotic — bringing him home 314

Welcoming your pet home — making him comfortable................315

Chapter 22: Exotic Care and Feeding 317

Bright Eyes and Scaly Tails 317

Finding a good exotic pet vet..318

What to expect during the first exam 319

Recognizing special health problems
    adopted exotics may have..320

Noticing when your exotic is sick and needs a vet.......................321

Identifying reasons not to be alarmed...322

Exotics and kids: What you must know..323

Exotic Meals: Feeding Your Exotic Pet 324

Snacks for snakes 324

Lizard lunch 325

Turtle tidbits 326

Amphibian appetizers..326

Arachnids and other "bug" basics 327

Hungry hermit crabs..327

Herp Hygiene and Grooming 327

Chapter 23: Snake Charming and Herp Handling:
How to Train Your Exotic Pet 329

Exploring the Possibilities and Limits of Exotic Taming and Training.....330

How to recognize a tamed exotic 330

How to tame your exotic 331

Handling Your Exotic Pet 332

Snake couture 332

Lizard love..334

Turtle touch 335

Touchy toads and feely frogs..336

Tarantula taming 336

Hermit crab handling..337

Dealing with a Herp Bite..338

Part VII: The Part of Tens...................................339

Chapter 24: Ten Great Reasons to Spay or Neuter Your Adopted Pet 341

You Can Do It on the Cheap 341
Spaying/Neutering Makes Pets Healthier.......................341
Spaying/Neutering Keeps Pets Home 341
So What If Your Pet Is a Purebred? 342
Spaying/Neutering Improves Behavior 342
If They Never Do It, They Never Miss It 342
Reproduction Is Risky...342
Your Pet Won't Miss the "Family Jewels" 342
Eight Million Pets and Counting....................................342

Chapter 25: Ten Favors You Can Do for Your Adopted Pet 343

A Forever Home...343
The Right Diet . . . at Last 343
Indoor Shelter 343
Exercise, Exercise, Exercise...344
Attention 344
Physical Touch . . . or Not 344
Mental Challenges for Better Behavior 344
Family Member Status 344
Grooming and Good Housekeeping 344
Regular Vet Care 344

Chapter 26: Ten Ways to Support Your Local Shelter or Rescue Group 345

Volunteering...345
Donating Money or Talent..345
Fostering a Pet..345
Dropping Off Food and Supplies 346
Giving Gifts in Others' Names......................................346
Referring Your Friends...346
Staying Informed 346
Spreading the Word 346
Starting a Rescue...346
Adopting Another Pet 346

Index...347

Introduction

I have lived with many animals: dogs, cats, birds, hamsters, mice, snakes, lizards, fish, tarantulas and other large startling bugs. Some were rescued, some purchased, and some were adopted from shelters. I've also made many common pet-owner errors throughout the years. I even gave up a few of my beloved pets to rescue groups when I thought I no longer could keep them. And then one day, there I was, a pet writer without a pet. I hadn't had the heart to try any of it again until one day in 1999, when I walked into the Iowa City/Coralville Animal Care and Adoption Center.

I meandered along the rows of kennels looking at the enthusiastic Lab mixes, the baying Beagles, the pining pit bulls and I kept thinking, "They won't have a small dog; they won't have a small dog." And then I saw Sally, a slender, delicate, fine-boned rat terrier with Italian Greyhound features, golden-brown eyes, velvety ears that tipped loosely forward, and a tight white coat with orange markings. She was all of 11 pounds, sitting still, all alone in the middle of the spacious kennel, staring at me. I stopped. She stared. I stared. She stared harder. It was almost as though she were trying to persuade me, with the force of her terrier will, that I simply must take her home. "Uh-oh," I thought. "Here we go."

I brought my children to meet Sally. We visited three times before Sally came home with us. Of all the dogs I've ever kept — purebreds, strays, free-to-good-home fellows — Sally is special. She seems to know that I will keep her forever, that her home is finally a forever home. Sure, she needed training and had a few bad habits, but we went to obedience class, worked hard, housetrained, learned tricks, went on walks, and now she rests contentedly at my feet while I work. Eventually, I brought home another little terrier mix named Jack, who has glaucoma and probably will be blind before the tender age of 3. Sally, the good big sister that she is, is now a dog's guide dog in training, but most of all she's the best dog friend I think I will ever know.

My point about Sally is that of all the many places you can find a wonderful pet, some of the best are animal shelters and pet rescue groups. There you find animals discarded by pet owners who could not or would not, for whatever reason, keep them. Regardless of the problems — poor health, lack of training, overexuberance caused by loneliness, fear-based shyness, or nippiness — the right pet owner with the right knowledge can help a pet to heal. Thousands of pets are waiting because they were failed by people who relinquished their responsibility and gave up, got bored, got tired, or let life get in the way. Some of these people couldn't help giving up their pets. Nevertheless, what remains are the recycled animals, waiting for someone willing to make the commitment of time, energy, money, and heart to take care of them for the rest of their lives.

Sally changed my life for the better, and I am willing to bet that a shelter pet is out there waiting to change your life. *Adopting a Pet For Dummies* is designed to help you find, care for, nurture, feed, train, socialize, and love an animal that desperately needs a second home. Some of these animals have health and behavior problems, but with patience and the knowledge and guidance this book provides you can usually recognize and manage the problems shelter animals tend to experience. I help you decide which kind of pet is right for you, give you resources for finding the kind of animal you want, and help you to do the right thing for your new animal companion after you've decided to give a pet a second chance. Sometimes the best things in life are the things other people throw away.

About This Book

This book covers many kinds of animals, and if I'd intended it to tell you everything you'd ever need to know about finding, caring for, feeding, housing, and training dogs, cats, small mammals, birds, reptiles, and other animals you might conceivably adopt, well . . . you can only imagine how big of a book it might be. The book you hold in your hands, instead, is a starting line — a guide to pet adoption and the overarching care and training information you need to get started in your new life with your new adopted pet. For more information on the precise care needs of the individual pet you decide to adopt, please consult any of the many other *For Dummies* guides on pet care published by Wiley, from books about specific purebred dogs like *Labrador Retrievers For Dummies* by Joel Walton and yours truly, to books like *Cats For Dummies* by Gina Spadafori and Paul D. Pion, *Parrots For Dummies* by Nikki Moustaki, *Ferrets For Dummies* by Kim Schilling, *Rabbits For Dummies* by Audrey Pavia, and *Reptiles & Amphibians For Dummies* by Patricia Bartlett, which are filled with useful and much more detailed information about these kinds of pets.

Each section of this book relates to a separate issue about adopting a pet or caring for an adopted pet. Because adopted pets have certain unique challenges, this book focuses on what you need to know about animals that have already had at least one home that didn't work out. You find out information about:

- ✔ Knowing the differences between animal shelters and pet rescue groups and how to work with both.
- ✔ Determining what kind of pets are most likely available and in need of good homes (and why).
- ✔ Discovering what to expect when you adopt a pet — from fees and applications to first-day pet jitters and behavioral problems.
- ✔ Finding a great vet, a quality food, the right housing, and everything else your pet needs to be happy and healthy.

✔ Introducing your new pet to its new life with your family, friends, children, and other pets.

✔ Tackling the problems that caused your pet to lose his first home, so you can both rest easy knowing that you've found an animal companion for life and that your adopted pet has found his forever home.

This book is unique because you can open it anywhere and just start reading. Find the animals that interest you, skip to the part about purebred dog rescue, or thumb right on over to parrots, ball pythons, or guinea pigs. The table of contents and the index guide you in your quest to find the information you need. Or, you can do it the old-fashioned way, reading the book from cover to cover. It's up to you.

Conventions Used in This Book

The following conventions are used throughout the text to make things consistent and easy to understand:

✔ All Web addresses appear in `mono font`.

✔ New terms appear in *italic* and are closely followed by an easy-to-understand definition.

✔ **Bold** is used to highlight important terminology and the action parts of numbered steps.

As for the pets, traditional wisdom tells us writers to call animals "it," but that simply doesn't reflect the way I feel about pets. Perhaps it doesn't seem particularly descriptive to you, either. In this book, I've used "he" or "she" to describe all the animals when necessary — even the ones that are neutered. I generally refer to dogs as "he" and cats as "she" — just because — and then for the most part, just for the sake of balance and simplicity, I've alternated genders with each section. In any event, I hope you won't be offended if the gender I use to talk about a pet is different than the one that applies to *your* pet.

What You're Not to Read

Of course, you can read every word of this book if you like. In fact, I'd be flattered if you did. However, this book is written so you don't have to do that if it doesn't suit your needs. Instead, you can find information easily and easily understand the information you find. If you see sidebars (they're shaded in gray), consider them extra tidbits of information rather than urgent material you absolutely must read. You can also skip the stuff on the copyright page and any chapter that isn't relevant to you. If you adopted a cat, skip the chapters on dogs and snakes and guinea pigs. If you adopted a rabbit, ignore the stuff about cats and parrots and tarantulas.

Foolish Assumptions

I thought about you a lot when I wrote this book, and what kind of pet you might be thinking of adopting and whether you have already adopted your pet. As I wrote, here's what I assumed about you:

✔ You adopted, or are considering adopting, one of the more common pets to be relinquished at an animal shelter or with a rescue group. If you adopted a dog or cat, it probably is a mix or a popular purebred. If you adopted a bird, small animal, or exotic pet, it probably is one of those most often sold in pet stores and consequently most often given up to rescue. I'm guessing you haven't adopted an extremely rare parrot, venomous snake, or any of the other exotic pets plenty of advanced hobbyists have but most beginning pet owners don't know about, so I don't talk much about those rarer types of pets.

✔ You adopted, or are considering adopting, a pet not because you hoped to get an animal on-the-cheap but because you really wanted to help a pet in need. You care about animals and are sincerely committed to devoting the time, money, and attention that your new pet really needs to be happy and healthy.

✔ You want this relationship to work. No, not between you and me, silly . . . between you and your pet! That, of course, is what this book is all about: making your relationship with your new adopted pet work, so your adopted pet never has to lose another home again.

How This Book Is Organized

This book is divided into seven parts, easily parceling the information you need into convenient sections. Whether you need to know about the adoption process, where to find a snake, or how to groom a long-haired cat, you'll know just where to turn. The following sections explain where to find what.

Part I: All About Pet Adoption

In this first part of the book, you find out all about animal shelters and rescue groups: how they differ, what they are, what they do, and how to work with them to find your perfect pet. What should you ask them? What will they ask you? What will you need to pay, certify, prove, and swear to before they let you take an adopted pet home? This chapter tells all.

Part II: Welcoming a Dog into Your Life

This part of the book focuses on dogs, one of the most popular and populous animals in shelters and rescues. You discover how to choose the right type of dog for you, how to recognize common health and behavior problems in adopted dogs and what to do about them, how to keep your dog healthy and well fed, and how to train your dog, including the best ways to conquer those annoying behaviors that may have landed your new adopted dog in the shelter in the first place.

Part III: Here Kitty Kitty: Rescuing a Cat

Animal shelters are typically filled with cats, from strays and feral cats to pets that have lived indoors for years. This part of the book helps you choose the right cat for you and recognize the health problems and behavior issues common to adopted cats. You find out how to manage these issues, feed and care for your cat, and even how to train your cat, from using a litter box to coming when you call.

Part IV: Befriending a Little Critter

In this section, you explore everything about the little critters: bunnies and ferrets, rabbits and rats, guinea pigs, hamsters, gerbils, mice, and rarer exotic small pets like chinchillas and hedgehogs. You'll find sections on care, feeding, behavior management, and how to find a vet that specializes in small animals, because these little guys need special care.

Part V: Bringing Home a Feathered Friend

Noise and mess land many a once-happy parrot or parakeet into the shelter or bird rescue group. This part of the book gives you the lowdown on exactly what bird-keeping involves. You discover the different kinds of birds and what they're like as pets, how to care for and feed them, and how to solve the behavior problems that often plague people who live with birds. From feather plucking to squawking and screaming, this chapter is your guide to finding peace with your parrot or other bird.

Part VI: Giving an Exotic a Second Chance

Some people don't consider them pets, but herpers and other reptile and bug hobbyists think they're just great. This section of the book guides you to finding the right exotic pet for you, whether one of the thousands of abandoned iguanas or snakes to tarantulas and other bugs once considered thrilling but eventually considered too much trouble. You discover how to find an exotic pet vet, how to care for and feed your exotic creatures, and how to manage them in your home responsibly and in a way that brings you enjoyment and allows your exotic pet a safe and stress-free existence.

Part VII: The Part of Tens

From this trademark Dummies set of chapters, you get no-nonsense information in condensed form: handy lists of ten things you need to know about why you need to spay or neuter your pet, favors you should do for your adopted pet, and finally, ten wonderful ways to support the heroic efforts of your local animal shelter or pet rescue group.

Icons Used in This Book

To make this book easier to read and simpler to use, I include some icons that can help you find and fathom key ideas and information.

This icon points out helpful things to know — things you can actually do to help solve a problem or improve a situation or things that will save you time or money.

This icon is a little nudge to remind you about something that is so important that it bears repeating. These are things everyone who adopts a pet needs to know and live by.

This icon is an alert to anything that can be potentially dangerous for you or your adopted pet.

Where to Go from Here

This book is organized as if it were several small books packaged conveniently together. If you want to know about how to begin going about the process of adopting a pet, start with Chapter 1. If you already adopted a dog but are wondering how to solve some of your pet's obnoxious behaviors, flip to Chapter 7. Does your new kitten need vaccinations? Head to Chapter 10 to find out. Or maybe you need to know how big of a tank your new iguana needs. Skip to Chapter 21. Or, read the table of contents or look up key words in the index to find exactly what you need to know, exactly when you need to know it.

Part I

All About Pet Adoption

"I think I had more of a parrot in mind."

In this part . . .

*I*f you haven't adopted your pet yet, then the beginning is the place to start. This part of the book tells you all about animal shelters and rescue groups. They aren't the same, but they have the same goal: taking in pets without homes and finding them new, permanent homes with loving, responsible caretakers. You also find out why animal shelters and rescue groups grill you about your home, life, work schedule, and more before ever turning over a pet to you, and what *you* need to ask *them*. The more you prepare for your new pet, the better the experience will be, so count on this part to prepare you for exactly what you're getting into when you turn to an animal shelter or a pet rescue group to provide you with a pet.

Chapter 1

Exploring the Pet Adoption Option

In This Chapter

▶ Deciding whether you really want a pet

▶ Analyzing your lifestyle and personality to determine the perfect kind of pet for you

▶ Examining the specific commitments, legal implications, and first-year costs of owning a pet

*A*dopting a pet is good for everyone. You get that soul mate you've been pining for, and a pet without a family gets you. But taking on the responsibility of an adopted pet isn't merely a matter of slapping down the check card for sundry adoption-related expenses and taking home the pet that strikes your fancy at the moment. You're bringing home a living, breathing, conscious being . . . and not just any conscious being. This animal already has lost a home and needs what animal shelters sometimes call a forever home — a full commitment.

This chapter helps you to decide whether you're definite about wanting to adopt a pet, whether you're ready for the responsibilities, expenses, and time that adopting a pet requires, and what pet you really want — as opposed to what pet you may think you want — before you think too seriously about it. This chapter also introduces you to the basic differences between shelters and rescue groups so you can begin to consider which adoption option you want to pursue.

Making Sure You're Ready to Be a Good Pet Parent

Who wouldn't want a pet? They're cute, they're companionable, they don't talk back. Then again, you need to feed them, clean up after them, take care of them every single day . . . hey, wait a minute. Are you sure you want a pet?

If the people who work and volunteer for animal shelters could change one thing about the world, many of them would make people think much longer and harder about whether they really want a pet in the first place. All too often, people adopt pets only to find they don't have the time, money, or patience to take care of them properly, and they end up returning the pet to the animal shelter.

Playing the name game

People enjoy naming their pets, but your pet's name may matter more than you think. Just ask the woman who named her Siamese cat *Killer,* or the person who dubbed a Jack Russell Terrier with the middle initial *T.* for *Trouble.* Sure, sometimes such names are ironic (like the 15-foot Burmese python named *Tiny*), but names can make a difference. Everybody expects a cat named *Jack the Ripper* to leave a wake of destruction, and meeting their (pet owner) human's expectations is one thing pets are good at. In ways you don't even realize, people subtly encourage behaviors that suit a pet's name and subtly discourage the opposite behaviors. So, think carefully about your pet's name and choose one that embodies the pet you really want. *Butch* might be a better name for your Bulldog than *Mr. Slobber.*

And what about the adopted pet that already has a name? Some people like to keep the name familiar to the pet, but others don't like the previous name or feel it is unsuited to the pet's personality. If your pet seems to like your new and improved name, I say go for it.

Pets have many great qualities, but they're also plenty of work and responsibility. Living with a pet isn't the same as living with, say, a blender. Sure, you have to wash a blender, and it can be the source of good things, but you can also stick it in the cabinet for weeks at a time, and it won't mind at all. Being a good pet parent means providing a pet with all the things it needs to stay healthy. Pets need mental as well as physical exercise, a clean environment, healthy food, and clean water. Being a pet parent means being responsible, keeping a schedule, and making arrangements for your pet's care whenever you have to be away. Are you ready for that kind of responsibility? The following sections can help you decide.

Considering the time commitment

Adopted pets in particular often need extra time to adjust to a new situation, especially when you first bring them home. They look to their owners for help with the transition. From there, new pets need guidance and companionship to lead happy, healthy, safe lives. And those lives can last for quite some time. Check out Table 1-1 for the average life spans of popular pets.

Table 1-1	Average Pet Life Span Chart*	
Pet	*Approximate Weight or Type*	*Average Life Span with Proper Care*
Giant dog	80–150 pounds	5–8 years
Large dog	50–80 pounds	9–12 years
Medium dog	20–50 pounds	12–14 years

Pet	Approximate Weight or Type	Average Life Span with Proper Care
Small dog	10–20 pounds	12–15 years
Toy dog	5–10 pounds	14–18 years
Teacup dog	Less than 5 pounds	12–15 years (often with health problems)
Indoor cats	Most breeds	14–16 years
Outdoor cats	Most breeds	3–5 years (due to accidents or disease)
Indoor rabbits	Most breeds	9–12 years
Outdoor rabbits	Most breeds	4–6 years
Ferrets	All	5–8
Guinea pigs	Most breeds	5–8
Hamsters	Most breeds	2–3 years
Gerbils	All	3–5 years
Small birds	Finches, canaries, parakeets	5–10 years
Medium birds	Cockatiels, conures, lories	15–20 years
Large birds	Cockatoos, Amazons, Macaws	30–50 years or more
Small snakes	Garter snakes, corn snakes	7–20 years
Large snakes	Pythons, boa constrictors	20–30 years
Small lizards	Anoles	3–5 years
Medium lizards	Geckos, bearded dragons	10–15 years
Large lizards	Iguanas, monitors	15–30 years
Tarantulas	Males	1–5 years
Tarantulas	Female	15–20 years, some 30+

All values are approximate, individual pets may vary significantly.

If you lead a busy life, work most of the day out of the home, or come home late and leave again early in the morning, think long and hard about the commitment before you adopt a pet. Some pets take more time than others — a hamster, for example, takes less time than a dog. But most adopted pets take a significant amount of time and financial commitment, and it isn't fair if you aren't willing to give your pet what it needs. Adopted pets already have endured stressful transitions. Be sure that you have time before putting your new pet through any more unnecessary changes.

Being mindful of housing restrictions

Pets aren't welcome everywhere. If you rent your home, be sure that your landlord allows pets. Many adopted pets are returned to the shelter or even abandoned when they're sneaked into a home environment that doesn't allow them and are then discovered.

As part of the adoption process, many animal shelters and rescue groups require proof of home ownership or an official letter from the landlord stating that he or she will allow a pet to live on the premises. Don't expect to be able to adopt a pet without first getting this paperwork in order.

Landlords and neighbors

Even when a pet is officially allowed in a rented home, adopted pets still can cause problems. Barking dogs, roaming cats, squawking parrots, and the presence of, say, a large python, are enough to make neighbors nervous, annoyed, or downright furious. Complaints and even calls to the police can be cause for a landlord to threaten or even move forward with an eviction. Other things that bother neighbors include failure to clean up waste, odor from pet litter boxes or cages, and failure to keep pets under control while off the leash. These concerns all are serious, and after you start a war with your neighbors or your landlord, life can get pretty stressful for everyone.

Making sure that you manage your adopted pet in a way that won't infringe upon the rights of your neighbors or break any terms, explicit or implied, in your lease is best for you, your neighborhood, and certainly your pet.

Lease laws and leash laws

If you get into a tangle with your landlord or neighbors, you need to know your rights. Sometimes other people who simply don't like pets will unfairly persecute you. This situation is completely different than perfectly justified complaints that you aren't managing your animal.

Every state and local region has its unique set of laws and ordinances regarding pets, what constitutes a pet, and where and when you are liable for your pet's behavior. For instance, in some states, killing any dog that harasses a domestic animal is perfectly legal, if the dog isn't wearing a rabies tag. Pet owners typically are liable for any damages their pets inflict on anybody or anything. That means if your Golden Retriever isn't wearing his tag and he escapes from your yard and chases your neighbor's cat, your neighbor is legally allowed to take action.

Find out the exact laws in your area by contacting your city or state government office. Ask about:

✔ Leash laws

✔ Noise ordinances

✔ Liability issues related to pets

✔ Tenant and landlord rights regarding pets

If you find that laws exist that you aren't willing to follow, then please don't adopt a pet.

Affording a pet

Maybe you're perfectly willing to take on the responsibilities associated with owning a pet. You have the time, the space, and the capacity for affection, but do you have the cold hard cash? Pets are pricey, especially during the first year. Even if you're adopting a pet for a meager adoption fee, that pet still needs the care, food, and supplies necessary for a healthy, safe life. Consider the costs involved during the first year of life for various pets before making a commitment to adopt one.

Table 1-2 gives you estimates on first-year costs of various pets. Because different shelters and rescue groups vary in costs according to services and by region of the country, because veterinarians charge different amounts depending on where they're located, and because supplies vary dramatically according to what you buy and how much you choose to spend, these expenses are merely rough but approximate estimates.

Table 1-2	**First-Year Costs of Adopted Pets**				
Expense	*Dogs*	*Cats*	*Small Animals*	*Birds*	*Exotics*
Adoption fees	$50–$200	$25–$150	$5–$50	$10–$200+	$10–$200
Spay/neuter costs	$0–$100	$0–$100	$0–$100	—	—
Vaccinations	$100–$200	$100–$200	$0–$100	—	—
Other vet care	$0–$200	$0–$200	$0–$200	$0–$200	$0–$200
Food	$400–$600	$300–$400	$50–$300	$50–$200	$100–$400
Supplies	$100–$500+	$100–$500+	$100–$300+	$200–$400+	$100–$300+
Housing, including bedding, heating, and lighting	—	—	$50–$100	$50–$500	$50–$200

(continued)

Table 1-2 *(continued)*

Expense	Dogs	Cats	Small Animals	Birds	Exotics
Training classes	$50–$200	—	—	—	—
Grooming fees	$0–$200	$0–$200	—	—	—
TOTAL:	**$700–$2,500+**	**$525–$1,500+**	**$205–$1,100+**	**$310–$1,500+**	**$260–$1,300+**

Be sure to take into account that pet expenses continue throughout their lives, and as they age, they may cost more money as their need for more veterinary care increases. Adopting a pet with special medical or emotional needs may tack on additional costs for extra veterinary care or help from a specialized trainer or animal behavior consultant. When considering costs, looking at the big picture and considering the animal's entire probable life span are good ideas.

The Good Part: Adopted Pets = Love

With all this nay-saying, it may sound like the message in this chapter is that you shouldn't get a pet. *Au contraire!* Pets are wonderful, and adopting a pet that needs a home truly is a noble deed. The message in this chapter is really more akin to the message delivered to Boy Scouts: Be prepared. Hundreds of thousands of people successfully keep and enjoy pets, and you can be one of them. If you know what you're getting into, living with an adopted pet can bring many good things into your life. Here are a few:

- ✔ **Pets make you healthier:** The rumor is true: Pets really do make people healthier. Studies show that pet owners have lower blood pressure and reduced stress, get more exercise, and visit the doctor less often than people who don't own pets. Consider adopting a pet to be an investment in your good health and longevity. (You will, of course, return the favor by keeping your pet in good health!)

- ✔ **Pets make you happier:** Studies show that people who have pets suffer less often from depression and have greater psychological stability than people who don't have pets. Less depression means more happiness . . . and how can you fail to be happy when your dog, cat, or even your sociable rat gazes at you with so much interest and adoration?

- ✔ **Pets teach you how to love better:** When you take on the responsibility of caring for and nurturing something or someone, you discover a little bit more about love. This affection goes far beyond the extra credibility you get with the opposite gender when they see you walking your dog through the park. Pets impact your life, your personality, and your entire being. They pull you out of yourself and into a relationship with them, and their dependence on you helps you to see beyond yourself. You find out about sacrifice, about how to be less selfish, and about how to give. Maybe that's why so many people get pets, then graduate to having children. Pets help you understand what it means to love something other than yourself.

Perfect Pet Profile Quiz: Find Out What Kind of Pet You Really Want

You're serious about adopting a pet, but maybe you're still not sure what kind of pet works best for your lifestyle and personality. Try this ten-question quiz. You may be surprised to find out that you really *are* a cat person or a snake person or that you're really more suited for a guinea pig. Pick the answers you think are best for each of the questions and circle the answer(s) (you may have to do it more than once) that correspond to the number and pet types for each question in Table 1-3. (I help you add up your answers when you're finished.)

1. **When you think of a pet, you're most cheered by the thought of something:**

    A. Warm, fuzzy, and snuggly.

    B. Wiggly and energetic.

    C. Aesthetically pleasing, beautiful, and breathtaking.

    D. Cool and shocking.

2. **When it comes to interacting with a pet, your basic philosophy is:**

    A. Pets should be seen and not heard.

    B. Pets should add to the décor of the home.

    C. Pets should be with their people all the time and participate in their lives as much as possible.

    D. Pets should be affectionate but also independent. Too much neediness is irritating.

3. **During the week, you:**

    A. Work most of the day, approximately 8 a.m. to 5 p.m., and never come home for lunch.

    B. Work most of the day, but can easily come home for lunch and stay there for at least 30 minutes.

    C. Work part time and are away from home no more than four to six hours each day.

    D. Work at home and are almost always there.

4. In your opinion, pet care should involve:

A. Providing daily food and water, and an annual vet check.

B. Providing the best food, purified water, the appropriate holistic supplements, pet massage, daily grooming, interactive games that stimulate mind and body, vigorous but appropriate exercise, and plenty of time for bonding, not to mention the best available veterinary care.

C. The construction of an elaborate habitat kept scrupulously clean, with interesting and stimulating toys and things to do, and a high-tech feeding and water system that minimizes mess.

D. Feeding once in awhile. Oh, and water.

5. You describe yourself as:

A. Marathon man/woman. If you're going to run, hike, bike, or swim, you may as well do it big.

B. Outdoorsy. Nothing like a hike in the woods, a nice campfire, and hanging your backpack from a tree to discourage the bears.

C. Moderate. A nice walk, a gentle meal, eight hours of sleep, and a regular schedule. Life is much nicer that way.

D. Deskbound. The whole world is available on your computer. Why exert any more energy than necessary? So what if you sometimes forget to eat . . .

6. When it comes to grooming:

A. You'd love to spend some nice relaxing time brushing and combing a long beautiful coat every day.

B. You'd rather keep grooming chores to a minimum. Short coats are best! And don't they make hairless dogs and cats?

C. You have better things to do with your time, and you aren't much interested in a pet that can't even groom itself.

D. You can hardly groom *yourself!*

7. How do you feel about pet hair and/or feather fluff?

A. A big furry dog, a fluffy cat, or a big exotic bird with fantastic plumage is well worth a little extra time with the vacuum cleaner.

B. You don't mind as long as it matches your clothes and furniture.

C. Hate it, hate it, hate it. No animal would dare shed a single hair or stray feather in your house!

D. Ah . . . ahhh . . . ahhhh . . . CHOOO!

8. You are allergic to:

A. Pet dander, pet hair, and feathers.

B. Shellfish, peanuts, or strawberries.

C. Small children and loud noises.

D. Conformity.

9. Training classes are:

A. For responsible pet owners.

B. For those strange people who actually want to own dogs.

C. A waste of time and money — dogs don't need them.

D. Prejudiced against cats.

10. The best reason to have a pet is:

A. To form a mutually beneficial bond with another living being.

B. To add life and fun to your existence.

C. To help a creature in need.

D. To win friends and influence people.

Just answering some of these questions may have helped you to get a clearer picture of the kind of pet you really want in your life, but score your answers and see, more specifically, what they reveal. In the chart below, circle the answer you chose for each question, and then see which column has the most circles. You may have a lot of circles in more than one column, which means that several different types of pets are right for you.

Table 1-3		Perfect Pet Profile Quiz Answers			
Question	*Dog Person*	*Cat Person*	*Critter Person*	*Bird Person*	*Exotic Person*
1	A, B	A, B, C	A, B	C, D	C, D
2	C, D	C, D	A, D	B	A, B
3	B, C, D	A, B, C, D	A, B, C, D	A, B, C, D	A, B, C, D
4	A, B	A, B	A, B, C	A, B, C	A, B, C
5	A, B, C, D	C, D	C, D	C, D	C, D
6	A, B	A, B, C	B, C, D	B, C, D	B, C, D
7	A, B	A, B	A, B, D	A, B	A, B, C, D
8	B	B, C, D	B, C, D	B, C, D	A, B, C, D
9	A	A, B, D	B	B	B
10	A, B, C	A, B, C	A, B, C	A, B, C	A, B, C

Some of the answers in this quiz are in fun, but consider whether you really are opposed to pet hair and remembering to feed and water your pets. If so, you need to consider a pet rock, instead, at least for now. Otherwise, you may have noticed that many of the columns in this chart encompassed a variety of answers. That's because within each pet category, you have a variety of choices. Short-haired dogs and cats don't need much grooming, but long-haired cats and dogs do. Some small animals and large birds produce pet dander, hair, and feathers. Others are small enough that shedding is negligible. Some animals need a lot of attention, and others are more independent.

Throughout this book, you have a chance to discover in more depth exactly what needs different types of animals have within each pet category, but to give you an overview of what to expect with each kind of pet, consider the pet-specific parameters in the sections that follow.

Beyond the Glamour: What It Means to Adopt . . .

Adopting a pet in general involves many considerations, but adopting a particular kind of pet involves a whole slew of new things to think about. Merely realizing that you're a dog person or a bird person or an exotic-animal person isn't enough to justify adopting a pet. You must also consider some creature-specific factors that can help you determine whether you're ready and whether you're at a point in your life when adopting a pet of the type you think you want really is practical.

A dog

More households have dogs than any other pet in America — 43.5 million households, according to the American Pet Product Manufacturer's Association. But dogs also are the pets that take the most work, time, care, and expense. Dogs need plenty of attention, regular vet care, good food, chew toys, training and socialization, and exercise. Being pack animals, dogs must feel like they're a part of the family, or they won't thrive. Even if they know they're the lowest family member on the totem pole, dogs want to know their place so they can feel secure. Dogs also need basic daily maintenance.

Many dogs, especially as puppies, can't be left alone for more than a few hours without needing a bathroom, and they should never be left alone outside. They can chew up your house, bark and howl, learn how to open cabinets, jump over baby gates, and generally cause a ruckus. Dogs need exercise in the form of walks and/or active games. But dogs also are incredibly rewarding companions, and a well-trained, well-socialized, and well-behaved dog is one of life's great joys. Getting your dog to that place isn't always easy, however. It takes work and a lot of attention!

Adopted dogs in particular can be needy and require extra work, patience, and a big effort to train and socialize in the beginning. Some fear being abandoned again, some may have health problems, and some may be distrustful of people. On the other hand, your adopted dog may be the picture of good manners, having already enjoyed good training and socialization by previous owners. Even so, all dogs want to be with people. They are social animals and won't enjoy being left alone in the backyard. Getting a dog means deciding that you want to hang out with a dog. It may sound obvious, but many people overlook this basic fact. If you want to hang out with a dog, great. If you think that may get tiresome, keep reading.

A cat

More households may have dogs than cats, but pet cats outnumber dogs in America — 90.5 million pet cats far exceed the paltry 73.5 million pet dogs! Cats are notorious for being more independent, less needy, and more self-sufficient than dogs, making them many pet owners' pet of choice. However, not all cats are independent. Some breeds and some individuals of any type can be demanding, meowing and butting at your hand for a targeted stroking session when you really need to be typing at the computer. In fact, cats may want to help you type at your computer. Don't rely on their accuracy, however.

Some cats are maddeningly allusive, denying your requests for affection when you're finally done typing and ready to pet them. Agile and playful, curious and clever, cats can get into trouble if they don't have enough to do. Some cats really want a playmate, and having one can be a great way to fulfill a cat's social needs, although be prepared for mad dashes around the house, with each cat a mere streak of fur in your peripheral vision. Other cats want nothing to do with a second feline, needing and desiring only you. With cats, you have to be open, flexible, and ready to accept the unique and often eccentric personality you get. If you don't have the patience for such indulgence, keep reading.

A small mammal

If you like to look at cute fuzzy critters but you don't want them demanding your attention all the time, perhaps a small animal is for you. Rabbits, guinea pigs, hamsters, gerbils, and mice endure, occasionally even enjoy being handled, and benefit from supervised exploration outside of their cages. Ferrets and rats, on the other hand, can be more demanding and want more intensive interaction. Even though small animals may not require a bunch of handling, they nevertheless require plenty of maintenance in the form of habitat cleaning.

All small animals need a cage or other safe enclosure that is spacious enough for them to move around in and explore and equipped with stimulating toys and other interactive exercise equipment. However, even the classiest of critter condos isn't going to be healthy when it's full of animal waste. Most critter cages need to be scrupulously and safely cleaned at least once a week, refilled with clean litter, and always supplied with fresh clean water and good food. If you're not willing to do that kind of weekly chore, keep reading.

A birdie

Pet birds are gorgeous, exotic, tropical creatures with stunning plumage, but their downy feathers are likely to accumulate in every nook and cranny within 50 feet of their cages, and many birds sing, squawk, whistle, twitter, and even scream when they're bored, hungry, or just because they feel like it. To stay healthy, birds need more than a bowl of seed every day supplemented with fresh fruits and vegetables — which require preparation. Birds must always have fresh water, and most birds require attention.

Birds that come out of their cages need to have their wings clipped for safety reasons (see Chapter 17). Larger parrots need time out of their enclosures and probably want to interact with you. And birds can live for several decades! Birds also need training, if you don't want to be nipped, that is, and regular vet care from a vet who's experienced with birds to stay healthy.

Some people think avian interaction is just great, but many others find that they don't have the time and, most of all, simply cannot stand the noise! Squawking from a large parrot or even a relatively diminutive conure (a kind of large parakeet) can be extremely loud. Even tiny budgies (small parakeets) are likely to spend much of the day twittering and singing. If you like these sounds, and if they add an exotic flare to your day, that's great. If such noise drives you crazy, or if you can't stand the idea of feather fluff and seed shells on the floor, keep reading.

An exotic

So you want to amaze your friends and intimidate your enemies with a giant snake or a prehistoric-looking iguana or a big hairy tarantula. That's probably not the best reason for adopting an exotic pet. Snakes, lizards, and arachnids don't require the constant care and attention that some pets do, but they need clean cages and careful handling. Some species shouldn't be handled at all, while others tolerate but don't require it. They do, however, require a proper and complete diet and clean, fresh water. Many exotic pets also have specific care needs, such as heated surfaces or certain types of lighting. Without them, the animals can quickly die. Before deciding on adopting one of these types of pets, you need to do some research so you know exactly what your adopted exotic pet needs.

Adopting an exotic pet means accepting a certain degree of responsibility. Many people are afraid of snakes, lizards, and spiders, and some of these animals can actually pose a risk to humans. Making sure your exotic pet never escapes or harms anyone is your primary responsibility, but you also must be aware of local laws and ordinances that govern exotic pets. In some areas, you're simply not allowed to own them. If you try to duck the law and keep one as a pet anyway, you risk getting caught and having the animal taken away or possibly even destroyed, if it harms someone. Are you ready for that kind of responsibility? If not . . . perhaps you really don't need any pet at all.

Finding Your New Best Friend through Shelters, Humane Societies, and Rescues

If you decide that you really do still want a pet and that you're practically born to be a pet owner, then it's time to examine your adoption options. The three types of adoption resources essentially are animal shelters, rescue groups, and humane societies. In spirit, all these organizations are the same, comprised of people who devote their spare time, or in some cases almost all their time, to rescuing animals. Each has pets available for adoption, but each differs in its approach to adoption, its requirements, and its procedures.

In the next two chapters, you find out in much greater detail exactly what animal shelters and rescue groups do. In general, however, the differences are described in the sections that follow.

Uncovering the basics of animal shelters

Animal shelters usually operate as city or county agencies, taking in animals that are abandoned, found wandering, or are without apparent owners and causing a nuisance. Animal shelters adopt animals, and some euthanize animals that are not adopted or adoptable. Some animal shelters are considered *no-kill shelters* that don't routinely euthanize animals (unless, in some cases, the animals are ill or dangerous), but that also means they turn away many animals. Animal shelters usually are located in dedicated facilities where potential adopters can go to look at the animals and where people who have lost their pets can go to find out whether their animal has been picked up by animal control. Animal shelters usually have dogs and cats, but many also have small animals, birds, and exotic animals that people abandoned because they no longer can care for them. Animal shelters usually are listed in the phone book.

Animal shelters often include the term "Humane Society" in their names, but human societies are not officially affiliated with each other under any national umbrella. The Humane Society of the United States is a separate group generally advocating and lobbying for animal welfare issues.

Being a Good Samaritan: Adopting a special-needs pet

If you've decided you have the resources to adopt a pet, consider taking the extra step to save an animal with special needs. Cute kittens and puppies are relatively easy to place; harder to place, and much more frequently euthanized, are pets with special needs — older pets or pets with medical problems or disabilities. Of course, special-needs pets may need serious medical care and can cost a pet owner much more in vet bills, special food, and heartache. Yet, some people feel that they're the ones to give these needy animals a loving, caring home.

Taking on a special needs animal definitely is a commitment above and beyond the sizeable commitment pet ownership alone entails. Yet, it also has special rewards. People who adopt special-needs pets often claim to have learned valuable life lessons from their disabled pets. Blind cats, deaf dogs, small animals missing a limb, birds that have been abused, each of these animals often show remarkable ability to rally, survive, thrive, and develop meaningful relationships with their caretakers.

Research carefully the care needs of any special-needs pet you're thinking about adopting, but if you can handle those needs and afford the necessary care, by all means, be the one to step forward and give a disabled pet a home. You can change a special-needs pet's last days into years, or at least fill those last days with loving human contact.

Demystifying the rescue group

Rescue groups aren't so different from the humane societies and shelters discussed in Chapter 2, except that they usually shelter a specific breed or type of animal and develop an interest in that type of animal that, in turn, increases the chances of appropriately placing their pets. Some groups, for example, are devoted specifically to a particular breed of dog, small animals, large parrots, or exotic pets such as reptiles. However, the one common denominator among shelters, humane societies, and rescue groups is their devotion to helping animals that need them.

Rescue groups usually are started by one or two people, or perhaps a club, with a sincere commitment to pets. These rescuers often get involved because they develop a reputation for knowing a lot about a breed or particular type of animal and are willing to take on animals that are abandoned or that people can't keep. Rescuers are impossible to categorize beyond their devotion to their chosen animals. Some are dog breeders, exotic pet hobbyists, and animal welfare activists. Others work in veterinary clinics or pet stores or have other unrelated jobs and do pet rescue work in their spare time.

Nevertheless, the affinity that rescue groups have for specific animals develops into a more or less structured network of rescuers and foster homes that puts interested adopters through a rigorous screening process to assure good matches between pet and owner.

Chapter 2

Seeking Shelter: Finding and Using Animal Shelters

. . . .

In This Chapter

▶ Looking at the different types of animal shelters and what they do

▶ Finding and recognizing a great animal shelter

▶ Assessing potential pets

▶ Questioning the shelter about policies, procedures, and pets

▶ Gathering all the information and documentation you need

. . . .

*A*nimal shelters do a great service for people and animals. Many communities have animal shelters, and some may even have several, but unfortunately, not every community has one. If you have an animal shelter in your community, consider yourself lucky! If not, local police routinely are relied upon to take care of animal-control issues. Regardless of whether they're run by the city or county or privately operated and funded via donations, animal shelters serve an important function. They take in the pets that people don't want — the strays wandering through the streets or countryside — and the lost pets whose owners are frantically seeking them.

A shelter is a great place to go if you want to adopt a pet, but you can't just waltz into most shelters and waltz out with a new puppy, kitten, parrot, or iguana. Shelter workers have seen up close what can happen when people buy or adopt pets on impulse. Those pets often end up right back at the shelter, and as a result many animal shelters have instituted strict rules about adoption. Shelters usually have a multistep process for adopting a pet. They need certain information from you, and you also need to get certain information from the shelter. Not all shelters are the same; their procedures vary and so do the quality of the facility and the knowledge of the staff.

This chapter is your roadmap to the pet adoption process through an animal shelter. In it you'll find information about:

    ✔ How shelters work.

    ✔ What to expect when you try to adopt a pet from a shelter.

✔ What you need to take with you to a shelter adoption.

✔ What questions to ask before adopting a pet through a shelter. I provide a similar list of questions on the handy Cheat Sheet at the front of this book. Tear it out and take it with you for quick reference.

Many people find the pets of their dreams from their local shelters, but many others encounter only regrettable circumstances and situations, so you need to be prepared and know what you're doing. Start here.

Animal Shelters Explained

Animal shelters come in two basic forms:

✔ Animal control agencies run by local government designed to protect people from animals, take in strays, and manage animal issues and problems within the community.

✔ Humane societies and other privately run shelters that are founded and managed by individuals who want to protect animals, advocate for animals, and find homes for animals that need them.

In general, both types of animal shelters do the same things; they take in animals without homes, arrange for adoptions, sometimes euthanize animals that cannot be adopted, and often rehabilitate animals to make them more adoptable by providing healthcare, spaying or neutering them, and working with them to socialize and train them. Not only do animal shelters provide you with a place to find pets that need new homes or look for your lost pet, but they also manage animal control issues where you live.

Animal shelters often work in conjunction with rescue groups that specialize in providing homes to specific kinds or even specific breeds of pets. These rescue groups often are better equipped for finding a home for purebred dogs or cats or less-common shelter animals like parrots or snakes, because they specialize in the unique needs of these animals and have more extensive connections and resources to find homes for their particular types of animals. (For more about rescue groups, see Chapter 3.)

Most of the animals at typical shelters are dogs and cats, but they often accept other small animals like ferrets, rabbits, birds, reptiles, and other exotic animals. These less common animals usually come to the shelter not as wandering strays, but rather because their previous owners bought them on a whim without first researching what was involved in caring for them. These animals suddenly are left without homes through no fault of their own.

Some shelters are privately funded in communities that support them, even though they're under the control of local government. Some have nice new facilities with plenty of donated food and toys and actively advertised adoption programs. Some employ trainers and veterinarians so that every incoming animal is screened, health-checked, and socialized. Some shelters have obedience-training programs for dogs to make them more adoptable, and they carefully screen pet behavior to determine how suitable each animal is for adoption.

Not all shelters, however, are so well equipped. In some areas, shelters are so overworked, understaffed, and depleted of resources that they can't give pets the best of care, let alone evaluate each individual animal to get a good idea of its adoption potential. Many shelters constantly deal with a lack of funding. Running a shelter takes a lot of know-how, from running a business and advertising to being a savvy accountant and business manager. Shelter work is a difficult business to be in, and yet shelters offer an invaluable service to their communities. The people who work at shelters serve pet owners and pets, often purely on a volunteer basis. (If that isn't reason enough to remember the local shelter at holiday giving time, I don't know what is!)

What is your local shelter like? The best way to tell is to visit, check it out, look at the animals, and ask questions before deciding to adopt. You can find out a lot about a shelter just by looking.

Thinking twice about the success of shelters

Many people refuse to visit animal shelters because they find it too sad or depressing. They shouldn't feel so bad because so many lucky animals are saved from a dangerous life on the streets, where they're at risk of traffic accidents, attack by other animals or humans, and subject to the elements. Many lost pets likewise are found and reclaimed by distraught owners simply because they were brought into animal shelters. Most important, adoptable pets find homes, and sick or dangerous animals are humanely relieved of their suffering.

Many people also think animal shelter employees are somehow the bad guys. If your average shelter employee had a nickel for every time somebody said, "I could never do your job. I love animals too much," that employee probably would want to chuck those nickels right back at the unthinking visitors. Shelter workers have tough jobs full of heartbreak and loss, but they do it because _they_ are the ones who love animals "too much." Volunteer at your local shelter to see what I mean. Need more proof? Did you know that:

✔ 18 percent of pet dogs in the United States are adopted from animal shelters.

✔ 16 percent of pet cats in the United States are adopted from animal shelters.

✔ About half the dogs and cats that come into animal shelters each year are adopted — hurrah! Of course, sadly, the other half must be euthanized because they either were not adoptable or nobody decided to adopt them.

Shelters are great places to find a pet to adopt, even if you're looking for a purebred dog. Between 25 percent and 30 percent of the dogs taken in by shelters are purebred.

Exploring what no-kill shelters offer

Some animal shelters advertise as "no-kill" shelters, meaning they do not euthanize animals. Although the idea of a no-kill shelter working hard to place every animal it accepts may sound like a worthy one, the downside is that no-kill shelters accept only animals that are deemed adoptable. Animal shelters — usually those run by local government — accept all animals, and that means they sometimes have to euthanize the ones that are not adoptable because of severe health or behavior problems. All shelters try their best to adopt out the animals that will make good pets; however, many animals suffer from abuse or abandonment, become lost, or are allowed to stray and may no longer be adoptable. At least animal shelters take them in and ease or eliminate their suffering.

A shelter is a great place to adopt a pet, and I almost always recommend people look at the shelter first before choosing or buying a pet from another source. But adopting an animal companion from a shelter isn't for everyone, and you definitely need to consider the pros and cons that follow before you decide whether a shelter is the right place for you to adopt your pet.

Shelter pros

A few of the wonderful reasons for adopting a pet from a shelter (and sometimes a rescue group — see Chapter 3), as opposed to buying one from a pet store or a breeder, are that you can

- ✔ **Save one of the millions of animals that are euthanized in shelters every year.** When you adopt a shelter animal, you give one of these adoptable pets a second chance at a new, healthy life and a happy home.

- ✔ **Discover that the pet you thought you wanted isn't the one you need.** An in-need shelter pet may be a much better fit for you — for example, you may think you want a puppy but discover that an older dog is calmer, better trained, and more bonded to you.

- ✔ **Pay less for your pet.** Adoption fees typically are far below what pet stores charge.

- ✔ **Find out more about your new pet than you can from a pet store.** Responsible shelters provide you with plenty of care information, support, temperament evaluation, and more.

- ✔ **Get more specific information about a shelter animal from shelter workers.** Talk to the people who have been spending time with the pet to find out about what the animal is like and what he needs.

- ✔ **Feel good about contributing to and supporting a process that supports the welfare and management of stray animals in your community.** You can get involved with the process in many ways, from adopting pets to donating money to volunteering your time. In fact, most shelters include many volunteers on their staffs, solicit donations, and conduct fundraisers. They often need your help. In fact, humane societies and privately run shelters usually depend almost entirely on donations and volunteers.

✔ **Find a lost pet.** Shelters often are responsible for reuniting lost pets with their owners.

✔ **Give up an animal that you've found or that you're unable to keep.** If, for some unfortunate reason, you're unable to keep a pet, you can turn it over to (or return it to) the shelter. If a stray wonders into your life, you can turn it over to the shelter — and maybe later adopt it.

Some shelter pets have special needs, and if you're willing to manage those needs, you can save a pet that otherwise may not find a home — and that feels great.

Shelter cons

I can't think of many cons to adopting a pet from a responsible shelter that properly screens potential pets for health and temperament and works hard to match pets and owners appropriately, but a few downsides to adopting a pet from a shelter can be problematic for you. You need to think carefully before adopting a pet from a shelter because:

✔ **You're unable to find the exact kind of pet you want.**

✔ **You're unable to adopt the pet you want immediately.** Shelters often must adhere to a waiting period so you don't rush into a decision and so pet owners have time to reclaim any incoming animals that may be lost.

✔ **You're faced with answering a lot of personal questions and submitting a lot of paperwork.**

✔ **Shelters aren't always rolling in dough.** Just because the government funds an animal-control agency doesn't mean it's getting everything it needs. Some shelters are underfunded and may not be able to maintain spacious facilities or spend much time screening or training the animals. Most shelters do all they can with the resources they have, but all too often, those resources are pretty slim.

✔ **Your new pet may turn out much different than you expected.** When you bring any animal home, you may find it's much different than it appeared to be at the shelter.

✔ **Some shelter pets have special needs that you may not be willing to deal with.**

✔ **You may be rejected for the pet you want if you don't meet the shelter's requirements.**

Finding a Great Shelter Near You

Great shelters are not usually hard to find. Many cities and towns have excellent animal sheltering facilities that work hard to pair the right pets with the right people. Where do you find a reputable shelter? Even if you don't have one in your immediate vicinity, you may have one nearer than you think. You just need to know where to look.

Sometimes the only nearby shelter is in great need of funds, volunteers, and resources, one that may not be able to provide careful screening, microchip identification, spay/neuter services, or even veterinary checkups before an adoption. These shelters may be busy, hurried, and so stressed that they may even let you walk in and walk right back out with a pet. That doesn't mean you shouldn't adopt a pet from such a shelter; animals in low-budget shelters with little staff aren't any better or worse than the animals in sufficiently funded and staffed shelters. You simply may not be able to find out as much about the animal, and that means you need to be extra vigilant in choosing an animal that's right for you. If the animal turns out to have an insurmountable problem, you may have to return it. However, with the know-how you're getting from this book, you can choose an animal that works in your situation. See the "Checking out the facility" section later in this chapter for help with adopting a pet from a less-than-perfect shelter.

Checking the Yellow Pages and Internet

"Letting your fingers do the walking" is the first step to finding a shelter near you. Look in the phone book under "Animal Shelter" or "Humane Society," or check under city or county government sections for "Animal Control." Doing so provides you with a link to your local animal control agency, but it may not be your only option.

One great thing about the Internet is the way it has facilitated pet adoptions. Several excellent Web sites link shelters across the country and quickly let you know exactly what shelters and rescue groups exist in your city, state, or region. Using these sites, you can search online to find out what pets are available anywhere in the country. You can search by species and breed, and some sites even have pictures and descriptions of the animals, including whether they work well with children or other pets. This information can help you spot potential pets, which you can then meet in person, already armed with some basic knowledge.

Web sites are no substitute for an in-person visit, but they certainly let you know what's out there. They even put you into contact with other nearby shelters that you otherwise may never have found. These sites often list animal-control shelters, privately run shelters, and rescue groups. Finding the perfect pet may be worth a day trip. Here are comprehensive Web sites designed to put you in contact with shelters near you:

✔ **Petfinder:** www.petfinder.org

✔ **Pets 911:** www.pets911.com

✔ **World Animal Net:** www.worldanimalnet.org

✔ **1-800-Save-A-Pet:** www.1-800-Save-A-Pet.com

✔ **The American Society for the Prevention of Cruelty to Animals (ASPCA):** www.aspca.org

✔ **Humane Society of the United States (HSUS):** www.hsus.org

Rounding up recommendations

Another great way to find a good shelter is by asking friends, co-workers, or local animal-care professionals — pet sitters, doggy day-care owners, and groomers — what they know about local shelters. They often can recommend the best places to adopt pets or share with you their own experiences with different local or regional shelters. If you already have a shelter in mind, talk to people who have adopted pets there, and if you can find them, talk to people who have been denied adoptions. These people may not be happy about their experiences, but if the shelter denies someone who didn't have the right environment or situation to adopt a particular kind of pet, that actually is a positive sign that the shelter is keeping the best interest of the animals in mind.

If you don't know of anyone who adopted from a particular shelter, the shelter should be able to provide references or put you in touch with someone who has. Checking these references can be especially helpful when you're adopting from a shelter in a different town or city. Other sources to consult for more recommendations about or background on a shelter include:

✔ **Local veterinarians.** Vets in the area have probably met and treated animals adopted from local shelters. They may have special insight into the way particular shelters handle the health of their animals. Although they may or may not like the shelter's procedures, vets may also have good insight into the health and temperament of some of the animals people have adopted from local shelters.

✔ **Local dog trainers.** Dog trainers, especially the ones who teach basic obedience courses, have probably seen many of the pets coming from shelters and may have a unique perspective on the way shelters assess adoptability and behavior.

✔ **Pet stores that don't sell cats and dogs.** These stores have probably sold pet supplies to many people who have just adopted a pet from the shelter. Some pet stores work in conjunction with local shelters, even sponsoring shelter animal adoption events. Pet stores may have information about and be able to recommend shelters.

Your shelter needs you

Animal shelters are notoriously understaffed and underfunded, and many of them rely on volunteers to keep doing the good work they do. Are you one of those volunteers? Volunteering at your local shelter is one of the best ways to understand how shelters work, to make a significant contribution to animal welfare, and to meet many potentially adoptable pets. Shelters need people to walk dogs, play with cats, feed and water animals, even apprentice as dog trainers. People with special knowledge about small animals, birds, or exotics may be in demand to help out with these less common pets, and people interested in exotic pets may find shelters the perfect place to find out about them before adopting. You can feel good about making a difference in your community while helping animals. In addition, for people who want to adopt every stray dog and cat they meet, volunteering gives you an opportunity to get to know and spend time with many animals without the burden of bringing them *all* home.

Walking through the Adoption Process

After you locate an animal shelter or shelters near you, you can visit, have a look around, ask questions, look at the animals, and inquire about the adoption process. Every animal shelter is different, but most operate according to some basic principles. This section hooks you on a leash and walks you through the process so you know just what to look for and what to expect from the shelter.

Checking out the facility

When you first visit an animal shelter, you may want to make a beeline for the nearest kennel of puppies or kittens. Whoa, Nelly! Hold on a minute. You can tell a great deal about a shelter just by looking around a bit. Here are some signs that the shelter you're checking out is a good one:

- ✔ Animals are kept in clean, spacious, well-ventilated kennels.
- ✔ Animals get time outside their kennels to go on walks or play in outdoor kennels.
- ✔ The shelter offers adoption counseling to help you find the right match for your needs and situation.
- ✔ The shelter employs or is affiliated with a local veterinarian, a local dog trainer, and a local animal-behavior consultant or veterinary behaviorist.
- ✔ The shelter spays or neuters animals or gives adopters vouchers to have this service performed by a local vet at a reduced cost or even for free.
- ✔ The shelter implants microchips in its pets for identification.

✔ The shelter works on socializing and training or taming animals and evaluates temperament and behavior carefully to help make the best pet/owner match.

Before you adopt an animal from a shelter that doesn't screen for behavior or provide veterinary care before adoption, be sure to:

✔ Take any animal you may want to adopt to the vet before you take it home and *before* you sign any paperwork committing you to adopt the pet. Get clearance from your vet that the animal is healthy, in good shape, and free from diseases and parasites. This visit may be costly. Expect to pay for tests, vaccinations, dewormings, and treatment. If you decide not to adopt the animal, take copies of all the veterinary records back to the shelter and hand them over. You may be able to deduct the cost of the vet visit on your taxes as a charitable donation. Ask your accountant whether you can.

✔ Spend several visits with the animal to get a better sense of its temperament. Pets need to act confident but not aggressive, and may act reserved but not overly shy or cowering. Extremely shy or aggressive pets can turn out to be even shyer or more aggressive when you get them home and they get used to you. On the other hand, sometimes shy or pushy animals calm down and settle into a new home nicely. These pets are stressed at the shelter but gain confidence and self-possession when they realize they have somewhere to stay. You need to realize that adopting a shelter animal comes with risks and that you'll be adopting a pet with some unknowns.

✔ Be careful about unscreened animals if you have children, live near children, or if children often visit your house. Don't put your children or other children at risk.

✔ Look for animals that appear healthy, with shiny eyes free of discharge, healthy skin, coats or feathers (if applicable) without bare patches, and without fleas, ticks, or mites.

✔ Consider adopting a special needs pet. Even if an animal has health or temperament problems, you may decide to adopt it anyway. Only do so if you're prepared to put in some serious time, money, and work rehabilitating the animal. The last thing such animals need is to think they have a home and then again be given up and returned to the shelter.

Looking at the pets

After you've had a look around the shelter and asked a few questions, you'll be eager to look at the pets. Shelter workers expect this exuberance, so ask whether you can see the animals, and they will be happy to direct you to the kennels, cattery, or other facilities. Shelters typically are arranged with a front office and then rows of kennels housing the animals. Some have special rooms for pets that are being treated for medical problems or that need special care. Cats may be housed in an open cattery with cat trees and scratching posts;

less sociable felines may be in cages or crates. Other animals such as small mammals, birds, and reptiles, may be housed in the front office to draw attention to them or in separate rooms where potential adopters can go to look at them. If you're interested in animals other than dogs or cats, ask the shelter workers whether they have such animals, and they'll be glad to show you.

If you don't see the kind of animal or breed you're looking for at the shelter, don't assume the shelter won't get that animal or breed. Most shelters take in new animals all the time. Although some shelters don't have time to keep lists of special requests and call people when those animals arrive, some shelters will oblige. You just have to ask. If you want a Chihuahua or a Persian or an Amazon Gray parrot, you may be able to get on a list to be notified when such a pet comes in and is made available for adoption. If the shelter doesn't provide that kind of service, just keep visiting and looking. Your perfect pet probably will appear eventually. Or, look into breed rescue (see Chapter 3).

Shelters usually have special rooms where you can take the pet out of its kennel, spend some one-on-one time, and have a great opportunity to get a closer look for signs of good health and pleasant and appropriate pet temperament (for more on assessing the health and temperament of individual pets, see Parts II through VI of this book on the different types of animals). These special rooms also give you a chance to interact with the pet to see whether you think it's the kind that you'd like to live with.

Although you may think you know immediately what pet you want, give it some time, and come back for another visit or two. First impressions are often correct, but not always. Bring all your family members, and if possible, even your other pets. Let everyone get to know your potential pet before jumping into the adoption process.

Asking the right questions

After you've looked at some pets, you'll want to find out more information about the shelter's adoption process. That's when you need to ask some serious questions. If you have a specific pet in mind that you think you may want to adopt, be sure to ask questions about that pet. Parts II through VI address different types of pets and can guide you in the kinds of questions to ask about a particular type of pet. Some general questions to ask about the shelter process include:

- ✔ Do you have the pets spayed or neutered, or do you require that adopters spay or neuter the pets? If so, do you offer a voucher to have the procedure done locally at a discount?

- ✔ Do you embed microchip identification in the animals? How much does this procedure cost?

- ✔ What information and supplies do you provide with an adopted pet?

- ✔ Can you recommend a good trainer or behavioral consultant?

✔ What information and paperwork do you require from people who are adopting pets?

✔ What are your adoption fees? Are there other costs involved?

✔ Do you have other requirements that I must meet before I can adopt a pet?

If you receive agreeable answers to these questions, ask the shelter for a list of everything you need and everything you're required to do, before you come back to adopt the animal. Most shelters require a certain amount of paperwork (see later section about "Sealing the Deal"), and they may require you to agree to do certain things after you take possession of the animal, such as having the animal spayed or neutered. Every shelter is different and should tell you without reservations what its specific requirements are.

Avoiding second thoughts: The waiting period

When you're anxious and eager to bring home your new pet, the waiting period that many shelters require can be frustrating. Although you want your pet *now,* the waiting period is actually a good idea. Although not every shelter requires it, some shelters enforce a waiting period specifically to guard against impulse buys and buyer's remorse.

People tend to get excited when they see a cute dog, cat, or exotic animal they've always dreamed of owning. In a frenzy to *get that pet,* people sometimes rush into a decision without really considering whether they're ready to take on the responsibility. Waiting periods may be only a few hours or even up to a couple of days, but be patient and use the time wisely for what it is intended: to think seriously about whether you're ready for the long-term commitment of adopting and caring for a pet . . . no matter how adorable. If you're quite sure you want the pet, you may also use this time to collect the paperwork the shelter requires, prepare your home, and get all the supplies you need when you bring your new pet home. In some cases, there can be some competition for adoptable pets, so you might also ask whether anyone else is also considering adopting the animal you like. If you are first in line, then you needn't worry that someone else will adopt the animal during your waiting period.

Sealing the Deal

Making the decision that you are indeed ready and willing to adopt an animal is an important part of sealing the deal, but it isn't the only part. You also need to collect some important information. You fill out an adoption form that asks you many questions, and you may have to provide some paperwork to turn in along with the adoption application. Although every shelter does things a little differently, a typical pet adoption process probably involves the following:

✔ Filling out an application form that includes basic information about you, your living situation, other people and pets in your household, and where you plan to keep the animal. The application may also ask whether you have a fenced yard, plan to let a cat roam, or have proper enclosures and other environmental requirements for small animals, birds, reptiles, or other exotic pets.

✔ Showing proof that you own your home or that your landlord knows you're adopting a pet and gives you permission to do so — usually in the form of a signed letter, a phone call, or personal visit. If you show proof of home ownership, the shelter may contact the assessor's office to verify that proof.

✔ Showing proof that you are not a student. Some, though not all, shelters won't adopt pets to students, because they're notoriously prone to leaving pets behind after graduation.

✔ Agreeing to take certain steps in the future, including:

• Having your pet checked regularly by a veterinarian

• Having a microchip implanted in your pet for identification and so that it can be tracked if lost

• Having your pet spayed or neutered

In many cases, you must sign a contract that specifically states you will do any or all of these things. Sometimes you even have to pay a deposit that you get back whenever you show proof that you've had these things done. Other times the shelter takes care of these services before releasing the pet for adoption, and the costs are fully or partially covered by your adoption fee. When shelters perform these services, adoption fees obviously are higher.

✔ Agreeing either verbally or in writing to take proper care of the animal by providing good nutrition and veterinary care and by having the animal adequately vaccinated, as required by law and as recommended by a vet.

✔ Verifying either verbally or in writing that the animal is for you and not a gift for someone else and that you intend the animal to be your pet and not your guard dog, barn mouser, or breeding stock.

✔ Agreeing that the pet will live inside and not be kept outside.

✔ Providing proof that you have a fenced yard or the right kind of facilities to keep the animal.

After you fill out all the paperwork, collect your copies, pack up any supplies and other information that come with your pet, and take your pet home!

Come prepared to transport your animal home safely. Dogs and cats need to be in kennels that can be secured inside a vehicle or strapped safely into a pet seatbelt, both of which you can purchase at the pet store or online (for example at ruffrider.com). Animals in cages also need to be safely secured with a seatbelt or other secure device. Bring your own mode of transporting your new pet, because most shelters won't provide one for you.

Chapter 3

Rescue Me! All About Pet Rescue Groups

In This Chapter

▶ Discovering what a rescue group is and how it differs from an animal shelter

▶ Assessing and approaching rescue groups: The best way

▶ Checking out a rescue group, and being checked out by a rescue group

▶ Getting to know the pets

▶ Volunteering as a rescue group foster caretaker

Maybe you really want to adopt a pet that needs a home, but you have your heart set on something specific: a yellow Labrador Retriever, perhaps, or a fuzzy Pekingese, or a Maine Coon cat, or maybe a lop-eared rabbit, a teddy bear hamster, or a ball python. If you know what you want in a pet and your requirements are specific, a rescue group may be just the thing for you.

Rescue groups do more than merely specialize, singling out one type of animal or breed for rescue. They also provide a more personal approach to pet rescue. Typically operated by volunteers and usually without a dedicated facility, rescue groups essentially are networks of animal devotees that keep in contact with each other to rescue and find new homes for their favorite breeds or animals. These people are committed to the welfare of their charges and won't allow just anyone to adopt from them. Prepare to be grilled!

On the other hand, don't be nervous — unless you're particularly delectable with a coating of sauce. Yes, rescue groups have stringent guidelines for adoption, but only because they care so much — a good thing! After the members of a rescue group recognize how committed you are to doing the right thing for your adopted pet, they'll appreciate you more, and you'll appreciate their efforts to help you find the perfect fit. This chapter helps you find a rescue group that meets your needs and advises you on how to meet, work with, and adopt a pet from one.

Weighing the Pros and Cons of Adopting from a Rescue Group

Working with a rescue group can be a great experience. You may develop a close relationship with the people you're working with as you get to know them and they get to know you and all decide which pet works best in your particular home situation and for your particular lifestyle and personality. Every rescue group is slightly different, and the costs vary, too, depending on the type of animal, what supplies come with the pet, how much medical care the animal already has received, and how long the animal has been in foster care with the rescue group. Some rescue groups have set fees for adoption that can range from $5 for a hamster or a rat to more than $1,000 for a large parrot complete with large cage and supplies.

The rescue group's procedures and policies depend not only on local laws but also on who started the group, how the group was organized, who manages the group, and even the personalities of the various people fostering pets waiting for homes. In fact, the character of the rescue group is much more closely tied to the personalities of the people running it than it is with a government-run animal shelter. But both are concerned about screening you to make sure you're right for the pet you want. Rescue workers rescue animals because they love them, and they don't want to entrust the animals they rescue with someone who won't provide them with a good home.

 Before choosing a rescue group, be sure to meet the people in charge in person. Ask for references and ask to see where they keep the animals. Although most rescue groups are devoted to saving pets and placing them in good homes, a few unfortunately use the rescue-group reputation as a front for stealing or hoarding animals and selling them for a profit, a practice that horrifies legitimate rescuers. Know what you're getting into before you support an illegal operation or unknowingly contribute to animal neglect and abuse.

But even the best rescue groups aren't for everyone. Before you decide, you need to weigh the pros and cons of rescue groups. If you think the pros outweigh the cons, then read on for more information about finding a rescue group that works with the kind of pet you want to adopt.

Rescue group pros

Not all of the benefits on the pro side of the slate are specific to rescue groups. Some apply to shelters, too. Nevertheless, among the many great reasons for adopting a pet through a rescue group are that you can

✔ Find the specific breed or animal you want.

✔ Work one-on-one with someone and develop a relationship with people already knowledgeable and interested in the breed — people who are just as passionate as you about rescuing animals.

✔ Rest assured (usually) that the rescue group has carefully monitored the animal's health and temperament and can give you a good idea of what the pet is like.

✔ Reap the benefits of the rescue's preadoption care, which often includes having the animal examined by a vet, spayed or neutered, treated for any health problems, and brought current on all vaccinations.

✔ Talk to people providing foster care to the pet. Because they've already been living with the pet, they can give you plenty of specific information about what the animal needs.

✔ Feel good about contributing to and supporting a process that is truly committed to finding homes for adoptable animals in a responsible way.

✔ Ultimately rescue an animal that needs a new home.

✔ Volunteer to help with the rescue group or become a foster-care provider for other rescued animals.

Fostering first: The adopter's test run

You know that adopting a pet is a big responsibility, but one of the best things about working with a pet rescue group is that you have an opportunity to be a foster caretaker for your breed or animal of choice. Doing so gives you experience in what living with a particular animal, breed, or species is like in general. Plus, you're providing your rescue group with a valuable service. Foster caretakers often are in short supply.

To volunteer as a foster caretaker, contact your local rescue group and explain that you're interested in providing foster care for rescued pets. You need to have the right environment for the pet and be prepared to provide a safe, caring home. If you don't have training or experience with the particular type of animal, the rescue group may train you first. Rescuers don't want to leave their pets with just anybody, so you can expect to be given just as thorough a screening as when you're being considered for a pet adoption. Ask what the terms are, what you're expected to do and pay for, and what the rescue group covers. Ask how much the rescue group typically knows about the animal's health and temperament before it comes to you, and how much you're responsible for assessing those traits. Furthermore, ask what happens if you decide that you want to adopt an animal for which you're providing foster care.

Providing foster care enables you to meet and interact with many different animals coming into your home in need and then leaving to go to their forever homes. The job of a foster caretaker is rewarding, even if it is hard at times to say goodbye. One of those foster animals may just turn out to be *your* forever pet. Or, you may decide you do pets even more of a service as a serial foster parent, caring for and helping to rehabilitate animals as they're rescued and then seeing them safely off to their forever homes with other caring adoptees.

Rescue group cons

As much as I'd like to tell you that the pros are all you have to worry about, if these pesky cons turn out to be deal-busters for you, you probably ought to consider other adoption options. Like the pros in the previous list, some of the drawbacks of rescue-group adoptions also apply to shelters. Depending on the rescue group (or shelter), you may find yourself:

- ✔ Traveling a great distance to hook up with the rescue person who has the animal you want.
- ✔ Answering many personal questions.
- ✔ Paying more than you planned for the pet and supplies.
- ✔ Allowing a rescue person to come to your home, check you out, and approve you for an adoption.
- ✔ Dealing with people who are incredibly devoted to animals but may not necessarily always be good at dealing with people.
- ✔ Feeling insulted. Rescuers typically have great passion but they've encountered plenty of unsavory human behavior and may deal with you by assuming the worst until you prove otherwise.
- ✔ Falling in love with a pet but being rejected as having an unsuitable environment for the pet you want.

Here's how to decide: If you don't like these kinds of personal intrusions, you may be better off working with a shelter. However, an animal rescue group may be just the way for you to go, if you:

- ✔ Admire what rescue workers do.
- ✔ Think the efforts of rescue workers are in the best interest of the pets (almost always true).
- ✔ Like the way rescue workers help you find a custom fit.
- ✔ Want to try providing foster care for rescued animals to help the cause while trying to choose the right pet for you.

Scouting Out a Particular Rescue Group

If you've decided to go with a rescue group, you can start hunting for the ones that deal with the type or breed of animal you want to adopt. Even if you've never heard of a rescue group in your area, one may exist right under your nose. Rescue groups don't always advertise, so you have to talk to the right people. This section guides you to finding the people who are looking for someone just like you.

Asking around

When you know what kind of pet you want to adopt, you can jump right in and contact local, regional, or national clubs organized by fanciers of the animal you want. Sounds simple, right? And for the most part it is. For example, a local dog obedience club may keep a list of purebred rescue groups in your area. The local herpetological society may be able to direct you to a great iguana rescuer.

Your veterinarian can be another great resource. Rescue groups often supply their information to vets, and vets often see and treat rescued animals, so they can frequently direct you to a contact person working with the kind of animal you want.

Responsible and ethical small-scale or hobby breeders of the animal you want typically are willing to put you in touch with local rescue groups associated with that breed. For that matter, some small breeders also work in rescue. (If a breeder tries instead to sell you an animal, walk away!) Even though they may breed purebred animals, devoted breeders also care about the forgotten animals of their chosen breed and usually do everything they can to help place them in good homes.

You can also ask around at local pet stores (the ones that don't sell the kind of animal you want), or at your local animal shelter. Because animal shelters often work with rescue groups to find homes for purebred animals, they often can provide you with contact information.

Surfing the Net

Consider the Internet as your staunch ally in locating a rescue group. Do you want to find an all-breed rescue? A purebred rescue? An exotic-pet rescue? Are you looking for something local, regional, or national? The Internet is full of contact information about specific rescue groups, and several clearinghouse-style Web sites keep huge databases of rescue groups and animal shelters across the country and around the world. Here are some links to help narrow your search. Many of these links have national coverage with Web-site search engines where you can enter your city or zip code and get a list of rescuers near you.

- **Pet Finder:** www.petfinder.org
- **Pets 911:** www.pets911.com
- **American Kennel Club purebred dog breed rescue links:** www.akc.org/breeds/rescue.cfm
- **Netpets Dog Rescue Groups page:** www.netpets.com/dogs/dogresc/doggrp.html
- **Feline Rescue Network:** www.acfacat.com

- ✔ **Rescue Network for Pet and Wild Animals:** rescuenetwork.org

- ✔ **American Ferret Association:** www.ferret.org

- ✔ **Ferret Central Shelter/Rescue Links (national and regional):** www.ferretcentral.org/orgs.html

- ✔ **Guinea Pig Rescue Links:** www.cavyrescue.com/rescues.htm

- ✔ **House Rabbit Society rescue resources:** www.rabbit.org/adoption/index.html

- ✔ **Rat and Mouse Club Rescue:** www.rmca.org/Rescue/

- ✔ **Rat Rescue Forum:** www.ratrescue.com/forum/

- ✔ **RatRights:** www.ratrights.org

- ✔ **The Rodent Club Rescue:** www.rodentclub.com/rescue.htm

- ✔ **Avian Rescue Online:** www.avianrescue.org

- ✔ **Avian Web Adoption Page:** www.avianweb.com/Rescue.htm

- ✔ **Bird Placement Program:** www.birdrescue.com

- ✔ **Herp Societies and Rescue Programs:** www.anapsid.org/societies/index.html

- ✔ **Exotic pet/alternative pet rescue:** www.altpet.net/Rescue/

Surviving the Screening Process

The picture on the Internet was so adorable that now all you can think about is adopting that fluffy dog, cunning kitten, or precious parrot. But before you get to meet the pet that piques your interest, the rescue group handling the adoption wants to have a few words with you. And you thought interviewing for your last job was tough.

Actually, getting screened by a rescue group isn't bad. Rescuers are careful only because they're protective of the pets, and they want to be sure you are a good match. If they don't think you are, maybe they're right! The key is not to be offended, even if you think some questions are nobody's business or you don't like the rescuer's zealous nature. Not every rescuer grills you, but many will, primarily because they've encountered many deadbeats and potentially disastrous situations, and they've had to turn down many potential adopters. Proving that your home will make a great one for a rescued pet is up to you.

Screening works both ways. Many people who felt like they were under the microscope never spent time screening the rescue group and finding out how much it really knows about the pets. In the same way that you expect to be carefully screened, you also need to carefully screen not only the rescue group with which you're working but also (and perhaps even more so) the pet you think you may want to adopt.

In most cases, you talk to someone on the phone first, who asks you some questions and has you fill out an application. The rescue group reviews your application, and if workers like what they see, they may visit you at home to determine whether you can provide a proper environment for the pet. Only when they think you're a good potential pet guardian do they let you meet the animal that they (or you) think is the right one for you.

Making contact and checking references

The first time you contact a rescue group may be by phone, by e-mail, or through a Web site on the Internet. Maybe you found a particular pet on the Internet, and you fell in love with a picture. Or, the rescue group may even contact you, if they hear, through the grapevine — such as through shelter workers, local vets, or a local club — that you're looking to work with a rescue group. They may even send you a picture and profile of a particular pet.

Regardless of how you make your initial inquiry, you'll probably first talk on the phone to a contact person who screens people who obviously are not serious about adopting a pet or clearly are not behaving like potentially responsible pet owners. You want a pet, so you want to make a good impression. Be specific and polite. Explain that you're interested in adopting a pet through the rescue program, and that you'd like more information about the group, how it finds animals, how long it has been in operation, how many people work with the group, and whether it can provide you with references, such as other people who have adopted pets through the group and any vets who have dealt with animals that have come through the rescue. If you hear good reports, you can feel more confident that you're working with someone who's responsible and can help match you with the right pet.

That said, don't rely solely on the opinions of others. After making initial contact, meet with the rescue group organizer and ask some pointed questions about:

- ✔ How the rescue is set up
- ✔ What requirements the rescue group has in terms of fees, contracts, home visits, spay/neuter procedures, training, or any other issues
- ✔ How animals are evaluated for health and temperament
- ✔ How the group decides where to place rescued animals

Your initial screening of the rescue group demonstrates that you're as serious about working with people who care about animals as they are. If the rescue group balks at providing you with any of this information, consider it a red flag.

People who rescue pets receive many phone calls, sometimes at all hours of the night. For many of these people, the phone rings into their homes, interrupting their dinners, their family time, and even their sleep. Please be considerate about what time you call rescue workers, and if you're calling outside your state, pay attention to differing time zones.

If you find that a rescue group's practices are questionable or anything else bothers you, don't feel obligated to work with that organization. If, on the other hand, you think you've found a real treasure of a rescue group, then congratulations, it's time to move one step closer to meeting the pets by allowing the rescue group to find out what a stellar adoptive pet owner you'll make.

Answering questions, questions, and more questions

After you've asked questions and checked references, the table turns, and it's the rescue group's turn to check you out. And will they ever!

Rescue groups have great expectations. They want you to provide the perfect new home for a rescued pet. Bear in mind the group's priorities and the neglected animals its workers have seen. Doing so helps you to understand why rescue-group representatives ask you specific and sometime prying questions and why they may even seem suspicious of your motives. Remember, the rescue group has seen plenty of bad eggs, and the point of the entire process is to ensure your potential pet gets the best possible home.

A rescue group relies heavily on your answers to a long list of questions when determining whether you'll make a good adoptive pet parent. The group may also request a home visit (which I help you prepare for in the "Preparing for a house visit" section later in this chapter) and may ask you to answer questions either verbally or on an application form. Reviewing the list of possible questions that follows can help you prepare for the Q-and-A session. Some of these questions obviously apply to more common rescue subjects like dogs and cats. Your rescued chinchilla won't need a fenced yard, and you won't need to take your rescued iguana to obedience class (unless you really want to). The rescue group wants to know details, including:

- The full names, ages, occupations, and brief personality profiles of everyone living in your household, including children and other pets.

- How long you've lived in your current home and how long you've been employed at your current job — the rescue group wants to weed out transient types likely to dump a pet when they move on to the next adventure.

- Details about your home and yard, including size, setup, type of neighborhood, proximity to busy streets, and whether you have a fence (if relevant).

- ✔ Whether you own or rent your home, including proof of ownership.

- ✔ Whether your landlord approves of the kind of animal you seek, including proof in the form of a signed statement and landlord contact information for verification.

- ✔ Your knowledge of local ordinances concerning pets (to find out this information, call your city hall or courthouse and ask where you can get copies of animal-related ordinances).

- ✔ Where, specifically, you plan to keep or house the animal and where it will sleep.

- ✔ How long the animal will be left alone each day.

- ✔ How often caged animals will get to spend supervised time outside of their cages.

- ✔ Your daily activities, schedule, and hobbies.

- ✔ A general description of what you're like (Do you like pina coladas? Getting caught in the rain? Do you often stay out all night or forget to water your plants?).

- ✔ Whether anyone in your family has any allergies.

- ✔ A detailed explanation of why you want the particular breed or type of animal.

- ✔ Whether you'd consider a pet with special needs, such as a medical or behavioral problem.

- ✔ What color, sex, and age of an animal you're looking for and reasons for each preference and how flexible you are about these factors.

- ✔ How much you're willing to spend each year on vet care, food, grooming needs, supplies, and other expenses. As little as possible? Whatever it takes? How often you think the animal will need vet care.

- ✔ What kind of food you plan to feed the animal.

- ✔ Your future plans for grooming (the pet, not yourself).

- ✔ Whether you're also looking for pets through other channels, such as pet stores, breeders, or animal shelters, and why you're looking there.

- ✔ Whether the pet will ever be taken into public areas or come into contact with children, dogs, cats, horses, or other pets of the same type.

- ✔ How you plan to socialize and train or tame the animal.

- ✔ Who the primary caretaker will be.

- ✔ What activities you'd like to do with the pet.

- ✔ What kind of enclosure you'll use, if any (such as a dog crate, birdcage, or critter cage).

- ✔ How you plan to handle times when you are away for extended periods, such as vacations.

✔ What you plan to do with the animal if you have to move.

✔ How you plan to help the animal adjust to its new home.

✔ Whether you have specific concerns about certain behaviors, such as barking, scratching, or refusal to be handled.

✔ A list of all the other pets you have ever owned, including type of animal, sex, age, whether they were spayed or neutered, and if you don't still have them, why?

✔ Whether you ever owned a pet similar to the one you want to adopt, and if you have, whether you still have it. And if you don't still have it, what happened to it?

✔ How you heard about the rescue group.

✔ How much you know about basic veterinary care, pest control management, or conditions common to the breed or animal.

✔ Who will inherit the pet in the event of your death.

✔ Whether you can provide several references (and they will call your references!), including the veterinarian you use for other pets.

Does that list seem excessive? You may even encounter some additional questions not on this list. Most rescue workers believe that if everybody had to answer questions like this before buying or adopting a pet from anywhere, no more dogs, cats, or other animals would have to be rescued — and they might be right.

If rescue workers like your answers and your references check out, then typically you get to meet the pet in which you're interested or some pets the rescue group thinks are a good match for you. If, however, they judge that you can't adequately provide for the pet, then your application may be turned down. Instead of being angry, ask them nicely to explain why your application was rejected. Consider whether they may be right. Maybe that pet isn't for you afterall, and you need to keep looking. Or maybe you and that particular rescue group just don't work well together. Just because one rescue group turns you down doesn't mean they all will, and this experience can give you some insight into whether you're ready for a pet or whether you need to consider a different kind of pet.

Preparing for a house visit

If you pass the interview/application stage, rescue workers probably will want to visit you at home. They'll also want everyone who lives in your home to be present and available, because they need to meet everyone who comes into contact with the pet on a regular basis. Some people get nervous about home visits, but it's no different than what any adoption agency would do if you were adopting a child. They want to be sure you have a safe, sound environment and that the way you presented yourself on your application matches the reality of your everyday life.

You don't need to do too much to prepare for the visit other than clean up and, if possible, have facilities for the pet already in place so you can show the rescue workers the dog kennel, cat tree, ferret enclosure, parrot cage, or whatever else may be relevant.

If you have children, be aware that many people have been turned down for adoption when they have children running wildly about disobeying their parents. Rescue workers see the way people raise their children as a direct reflection on the way they'll raise and care for a pet. Tell your darling rugrats to be on their best behavior. Of course, if they really do run wild and you really do have a hard timing taming your offspring, you may be better off focusing on them before adopting a pet. Don't be offended, I speak from experience. Some people also are turned down if their perfectly lovely little children are too young for a particular pet or if a pet doesn't do well with children — which ultimately is best for everyone, of course.

If you are turned down for any reason after your house visit, again, ask the rescuer to explain why. If it has to do with you, you then know what problems or conditions to remedy. If it has to do with the particular pet, you may want to start thinking about a different kind of pet.

Meeting the pets

So far, so good. The rescue group likes you, and you like the people running the rescue group. Finally, you get to meet the pet whose picture you saw on the Internet. Or, if you haven't seen a particular pet, you get to meet a pet that you and the rescue group decide sounds like a good match. Until they're adopted, most rescued pets live in homes with foster parents who either work with or operate the rescue group, so now the tables are turned again, and it's your turn for a home visit to scrutinize not only the pet but also evaluation skills of the rescue group and foster parent. Are they telling you everything about the pet that you really need to know?

Rescue workers who find good adoptive parents are motivated to place their beloved animals in good homes, and although some are upfront about problems, with others, you may need to do a little digging. If the pet is new to the rescue, rescue workers may not have had an opportunity to evaluate the animal's health and behavior thoroughly. You can evaluate the pet for cleanliness and external signs of good health. The pet needs to be friendly and interactive (if relevant for that kind of pet) and not shy or aggressive.

Sometimes, if an animal is newly rescued and hasn't been in the foster home for long, it may still be insecure or adjusting — a natural reaction. The longer an animal lives in a foster home, the more the foster caretakers are able to tell you about the animal.

If the foster parents have nothing but wonderful things to say, be on your guard. Most animals have a few qualities that can be difficult to manage, and many animals are in rescue because of these qualities, whether it is a dog who urinates every time she gets scared (called submissive urination), a cat who refuses to use the litter box, a conure with a particularly cacophonous voice, or an iguana who thinks fingers are delicious. Here are some questions to ask:

- ✔ Can you tell me about this animal's temperament? What do you enjoy about him?

- ✔ Does the animal have any fears or dislikes?

- ✔ Have you noticed any tendency toward aggression, biting, pouncing, nipping, or even just guarding food, treats, or toys with a little growl or snarl or whip of the tail? If a bird, is it beaky, tending to bite everything?

- ✔ Is this animal shy or outgoing? Does he seem to enjoy the company of people or just certain people? How does he react to new situations?

- ✔ Does the animal have any behavior problems that need to be worked on? Have you been working on them?

- ✔ What healthcare has the pet already had? Have you noticed any signs of ill health that I need to look into with my vet?

Foster caretakers are important resources for you in deciding whether you want to adopt an animal. They interact with the animal every day. Ask them as many questions as you can about the animal's behavior. Things they may not see as a problem may be a problem for you, such as submissive urination or shyness. Some animals may have unexplainable fears of certain sounds or types of people.

Beyond what you are told, you can also observe things on your own by interacting with the animal. Do you like what you see? Does the relationship seem workable? Don't decide right away. Give the animal some time to get to know you. Rushed decisions often are the ones people regret. Please don't give in to the urge to take that animal home right there and then. The animal may be the cutest thing you ever saw, but if you go home, think about it, come back, and visit another time or two, you get a much better sense of what life with that animal will be like. Foster caretakers, rescue workers, the pet, and you all benefit from a relaxed, unhurried approach. The more interaction you have, the more you'll find out about whether you and the pet are meant to be together.

Making a Commitment: Signing the Rescue Contract

You can promise rescue workers, and your new pet, the moon if you want to, but signing a contract makes it all a little more official. Rescue groups sometimes make you sign lengthy contracts in which you promise to take good care of the pet in some specific ways. Some contracts require you to pay a deposit and when you come back with proof of spay/neuter procedure, vaccinations, obedience classes, or whatever else is required, the deposit is returned.

Rescue contracts can be intimidating, and it may seem like you have to promise to do an awful lot. Don't sign unless you agree, but consider the importance of what the rescue group is asking. Before granting an adoption, rescue groups may require you to agree to:

- Having the animal spayed or neutered

- Never breeding the animal

- Never selling or giving away the animal

- Returning the animal to the same rescue group if for any reason you can't keep it

- Keeping current on all vaccinations

- Deworming and other regular pest control measures, including flea, tick, or mite control

- Providing the animal with annual veterinary checkups and all necessary care as advised by a veterinarian

- Attending basic obedience classes (for dogs)

- Keeping the animal from roaming outside (such as with cats)

- Not housing the animal outside (such as with dogs or rabbits)

- Housing the animal safely and responsibly in an enclosure with adequate space and ventilation (such as with small mammals, birds, reptiles, and spiders); never tethering the animal to a chain and leaving it outside unsupervised

- Agreeing not to declaw a cat, rabbit, ferret, or dog — yes, some vets will even declaw dogs

- Providing all necessary care and expense for the safe, secure existence of the animal

Beyond agreeing to certain conditions, rescue groups typically charge a fee for adoption. The fee is not intended for anyone's profit, but simply to cover expenses the rescue group incurs taking in, treating, and caring for the animal. Truth be known, adoption fees often don't even begin to cover these expenses, which usually come out of the rescue volunteer's own pocket. Fees vary so be sure all fees are in writing. If everything goes well, and you, the rescue group, and the pet are all happy with the combination, and if you agree to the rescue group's terms, contract items, and fee, it's time to sign and take your pet home. To find out about preparing your home for you new pet and what supplies to buy, see the chapters later in this book that are geared toward specific types of pets.

You need a safe way to transport the animal home, too, usually an appropriately sized portable kennel or cage. Dogs and some cats are comfortable riding in pet seatbelts that you can buy at your local pet store or order online (try ruffrider.com). Please don't ever transport a dog loose in the back of an open-bed pickup truck! Animals in cages also need to be safely secured with a seatbelt or other secure device.

Part II

Welcoming a Dog into Your Life

The 5th Wave · By Rich Tennant

You the couple interested in adopting the German Shepherd?

ANIMAL SHELTER

In this part . . .

So many dogs, small and large and everywhere in between, with short coats, long coats, big ears or small, barkers and bayers, and the quiet shivery ones . . . well, this part of the book helps you choose the right breed or breed type for your life, and it tells you everything you need to know about caring for, feeding, managing, and training your adopted dog. You find out about vaccinations, spay/neuter surgery, good vets for dogs, and how to solve behavior problems. You dig into what so-called problems aren't really problems at all, but rather just normal dog behaviors. Consider this part your translation guide to all things doggy as you care for, nurture, and welcome an adopted dog into your home.

Chapter 4

Choosing Your Dog

In This Chapter

▶ Deciding on your dog's age and sex

▶ Recognizing signs of a healthy dog

▶ Detecting signs of great pet temperament

▶ Considering a mixed-breed or purebred dog

So many adorable dogs gaze at you from the shelter kennels, barking and wiggling, or coyly blinking and flirting, each trying to get your attention. If only you could take them all! But, of course, you can't. What you can do is focus on exactly what you want and need in a dog, and what kind of dog works best in your home and with your lifestyle. The fact that the animal shelter is full of dogs is proof that too many people buy dogs that aren't right for them. This chapter helps you make smart decisions on each of these issues, so that when you choose your dog, you know you've done the right thing. Sure, you should listen to your heart, but let your brain have a say, too.

Puppies Are Precious, but . . .

Just look at that fluffy wiggling ball of fuzz, those big innocent eyes, that madly wagging tail. Many people who want to adopt a dog are hoping to adopt a puppy, and that's no surprise. Puppies can be practically irresistible. Shelters have a much easier time placing puppies than they do older dogs. The downside, however, is that many of these puppies wind up back at the shelter as soon as they hit that difficult adolescent period, when they're big, rambunctious, and particularly challenging.

Before you decide that you *know* you want a puppy, make sure you take a good hard look at your options. Sometimes breed, size, or temperament of a dog is more important than its age. A chubby, round yellow Labrador Retriever puppy may be the cutest thing you ever saw in your entire life, but how will you feel when he grows to 75 pounds of explosive energy, knocking favorite knickknacks off your coffee table with his big wagging tail? Adopting either a puppy or an adult dog each has its distinct advantages and disadvantages, so consider the pros and cons I present in the sections that follow before making a decision.

Pros and cons of adopting a puppy

They're tiny, they're cute, and they tug at your heartstrings with that ferocious little tug-of-war puppy growl. But do you really want to adopt a puppy? Consider the pros and cons in the following lists.

The pros of puppy adoption provide you with:

- Control over exactly when and how well the puppy is socialized and trained, so your puppy learns good behavior early on and thus avoids bad experiences
- An opportunity for you and your puppy to bond right from the beginning
- A fun, playful, and adorable companion
- Plenty of attention from people who just want to pet the cute puppy
- Short-lived high energy that mellows into mature adolescence in one to two years
- A longer amount of time together than when you adopt an older dog

The cons of puppy adoption strap you with:

- A pet with behaviors you don't like, if you fail to control exactly how well the puppy is socialized and trained.
- The chore of housetraining your puppy, a time-consuming and sometimes frustrating task. If you stop paying attention, even for a moment, you'll have puppy puddles and piles to clean up for what seems like forever.
- Chewed up, well, everything. Puppies need to chew . . . a lot. You must provide them with things to chew and be very careful to keep things they are *not* allowed to chew out of reach.
- A seeming inexhaustible need for more exercise and stimulation than most adult dogs. Puppies, by nature, are energetic.
- Ill-mannered behaviors. Of course, manners are all human, and puppy behaviors are entirely natural, but even so, in our human world, puppies have no manners whatsoever. They may nip fingers, jump on people, bark at everything, pull on the leash, steal and chew up your stuff, pick on other pets, dig holes in your yard, try to escape the fence to play with the neighbors, and keep you up at night because *they* want to play. You have to teach them *everything*.
- A potentially scary picture of the unknown. Without ever seeing a puppy's parents, you have no idea what the puppy will look like when it grows up — especially true in the case of mixed breeds. Many shelter puppies that look like purebreds grow up to look much different as adults.

Pros and cons of adopting an adult dog

Adult dogs can make absolutely wonderful adopted pets. After adopting a puppy, many people decide never to do *that* again, and vow to adopt only adult dogs in the future.

Many adult dogs in shelters are wonderful, well-behaved family pets that lost their homes because of no fault of their own. Some are there because of some perfectly natural dog behavior their owners just didn't know how to manage. Others are there because divorce, a move, or an owner's death resulted in these pets losing their homes. Others are there because they are no longer the cute puppies to which their owners first were attracted. The most common age for dogs to be surrendered to shelters is in the difficult adolescent phase and early adulthood, usually between about 9 months and 2 years, when dogs typically develop some challenging behaviors backed up by a full-grown size. Rather than work on these issues with training and socialization, pet owners often just give up.

Before you decide that you want an adult dog, carefully consider the advantages and disadvantages and weigh them within the context of your own lifestyle.

An adult dog may be the perfect fit for you because it may already be:

- ✔ **Housetrained.** Many dogs housetrain young and never forget.

- ✔ **Finished teething.** Adult dogs typically don't chew and nip the way puppies do, although there are exceptions.

- ✔ **Well versed in basic training.** That is, they *know* how to walk on a leash, obey basic cues like "Sit" and "Come," and generally behave appropriately in the house.

- ✔ **Well socialized.** In other words, friendly and accustomed to many different kinds of people and situations.

- ✔ **More laid back.** Adult dogs aren't quite as wild and energetic as puppies.

- ✔ **Almost through adolescence.** Although adolescent dogs initially may be high energy, this condition won't last much longer, especially when you provide plenty of outlets for that energy.

- ✔ **More adaptable and willing to bond closely with anyone who takes them in, feeds them, and gives them a home and some attention.**

  Many people claim that adult dogs they adopted from shelters and rescue groups seem to know they've been given a second chance and that the people adopting them have done something wonderful by taking them in. These pet owners often claim they get a strong sense of gratitude from their dogs.

- ✔ **A quick study.** Adult dogs typically learn quickly and enjoy training sessions as a fun way to spend time with you. You can teach old dogs new tricks.

- ✔ **More readily available.** Shelters have a harder time placing adult dogs. Adopting one saves an animal that may otherwise never find a home.

Despite all the wonderful things that can come with adult dogs, they may also present challenges that you need to be aware of before you decide to adopt one. Some of these challenges are

- ✔ **Behavioral problems.** Resource guarding is one — snapping when you try to take away food or treats. Others are housetraining problems, dislike of children, or more serious issues like aggression or self-mutilation in response to anxiety.

- ✔ **Bad habits that take extra training to undo.** Excessive barking, digging in the yard, or chewing on your shoes are examples.

- ✔ **A lengthy adjustment period because the dog was in another home for so long.** Dogs may mourn lost loved ones or seem depressed.

- ✔ **Difficulty bonding.** Some dogs need to be taught to trust humans again.

- ✔ **Too short a time in your life.** You may only have a few more years with an adult dog. Larger breeds, especially, have life spans of only 6 to 8 years to begin with. If your adopted Great Dane is already 4 years old, well, you do the math.

Deciding on a Male or Female

Just as some shelters have a harder time finding homes for adult dogs than they do for puppies, many have a harder time finding homes for male dogs than they do for female dogs. Pet owners often say they want a female, a factor that at times is even more important to them than the breed. Yet males and females exhibit virtually no consistent difference in behavior. In some breeds, males actually make more affectionate pets, and females are more independent and have a higher drive to work. In other breeds, males tend to be more aggressive and the females more laid-back. But even these generalizations have many exceptions. And, when pets are spayed or neutered, some of these differences become even less significant.

Trying to predict a dog's personality based on its gender is impossible. That's why choosing a breed or breed mix or any individual that has qualities you enjoy is much more important than choosing a male over a female. Look at the breed, age, grooming needs, and temperament of a dog before you consider gender. You may be thankful that you didn't limit your choices so much when you find your canine soul mate is the sex that's opposite of what you thought you wanted.

Identifying Signs of a Healthy Dog

No matter what age, size, sex, or breed you're looking for, the health of the dog you're considering is one of the most important factors to evaluate before you adopt. Although many adopted dogs have minor health issues that are easy to resolve — a skin irritation, ear infection, or minor arthritis, basic sound health keeps basic vet bills at a minimum. If you adopt a dog with serious health problems such as chronic kidney trouble, heartworms, glaucoma, or heart disease, the vet bill can quickly skyrocket. Maybe you're willing to take on that expense for the sake of an ailing pet, but unless you're specifically prepared to adopt a dog with special medical needs, adopting a healthy dog probably is one of your top priorities.

Fortunately, most shelters and rescue groups have dogs checked by veterinarians and treated for any health issues before making them available for adoption. If you want to adopt a dog that has a minor health problem such as ear mites or a skin rash, you can ask the shelter to have these issues treated first. Although the shelter may not have the resources for such treatment, if it's something the shelter's vet overlooked, it may be willing to take care of the treatment for you. You can expect the shelter to have records of all vaccinations, dewormings, pest control measures, tests, medications, and any other medical diagnoses or treatments that have been administered during the dog's stay at the shelter. In some cases, the dogs' previous owners may be another source of information, providing medical records or at least the name of the vet caring for the dog before it was surrendered.

Beyond written documents, however, you can tell a great deal about a dog's health just by looking. When you evaluate a shelter or rescue dog, look for the signs of bright, vibrant health that I describe in the following sections.

Bright eyes and bushy tails

On first examination of a dog, you need to notice a few obvious signs of good health, including:

✔ **Bright eyes:** Eyes need to be bright and clear with no cloudiness and no discharge. Dogs older than 5 or 6 years old may have slight eye cloudiness caused by progressive hardening of the lenses, appearing as a barely detectible blue in the pupils and eventually a grey. This symptom is normal for older dogs, but milky opaque lenses are a sign of cataracts that cause blindness and need to be fixed, requiring expensive surgery. *Note:* Some breeds tend to have tear stains, including Poodles, Shih Tzu, Maltese, and other white or light-colored dogs. Tear stains are not usually a sign of ill health; they can even be remedied with some special products. However, a thick gooey discharge and redness or irritation in a dog's eyes may be a sign of an eye infection that requires medication.

✔ **Tight eyelids:** Eyelids need to fit tightly around the eye and not hang loose, except in the case of loose-skinned, droopy-faced dogs like Bloodhounds and Bassett Hounds. Some dogs have *entropion,* a genetic condition in which the lower eyelid curls inward, irritating the cornea, or another similar condition called *ectropion,* where the lower eyelid curls outward, hanging and enabling debris to become trapped under the lid. These conditions are easily fixed with a simple surgery, but they need to be addressed.

✔ **Discharge-free noses:** The dog's nose also needs to be free of any discharge, and the dog shouldn't be wheezing or coughing. These symptoms can signal a respiratory infection or other problems. A cold wet nose isn't necessarily a barometer of good health despite the old wives' tale, and a cold wet oozing nose is certainly not a sign of good health.

✔ **Polished ivories:** Take a look at those teeth. They should be white and clean and mostly free of tartar buildup. If they aren't, you need to do something about it. Tartar isn't necessarily a reason not to adopt a dog. Clean teeth are important because dental bacteria can travel through the bloodstream, infecting the dog's heart, causing heart disease, and decreasing life span. Teeth with a lot of tartar may need to be professionally cleaned by your veterinarian while your dog is under anesthesia. Generally a safe procedure, anesthesia can be risky for some breeds and for older dogs. This procedure also can get pricey. If your dog has just a little tartar, your vet may be able to scrape it off without putting your dog under.

✔ **Clean, infection-free ears:** Ear infections, usually caused by yeast, are common in dogs, especially dogs that have been wandering outside for extended periods and dogs with floppy ears (moisture and bacteria can get trapped inside the ear). Even dogs with short, prick ears can get ear infections because the ears are wide open to the introduction of bacteria. Another common ear problem is ear mites. Signs that a dog has an ear infection, or mites, include scratching, head shaking, and pawing at the ears. Ear infections must be treated by a vet but usually are easy to resolve.

Skin-tastic

A dog's coat — whether short, tight, and smooth as silk; long, flowing, and glamorous; or harsh, crispy, and wiry — is his crowning glory. The condition of the coat can also be an important indicator of the dog's overall health. Many health problems manifest in the skin and coat.

Parasites like fleas, ticks, and mange mites not only are uncomfortable and cause itching, but they also can transmit serious, even fatal diseases and result in rashes, allergic reactions, and massive hair loss and sores, including the red, inflamed, painful areas called *hot spots.* Skin infections — common in animals that are injured while wandering — can be caused by staph or other bacteria or by a wound that becomes infected. Likewise, immune system and other systemic problems can cause dull coats, hair loss, and skin problems.

Any of the following skin-and-coat conditions can indicate a health problem that needs to be addressed:

- ✔ **Patches of missing hair:** Even small patches of missing hair can signal a skin infection that requires treatment. Large patches can signal mange, which is caused by tiny skin mites.

- ✔ **Signs of fleas:** You may see tiny black specks — flea dirt — or the little brown hopping bugs themselves.

- ✔ **Ticks:** Ticks can be as tiny as pinheads, or when attached to the skin, swollen with blood to the size of acorns.

- ✔ **Signs of mites:** Mites are tiny black bugs that you may be able to see. They are smaller than fleas. Signs of mites include itching, ear irritation, red scaly patches, rashes, and hair loss.

- ✔ **Hot spots, those red, itchy, inflamed, weeping wounds caused by excessive scratching:** Hot spots can be the result of many possible causes. The most common are allergic reactions to fleabites, food, or other environmental irritants, or an irritated or infected injury. Although usually not serious, hot spots are incredibly uncomfortable for the dog and can be difficult to resolve because the dog will keep scratching and licking the wound.

- ✔ **Dull, thin coat:** A dull coat can signal diseased skin. Keep in mind, however, that this symptom also can be a sign of something as normal as a seasonal coat change or a post-delivery hair loss (in some breeds, the female loses much of her coat after having a litter of puppies). If coat changes signal a serious disease, such as hypothyroidism, it will have to be treated by a veterinarian.

- ✔ **Lumps or bumps in the skin or under the skin:** These afflictions may be cysts or tumors that may be simple to remove or that may be cancerous.

Bringing up the rear

Just what is under that tail? Take a look. A dog's rear end needs to be clean and free of discharge and signs of irritation or infection. Dogs with worms sometimes have infected rears, and in some cases, tiny worms are visible around the anus. If you get a chance, you also need to take a peek at the dog's stool (just don't do it right before lunch!). Some worms are visible in the stool. The stool should also be firm. Loose, very dark, or bloody stool can signify a problem with worms or other intestinal conditions.

Puppies commonly are infected by parasitic worms in-utero and, if not treated, they can carry these worms into adulthood. Problems with worms can be resolved with medication. Likewise, newly admitted dogs commonly get temporary diarrhea even with mucus or blood in it, caused by the stress of caging, new noises, loss of family, and dietary changes. This condition usually resolves itself in the first week. If you see abnormal stool in the cage, tell the staff and ask how long the dog has been in the shelter. If he's been there longer than a week, ask if a parasite check with a microscope has been done and/or if the dog has been dewormed.

The great big world: How the dog interacts

A dog's temperament is crucial in determining health. Dogs that are shy, hesitant, guarded, cowering, or growling and aggressive may actually be in pain or discomfort because of a health problem that isn't otherwise detectable. Temperament also is an indicator of personality (explained in the section that follows), but don't overlook the possibility that poor health is causing any temperament problem you see.

Although any of the following signs can simply be related to the stress of the environment or the dog's situation (the following section tells you more about evaluating temperament), factors that look like temperament problems but can actually indicate a health problem are:

- Cowering, extreme shyness, hesitation, or reluctance to be touched
- Backing away, hiding, or avoiding people and other dogs
- Whining, whimpering, crying, or agitation
- Constant scratching
- Circling, pacing, panting, or other nervous behavior
- Excessive drooling, especially accompanied by panting
- Growling, nipping, and other signs of aggression, although no dog behaving aggressively should be offered for adoption so please alert shelter workers if you notice signs of aggression

Temperament Testing

Many shelters do temperament testing on the animals they hope to offer for adoption, so they get a clear idea of the kind of pet home that best suits the pet and can separate pets that simply won't be able to thrive in a pet home because of a bad temperament. The temperament testing that shelters usually do can be as simple as checking the dog's behavior with other dogs and people, giving it basic commands to see whether it has any previous training, and testing the dog with cats and children.

Some shelters do more intensive temperament testing following specific methods recommended by certain trainers. Ask your shelter what type of temperament testing it has done and whether you can read the test results. I'd be wary of a shelter that refuses to let you read the results, because it may be trying to hide the fact that it doesn't do any temperament testing. The dog may nevertheless be perfectly adoptable. However, you want to know as much as possible about the animal you plan to adopt.

Evaluating a dog's temperament is extremely important. It can spell the difference between a trustworthy, trainable family pet and disaster in the form of injured people, angry neighbors, lawsuits, eviction, and a death sentence for the dog. A pet dog with a bad temperament is a serious liability. Bad temperament isn't the same thing as behaviors you don't like, such as lack of housetraining or barking too much. Bad temperament means the dog cannot be trusted around humans or other pets because of aggression or that the dog is so painfully shy or unsocialized that his quality of life suffers and he can't form healthy relationships with people. Shy dogs often bite out of fear, too. Clearly, animals with bad temperaments don't make good pets.

Beyond bad temperaments are variable temperaments. Some dogs are outgoing; some are reserved. Some are vocal or pushy or assertive; some are shy, retiring, and quiet. Temperament is akin to personality. It comes in many different guises, and understanding a potential pet's — and your own — temperament helps you choose a dog with which you can live, get along, and relate.

Not everyone agrees that accurately analyzing the canine temperament is even possible in just a few minutes or after just a few meetings. In general, remember that determining a dog's temperament is never a quick-and-easy thing to do. It involves a careful process of observation of and interaction with the animal. Some signs of bad temperament are obvious — growling, snarling, constantly quaking with fear — but many signs are not. Other aspects of temperament tend to unfold slowly as the dog becomes more comfortable in your presence. That's one reason why spending several extended visits with a dog before agreeing to an adoption is such a good idea. The more comfortable the dog is around you, the more his real temperament — shy, reserved, outgoing, fearless, aggressive, utterly friendly — will come out.

Exploring the effects of breed temperament

Assessing the temperament of any given dog is a tricky issue at best. Complicating matters are temperaments that once were accepted as part of a dog's breed but now are no longer suitable for the same animal as a pet. Sled dogs, hound dogs, guardian dogs, herding dogs, and many other types of working dogs, for example, needed extremely high levels of energy and endurance, an instinct to run long distances to track down game, strong territorial instincts, or instincts for nipping at heels to keep livestock in one place to earn their keep. When adopting one of these dogs, you need to know about these breed traits.

The breed or mix of breeds in a dog has a big impact on that dog's temperament and its physical traits — its coat and size, for example. Dogs with some sporting dog in them (like Labrador Retrievers, Golden Retrievers, and German Shorthaired Pointers) are relatively large and high in energy. Labrador Retriever mixes (see Figure 4-1) are among the most common dogs in animal shelters, often because people expect a placid temperament but are overwhelmed with the activity needs of a younger Lab or Lab mix.

Figure 4-1:
Lab mixes make devoted, intelligent, trainable companions as long as you give them lots of exercise.

Knowing a dog's natural tendencies is an important key to matching it with an individual or family. You can't expect a Border Collie to be a couch potato or a Jack Russell Terrier not to bark; it simply isn't in their nature. If you do, you're just setting yourself up for failure and setting your dog up for another disappointment.

Ask the shelter or rescue group for help finding out the breed or mix of the animal you're thinking about adopting. Most shelters and rescue groups label dogs as a breed or breed mix to give you an idea of what you can expect. Consider this information a guideline for helping you to choose a dog, but remember that no test can predict or guarantee exact behavior a few months down the road. Some general trends in breed temperament include the following, but remember that many exceptions exist for every rule:

- ✔ **Sporting breeds:** Retrievers, Pointers, and Spaniels are high energy and need plenty of activity, but they're generally easier than many other breeds to train.

- ✔ **Large working breeds:** Rottweilers, Doberman Pinschers, Great Danes, and Boxers tend to be territorial and protective. They need to be thoroughly socialized to keep them from becoming aggressive.

- ✔ **Terriers:** Jack Russell Terriers, Fox Terriers, Westies, and Schnauzers are high energy and bark a lot. They like to dig, jump, and can rarely be deterred from chasing small furry animals.

- ✔ **Hounds:** Beagles, Dachshunds, and Greyhounds follow scents or moving targets without regard to you or traffic or anything else. They are independent and can be difficult to train.

- ✔ **Northern breeds**: Siberian Huskies and Malamutes are extremely high energy, independent, and notoriously difficult to train. They are great at sports like sled pulling but can become destructive without enough mental and physical challenge.

- ✔ **Toy breeds:** Chihuahuas, Shih Tzu, and Maltese tend to bark a lot and can be prone to shyness as a protective mechanism caused by their diminutive size or aggression when they're unsocialized or overly protected. See Figure 4-2 for an example of a toy breed mix.

- ✔ **Herding breeds:** Border Collies, Shelties, and Australian Shepherds are highly intelligent and trainable but need a challenging job and plenty of exercise, or they can become destructive. Some herding breeds tend to nip at heels to keep children, other pets, or anyone else in the herd.

Figure 4-2:
Small mixed breeds like this Miniature Pinscher/ Pug cross probably have some toy breed and/or terrier in their genetic mix. Most are playful, friendly, and tend to bark a lot.

For more information about breed characteristics, check out the sections on "What Kind of Dog Is That? The Joy of Mixed Breeds" and "Adopting a Purebred Dog" later in this chapter.

Understanding the basics of temperament

So how do you know what's good or bad about a dog's temperament?

First of all, observe how the dog acts in the shelter or foster home. Is he active or laid-back? Does he seem nervous or calm? Does he follow or stay closely focused on people or is he more concerned with doing his own thing, exploring independently, or relaxing as if deep in thought?

Next, observe the dog as you interact with him. Is he interested in you or relatively indifferent? Does he try to engage you in active play and cuddle with you, or does he try to avoid you? Does he readily accept petting, or does he shy away? Does he jump all over you, or stand nicely, waiting to see what you may do next?

Observing these behaviors takes time and effort, so don't expect to be able to immediately adopt a dog after your first meeting, especially if you have any reservations about the dog's temperament. Spend several get-acquainted sessions with the dog to gain a more accurate feel for its individual personality. If you know your dog's breed or can guess what breeds may have contributed to his mix, you can research the typical temperaments for which each breed is known and compare them to the way your potential pet acts.

Although every dog has a unique personality, a few red flags can signal temperament problems that can become difficult to manage in a pet situation. As you watch how a candidate for adoption responds to the world, look out for the following warning signs:

- ✔ **Extreme shyness:** A dog with a good pet temperament won't act fearful and refuse to let you touch him. Hiding, cowering, crying, and flinching from touch are bad signs. Extremely shy dogs may live stressful lives, suffer from ill health, and never really bond with their owners. They can also bite out of fear.

- ✔ **Aggression:** A serious temperament flaw, aggression puts many dogs into the unadoptable category. Signs of aggression include teeth baring, growling, lunging, nipping, snapping, biting, and chasing. Aggression can be caused by extreme fear, an overdeveloped sense of dominance, a lack of trust for humans, past abuse, or a congenital bad temperament.

  Avoid any dogs that show signs of aggression toward children or small pets. If, however, you decide to adopt a dog that shows aggressive tendencies, be prepared to provide plenty of targeted training with the help of a professional who specializes in overcoming aggressive behavior problems. Don't take on a project like this if you have children or if children frequently visit your house.

- ✔ **Hyperactivity:** Many dogs, especially puppies and adolescents, have high energy and require a lot of exercise and interaction. This is normal. Dogs that are truly hyperactive usually are so high energy that they rarely calm down and are virtually uncontrollable. They have a hard time focusing on you, listening to you, or interacting with you even after you've spent several hours with them. Pet owners will have a hard time fulfilling their exercise needs or training them.

Discerning the difference between a high-energy dog and a hyperactive dog can be difficult at first. Some dogs are hyperactive in adolescence and calm down when they're older, but you probably won't be able to tell for sure. Some breeds naturally are active, such as sporting dogs like Retrievers and Pointers and herding dogs like Border Collies and Shelties. Others received so little attention for so long that they simply are frantic to get any attention they can from you. None of these cases is a sign of a hyperactive temperament. So before you cross these dogs off your list, remember that many of these dogs just need a loving home, plenty of exercise, and some good old-fashioned attention.

These general observations probably give you a basic sense of your dog's temperament, but you also need to hear what shelter or rescue workers have observed about the dog you're considering. They've probably interacted much longer and more intensively with the dog than you have and thus can offer you some good insights.

Go-getters, chill-outers, and wait-and-seers

By observing the dog's temperament as suggested in the preceding section, you can begin getting a sense of the dog's personality. He may be outgoing or shy, self-confident or needy, active or sedentary, social or reserved. These various personality traits, explained in a bit more detail in the list that follows, can help you determine whether you and the dog are a good match:

✔ **The go-getters:** These dogs are always on the move, always excited about the next new game, project, or travel opportunity. They relish the unfamiliar adventure. Go-getters love to hike, run, play sports, and depending on the breed or breed combination, engage in high-energy dog sports like agility, flyball, canine freestyle, rally, dock jumping, earthdog, disk sports, water retrieving, tracking, or hunting tests. They're active, energetic, and great matches for people who lead active, physical, athletic lifestyles.

✔ **The chill-outers:** Although as puppies and adolescents, dogs tend to be at their most active, some individual dogs are more laid-back — chill-outers, if you will. Like some people, they tend not to get all riled up but, instead, are typically adaptable, easy-going, and prefer hanging out or cuddling up with you on the couch to going for a five-mile run. Sure, they need exercise and enjoy a rousing game of fetch the same as the next pooch, but they generally are less likely to run you ragged. This canine personality is perfect for the more sedentary, stay-at-home type of pet owners who want a companion rather than a four-legged dynamo bouncing off the walls from boredom.

✔ **The wait-and-seers:** These dogs like to hang back a little until they're sure about things. Rather than plunge into the next new event, they're more hesitant. Whether pausing until they recognize something familiar or waiting for the go-ahead from their trusted keeper, these dogs are simply a little more reserved. When meeting someone new, they won't typically dash up to the stranger with their tails wagging. They may wait patiently or even stiffen and be on guard until they're sure the new person is okay.

Some breeds tend to be wait-and-seers, particularly guardian breeds with their long history of serving as watchdogs to owner and property. Some toy dogs also react this way, perhaps out of a sense of self-preservation. When you weigh four pounds, you have to be careful with whom or in what you get tangled. These cautious, reserved dogs make admirable and intelligent pets, constant companions for people who can spend plenty of time with them because they typically bond closely to one or two people. If well socialized, they can be trusted to act appropriately when around people, not nipping or growling when someone friendly tries to approach you or them.

Regardless of the dog's personality, you need to look for a type of pet with which you can deal and relate. Just as in human relationships, some personalities simply mesh well together, while others clash. The dog-human team that meshes has a strong foundation for building a healthy, close relationship for the rest of the dog's life.

What Kind of Dog Is That? The Joy of Mixed Breeds

Most dogs in animal shelters are mixed breeds. These dogs can give you all the joys and all the challenges of purebreds. They can be calm or active, grooming them can be easy or time-consuming, and they can be challenging or a breeze to train. Above all, mixed breeds are dogs, just like purebreds. They respond best to plenty of affection, attention, mental and physical activity, and consistent, positive training.

Although mixed breeds are harder to place than purebreds — perhaps because they're considered common — they're anything but disposable. A mixed breed can be a wonderful addition to your life and family. In fact, mixed breeds have a particular appeal to many pet owners. These Heinz 57 dogs come with a potpourri of wonderful traits, and each has a personality all its own. Nobody can stereotype your adorable mutt like they may be able to do with a purebred.

When you adopt a mixed breed dog, you probably want to know what kind of dog you're getting, or, if it's a puppy, what kind of a dog it will grow up to be. For that you need to do a little detective work.

First up is figuring out (or trying to) what kind of dog your mixed breed *is* — in other words, what breeds created it? Mixed breeds can look much like a particular breed or have an appearance that's a mystery to all. Nevertheless, the best way to tell what your mixed breed dog is made of is to take a good close look at breed photos and see which ones resemble your dog. Remember, however, that this method can be misleading, because many purebreds originally were mixes of other, older breeds.

Chances are the dog you want to adopt is a mix of some of the more common breeds. In fact, most mixed-breed dogs in shelters come from some combination of two or more of the following breeds: Labrador Retriever, Golden Retriever, Rottweiler, German Shepherd, Beagle, Border Collie, Australian Shepherd, Chow Chow, American Pit Bull Terrier, Rat Terrier, Fox Terrier, and Chihuahua. You're likely to see other breeds mixed in too.

Are mixed breeds healthier?

You may have heard both sides of the argument about whether mixed breeds are healthier than purebred dogs.

One side claims that mixed breeds are more "natural," and therefore healthier, and that mixed breeds have better *hybrid vigor,* meaning their gene pool is larger and comes from a more diverse dog population. This trait, proponents say, naturally reduces the chances that genetic diseases will occur. In the smaller gene pool of a purebred population, they add, chances are greater that both parents (when mating) carry a recessive gene for harmful genetic mutations.

The other side disagrees, claiming that purebred dogs don't develop genetic problems any more often than mixed breeds and asserting that you simply are more informed about *which* genetic problems purebred dogs bring to the table and are more likely to develop. Because purebreds often are products of breeders working hard to eliminate genetic disease, this side claims their dogs may be even healthier than mixed breeds randomly breeding without any attempt to eliminate harmful genetic mutations.

So far, no definitive and widely accepted study has proved either side right or wrong, even though people have strong opinions on both sides. Until real proof is found, your best bet is finding a dog that you like with a great temperament that a vet approves as healthy. Any dog can develop a serious disease later in life, so instead of worrying too much about that, just do your best to choose a healthy dog and practice good preventive healthcare. (For more about caring for your dog's health, see Chapter 6.)

To determine what stock a dog came from, you can also watch how the dog behaves. Territorial, reserved dogs probably have some guardian breed in them. Dogs with a tendency to move children in one direction or nip at heels tend to have some herding breed in them. Small dogs that bark a lot and take chasing squirrels seriously probably have a terrier background. Larger blocky friendly dogs that have floppy ears and smooth or feathery coats, love water, and pay close attention to birds probably have sporting-breed bloodlines. Very small dogs probably are at least part toy breed. (For more about each of these breed groups, see the "Adopting a Purebred Dog" section later in this chapter.)

Another thing to remember about mixed breeds is that mixed-breed puppies may change considerably when they grow up. Certain combinations (of one breed with another) can be misleading. A tiny white puppy can grow up to be a 100-pound grayish-black giant. Patterns can change and disappear. Coat texture can change. And size . . . well, that's anybody's guess. Some people say you can tell a puppy's ultimate size by the size of his feet, and this works sometimes, but it isn't failsafe. Of course, adopting an adult mixed-breed dog eliminates this guessing game, because after about a year, the dog has reached full size and grown in his adult coat. He probably won't change much more.

Adopting a Purebred Dog

Maybe you've always dreamed of having a fleet-footed Saluki, or you really want to adopt a Schnauzer like the one your parents had when you were growing up, or maybe you just melt at the site of a tiny white Maltese with long silky fur. You don't have to give up that dream just because you're committed to adopting a dog that needs a new home. According to the Humane Society of the United States, 25 percent to 30 percent of the dogs in animal shelters are purebreds, and while some of these may not win any dog shows because of cosmetic "defects" like ears that are too short or spots in the wrong place, they can give you all the joy of a purebred along with the good feeling of rescuing a dog in need. Purebred rescue groups can make your search for the perfect purebred even easier by helping you to find the purebred you desire with a personality that best fits into your lifestyle. (See Chapter 3 for more information on finding a purebred rescue group.)

Many people, however, decide on a certain breed without knowing what that particular breed needs. Just because you like the look of a breed doesn't mean you'll like the behavior of that breed, so before you adopt a purebred, find out what traits that breed is likely to have. For starters, the sections that follow describe some general guidelines to get you thinking seriously about whether the purebred of your dreams is really the dog you want.

All about breed groups

Every purebred dog falls broadly into one of several different groups or breed types that clue you in to a little something extra about the dog before you adopt it. If you see traits you really don't want in a dog, don't choose one from that group. Each of the groups listed in the sections that follow includes some examples of breeds that fit into each respective category, but not all of the hundreds of breeds are included. If you don't see the breed that interests you, look it up on any of the following Web sites to see what breed group it falls under. These Web sites also provide you with much more detailed information about each of hundreds of individual breeds:

- **American Kennel Club (www.akc.org):** The oldest breed registry in the U.S., AKC recognizes 154 breeds in seven groups: Sporting, Working, Hounds, Terriers, Toys, Nonsporting, and Herding.

- **United Kennel Club (www.ukcdogs.com):** The UKC recognizes 308 breeds in eight groups: Companion dogs, Guardian dogs, Gun dogs, Herding dogs, Northern breeds, Scenthounds, Sighthounds and pariah dogs, and Terriers.

- **Fédération Cynologique Internationale (www.fci.be):** This international organization recognizes 332 breeds in ten groups: Sheepdog and Cattle Dogs; Terriers; Spitz and primitive types; Pointing Dogs; Companion and toy dogs; Pinscher and Schnauzer, Molossoid breeds, Swiss mountain and cattle dogs, and other Swiss breeds; Dachshunds; Scenthounds and related breeds; Retrievers, flushing dogs, and water dogs; and Sighthounds.

Good buddies: Companion dogs

Any dog can be a great companion, but dogs that fall under the category of companion breeds are the ones that have been bred for centuries, not to pull sleds or herd sheep or guard the house but specifically for the important job of being a companion to humans. Many are tiny lap dogs; some are slightly larger. Coat types range from the shortest Chihuahua coat to the longest, flowing Shih Tzu coat. These dogs have a special knack for being adorable. Some need a lot of grooming, but the people who enjoy companion breeds don't mind. These dogs are perfect for people who want to lavish them with attention.

Companion dogs don't do well when left alone all day, but if you work at home, they happily sit on your lap or at your feet for hours. Many of them bark a lot, and some are downright yappy. Just because they're little and cute doesn't mean that they don't need obedience training. These little guys can develop great big Napoleonic complexes unless they're taught the rules. They can be harder than larger breeds to housetrain, and prefer sitting and sleeping next to you, *on* the furniture and *in* your bed.

Examples of common companion dogs include Yorkshire Terriers, Poodles, Shih Tzu, Chihuahuas, Pugs, Pomeranians, Maltese, Lhasa Apsos, Miniature Pinschers, Bichon Frise, Cavalier King Charles Spaniels, Papillon, Pekingese, French Bulldogs, Bulldogs, Havanese, Boston Terriers, and Italian Greyhounds. See Figure 4-3 for an example of a Japanese Chin, a purebred companion dog you may find at a shelter.

Figure 4-3: Long-coated toy breeds often are abandoned because their owners can't spend time grooming them properly, but with patience, they can become devoted companions.

Imposing Guardian breeds

These large, powerful dogs make excellent companion dogs and sometimes perform other tasks like pulling heavy loads, but they've served humans for thousands of years primarily as guardians. Long ago, when such barbaric practices were legal, these dogs also fought for sport. Exceptionally strong animals, they retain an instinct to protect their humans and their property. Because Guardian breeds are so strong, training and active socialization at an early age is absolutely crucial. Many of these breeds are big softies with their owners and friendly with friends . . . but evil-doers beware.

These dogs never should be left outside alone in the yard all day. They need frequent human interaction to make the most of their intelligence and plenty of exercise and owner interaction so they don't become bored and destructive. Many Guardian breeds don't bark much unless they have a good reason or they're left alone too often. They also tend to have a good natural instinct about people. Early socialization helps refine this instinct so the dog becomes trustworthy around children, neighbors, and friends.

Examples of common Guardian breeds include Boxers, Rottweilers, Doberman Pinschers, Great Danes, Mastiffs, Neapolitan Mastiffs, Bullmastiffs, St. Bernard's, Newfoundlands, and Great Pyrenees.

Active Sporting breeds

Sporting breeds, sometimes called gun dogs, include Retrievers, Pointers, Setters, and Spaniels. These dogs and their ancestors have hunted next to humans for thousands of years. They have a keen eye for birds and other game animals and strong instincts for finding them, flushing them out, and retrieving them after they're shot. Some people describe seeing Retrievers or Pointers react for the first time to the sound of a gun as if it were a potent ancestral memory. Many sporting dogs know exactly what to do when hunting, even if they've never been trained to do it, and many are natural water Retrievers that love to swim and fetch things from the water.

Because they can hunt for hours, Sporting breeds are extremely active and need plenty of exercise. They can be the perfect pet for families that take them out to run, play, or compete in dog sports. Friendly and eager to learn, sporting dogs are happiest and healthiest when they can interact with people. They're among the most popular choices for families because they enjoy children as active playmates. Early training teaches sporting dogs the rules while they're still small enough to handle physically.

Examples of common Sporting breeds include Labrador Retrievers, Golden Retrievers (see Figure 4-4), Cocker Spaniels, German Shorthaired Pointers, English Springer Spaniels, Weimaraners, Brittanys, Vizslas, Chesapeake Bay Retrievers, Irish Setters, and Portuguese Water Dogs.

Figure 4-4:
Golden Retrievers are the second most popular purebred pet (after Labrador Retrievers), but many pet owners find they can't handle the Golden's high energy.

Born to run: Cold-hardy Northern breeds

Arctic dogs tend to have prick ears, curled tails that swoosh over their backs, heavy frost-proof coats, and strong feet made for running and padded with fur. These dogs have extreme drive and have served many purposes in frigid climates, pulling sleds, guarding, hunting, and warming the beds of their companions.

Northern breeds tend to be independent with a strong survival instinct and, in many cases, a strong instinct to run. They don't tolerate warmer weather but love the cold often sitting for hours out in the snow. They're clever escape artists, so they need secure fences and supervision and always need to wear identification. (All dogs should, for that matter, but it's especially important for escapees.) Good owners for Northern breeds include active families, people who live in areas where these dogs can safely run, and people who want to get involved in fun sports like dog sledding, skijoring (dogs pulling cross-country skiers), carting, and weight pulling. If you want a challenging dog that sees you as an equal but is willing to follow your rules if you earn his respect, this may be your group.

Examples of Northern breeds include Siberian Huskies, Chinese Shar-Pei, Alaskan Malamutes, Akitas, American Eskimos, Chow-Chows, Keeshonds, Norwegian Elkhounds, Samoyeds, and Shiba Inus.

Eye on the prize: Sighthounds

Sighthounds are among the oldest types of dogs. These long, lithe, speedy runners have supersharp eyesight and long were bred to spot prey from far away — even across dessert sands — and chase it down, fast. Greyhounds are among the original Sighthounds, but many other Sighthounds have evolved from greyhounds.

Sighthounds are an interesting combination of independent and sensitive. They won't smother you or beg for affection, but they may sit nearby pining for your attention. Sighthounds need secure fencing and strong leashes, or they can dash into traffic after a squirrel or rabbit. When chasing something, they don't notice anything else, thus few Sighthounds ever are trustworthy off leash no matter how well trained. They won't even hear you yelling "Come!" Sighthounds are often depicted in art because of their slim curvy forms and beautiful lines.

Examples of common Sighthounds include Greyhounds, Afghan Hounds, Whippets, Salukis, Scottish Deerhounds, Irish Wolfhounds, Basenjis, and Rhodesian Ridgebacks.

The nose knows: Scenthounds

Scenthounds have an extreme sense of smell and can pick up the scent of a crumb of toast in the bottom of the kitchen wastebasket and go after it. Although typically mellow and affectionate, when they catch a scent, they become incredibly single-minded, and like the Sighthounds, won't hear you calling them back away from traffic or other hazards if they are on a trail.

Scenthounds may bay, bark, or snuffle along the ground with no thought of glancing up and probably will chase small animals if they smell them. They're incredibly food motivated and clever about scoring a plate of food from the counter when nobody's looking. Pet owners must be careful not to let food-hounds become overweight. Scenthounds love competitive tracking events and are naturals at this sport.

Examples of common Scenthounds include Beagles, Dachshunds, Basset Hounds, Bloodhounds, English and American Foxhounds, and all types of Coonhounds.

Feisty Terrier breeds

These bright, energetic little fellows like to bark, and do so loudly and often. They've been bred to maximize their vermin-catching potential so they get excited and motivated — and loud — when they spot a squirrel, a rabbit, a mole, or a mouse. They won't be deterred unless you scoop them up and take them inside, but good luck catching these quick springy dogs. Terriers can try the patience of anyone who is sensitive to noise and high energy. Smart and independent problem-solvers, they need plenty of opportunities to race, chase, and play. They adore people and need (and even demand) a lot of attention. They can quickly morph into the role of lapdog, like to travel, and always are interested in what you're doing.

Some terriers are enthusiastic chewers and diggers, and they all need secure fences to keep them from harm when chasing anything they perceive to be vermin. Don't be surprised if they even bark at blowing leaves, dust bunnies, and any and all visitors, known or unknown. Terriers make excellent watch-dogs, even if they are too small to be guard dogs. The group of Terriers mixed with Bulldogs have a bad reputation but can be among the sweetest and most well behaved of Terriers if they're well socialized and trained. Terriers tend to be generally aggressive and need careful supervision around other dogs.

Examples of common terriers include West Highland White Terriers (Westies), Miniature Schnauzers, Scottish Terriers, Cairn Terriers, Fox Terriers, Rat Terriers, Jack Russell Terriers, Parson Russell Terriers, Airedale Terriers, American Pit Bull Terriers, Bull Terriers, American Staffordshire Terriers, and Staffordshire Bull Terriers.

Superfocused Herding breeds

This group has been herding sheep and cattle for thousands of years, so the instinct to herd is strong. These dogs may nip heels or use their bodies to push people and other dogs in the direction they think they should go. They are protective of children and worry that their "flock" may come to harm, so they may bark or physically pull children away from perceived threats. Many have dragged children from their roughhousing or from water with their teeth. Remember Lassie running for help when Timmy fell in the well? Classic Herding breed.

Herding breeds have intense focus and high energy. They need frequent exercise and complex mental stimulation to feel at ease. Many people feel overwhelmed by the Herding breed's high activity and clever independence. These dogs can out-think many humans, so stay alert! Herding breeds love to compete in challenging, high-energy dog sports like agility and flyball, and in organized or actual work-related herding. Many instinctively know how to herd without training, but all Herding breeds need early obedience training to help channel their formidable intellect and high energy.

Examples of common Herding breeds include Collies, Shetland Sheepdogs (Shelties), Border Collies, Pembroke Welsh Corgis, Cardigan Welsh Corgis, Australian Shepherds, Australian Cattle Dogs, Old English Sheepdogs, and German Shepherd Dogs (some people categorize these as guardian dogs).

Chapter 5

Helping Your Adopted Dog Make the Homecoming Transition

In This Chapter
▶ Puppy-proofing your home first
▶ Buying the supplies you need . . . and a few just for fun
▶ Introducing your adopted dog to his new life
▶ Spotting transitional problems that may require professional help
▶ Stressing routine for a better-adjusted dog

Congratulations, you've found the dog for you! But wait . . . don't bring him home just yet. You have some preparation work to do.

Fortunately, you can make a big difference in how well your new dog adjusts to his new surroundings by making use of a few targeted strategies. On his first day home, your new best friend may not believe that he's finally in his forever home — and with his own cozy bed and shiny new food bowl and everything. But your new dog may be a bit nervous, even scared, when he first comes home with you, despite the fancy new collar and deluxe chew toys. Lucky for you, this chapter tells you exactly what to do to ensure that your new four-legged friend's homecoming is a happy one.

Preparing Your Pad

If you don't already have a dog, you need to do some pooch-proofing before you bring your new friend home — to keep your new dog and your old possessions safe. Pooch-proofing is important for exploring, chewing, mischievous puppies and for adult dogs who haven't quite learned what goes and what is unacceptable in your home. These precautions are particularly important for dogs who never spent much time indoors until now. Although an adult dog may not even consider gnawing on the legs of the kitchen chair, eating your shoes, or rooting through the garbage, you won't know for sure until you bring her home. Better to pooch-proof, just in case.

You also need some stuff to keep your dog healthy, well exercised, and amused. For people who like shopping, this part of bringing your new dog home is fun.

Puppy-proofing first (even for adult dogs)

Before bringing a dog into your home, you need to come to terms with the many things that a short four-legged animal can get into. Any dog in a new environment is bound to explore, and some dogs explore more — shall we say — *enthusiastically* than others. Puppies, in particular, explore the world with their noses and mouths, and that may mean chomping on choking hazards, chewing through electrical cords, and munching on your favorite nonmunchable possessions. Energetic puppies and older dogs unaccustomed to being inside also are at risk of falling, having things fall on them, and getting stuck in the strangest places. Some of these situations can be dangerous for the puppy, such as getting stuck inside a recliner or underneath a car in the garage.

Your home doesn't *have* to be a house of hazards for your new dog. You just need to take some precautions first. On the other hand, just because you have a new dog doesn't mean you have to resort to vinyl flooring and covering all your furniture with sheets. You do, however, need to look around and eliminate potential hazards. Here's what to look for when pooch-proofing:

- ✔ **Choking hazards:** Look across all of your floors; do you find any paperclips, bits of paper or string, rubber bands, or other objects a young puppy may find tempting enough to sample? Pick them up right away; they're choking hazards.

- ✔ **Unsteady objects:** What if you knocked the base of that side table with your wagging rear end? Would that lamp fall on your head? Can big puppy paws reach the edge of that coffee table and knock off all those breakable knickknacks? Either make those unsteady objects steady enough to withstand the onslaught of your new dog or move them out of your pooch's sphere of influence.

- ✔ **Strangulation hazards:** Does the dangling curtain fringe beckon, begging your pup to grab it with his teeth and give it a good shake? Are the mini-blind cords hanging within reach of dog necks? Find a way to remove these potential strangulation hazards from your dog's reach by taping them down, tying them out of reach, or removing them altogether.

- ✔ **Electrocution hazards:** Can you imagine what those sharp little puppy teeth can do to an electrical cord Yep, you're right. A puppy can bite through a cord in seconds, causing severe burns and electrocution. Make sure you tape cords down or put them behind furniture so puppy isn't tempted by an electrocution hazard.

- ✔ **Tempting trash:** Is the garbage can, with its luscious aromas, standing open for your dog to topple, spilling its feast of cast-off goodies? The tempting trash from some garbage can really harm a dog that may be used to scrounging for meals. Some particularly hazardous examples are tasty but dangerous cooked bones that can splinter in your dog's intestine, rotten food, and choking hazards such as milk bottle caps and little metal tabs from the tops of soft-drink cans.

✔ **Poisons:** Did you know that anything that can poison a human toddler can also poison a dog? Put safety locks on cabinets that are within the reach of your new dog, particularly the ones that contain poisonous household chemicals like cleaners, pest poisons, medications, cleaners, and even toiletries like your shampoo, lotion, and sunscreen. (For information about what to do if you suspect your dog has been poisoned, see Chapter 6.)

✔ **Your prized possessions:** Did you know that a puppy is like a major league cleanup hitter with the bases loaded, two outs, and a mouthful of salty sunflower seeds? They both love and need to chew on things. For puppies, chewing feels good during teething, and some mouthy breeds like Sporting breeds, Hounds, and Terriers chew throughout their lives. However, dogs don't know that your child's favorite stuffed bunny or expensive piece of sports equipment is any different than the fleece stuffed toy or rubber chewie that you often give them. An adopted dog that never was taught the difference between dog toys and human things may have a hard time telling the difference at first . . . or always, so put your *prized possessions* away!

Avoiding poisons

Many of the things that are poisonous to humans also are poisonous to dogs, but dogs can react — sometimes severely — to substances that are completely benign for humans, such as chocolate and onions. Here is a list of foods, plants, medications, and poisons that are particularly dangerous for dogs. Don't let your dog ingest any of the following:

✔ **Chocolate:** Dogs can react severely to both the caffeine and the theobromine in chocolate.

✔ **Raisins or grapes:** Some dogs suffer acute kidney failure and death caused by these foods, even in small amounts.

✔ **Onions:** Onions can cause severe anemia in some dogs.

✔ **Prescription and nonprescription medications for humans:** Many human medications are very dangerous for pets. For example, acetaminophen, the active ingredient in Tylenol, can cause liver failure and the destruction of red blood cells (cats are even more sensitive to acetaminophen than dogs). It's just a good idea to avoid giving your dog any medication intended for humans unless you have been advised to do so by your vet.

✔ **Antifreeze:** A few drops of antifreeze can kill a dog, and worse yet, it tastes and smells appealing to dogs, so watch for stains in your garage or driveway.

✔ **House and garden flowers, ferns, shrubs, and other plants:** Check out the ASPCA Animal Poison Control Center's Web site page that lists many common plants that can be poisonous to pets. Find it at www.aspca.org/toxicplants/M01947.htm.

Most puppy-proofing is a matter of common sense and can be essentially summarized in one Golden Rule of puppy proofing:

If you don't want your dog to chew it, then put it out of reach.

A lot of dog owners discover this lesson the hard way. If you leave things like toys, clothes, slippers, new shoes, or wallets out where your dog can get at them, don't blame your dog for thinking he can help himself. It is an impressively self-controlled canine who can resist these things when nobody is watching. This threat is an excellent motivation for children to keep their rooms clean or at least close their bedroom doors so the puppy can't get in. Otherwise, they risk chewed up and ruined laundry and toys. (I can't tell you how many pairs of underwear my puppy has chewed holes into in the last year, and you probably really don't want to know.)

Dog destruction doesn't just apply to your furniture and wearables. It applies to your food. Dogs of any age are incredibly clever when they smell something delicious. Adopted dogs may've spent some serious time scrounging for every piece of food they could find and going for long periods of time without any food at all before they came to live with you. These dogs can become extra clever at scoring tidbits, so you always have to be one step ahead of them. Don't leave your dinner on the counter if your Great Dane can rest his head on the counter and stare at it. That's just more temptation than the average dog can withstand.

Supervision is a key element to puppy-proofing. Although you may not be used to keeping an eye out for what your puppy is doing at all times, doing so is essential for your dog's safety, not to mention a crucial part of housetraining (see Chapter 7 for more about that). Until you know exactly what your puppy is likely to do, watch her.

Gathering doggy accoutrements

Dogs get by perfectly well with only a few basics, but you may want to consider a few luxury items, too. *Hint:* Chew toys are *not* luxury items; they're a necessity, especially for puppies.

Stocking up on doggy necessities

Dogs don't require thousands of accessories, and you certainly don't need to spend a fortune to equip your dog. However, to be able to manage and train your dog successfully, you need some basic tools that your friendly local pet store should be able to supply.

> ✔ **Identification tags:** ID tags are the most important dog accessory you can buy. Engraved with your dog's name and your address and phone number, an ID tag can be your dog's ticket home if he ever gets lost. A pet tag is important even if your dog has a microchip implanted from the shelter

or the vet. Anyone can find your dog when it strays, but that doesn't mean anyone can or will take your dog to a shelter or vet to scan for the microchip. An identification tag on the collar makes finding the animal's owner easy. Put it on your dog and never take it off.

✔ **Buckle collar and six-foot leash:** Choose nylon or leather with a metal or plastic buckle, decorated or simple. For some small breeds or dogs that pull a lot, consider a harness in addition to a collar, but make sure you still can include identification tags.

✔ **Crate or kennel:** Choose a crate or kennel that is big enough for your adult dog. A *crate* is a plastic carrier with a wire front. Crates are sometimes called kennels, but "kennel" also refers to a wire cage. Your dog needs to be able to stand up, turn around, and lie down comfortably inside. If you have a puppy that will grow quite a bit, buy a crate or kennel to fit the dog's adult size (if you know what it will be) and temporarily block off part of the crate to make it smaller. Otherwise, the puppy may use one end for a bed and the other end for a bathroom. The crate or kennel is absolutely essential for housetraining (see the section on housetraining in Chapter 7) and general management, because it becomes your dog's beloved den (see the section on "Showing your dog to his den" later in this chapter), and she will love it even more than you do. If you travel a great deal, look for a crate or kennel that can be buckled into the back-seat of your car or van.

✔ **Dog seat belt:** No, this device is not a luxury, but rather an important safety item. If your dog's kennel is too large to fit in the backseat or to buckle in, look for one of several different high-quality dog seat belts that attach to your car seat belt. Dog seat belts keep you and your pet safe in the car. Your dog will neither jump on you, distracting you while you're driving, nor injure anyone else in the car in the case of an accident. With this device, you can *all* buckle up safely.

✔ **Food and water bowls:** Metal and ceramic are easier to clean and less likely to harbor bacteria, and they're not tempting to chew.

✔ **A high-quality dog food:** Check out Chapter 6 for more information about choosing a good food.

✔ **Assorted brushes depending on your dog's coat:** A natural bristle brush can be used for short and medium-coated dogs, and wire-pin and slicker brushes work for long or fluffy-coated dogs. Bristle brushes are good for regular maintenance brushing, while pin brushes are good for double-coated dogs because they brush down to the skin. Slicker brushes are great for pulling out excess undercoat during periods of heavy shedding.

✔ **Shampoo made just for dogs:** You'll also want conditioner for long-coated dogs.

✔ **A nail clipper made for dogs:** This tool comes in sizes appropriate to your dog's size (the label says whether the clipper is for small, medium, or large dogs).

- ✔ **Pest control products to prevent fleas, ticks, and heartworms:** The best ones come from your veterinarian (for more on pest control, see Chapter 6).

- ✔ **Chew toys:** Puppies need to chew and need to have acceptable things to chew so they don't chew your things. Chew toys can include hard rubber teethers and edible chew toys like rawhide, pig's ears, hooves, and jerky treats.

Some vets advise against certain edible chew toys like rawhide for some dogs, because they can pose a choking hazard and/or stomach upset. If you aren't sure about which edible chew toys are safe for your dog, talk to your vet.

- ✔ **Interactive toys for bonding time:** Whether you throw a tennis ball or a flying disc like a Frisbee or play tug-of-war with a rope toy, be sure to get a few toys that you and your dog can play with together. These toys give you great ways to play with your dog in the doggy way that she enjoys and help build a quality relationship between the two of you.

Loading up — a little or a lot — on luxuries

So much for the must-haves, now what about those luxuries? Okay, so your dog doesn't really *need* that fancy dog bed that looks like a velvet *chaise lounge* from a French drawing room. But after all she's been through . . . Well, you can buy some truly amazing high-end products for dogs that no dog needs but that pet owners simply enjoy. You can spend a little on fancy stuff, or a lot. Here are a few options:

- ✔ **Clothes and hats:** Some dogs love them; others wouldn't be caught dead in the dog park wearing that stuff. If your dog enjoys doggy couture, look for matching sweaters for you and your dog, Halloween costumes and other holiday-wear, rain gear, leather jackets, even snow boots.

- ✔ **Pretty charms and dog jewelry including hair accessories like ribbons and barrettes:** Swarovski crystal collar, anyone?

- ✔ **Retractable leashes:** These leashes aren't a requirement, but they can be useful for letting dogs get more of the feeling of being off-leash while still staying safe. They extend 10 feet to more than 25 feet, but retract into a plastic holder with the push of a button. Don't use these leashes while training dogs to walk beside you on a leash. (For instructions on how to train a dog to walk beside you on a leash, see Chapter 7.)

- ✔ **Fancy dog furniture:** Although your dog needs to learn to sleep in her kennel, especially during housetraining, some dogs just love to lounge on their own special furniture. Some available options include feathered canopy beds, upholstered leather couches, hammocks and trampoline-type beds, huge fluffy donut-shaped beds, and little doggy tents. Many of these items are designed to enhance the décor of your home.

⮀ **Cool toys.** Dog toys have become truly innovative. Just browse the pet store or the Internet, and you'll see some clever, fun, interesting inventions, like:

- Balls with bigger rubber tongues attached — a hoot when your dog has the ball in his mouth.

- Slingshots for finally launching tennis balls far enough to give your active dog a really good run.

- Vibrating toys that move on their own.

- Toys that let you record a message so your dog can hear your reassuring voice when you are away.

- Toys that you can stuff with all kinds of treats that your dog has to work to remove (these built-in rewards can keep your dog interested for hours).

- Toys designed to make the realistic sounds of small prey animals to fulfill your dog's inherent hunting desires.

Catering to your dog's needs

Some doggy accoutrements are necessities for certain dogs and luxury items for others. Dog litter boxes, ramps and stairs, and special grooming supplies are among the more common ones.

Dog litter boxes are good for pet owners who can't easily take their little dogs outside, people with mobility issues, or pet owners who live in high-rise apartments in the city. Dog litter boxes are sized for different dogs and come with pelleted paper litter-box filler that absorbs moisture. When litter-box training your dog, you need to change the litter after each use. Another option is framed squares of sod or artificial turf so your dog gets the feel of going on the grass even while she's inside.

Ramps and stairs are good for dogs with sensitive spines like Dachshunds or senior dogs with arthritis that have trouble jumping up and down from couches, beds, and cars. You can buy beautiful padded ramps and stairs for inside, or more utilitarian versions for cars and even for swimming pools and boats to help your little swimmer get out of the water more easily. This item may actually be an important safety device, if you have a swimming pool and your dog can't easily get out of it. In that case, consider this item a must-have.

You can also buy grooming products with a personal touch. Coat conditioner and coat spray are essential for long-coated dogs. A square of velvet or a chamois to polish short coats is a nice addition. Some dogs look better when washed with special shampoos made to brighten white coats, darken dark coats, or soothe sensitive skin. Dogs with allergies or fleas may need special shampoos that help them resolve their health issues. Some companies make lines of dog spa products with natural botanicals. You can even buy doggy cologne to keep your pooch sweet-smelling.

Welcoming Doggy Home

After the house is prepared and well stocked, you can load up your adopted dog into the car (don't forget a dog seat belt or crate!), drive home, pull into the driveway, coax him out of the car and then . . . Wouldn't it be nice if your new adopted dog bounded happily into the house, engaged in a quick game of fetch, sniffed and licked the family, then curled up in his doggy bed for a nap, happy tail a-waggin'?

Even though such scenarios have been known to happen, they're not common. The more likely reaction you can expect from your adopted dog is that she will be a little nervous, maybe a little scared, probably curious, and maybe so excited that she can hardly contain herself. She may even experience a few more serious adjustment problems.

The trick to helping your dog make a smooth and quick transition to her new home is immediately establishing routines and sticking to them. Dogs pick up quickly on the rules of a new place, so the sooner they get that information from you, the sooner they can adjust to their new situations. Keep initial introductions calm and limited. Don't mob your new dog with people, toys, games, treats, and attention all at once. Dogs react to the moods and actions of the people around them, so if you want a calm, relaxed dog, then try to act calm and relaxed. If you act anxious, worried, or excitable, your dog picks up on your cues. If your dog thinks you have the situation fully and confidently in hand, she can relax a little bit and not have to worry about trying to manage things herself.

In most cases, calm behavior and a comfortable routine win out, quickly sending your adopted dog the message that all is right with the world again.

Dog, meet potty spot

Taking care of business is the first thing to do when you get home with your adopted dog. You know what business I'm talking about: the business of housetraining. Regardless of your dog's age, adults and puppies need to know where they are allowed to fulfill their, um . . . elimination requirements. Housetraining problems are among the chief reasons why people give up their dogs to animal shelters, so managing this issue right from the start is super important.

Choosing a potty spot

Before bringing your new pet home, you need to know in advance where you want her to go. If you have a yard, you probably want her to relieve herself there. But you also need to pick a spot in the yard that will be most convenient, a spot where people aren't likely to walk away from the pathway to the garden or gate. Secluded locations are better than spots right near the sidewalk or street. Some dogs don't care where they go, but others may feel vulnerable and won't want to do their business with cars whizzing by on the other side of the fence or other dogs wandering past with their owners and barking.

If you want to paper or litter-box train your pet, the spot where you place the receptacle needs to be ready to go before your new dog comes home. It needs to be placed in an area away from high foot traffic that's easy to clean, such as on a linoleum or tile floor and far from your dog's sleeping area. Dogs don't like to eliminate near where they sleep.

Telling your dog where to go

As soon as you get home, you may be tempted to take off your dog's leash and let her explore the house. Wait! Don't unclip that leash from that collar just yet. First, take your dog to the place where you want her to eliminate, either in the yard or the area of the house you've chosen. Keeping that leash on, have your dog sniff, circle, and check out the spot, but stay where you are until she relieves herself. Although this process can take a long time, wait. If you know your dog recently relieved herself and simply doesn't need to go, skip to the next section about introducing your dog to her den. You can go back and try this step again and again. And again! You'll find repetition of this step a worthwhile endeavor.

Rewarding a job well done

When she does go in the right spot, say hooray! Praise her, pet her, call her a very good dog because she just did something very good. She went where you wanted her to go, and that's a big step for a new dog in a new home. Make sure she knows she has pleased you.

Then, if you have a fenced yard, you can let her off the leash now to explore on her own. If you don't have a fence, lead her around the yard on the leash and let her sniff, check out the perimeter, and figure out what's what. Finally, bring her in the house. Or, if your dog's potty spot is inside and you're already in the house, you can let her have a chance to explore the rest of the house now.

Showing your dog to his den

Now is the time to grab some treats, because you're about to introduce your dog to her new best friend, aside from you, of course. Dogs are naturally den animals and need a safe place to call their own. One of your most powerful tools for helping your dog feel safe and comfortable in her new home is the dog den.

Whether you choose to use a plastic crate (see Figure 5-1), a wire kennel, or a portable wire enclosure — sometimes called an *exercise pen* or X-pen —, your dog needs somewhere to feel safe. Crates and kennels with latching doors can help with housetraining and travel, but if your dog already is housetrained and not destructive, you may not need to latch the door just yet. If the kennel is all wire, cover it with a blanket, leaving only the front open. Dogs feel safest when they can rest without feeling they need to watch their backs. Your dog probably wants to be near you, so situate the den in a room where your dog can at least hear, if not see you, when she's resting.

Figure 5-1:
One good choice for a safe spot or den is a plastic crate with solid sides and a door that can be left open or closed.

To attract your dog's interest, make sure the den is comfortable and soft, and then open the door. Get your dog's attention with a treat, or by leading her to the den by her leash. Then, toss a few treats into the den and step back. Don't force your dog to go inside the den, and don't shut the door after her if she does go in on her own. Leave the den open so she can explore. If she goes in to get the treat, praise her, but stay back. Let her know her den is a safe spot, not jail, and even you won't grab at her while she's in there. Talk softly and pleasantly to your dog as she explores her new den. Hide treats inside the den periodically, so your dog gets the message that she is likely to find something delicious inside that safe, comfy spot.

And what if your dog doesn't take to the den right away? Young puppies can quickly learn to accept the den, but can endure being in it only a few minutes at a time at first. Even if whining and crying, don't make a big deal about it, or risk increasing your pup's anxiety. Put her in the den, shut the door, stay nearby, talk casually but reassuringly to the dog, and then let her out again. Increase the amount of time your dog spends in the den just a few minutes at a time over a period of a few days. Pretty soon, your puppy gets used to the routine and recognizes the den as something safe and predictable.

In the case of an older adopted dog that has neither been in a crate before nor had any bad experiences with the crate, *not* forcing the issue is an important attitude for you to take. Just leave the den door open and let your dog adjust at her own rate. If the dog is truly fearful of the crate, then use the schedule training method for housetraining (see Chapter 7), and keep working to make the den an inviting place without putting any pressure on her.

If your dog's first experiences with her den — and with the entire house and yard — are filled with positive associations like pleasant calm interaction and plenty of yummy treats, you can set the stage for a happy home.

You can actually let your dog rest in her den awhile or you can move on to introduce her to her new family if she's ready.

Introducing your people

The more people your dog meets in a pleasant and positive environment, the better socialized she becomes. First of all, she needs to get to know you, her new favorite person. Next, she needs to meet the other people who live in your house. Finally, she needs to meet all kinds of other people, too.

Dogs that are familiar with many different people of different ages, sizes, hair types, colors, and mobilities become better judges of character than dogs that rarely see anyone beyond the people who live in the house. Dogs are social animals, and they find people fascinating even though prone to strange human habits. The more they know about the curious existence of their two-legged caretakers, the better they get along living in a human world.

Meeting the parents

Your dog first must get to know you and the other adults in your household. These introductions need to be positive, friendly, and not too overwhelming. Your dog is learning about you as you take him around the house and yard, showing him his new environment, but you also need to spend some time focusing on your dog on that first day, so that means:

- Sitting on the floor with your dog
- Letting your dog sniff you
- Petting your dog
- Talking to your dog
- Showing your dog some toys

See what happens when you throw a ball for your dog. Will she chase it? Retrieve it? Or ignore it? Try to figure out what your dog likes and doesn't like, what interests her or makes her nervous. The more you find out about your dog, the more she also will learn about you.

When introducing your dog to other adults, one person at a time is plenty for your dog to take in. Have your dog sniff and investigate the other adults in the house, and have the other adults give your adopted dog treats and gentle petting. Take cues from your dog. If she seems overwhelmed or nervous, take it slow, or save introductions for later. If she seems interested to meet everyone, then give her that interaction time.

Lapping up the kid time!

Kids love dogs, and kids get pretty excited about a new dog in the house. Dogs love kids, too — most of the time. Before you're completely familiar with your new adopted dog, however, prepare your child for how to interact with a new dog and carefully supervise all child-dog interactions. For that first introduction, clip on your dog's leash.

Before bringing an adopted dog home, children need to know that this newest four-legged family member may be nervous, overly excited, or even scared. Loud, quick-moving children can intimidate a dog, especially one that isn't familiar with children. Explain to your children that first impressions are important, and if the new dog's first impression of them is one of fear, then the new dog may not want to play with the children. Children need to approach a new dog quietly, slowly, and with soft gentle voices.

Children likewise need to play with a new dog (or any small dog or puppy) while sitting with her on the floor, rather than trying to pick up the puppy and carry her around. Have the child sit, then let the dog approach the child while the dog is on a leash held by a responsible adult. Keep control over the dog so she doesn't jump on the child, and make sure that the child handles the dog gently. Depending on age, you can let children feed the dog treats or offer her a new toy, but only under strict adult supervision. You don't want your new dog bullying your child to get the treats. With your help, the child needs to be in control of when the dog gets the treat. This kind of positive first meeting sends a message to your dog that short little humans are just as nice and safe and rewarding as the taller ones. Your dog can become your child's best buddy, but maintaining control over the situation is important so the relationship starts off on the right paw.

If your dog reacts too roughly or even fearfully or aggressively toward a child, take the matter seriously and don't let child and dog interact unsupervised, ever, until the matter is fully resolved. Consult a professional trainer or behaviorist for advice. See Chapter 7 for more information about handling behavior problems in adopted dogs. Take aggressive behavior seriously and tackle the problem immediately. Aggression doesn't just go away on its own. Don't risk any child's safety.

Relying on friends to help socialize your dog: The welcome-home party

Even if you have a big family, meeting other people is important for your new dog. It can happen on walks through the neighborhood or trips in the car, but another great way to socialize your dog with all kinds of people is having a dog party. Ask a variety of friends over for snacks and playtime with your new dog.

That doesn't mean that you just let your friends mob your adopted dog. Remember that all your dog's initial interactions with people need to be calm and positive. Give your friends treats to give your dog. Have them approach her one at a time for petting and play. As everyone gives your dog focused and happy attention, your dog gets the impression that people are just great to be around and well worth pleasing.

Before socializing your dog, make sure she doesn't have any aggression issues, such as snapping to protect food, or fear issues, such as anxiety around certain kinds of people. Putting your dog in situations in which she feels nervous, cornered, or surrounded by too many people before she's ready can actually make her more fearful or anxious. You're the best judge for determining whether your dog is ready for this kind of stimulation and socialization. If you aren't sure, try inviting friends over one at a time for awhile to find out how your dog reacts. And keep the treats coming.

Introducing other pets

Meeting the humans in the house is one thing; introducing other pets is another. Some dogs get along just fine with other dogs, but others have issues with their perceived competitors. Some dogs don't think twice about cats, but others see cats as prey animals and great chase opportunities. Some cats, on the other hand, are not accepting and downright nasty about canines intruding on their happy homes. Small animals and birds can look a lot like prey animals, too. Your task: Carefully introduce your new dog to other pets in the household to prevent conflict and to subvert potential tragedy. Doing so can take some time, and some animals don't adjust to their new siblings for weeks or even months. Take it slow, be diplomatic, and supervise all interactions until everyone can be reliably trusted. After that, you may be qualified to sub for Kofi Anan at the United Nations, or at least you'll be better equipped for scheduling regular détente meetings between pets coming from opposite sides of the fence.

How dogs meet dogs

Most dogs tend to relate to each other in a hierarchical system of leaders and followers, and most dogs tend to be at least somewhat territorial. If you already have a dog that's used to being the only dog in the house, he probably will see another dog as an interloper and want to make darn sure that the new dog knows his place.

A new dog on new turf may defer to the previous resident dog. On the other hand, expect no guarantees of a conflict-free meeting. Dogs learn crucial dog-to-dog communication skills when they are still with their littermates between 3 to 6 weeks of age. Puppies that are deprived of this time together may not understand how to communicate well with other dogs. Like people, some dogs just tend to have stronger personalities and try to be the leader. If you put two such dogs together, you can have squabbles.

You can reduce the likelihood of a brawl by taking some or all of these steps:

- ✔ Adopting a female dog if you already have a male dog, or vice versa. Male and female dogs together are less likely to fight each other than dogs of the same gender. Spayed or neutered dogs also are less likely to enter the fray.

- ✔ Introducing the dogs first on neutral territory, such as at the shelter or the home of a friend.

- ✔ Remembering that the first dog may see your home as his territory and feel threatened that another dog is on his turf. Be patient and supervise all interactions until the dogs accept each other.

- ✔ Being patient. Dogs may take a few hours to become fast friends, but some dogs may never get along very well. The relationship probably will improve with time, but it can take weeks or even months.

- ✔ Keeping both dogs on their leashes, with each handled by a separate adult. You must be a strong presence and maintain control. When both dogs think a third party is in control of the situation, they may feel less anxious, fearful, or defensive.

- ✔ Letting both dogs spend some extended getting acquainted time on either side of a baby gate (see Figure 5-2), screen door, or other barrier that neither is able to jump over. Doing so can help dogs gain interest in each other without the threat of one dog invading the other's space.

- ✔ Giving each dog his own space, his own den, and room to run away to in case of a confrontation. A brand-new kennel or crate won't automatically be the resident dog's property, so it gives the new dog a place to feel safe. Keep the door open so the new dog can go in whenever he needs a safe spot, but keep the resident dog out of the new dog's den.

- ✔ Giving both dogs plenty of attention and separate training time, especially your resident dog, who may be feeling neglected. Make sure he knows you aren't replacing him!

- ✔ Taking it slow. Not everybody wants a new sibling. Let both dogs take time getting to know each other, and supervise all interactions until they work out their new relationship.

Figure 5-2:
A baby gate can help your new dog and your resident dog get acquainted.

If your two dogs get into a fight, don't stick your hand in the middle, because you can get hurt doing so. Keep a spray bottle filled with water handy and distract the dogs with a spritz or make a loud noise, like shaking a can of pennies or pebbles. As soon as they stop fighting for a moment, separate them immediately and put each in his respective den or separate room to cool off.

If you can't seem to resolve the issue, call a local dog trainer who uses positive reinforcement. A trainer can work with you and your dogs, giving you some strategies tailored for your individual situation.

Introducing kitty

Some dogs get along just great with cats. In many cases, however, dogs that aren't raised with cats see them as something to chase. Conversely, dogs that are raised with cats may let their guards down in front of a claw-wielding whirlwind, so be careful in that case, too. A new puppy probably can learn to accept your cat as a member of the family. An adult dog that has lived with cats successfully before also will probably be okay. ***Remember:*** A shelter or rescue worker may be able to provide information about the dog's history. An adult dog that isn't familiar with cats may pose a problem.

When introducing a dog and a cat, both need protection. Be sure your cat's claws are trimmed to prevent serious injury to your dog whose eyes are especially vulnerable. And make sure your cat has safe places to escape if the dog attempts to give chase. Finally, supervise all interactions until you're sure both pets can be trusted.

Some people keep their dogs and cats separated, giving each one a separate level of the house or its own room, but doing so can be complicated and a slip-up can cause disaster. Regular obedience training can help you and your dog communicate so that your dog understands what is and is not allowed in your home — and that includes cat chasing. A few dogs never are able to live peacefully with cats. If that happens to you, you may need to consider returning your new pet to the shelter or rescue group in favor of a dog that does get along with cats. Because returning to the shelter is stressful for the dog, I urge you once again never to rush into an adoption without a good chance that your new dog will fit into your home situation.

Small animals: Friends, not doggy snacks!

Some dogs have strong instincts for chasing and killing small animals. Terriers, for example, have been bred for centuries to strengthen their instincts for going after vermin — that's why they're called ratters. If you have hamsters, gerbils, rats, mice, guinea pigs, ferrets, or rabbits as pets, your dog may feel a compulsion to get to them, so you must be extra careful to keep these small creatures safe. Introduce them carefully, or keep the small animal in a place where the dog won't see it, and never leave small animals or birds alone with dogs, for the safety of both — a dog can kill a small bird, but to a small dog, a large parrot is a formidable foe. Make sure that cages are out of reach and inaccessible to your dog.

Downtime

After your dog has had a bathroom break (or two), seen his den, met the family and other pets, and done some power sniffing around his new digs, give your dog some downtime. Take your dog back to her special safe place, throw in some treats, and let her go inside. If she won't, herd her gently inside, and close the door. Praise her and talk gently and positively, and then without making a big deal about it, let her have a rest.

Your dog may whine, cry, or whimper pathetically, but never fear, you don't have to leave her in there for hours. Instead, leave her in the den for at least 15 to 20 minutes. She may settle down and have a nap, or just watch you for awhile. If she seems nervous, you can stay in the same room, but don't pay any attention to her. This time is specifically for your dog to be by herself, and your sympathetic attentions will only make her worry. Remind yourself that you aren't ignoring your dog. You're teaching her self-sufficiency and confidence, and you're teaching her that when she is in her den, her time is her own and nobody will bother her.

After a short rest period, you can let your dog out of the den again. However, take her right back to that potty spot outside, on her leash, until she does her business. Then, get on with whatever activities you have planned next. Repeat these short, positive, nonemotional den rest sessions throughout the day; your dog will quickly learn to appreciate and even look forward to them. Pretty soon, she may go on in there all by herself.

When night falls, tuck your dog into her den until morning, close the door to keep her safely inside, and prepare to endure a night or two of crying and whining. Your new puppy or even an adult dog may not understand at first that this is time for sleeping and that she can come out again in the morning, but after a few nights, she'll get the routine. Remember how much dogs depend on routine? Young puppies probably need a bathroom break during the night, once or maybe twice, but don't get up every time the puppy cries to commiserate. Send the message, instead, that this is how it works, and everybody likes it that way. Soon, your puppy will like it that way, too.

For adult dogs that truly resist the crate, set up a comfy bed beside yours, so your dog knows you're nearby (be sure to close your bedroom door so the dog isn't free to roam while you sleep). Your new adopted dog needs a sense of security, and night is one opportunity to reinforce that. The first few nights can be trying on any new pet owner, but just think of how the adopted dog feels. Most dogs adjust very quickly and sleep through the night sooner than a human baby would. Plan on a nap tomorrow, and be patient. In a week, chances are that nighttime woes will be a distant memory.

Recognizing Adjustment Problems

Adopted dogs often make the transition to their new homes with only minor problems. Occasionally, however, adopted dogs suffer from more severe transitional issues such as anxiety, fear, and extreme hyperactivity. Many of these problems can be addressed by merely acting calm and not making a big deal about your dog's behavior. He soon finds out that he's worried or fearful over nothing. But sometimes, what you do at home just isn't enough.

If your dog is suffering a serious transitional issue, you first need to have the dog checked by a veterinarian to be sure no health issues are involved, and if not, then seek the professional advice and aid of a recommended trainer who uses positive reinforcement.

After arriving in your home, you may see some indications that point to the need for professional intervention, if your dog:

- ✔ Injures himself trying to get out of his kennel or out of the house.

- ✔ Remains extremely hyperactive, racing around, barking, pacing, or panting, and won't calm down after two hours, even after you're calmed down and setting a good example.

- ✔ Becomes aggressive and bites or snarls for any reason.

- ✔ Shakes, shivers, and cries, and/or hides for more than a day, and you can't coax him out of hiding.

- ✔ Refuses to eat for more than two days (more than one day for puppies).

- ✔ Has a seizure. For information on how to recognize and handle a seizure, see Chapter 6.

If your dog experiences any of these conditions, seek professional help. You need to know that experiencing these conditions may mean your adopted dog needs a little extra patience and work, and in a few cases — not the majority, fortunately — dogs may never adjust and need to be returned. Talk to your trainer about what to expect and whether other family members (children, other pets) can be in a dangerous situation because of your dog. But also know that most of the time, adjustment issues can be successfully resolved. With a patient and caring owner like you, your dog has a great chance of settling happily in and, with time, learning to trust, love, and thrive.

Chapter 6

Caring for Your Adopted Dog

· ·

In This Chapter

▶ Discovering your adopted dog's unique nutritional problems and requirements

▶ Choosing the best dog food

▶ Finding and visiting a great veterinarian

▶ Spaying or neutering and vaccinating your dog: Why they're so important

▶ Recognizing health problems and knowing when to see the vet

▶ Grooming your dog to near-perfection, for beauty *and* good health

· ·

After successfully navigating the introductory phases of bringing a new dog into your home, you may feel a bit triumphant. Just look how beautifully your dog is adjusting to her den, to you, and to her new home. But all that work you just went through adopting your dog and bringing her home, well . . . that's only the beginning. Now that you're responsible for another living being, you naturally want to give your furry family member the best possible care and that means feeding her good food and seeing to her health-care needs.

People who don't practice stellar nutritional habits and rarely go to the doctor for annual checkups may find providing such care for a dog a little difficult. When your nutrition and health habits are lacking, how can you expect to practice good habits with your pets? Yet, this part of caring for your adopted dog is crucial, because she depends on you for her food and care. After all, the dog can't take herself to the vet or pour herself a bowl of kibble, can she?

An adopted dog's needs may be particularly crucial at the outset because of nutritional deficits and other health problems that need to be corrected. Nutritional and health issues common to adopted dogs usually are related to neglect, abandonment, or previous owners who didn't want to (or couldn't) pay for a treatment. Other issues, such as flea infestations, leg injuries, or malnutrition, may be related to time spent wandering. A special effort is required to uncover and treat these nutritional and health needs so that your adopted dog can rally to become a healthy, vibrant, energetic, shiny-coated family pet. Getting it done is all up to you. I tell you how in this chapter.

Keeping Your Dog Healthy

Your new adopted dog deserves the best possible care, now that she lives with you and depends on you to keep her healthy. Although some health problems are genetic and others are caused by your dog's past experiences, you still have plenty to do to correct and maintain your dog's health. In the following sections I explain how to start your pooch on the right paw and maintain her good health.

First things first: Choosing a great vet

You and your veterinarian are partners who want nothing more than good health for your pet. But not all vets get along well with all people or pets, so choose yours carefully. You want a vet who

- ✔ **Is familiar with the characteristics of the breed you have.** Each breed (Lab or Poodle, and so on) or breed type (toy or giant, for example) has its own special needs that can impact the type of medical attention it receives. Sighthounds, like Greyhounds for example, are sensitive to anesthesia, so surgery can be risky. Collies likewise can be so sensitive to a certain type of heartworm medication that they should be prescribed an alternative medication.

- ✔ **Has treated other dogs with conditions similar to your dog's.** If you've adopted a senior dog or one with special needs, find out what kind of experience your vet has with your dog's specific issues or whether he or she has treated dogs with other special needs, such as blindness or paralysis.

Ask yourself these important questions as you consider how *you* feel about a particular vet:

- ✔ Do you and the vet communicate well?

- ✔ Do you like the way the vet handles and talks to your dog?

- ✔ Is the vet's office staff friendly?

- ✔ Are the vet's location and office hours convenient and accessible?

Find out whether your veterinarian's office provides after-hours and/or emergency care before your dog ever needs it. Some vet's offices actually staff an on-call veterinarian; others may work with an emergency clinic that's always open. Either way, make sure you know who to call and where to go in the event your dog needs medical attention when the vet's office is closed.

Giving your new friend a good once-over: The first exam

Every adopted dog needs to visit a veterinarian right away — before ever coming home, if possible. The first visit is a chance for your vet to get to know your new dog; moreover, it's a time for the vet to give your dog a thorough checkup and do some tests to make sure everything is normal. When you set up the appointment, ask whether you need to bring anything, such as a stool sample from your dog.

At your dog's first exam, the veterinarian:

- ✔ Finds out everything that you know about your dog and his history.

- ✔ Pokes, prods, rubs, squeezes, feels your dog all over (paws, nails, eyes, ears, mouth, and rear end) in search of any abnormalities or external parasites.

- ✔ Does a fecal test to check your dog for worms and other internal parasites.

- ✔ Performs a blood test to check your dog for heartworm, that dangerous parasite transmitted by mosquito bites. This is not appropriate for puppies under 6 months, as the test is not able to pick up infestations this early in the life cycle. Do put puppies on heartworm preventive, and have the vet test after six months or the following spring in northern states when mosquito season gears up again.

- ✔ Treats your dog for intestinal worms. *Note:* If your new dog is a puppy, the vet probably won't go through the hassle of testing her because worms are such a common problem in puppies. The vet will just go ahead and give the puppy a deworming medication. Adult dogs are treated after tests reveal problems.

 Older dogs that aren't used to the way the vet touches them may shy away in fear. You can help prepare your dog for future visits with regular grooming sessions. Adopted dogs that have never received regular veterinary care may especially need this kind of conditioning. I explain how to acclimate your dog to regular handling in the "Grooming disguised as a checkup" section later in this chapter.

After the examination, the vet talks to you about your dog's health-care plan, explaining when it's time for vaccinations, whether your dog needs treatment for any problems, whether your dog may need to lose or gain a few pounds (see the section on assessing your dog's weight, later in this chapter), and what options you have for spaying or neutering your dog.

Scheduling spay/neuter surgery

Most shelters and vets recommend that pets be spayed or neutered as soon as possible. Six months is the common age, but some shelters even recommend the surgery be done younger, called "early spay/neuter." In many cases, the shelter or rescue group ideally will have the spay/neuter done before you take the dog home. If you are responsible for the procedure, get it done as soon as possible, before your pet settles in to the new routine. After the surgery, your dog will need to take it easy for a few days. Keep her calm, keep an eye on the stitches, and follow your doctor's post-op recovery procedures.

Because people who work for animal shelters and rescue groups see so many unwanted animals, they usually are vocal advocates for spaying/neutering pets. In fact, many shelters require spay/neuter in their contracts and also give adopters certificates for free or reduced spay/neuter surgeries to encourage them to make the healthy, safe choice for their pets. Spaying or neutering does more for dogs than prevent them from adding to the canine overpopulation problem however. It's also good for them! Spaying and neutering:

- ✔ Reduces or eliminates the risk of cancer of the reproductive organs. If the spay is performed on a female dog before the third heat cycle, the procedure greatly reduces the risk of mammary cancer. Spay at any time in the life cycle eliminates the possibility of uterine cancer.

- ✔ Eliminates the risks of pregnancy.

- ✔ Reduces the dog's desire to wander, fight with other dogs, or behave aggressively.

Vets do so many spay/neuter surgeries that the risks are minimal — much less than leaving a dog unaltered. Spaying or neutering your pet is the responsible thing to do, and the healthiest option. If you're still not convinced, talk to your vet about this important procedure.

Staying current with vaccinations

In addition to discussing spay/neuter surgery, your vet also wants to make sure your dog's vaccinations are up to date.

Vaccinations are a controversial issue. Some people, including many vets, believe adult pets are overvaccinated and think too many vaccinations pose health risks. Others believe vaccinations should be performed yearly to keep dangerous diseases like distemper from getting a paw-hold on the pet population like they did in decades past.

Adult dogs may not need annual vaccinations and can instead have *titer tests* — tests that check a dog's immunity levels — to determine exactly which vaccinations are needed. One exception is the rabies vaccine, which is regulated by law and may be required every one to three years, depending on where you live and the type of rabies vaccine the vet uses.

Puppies definitely need a series of vaccinations in the first year of life to protect them from many dangerous diseases as they're immune systems develop. Different vets recommend slightly differing vaccination schedules. Vaccines likewise vary according to the specific dog's risk factors. Your vet can be more specific about the vaccination needs based on your individual dog, the particular region of the country in which you live, and your individual circumstances. In general, however, the first-year vaccination schedule for puppies usually resembles the schedule in Table 6-1. *Note:* DHPP is a common combination vaccine that includes vaccines for distemper, adenovirus (hepatitis), parainfluenza, and parvovirus.

Table 6-1	Puppy Vaccination Schedule	
Puppy's Age	*Recommended Vaccinations*	*Optional Vaccinations*
6–8 weeks	Distemper, measles, parainfluenza	Bordatella
10–12 weeks	DHPP	Coronavirus, Leptospirosis, Bordatella, Lyme disease
12–24 weeks	Rabies	None
14–16 weeks	DHPP	Coronavirus, Lyme disease, Leptospirosis
12–16 months	Rabies, DHPP	Coronavirus, Leptospirosis, Boradetella, Lyme disease
Every 1–2 years	DHPP	Coronavirus, Leptospirosis, Bordetella, Lyme disease
Every 1–3 years	Rabies (as required by law)	None

Deworming and other tests

Your vet also makes sure your dog is dewormed and tests him for any other potential problems uncovered during the physical examination. Worms — from roundworms and tapeworms to deadly heartworms — are common parasites that can severely damage a puppy's health. All puppies need to be dewormed according to a vet's recommendation, but dogs of virtually any age that are exposed to mosquitoes need to take heartworm medication.

Heartworms are microscopic parasitic worms transmitted by mosquitoes into your dog's blood. They travel to the heart and grow, tangling themselves inside the heart and blood vessels. If left untreated, heartworms are fatal. Even if discovered in time, before the worms have grown too large, the treatment still is risky and expensive. Fortunately, medication to prevent heartworms is available in tasty treat-like pills that your dog takes every month.

The medication used to prevent heartworms can kill dogs that already have the parasite; therefore, testing for heartworms is a must to ensure that your dog is clear. Although the test isn't 100 percent reliable, it will likely reveal heartworms after they've lived inside your dog for six months or more, so a yearly test at the beginning of each mosquito season is important to detect any heartworm infection acquired in the previous year. Your safest bet is to keep your dog on heartworm preventive medicine year-round, not just during mosquito season.

Other tests your vet may want to do are related to any signs he or she sees that may indicate a health problem. Ask your vet to explain the tests, what they reveal, and how much they cost.

Ridding your pooch of pesky pests

Fleas and ticks, not to mention worms, mites, flies, and various other internal and external parasites, are a common problem with any dog, but especially dogs that have been wandering, spend a lot of time outside, or have been frequently exposed to other dogs. One of the first things the veterinarian does when he examines your new adopted dog is check for the presence of various types of pests and parasites and then suggest strategies for eliminating them.

These nasty critters can transmit serious diseases like tapeworm and Lyme disease, and they can jump onto you and bite you, too. Ridding your dog of these pests and preventing them from returning is important. Thanks to technology, keeping your pooch pest-free is easier than ever.

If your dog already has a flea infestation, you can get rid of them with a long thorough bath and a flea comb. Rinse and drown fleas, dry your dog, and then comb through the dry coat carefully, looking for any strays. Drop them in a cup of alcohol, and then flush them.

Ticks that are already attached to your dog must be removed immediately. The longer a tick is attached, the greater the risk that it will transmit a disease to your dog. Here are the steps for removing a tick:

1. **Soak the tick in alcohol.**

   You can use a cotton ball soaked in alcohol to accomplish this task. Doing so makes the tick loosen its grip.

2. **Carefully pull the tick out at a 45-degree angle to the dog's skin.**

   You'll need either tweezers or special tick forceps you can buy in the pet store. Don't pull straight up, or the mouth parts of the tick can break off and remain under the skin! If this happens, you may notice a red lump at the site where the tick was attached, caused by a reaction to the tick parts. Usually, this situation will resolve itself, but keep the area clean and monitor it for signs of infection, such as pus, swelling, or red streaks.

   You can remove a tick by hand, but in all cases wear rubber gloves. If an engorged tick bursts, tick bacteria can infect you through your skin.

3. **Drop the tick in alcohol to kill it, and then flush it.**

After removing fleas and ticks, apply a reliable monthly spot-on treatment that you can purchase from your vet. A few drops between your dog's shoulder blades protect him from fleas for a month. Various brands are available. Some kill only fleas, and others also kill ticks and repel mosquitoes that transmit heartworm, the dreaded West Nile virus, and other diseases. Your vet can recommend which brand is most appropriate for your dog.

You can also buy flea and tick products over the counter at the pet store. Some of these work better than others, and the spot-on treatments seem to be the most effective, but please read the label carefully. You can injure or even cause a fatal reaction in your pet if you misuse these products. You can look for prescription-only products like Advantage and Frontline on the Internet at discount prices. Although vets much prefer you get these products from them, in a setting where they can examine your dog and explain the proper usage, these products are less expensive on the Internet. (A vet at the company writes the prescription for you without ever meeting you.)

Get in the habit of applying the spot-on treatment when you give your dog his monthly heartworm pill. Your vet can recommend treatment for other pests, such as mites that cause mange — resulting in scaly skin and hair loss — or a fly infestation. Really nasty cases of pests will probably have been treated at the shelter before the dog was offered for adoption.

Noticing problems after you get home

Adopted dogs have many of the same problems that other dogs have, but they may be more prone to problems that result from wandering, being exposed to many other dogs, living in a kennel, being neglected or abused, and not being vaccinated against contagious diseases. For that reason, when you first adopt a dog, you may pay several visits to your veterinarian.

Although shelters do their best to adopt out healthy dogs, your dog may still bring home some health problems. Shelters treat obvious conditions like broken bones, wounds, major pest infestations, and serious diseases before their animals are adopted, but not-so-obvious health problems may not appear until later. These include certain parasites like heartworms, skin infections that get worse, generalized itching, sprained or injured joints and tendons, and respiratory problems. All these conditions warrant a trip to the vet.

Because your new dog is likely to need several visits with your vet, keep a list of problems you want him or her to check out. On this list, include any physical and behavioral changes you've noticed (many serious health problems begin with subtle signals). With this list and your keen observations, your vet is better able to diagnose and treat any problems — big and small — before they get out of hand.

The symptoms your new dog exhibits may indicate a slight or serious health problem, so how do you know when to call the vet? Even though your dog may be just fine, you're better off playing it safe and calling the vet if your dog exhibits any of the following symptoms:

- ✔ **Suffers from persistent coughing, wheezing, choking, and gagging, periodically throughout the day for more than one or two days.** These symptoms can signal a throat obstruction, respiratory disorder, or heart problem.

- ✔ **Limps or seems reluctant to exercise.** These symptoms can signal arthritis, a pulled muscle or tendon, or joint disease.

- ✔ **Shows signs of fatigue and/or disinterest in doggy activities that differ from the dog's normal behavior, lasting more than a few days.** Dogs with low energy can signal a thyroid problem, heart disease, or many other problems.

- ✔ **Yelps, nips, or bites when touched — as if in pain.** This symptom can signal a wide range of problems.

- ✔ **Shows a sudden increase or decrease in appetite and/or sudden weight loss or weight gain.** These symptoms can signal thyroid or other autoimmune problems, diabetes, or pain from any cause, including mouth or dental pain.

- ✔ **Shows a sudden increase in thirst for no apparent reason that continues over several days.** Drinking larger-than-normal amounts of water can be a sign of diabetes or other diseases.

- ✔ **Suffers from a lump, rash, or skin thickening or a sore that won't heal or that looks infected.** These symptoms can signal a skin infection that requires antibiotics or a skin or other cancer.

If your dog exhibits any of the symptoms on the following list, you need to go immediately to the vet or emergency vet clinic. Consider these symptoms signs of an emergency:

- ✔ **Gagging, choking, or any sign of an inability to breathe easily.** Your dog may have something lodged in his throat or be suffering from a severe respiratory problem.

- ✔ **Inability or unwillingness to move, severe lameness, and yelping when touched as if in severe pain.** These symptoms can indicate a broken bone or disk rupture. Disk rupture is most common in long-backed dogs like Dachshunds. Without immediate treatment, dogs can become permanently paralyzed.

- ✔ **Pacing, panting, and salivating for no apparent reason, especially with a distended abdomen.** These symptoms can signal bloat, a serious emergency in which the stomach swells with gas and twists.

Without immediate veterinary treatment, this condition is fatal. Bloat is most common in deep-chested breeds like Great Danes, Labrador Retrievers, and German Shepherd dogs.

✔ **Has or shows signs of having had a seizure, including fainting, a blank stare, sudden whole-body stiffness, rigid or jerking legs, sudden collapse, stumbling, drooling, or uncontrolled peeing and pooping.** These symptoms may point to epilepsy, which is treatable, or a brain tumor or other secondary response to disease.

✔ **Continuous vomiting and/or diarrhea beyond one or two episodes.** These symptoms can point to poisoning (see next item), intestinal parasites, or digestive disorders.

If you suspect your dog has been poisoned, time is of the essence. Either get your dog to an emergency veterinary clinic immediately, or call the ASPCA's Animal Poison Control Center. This service, which is operated out of the College of Veterinary Medicine at the University of Illinois, can help you treat a poisoning emergency faster than you can get to a vet. For $50, a vet helps you with your emergency over the phone. Call them toll-free at 888-426-4435.

✔ **Exhibits neurological changes**. Signs of neurological changes include stumbling or disorientation, confusion, failure to recognize you, seizures (see description of seizures earlier in this list), and collapse.

Following up with an annual exam

After puppyhood, your healthy adult dog still needs to see the vet, even if you're not vaccinating your dog every year. An annual exam is an important part of good health maintenance, because you greatly increase the chance of catching a problem while it's still easy to treat. Many diseases that are common to dogs first show themselves with only minor symptoms. A skin lump, a dull coat, and minor changes in behavior can be signs of an impending problem, so keep your vet informed by scheduling your dog for a physical every year.

Somebody's Hungry!

Your choice of pet food makes a big difference in the health of your dog. Pet foods range dramatically in quality from the supercheap to the superpricey. They're marketed for different ages, stages, sizes, and even breeds. How the heck do you know which pet food to choose from among the many that decorate pet- and grocery-store shelves? Read on!

Choosing the right food for your dog

With the help of your vet, you can determine what your dog needs to eat. If your dog is healthy, a premium adult maintenance diet is probably just fine. Read the label, look for recognizable meat protein sources listed among the first few ingredients, and get advice from your veterinarian if you aren't sure about which food is best for your adopted dog. But what do you do about overweight or underweight dogs, puppies, adult dogs, senior dogs, and dogs with special needs?

I tell you about better ways of feeding overweight or underweight dogs in the "Correcting a weight problem" section later in this chapter, or you can pick up a copy of *Dog Health & Nutrition For Dummies* by M. Christine Zink (Wiley).

Puppies, on the other hand, need a high-quality puppy food, but large breed puppies — even the skinny ones — must grow slowly, so after the first few months of life, most of these dogs need to be weaned off puppy food. Large breeds like Labs, German Shepherds, Rottweilers, and large mixed breeds are prone to bone and joint abnormalities as they age. If they grow too quickly, bones won't be as dense, and joints won't develop well. Feed large-breed puppies a high-quality food with moderate amounts of protein, fat, and calories.

Senior dogs and dogs with special needs, such as injuries or diseases, may have specific nutritional needs. Dogs that develop kidney problems may need a low-protein food, but other seniors need enough protein to keep their muscles nourished. Many good prescription foods address specific health problems and chronic diseases. Talk to your vet, who can advise you best about prescription diets to meet your dog's particular needs.

To a large extent, price *is* indicative of quality, but more expensive premium foods are actually more of a bargain than you may think. Cheap pet foods are full of fillers, including protein sources that aren't as digestible as more expensive protein sources like muscle meat. When dogs eat cheap foods, their stools (that's a fancy word for poop) are large, soft, messy, and quite frankly, stinky. When they eat premium foods, their stools are smaller, tighter, easier to pick up, and hardly smell at all. That's because dogs actually digest more of the food, and that means you won't have to feed your dog as much food to get the same or better nutritional value.

Premium diets come in dry kibble, canned, frozen raw-meat, or dehydrated patties. Each has its own benefits, and your choice usually depends on what you're willing to spend, how much time you want to take preparing the food, and whether your dog actually eats it. Dry kibble contains more fiber and helps keep teeth clean, but it contains less water, so dogs may need to drink more water to compensate. Canned food may taste better and contain more water, but some vets think it may contribute to tooth decay. It also gets expensive for large dogs, because it's less concentrated than kibble, so you feed your dog more of it. For some dogs, frozen and dehydrated raw diets can be healthy, if they're from a reputable company, but they can be expensive and need to be defrosted or rehydrated. Raw food is controversial — debate rages over whether it is more nutritious or more likely to harbor harmful bacteria — so talk to your vet about whether raw food is a good diet for your dog. One kind of food that most vets won't recommend is semimoist. Although these chewy kibble pieces may taste good to dogs, they're typically loaded with sweeteners and artificial colors and aren't a good nutritional choice — like junk food for dogs.

Addressing bad nutritional habits: What your dog doesn't need to eat

Adopted dogs that had to scrounge for themselves or even beloved pets that lost their homes but had owners who couldn't resist feeding them not-so-healthy people food may already have bad eating habits. Two key factors to remember for keeping your dog's diet in shipshape are that dogs do just fine eating a high-quality dry kibble and never should be given any kind of junk food like sweets or processed food intended for human consumption.

Some human foods are good for dogs and, like high-quality canned foods, can give kibble a little more appealing taste. However, junk food, which isn't all that great for humans, can be harmful to dogs, leading to malnourishment, obesity, digestive problems, and even disease. If you include healthy people food in your dog's food bowl, reduce the amount of kibble you give her and keep a close eye on your dog's waistline. I show you how to gauge your dog's waistline in the "Administering the body evaluation test" section later in this chapter.

Helping Fido's tummy transition

Regardless of how good the food that you choose for your dog happens to be, remember that some dogs have sensitive digestive systems and don't adjust well to changes in their diets. When adopting, find out what the shelter or rescue worker has been feeding the dog. Then, if you decide a different food would be better, introduce the new food gradually, mixing it with the old and gradually increasing the amount of new food over the course of a week to prevent digestive upset.

Deciding when to ring the dinner bell

Adopted dogs tend to have an almost desperate obsession with food. If they've gone for weeks, months, or even longer, barely getting enough to eat, they can be protective of food, fearful that someone will take it away, or eat ravenously, as though they may never get another meal. Your adopted dog may take a long time accepting the fact that food always is available. For that reason, feeding your adopted dog twice or even three times every day is a good idea. The more often food shows up in front of your adopted dog, especially at regular times, the more she will realize that you're a dependable source of food. Just remember to divide up the daily food ration into multiple feedings. Small frequent meals are good, but too many calories are not good for your dog. If your dog aggressively protects her food, try feeding her by hand. (For more about dealing with aggression, see Chapter 7.)

Keeping an eye on your dog's waistline

You can keep your adopted puppy or dog slim and at a healthy weight while improving the nutrients he gets every day, but doing so can be a tricky balancing act.

Many adopted dogs come to their new homes slightly underweight, but they often grow pudgy — sometimes quickly, because their owners can't resist those longing eyes, hungry faces, or those protruding ribs. How can you *not* want to feed such a pitiful creature just a little something extra? But obesity can cause many serious health problems in pets of any age, from puppies to seniors. Too much weight stresses bones and joints, strains the heart and other internal organs, crowds the lungs, and turns a simple walk around the block into a major chore. In fact, overweight dogs suffer much the same risks and consequences as overweight humans.

Malnourished dogs don't have it any better. Lacking crucial nutrients can lead to serious nutritional issues, too. Signs of malnourishment include a bloated abdomen, bleeding gums, and an emaciated body with ribs clearly visible.

Even so, many pet owners are startled to hear from their veterinarians that their skinny, "wasting-away" dog is actually at a healthy weight. Because so many pet dogs are overweight, people have grown accustomed to seeing dogs in a slightly padded condition and don't always recognize that for most dogs, thin is better.

So how do you know whether your adopted dog is overweight, underweight, or just right? With some dogs, the answer is obvious. They're either emaciated from a lack of food and other harsh living conditions or roly-poly and waddling down the street. With others, the answer isn't so easy to tell. Use the body evaluation test and the figures that follow as your guide.

Administering the body evaluation test

To determine whether your dog is the correct weight, compare his body condition with the graphical representations of how dogs typically look when they are overweight, underweight, or just right in Figure 6-1. Use this figure to guide you as you evaluate your dog using the following three-step process:

1. **Look at your dog from the side.**

   His tummy needs to tuck up from his chest and not be level with or hang below his chest. If you can easily see a dog's ribs, he's probably *underweight*. Many dogs in shelters are severely underweight because they starved while enduring harsh living conditions, expending huge amounts of energy to escape hazards, find food, and look for shelter. A few breeds are exceptions, including Greyhounds, Whippets, and Italian Greyhounds; their ribs show at a normal weight. Breeds with heavy coats need closer scrutiny because you probably can't see ribs even when the dog is underweight, so try the next two steps for a more complete assessment.

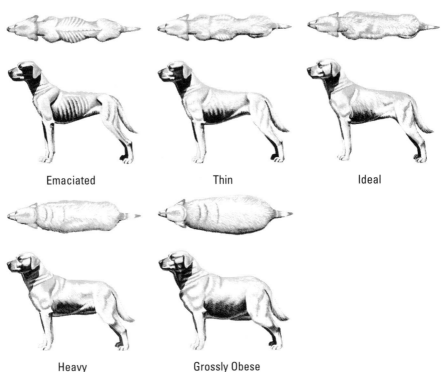

Emaciated   Thin   Ideal

Figure 6-1:
Purina's Body Condition Chart shows how to recognize whether your dog is overweight, underweight, or just right.

Heavy   Grossly Obese

Courtesy of Nestle Purina PetCare Co.

2. **Look at your dog from above.**

    As you stand over him and look down, your dog needs to have a visibly tucked-in waist, but his hipbones shouldn't protrude too severely. If your dog looks like a barrel, a sausage, or a small beach ball with legs, he's probably overweight. If his hips protrude sharply, he's probably under-weight. If he has a nice curve inward at the waist, he's probably at a good weight.

3. **Feel your dog's sides for the ribs.**

    This test is especially important for heavily coated dogs, whose fur often conceals excess or lack of sufficient weight. If you can feel no evidence that your dog possesses a rib cage, he may be overweight. If you can feel the ribs but they have a slight padding, like a light blanket over them, then your dog may be just right. If the ribs are obvious and feel like they're covered with only the thinnest layer of skin, your dog may be underweight.

Correcting a weight problem

If your dog is underweight, choose nutrient-dense dog food as recommended by your vet, such as premium puppy food or prescription food designed to help dogs gain weight. Or, if your vet recommends it, add healthy, nutrient-dense people food to his regular kibble, such as chopped meat, whole-milk plain yogurt, olive oil or flax seed oil, and fatty fish. You want calories, healthy fat, and plenty of vitamins and minerals in every bite of food you feed your dog — but not junk food or high-salt or high-sugar content.

Should you make your own pet food?

Do you love the idea of making your own pet food? Many people do it, but feeding your dog from the food you have in your cupboard isn't as easy as handing him a slice of pepperoni pizza and pouring him a glass of milk. Dogs don't have the same nutritional requirements as people, and if you leave out certain nutrients, your dog can suffer serious health deficiencies. Before making your first batch, do some intensive research, and decide whether you want to feed a cooked diet, a raw meat diet (sometimes called a BARF diet, which stands for Bones And Raw Food), or a combination of the two. Get the thumbs-up from your vet, and then gradually ease your dog into a home-cooked diet, so that your dog's digestive system has a chance to adjust. As you make the switch, keep an eye on your dog, making sure he looks healthy, feels good, and enjoys the food. Many people think making their pet's food is fun, enjoyable, and rewarding, but the subject is controversial, so do your research before taking on this task.

If your dog is overweight, you'll do him a big favor if you help him correct this problem with a little more exercise, fewer treats, and in some cases, a switch to a dog food made for overweight dogs. Your vet can advise you on the best ways to put weight on or take it off your adopted dog, but in general, dogs lose weight the same way humans do: fewer calories, good nutrition, and exercise.

Good Grooming Matters

Some adopted dogs have come from homes where they received regular grooming, but many were neglected in this important area and may need some help with their personal hygiene. (I address ridding your dog of the fleas and ticks he carries around in the "Ridding your pooch of pesky pests" section earlier in this chapter.)

Grooming is far more important than beautification, although a well-groomed dog is certainly a pleasure to behold. Grooming is part of good healthcare. A tangled, matted coat traps bacteria, hides pests, and encourages skin infections. Dirty ears develop yeast infections or mites, runny eyes stain your dog's adorable face, and toenails allowed to grow too long actually deform your dog's feet. Regular grooming gives you a chance to keep tabs on your dog and any changes in her skin, coat, body, and even behavior.

Grooming disguised as a checkup

Most dogs don't absolutely require daily grooming, but a few minutes set aside each day for grooming can become a comforting routine, a chance to bond with your dog, and an opportunity to get your dog used to regular handling. Besides, daily brushing decreases the amount of dog hair you have in the house. Brush more, vacuum less.

Each day at the same, take your dog to a special grooming spot on a counter, in the bathroom, on the front porch, or in a spare room you set up as a grooming station. Smaller dogs are easier to groom on a raised surface like a counter or sturdy table. Put down a bath mat or towel to prevent slipping on slick surfaces and do the following:

> ✔ **Rub your dog all over her coat and skin.** Doing so provides your dog with nice relaxing massage, gets her used to human touch, loosens dead hair for more efficient brushing, and reveals any unusual skin changes like lumps, rashes, or thickening — something that feels different than normal.

✔ **Check your dog the way a veterinarian would.** Look in her ears and at her eyes, pick up each foot and gently squeeze each footpad, examine her nails, lift up her tail, and feel her abdomen, gently prodding with your fingers in the soft tucked-up tummy skin below your dog's ribcage. When your dog is used to these procedures, she won't be disturbed when a vet does the same things. As you conduct your own exam, talk to your dog, praise her, and pet her, occasionally offering a treat. The entire experience needs to be fun, not frightening or annoying, to your dog. If you notice any abnormalities, like lumps, skin changes, or if your dog reacts as if a particular area is sensitive, give your vet a call to see whether you need to bring your dog in for a check. Now you can break out the brush.

Brush, comb, trim, bathe, and polish

Once every day, or at least once a week, brush your dog's entire coat using a natural bristle brush, or use a slicker brush (see Figure 6-2) during times of heavy shedding to help pull out a dead coat. For long-coated dogs, pay special attention to mat-prone areas behind the ears, at the place where the front legs meet the chest, and around and under the tail. For long-coated dogs, follow the brushing with a thorough comb-through, using a steel comb. Comb all the way down to the skin, to get out every tangle before it tightens and has to be cut out.

Figure 6-2:
Long-coated dogs need frequent brushing to keep mats and tangles out of their coats. This slicker brush is good for pulling out dead hair during times of heavy shedding.

If you encounter a tangle that you can't comb out, try spraying it with coat conditioner to loosen it. You can get this handy grooming supply at your local pet store. Don't get the tangle wet because wetness tends only to tighten tangles. You may have to slice it vertically with a scissors or mat splitter, another handy grooming supply you can get at your pet store. Then comb out the pieces. Be careful not to cut your dog's skin, and always cut parallel to the hair, rather than across the hair, so you don't leave a hole in your dog's coat.

Some dogs don't need baths very often, especially short-coated breeds that stay inside most of the time. In fact, too-frequent baths can cause skin irritation from the depletion of natural oils in your dog's coat. Long-coated breeds need baths about once every four to six weeks, with a good brushing first and a good blow-dry after, to keep their coats in good shape. When a dog gets into something stinky, a bath definitely is in order. Assemble all your supplies first and bathe your dog in the tub or outdoor children's pool with lukewarm to cool water, rinsing out all shampoo thoroughly. Blow-dry long coats to make them fluffy.

For short-coated dogs, rub down the coat with a chamois or velvet square for extra sheen after it is dry. Next, clean your dog's ears with a moist cotton ball soaked in water or ear wash made for dogs, available at your pet store. Wipe your dog's face and apply moisturizing eye drops if necessary for your breed (your vet will tell you if your dog needs this, but it is most often required of dogs with flat faces and large eyes). If your dog has a white or light-colored coat, she may develop tear stains under her eyes. You can buy tear-stain remover at the pet store to get rid of them. Keeping the eyes clean and dry minimizes future staining.

Trim your dog's nails using a nail clipper made just for dogs, as in Figure 6-3. If you clip off just the tips once each week, your dog quickly grows accustomed to this chore. Also, the *quick,* or small vein that runs partway down the nail, tends to recede farther back into the nail if you clip more often, reducing your chances of accidentally cutting this vein. You can see the quick in dogs with light-colored nails, but in dogs with black nails, you just have to guess. You're best off just clipping the ends of the nails.

If you do cut off too much nail and clip the quick, it will bleed, and your dog will feel an unpleasant pinch that can quickly turn a dog against nail clipping. Be careful, and keep some coagulating powder handy just in case. You can buy some at your local pet store.

Some adopted dogs are resistant to nail trimming and won't let you hold their paws. In that case, you may have to take your dog to a professional groomer for nail clipping, but if you can do it yourself, it's much easier, and cheaper. Start by getting your dog used to letting you just touch and then hold her paw. Praise and offer lots of treats. Go very slowly. When your dog is comfortable letting you hold her paw, try clipping just the tip of one nail, then giving a treat. Try for another nail tomorrow. Small steps with plenty of rewards and reinforcements are the best way to acclimate a dog to something new that she doesn't necessarily enjoy.

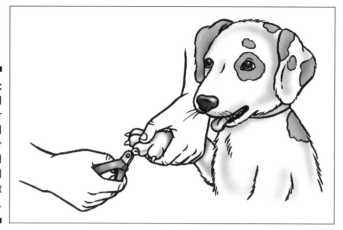

Figure 6-3:
Use a nail clipper designed just for dogs, and be careful not to cut the quick.

Don't forget good dental care! Lack of it can lead to dental bacteria, which can quickly travel to a dog's heart, causing heart disease. Clean teeth can actually increase your dog's life span. Brush your dog's teeth as often as you can — every day is best, but once a week is still good — with a toothbrush and toothpaste made especially for dogs that's meat flavored for palatability. If your dog doesn't like brushing, you can start by simply wiping her teeth once a day with a soft cloth or trying one of the toothbrushes that slips over your finger. Or, try ProCare Dental Gel, which requires no rinsing and only weekly applications. This gel helps keep tartar from building up in your dog's mouth. You can buy a variety of treats (including gel treats) that help reduce tartar, and some dog foods are designed to help keep dog's teeth clean. Ask your vet if one of these foods is appropriate for your dog.

If your adopted dog's teeth already have a lot of tartar, your vet can properly clean them. This procedure requires your dog to be put under anesthesia, and it can be expensive; however, severe tartar buildup can cause an infection leading to your dog's heart, so consider it a necessary pet health expense if your vet recommends it. After that, you can start your dog on the road to good dental habits.

Some adopted dogs don't like to have their teeth touched, but this skill is an important one for a dog to learn, because the vet has to look in your dog's mouth. So you need to try touching her mouth, lifting up her lips, and touching her teeth every day, to get her used to it. Then you can introduce the toothbrush and brush just a little at a time, giving your cooperative dog lots of praise. Good dental health is well worth the extra effort.

Chapter 7

Doggy Boot Camp: Basic Training and Behavior Management

In This Chapter

▶ Housetraining your dog with methods that really work

▶ Getting acquainted with some basic training cues and socialization strategies

▶ Finding a good obedience class and instructor

▶ Foiling escapees, barkers, jumpers, chewers, nippers, beggars, and diggers

▶ Dealing with separation anxiety and aggressive behavior

▶ Finding and using an animal behaviorist to help behavior problems

Sometimes humans must seem pretty confusing to dogs. People love it when their dogs gnaw on chew toys but hate when dogs gnaw on their nice, chewy leather shoes. People take dogs outside into a big, exciting world but expect dogs to stay right next to them without yanking on a measly 6-foot leash. What is it with humans, anyway?

Dogs and humans have chosen to live together over thousands of years of mutual evolution, but each still has habits that the other has a hard time understanding. That's where training comes in. Training an adopted dog is not much different than training any other dog — each reacts in its own way to different teaching methods. However, adopted dogs that experienced trauma may be particularly sensitive or have obstacles to normal routes of training, so you may need to progress at a slower pace, be flexible about what training methods are working or not working, and be extragenerous with your positive reinforcement. Patience and consistency are absolutely key to training adopted dogs. Everyone in the family must kindly but firmly enforce the same rules in the same way, and enforce them at all times, in all situations. That's the best way to communicate with your dog.

In this chapter, you explore training methods, obedience cues, and other information about human-dog interaction, including some tips about dog behavior in general and the behavior of adopted dogs in particular. Use this information to housetrain your new pet, to find a great training instructor, to manage some of those doggy behaviors you can't quite live with, and in general, to show your adopted dog how to act in a new home so you can build a strong foundation for a well-behaved pet.

Housetraining Made Easy

One of the main reasons people give up their adopted dogs is a problem with housetraining. Many adopted dogs have lived outside, in kennels, or alone in backyards for a long time without being housetrained. Others may have lived inside most of the time, but their owners never had the time or patience to be consistent about housetraining. And although some adopted dogs may already be housetrained, the stress of losing their homes and going through the shelter or rescue process (or both) can cause housetraining habits to lapse. Even so, you can teach your new puppy or a resistant adult dog how to relieve himself where you want him to go, rather than in the inappropriate spots he make pick out for himself.

Beginning with the basics

Housetraining isn't that hard, but you can't expect a dog to just housetrain himself. Housetraining communicates to your dog exactly what you need him to do. If dogs know what you expect of them, they're perfectly content to use the yard as a bathroom rather than that nice stinky spot behind the couch, but your dog won't know unless you tell him. Here is the basic process:

1. **Watch for signs that your dog needs to relieve himself.**

   The signs include circling, walking slowly with nose to the ground as if very intent on sniffing out a good spot, and of course, squatting or lifting a leg. Some dogs wander to a particular part of the house where they've had a previous accident, and some dogs stand by the door hoping you'll notice them in time.

2. **Put your dog on his leash and take him outside to relieve himself.**

   Always use a leash until your dog is reliably housetrained — doing so is more time-consuming than just letting him out the back door, but it's important for two reasons:

   • You can praise him *while* he's relieving himself, so he knows exactly what behavior you like.

   • You can reward him for a job well done by letting him off the leash to run around and play in the yard. That way, he quickly learns to take care of business first to be able to play.

   Dress appropriately. You'll have to stand outside while your dog does his business regardless of the weather.

3. **Give your dog a chance to go potty.**

   Be patient. Sometimes, you may have to stand outside holding the leash for a while.

   If more than 10 or 15 minutes pass, your dog probably isn't going to do anything on that trip, so take him back inside, put him in his crate for 15 to 30 minutes, and then take him outside again. Don't give him the opportunity to go in the house!

4. **When your dog relieves himself, associate it with a word like "potty."**

   For example, the moment your dog begins to urinate, say "Potty, good potty!" in a happy voice. Pick whatever word you want to use, but choose one that you can say comfortably in public. You're teaching your dog to associate that word with the action of relieving himself so that, later on, you can use the word to encourage him to go when it is convenient, such as on a car trip or when you need to leave the house and you want to make sure he goes potty first.

5. **While he's in the middle of doing his business, give him gentle verbal praise to reinforce that his current behavior is good.**

   Don't get too excited or you may distract him, and he may stop before he is finished to play with you.

6. **After he has done his job, act like your dog has just done the greatest thing you ever saw any dog do and give him rewards.**

   Tell him how good, smart, and well mannered he is. Pet him and let him off the leash. Play with him. Throw a ball. Let him chase you. Do whatever he loves, with great enthusiasm. Dogs love to please you, and if you look pleased as all get-out, they want to keep it up, especially if it means getting that extra positive attention.

Don't let up too soon. Many dogs never get fully trained because their owners stop taking them out on the leash or supervising in the house before they're reliably housetrained.

When housetraining, the most important thing you can do is always set up your dog for success. Whenever your dog relieves himself in the right place and you reward him for it, you're reinforcing something important. Dogs remember good things that happen to them, and if they get plenty of praise and affection when they relieve themselves outside, that is what they will want to do every time.

Take your dog to the place where you want him to use the bathroom at regular times each day — at least every couple of hours for puppies and always do so first thing in the morning, after active playtimes, after naps, and within 30 minutes after eating.

Adding crate training

Remember the crate or kennel you bought for your adopted dog to have her own private den? (See Chapter 5 for more about crates and kennels.) It's also an important tool for housetraining, especially for puppies. In fact, crate training probably is the most effective method of housetraining with the fastest results. But the term "crate training" is a bit of a misnomer because the key to crate training is what you do when your dog is actually *out* of the crate.

Crate training is all about supervision. When your new puppy or dog is roaming around the house or yard in the first few weeks she's at home, you need to spend plenty of time watching her and interacting with her. Your dog is just getting to know her new environment and needs your guidance, so help her understand which activities are good and which are not, and that includes relieving herself. Watch your dog, and if you see signs she's getting ready to relieve herself, you take her outside, then praise her when she does her duty. If *you* miss the signs, well . . . that's *your* fault.

But the crate comes in handy when you can't supervise. Dogs have an instinct *not* to soil their dens and don't want to sleep in their own bathrooms. Who would? Treat your dog's crate is if it were her den. Because nobody can watch a puppy or dog every waking hour, the crate, or den, serves as a sort of babysitter. When you cannot directly supervise your puppy, you rest her in the crate, where she isn't likely to have an accident. Dogs need interaction and exercise in addition to bathroom breaks, but if you use the crate correctly, your dog will quickly learn where you want her to relieve herself.

The problem with crate training is that people tend to leave puppies in their crates for too long, which is one reason some people think crate training is cruel. It is cruel to leave a puppy locked in a small space, no matter how comfy and full of treats, for long hours at a time. No young puppy should ever be left inside a crate for more than two or maybe three hours at a time, and no adult dog should have to sit in a crate for longer than four hours, except during the night, when up to eight hours is fine. Doing so sets up your dog for failure because her bladder can hold only so much. Besides it's unpleasant and unnatural for dogs, because they're social creatures by nature.

One barrier that some adopted dogs have to crate training is past bad experiences with the crate. Most dogs love their dens, but if yours continues to object to the crate after at least several weeks of crate training (for example, if your dog continually refuses to go into the crate or stays in it only for brief periods of time before demonstrating signs of frustration or anger, like whining, yelping, or frantic scratching to get out), then schedule training (without the crate) may be a better approach. I discuss schedule training in the next section.

If your dog is not fully housetrained and can't be trusted out of the crate, and if you're typically away from home for eight to ten hours most work days, you must either come home from work or hire someone to come over in the middle of the day to let the dog out for a bathroom break and some exercise and to give the dog some attention. Fortunately, many pet sitters now will come to your home during the day and give your dog plenty of TLC. Many doggy day-care centers also have opened around the country to take your dog during the day and give him attention, exercise, and socialization with other dogs. What a great idea! If you can't afford this option or don't want to bother, you probably are not at the right stage in life to have a dog. Please don't give crate training a bad name by abusing the crate's convenience.

To find a good pet sitter or doggy day-care center, look up "pet sitter" or "pet services" in the phone book or ask your veterinarian for recommendations. Ask for and check pet-sitter and doggy day-care references.

Adding schedule training

Schedule training essentially is applying a routine to housetraining. Dogs love routines, and if they always have a chance to relieve themselves at approximately the same times as part of a regular daily schedule, they typically respond quickly. Just like crate training, schedule training requires indoor supervision and taking the dog outside on a leash until she relieves herself, praising her, and letting her run around. Schedule training doesn't necessarily employ the crate, but it can.

Schedule training works because dogs typically relieve themselves according to a schedule. Puppies need to go much more frequently than adult dogs — every two to three hours. But these sessions aren't random, instead they typically occur first thing in the morning, within 15 minutes after eating any meal, after all naps and active play, during training sessions and walks, right before going to sleep for the night, and once or maybe twice during the night when they wake up. Adult dogs relieve themselves predictably, first thing in the morning, within 30 minutes after eating, in the evening, and after naps, active play, and training sessions. Adult dogs, however, shouldn't need to relieve themselves at night.

Dealing with mistakes

Whose mistake is it when a dog has a housetraining accident? Did you forget to let the dog outside in time? Did you keep the dog in his crate for too long? Did you leave the dog alone outside to relieve himself, and he was so anxious to get back to you that he forgot to go outside and had an accident when he came back inside with you? These scenarios are human error, not dog mistakes.

Some people think punishing a dog is helpful whenever he has an accident in the house. Others cruelly rub the dog's nose in his own waste. Doing so might be a good idea, if it worked. However the problem with that method is that it simply scares or alarms the dog and teaches him little more than perhaps that you have an aversion to the presence of dog waste and that he'd better hide it better next time — like under the bed or behind the couch. Punishment builds a barrier between you and your dog and reinforces an idea that your adopted dog may already have — that humans are unpredictable and untrustworthy. Stress to everyone in your household that the dog is learning something new, and that yelling or blowing up at the dog only makes the lesson take longer.

If you catch your dog in the act of making a housetraining mistake, quickly whisk him outside and then praise him as he finishes. Otherwise, just quietly clean up the mess and ignore your dog completely while you're doing it. Any attention, positive or negative, can be a form of reinforcement for some dogs. If you don't let your dog see you cleaning up the mess, he can't associate you or your actions with the inappropriate behavior. Clean up when he is out of sight or in his crate, and be sure to use an odor remover (available in pet stores), because dogs often relieve themselves where they smell signs that they or another dog have gone there before.

A few great products are specifically designed to clean and remove stains and odors from puddles, piles, and even vomit. Some products use enzymes to actually ingest the odor and stain molecules. Look for them in your local pet store, or ask other pet owners which products work best for them. You can even make an effective cleaner/odor-remover at home by mixing water and white vinegar in a 1:1 ratio and pouring or spraying it on the stain.

Teaching Good Doggy Manners

Teaching a dog good manners is the best way to assure that he can live successfully in a human household, and it requires a two-pronged approach: training and socialization. If you start early, train often, and never stop socializing your dog, you can help him become the best he can be, make a great impression on neighbors and the community, and create a better reputation for all pet dogs. How's that for a worthy cause? Read on to find out exactly how to do this.

Off to school: Finding a training class

Young puppies and adult dogs alike can benefit from obedience classes. Training classes are more than a good idea for adopted dogs; they're practically a requirement. In fact, some rescue groups require you to take your adopted dog to a training class. Training classes are important because they:

✔ Can fix many of the issues for which so many dogs are relinquished.

✔ Provide you with access to a professional trainer who helps you tackle individual issues you may have with your dog and teaches you strategies for handling behavioral problems.

✔ Expose your new dog to many other dogs and people, creating a friendly environment for socialization. You may even make some new friends.

Ask representatives of the shelter or rescue group whether they can recommend any trainers. Some shelters already have established relationships and work directly with trainers who may already know your dog. You can also ask your veterinarian, get recommendations from friends who already have taken their dogs through classes, or look up "dog training" in the phone book. You can also search the Association of Pet Dog Trainers' Web site for a good trainer in your area who uses positive training methods: www.apdt.com under "Trainer Search." This network of certified trainers is proactive about positive, reward-based training.

Not all training classes are the same, so before choosing one, you need to evaluate the ones that are available in your area. Here's a rundown on some of the classes that can be helpful:

✔ **Puppy kindergarten or puppy socialization:** These classes are excellent for puppies that are just learning about the world. Most will enroll puppies starting at the age of 8 weeks, so you can get started with your puppy right away. Fun, friendly, gentle, and not very rigorous, these classes focus more on socializing the puppy and teaching simple cues. They also offer help for common puppy behavioral issues like nipping and housetraining. Many encourage the children in the pet's family to attend.

✔ **Basic obedience:** For older dogs or puppies that have completed a puppy class, basic obedience classes focus on the basics of what pet dogs and their owners need to know to communicate effectively. Instructors teach the basic cues and answer questions about common pet issues. Some classes include fun activities like introducing dogs to an agility obstacle course.

✔ **Specialty classes:** Dogs with basic obedience knowledge get training in these classes for advanced activities, like rally, competitive obedience, agility, flyball, or to take the Canine Good Citizen test (for more about the test see the "Canine Good Citizens" sidebar later in the chapter).

Many classes require your dog to have all the core vaccinations, including the rabies vaccine and the combination shot that protects against the most common diseases (for more on what vaccinations are required and recommended, see Chapter 6). Sometimes an additional vaccine for *Bordatella* (the common cause of kennel cough) is required. It is important that puppies continue their series of shots while taking classes, because they have a window of vulnerability to diseases between 8 and 16 weeks of age, when they can still pick up diseases fairly easily from other dogs, despite their vaccinations. Because most vets don't give rabies shots until 6 months, some new puppy classes won't require them.

When evaluating classes, get to know the instructor before signing up. Instructors have a wide variety of training methods, and the best ones are the ones who not only emphasize reward-based training over fear-based punitive training but also are flexible in adapting training methods to the needs of individual dogs. Adopted dogs typically respond best to reward-based training, which helps rebuild their trust in humans and strengthens their bond with you. Look for trainers who recommend *buckle collars* (any collar with a clasp) rather than choke chains and never advocate physical force.

In a few cases, adopted dogs may not be good candidates for training classes. Dogs with aggression (see the "Who's the Boss? Managing Aggression" section later in this chapter) can put other dogs at risk in a class situation, and dogs with extreme fearfulness or shyness may be too stressed by a class situation to learn anything. Many trainers come to your home to help train your dog or teach you how to train your dog. In that case, look for a trainer who specializes in the issues your adopted dog is experiencing.

Socialization strategies

Socialization is one of the most important steps you can take to help your adopted dog be a good dog. Socialization is just as important as training, and the two go hand-in-hand to help make good dogs into great pets. Many adopted dogs never received enough attention in their previous homes. In fact, "not enough time for the dog" is another one of the more common reasons that people relinquish their pets to shelters and rescue groups.

Recognizing Canine Good Citizens

Your dog may not win any shows, but that doesn't mean he can't make a big impact on the world. Many adopted dogs thrive on learning how to be therapy dogs, visiting people in hospitals or nursing homes. Dogs can become certified as therapy dogs through several wonderful programs. As a prerequisite, some of these programs include a requirement that dogs earn their American Kennel Club Canine Good Citizen certification, achieved by passing a test that shows your dog knows how to behave in society. For more information on these programs, check out the following links:

Therapy Dog International: www.tdi-dog.org

Delta Society Pet Partners Program: www.deltasociety.org/dsa000.htm

American Kennel Club Canine Good Citizen information: www.akc.org/events/cgc/index.cfm

Socialization simply is the process of exposing the dog to many different kinds of people and situations. Adopted dogs that haven't met many people or been anywhere other than their homes or backyards often are startled, alarmed, or threatened by strange people, other animals, and unusual situations. You can't raise a well-adjusted child if she's kept in one room for her entire childhood any more than you can raise a well-adjusted dog that way. To socialize your adopted dog, first be sure you know whether you have to be extra careful around other dogs, children, cats, or certain kinds of people — some dogs tend to dislike men or women. Always keep your dog on a leash and protect him so that you keep his experiences of the world positive and reassuring. Then, venture out.

The first great socialization experience most dogs get is the daily walk. Walking through the neighborhood (with a leash, of course) enables your dog to experience many different sights, smells, people, and other animals. Dogs may bark, pull at the leash, or be obsessed with sniffing absolutely everything. That's okay. You can work on resolving these undesirable manners in your training. But make sure you expose your dog to the world every day.

Driving somewhere in the car gives you and your dog another socialization opportunity. Dogs who ride only to the vet tend to fear and loathe the car, but dogs that never know what fun destination lies ahead travel much better. Take your dog to parks, on hikes, on picnics, to soccer games, or just let him ride with you as you run your errands. Let him meet people everywhere he goes — always keeping him supervised and on the leash for control — and he quickly finds out what a fun and interesting place the world can be. Every experience beyond the normal routine helps show your dog more about the world and refines your dog's natural instincts about people, animals, and places.

If you travel with your dog in the car, always put him in either a dog seat belt or crate that straps into a seat belt for everyone's safety. Never, ever, leave a dog alone in a parked car on a warm or sunny day. Many dogs die of heatstroke each year when they're left unattended in parked cars, even with the windows opened a few inches. Some dogs don't travel well, possibly because of negative experiences with cars or other insecurities. If your dog suffers from greater anxiety going with you in the car than staying home alone, safely tucked in his den, then practice different socialization methods first, working up to car travel when your dog is ready and acts eager to join you.

In cases of dog aggression toward humans or extreme fear or anxiety, check with a canine behavioral consultant who can help maximize your socialization efforts, giving you targeted strategies to solve your problem. Never deal with aggression on your own, without the help of a professional. If you have children in the home, you should never adopt an aggressive dog, no matter how willing you are to work with it. For more about behavioral issues and how to find a canine behavioral consultant, see the section on behavioral issues later in this chapter.

Teaching the building-block training cues

"Sit" is such a simple word with such a powerful action. Yet most dogs in animal shelters and rescue groups don't know what it means. Basic training — including housetraining — enables dogs and humans to successfully coexist. This foundation is especially important for adopted dogs that may never have had the basis of a strong people/dog relationship.

A reliably housetrained dog that knows the cues "Sit," "Stay," "Down," "Heel," and "Come" can almost always live fully integrated into a human household. These same cues enable you to tackle almost any behavioral problem. You may learn how to teach these cues in obedience class, but remember that you can also teach them at home. Train daily so you and your dog can spend time together reinforcing good behavior. Well-trained dogs enjoy practicing the moves they know well; even dogs that haven't had any training also benefit from frequent practice of these five essential training cues.

After your dog knows these basics, the sky is the limit. You can advance to all kinds of fun activities. Remember that each training method employs a *reward,* which can be anything from a small treat, an opportunity to play with a favorite toy, verbal praise, petting, or whatever else motivates your dog.

Clicker training magic

Some training classes and trainers use clicker training as their primary method. *Clicker training* uses a small hand-held plastic clicker to make sounds that mark behaviors you want to reinforce faster than you can offer a treat or say "good dog." Clicker training is a precise form of training that is popular with reward-based trainers, because it works very quickly for many dogs and is based on positive rather than negative reinforcement.

Here's how it works: "Charge" or "load" the clicker by clicking it and then giving the dog a treat. Dogs quickly find out — sometimes in three quick clicks — that the click is something good. Thereafter, when the dog does exactly what you want — going potty outside, sitting, coming when called — you click during the exact second that the dog is doing the behavior you want and then reward with a treat. Dogs catch on with amazing speed. It's almost like magic.

For some adopted dogs, however, the sound of a clicker is startling and scares them. When using clicker training with these dogs, you may need to desensitize them to the sound of the clicker. Charge the clicker for several weeks or longer to securely establish the connection between the clicker and rewards. Click and treat only a few times a day, but when the dog acts scared, respond by acting relaxed and happy about the clicker. If the dog never gets used to the clicker, choose another sound or training method. Remember, flexibility is a key to success in training.

Treats are great motivators, but be sure to keep them small — tiny pieces of cheese or turkey hotdogs, for example — or use pieces of your dog's regular kibble, if that is enough of a motivation for your dog. You don't want training to cause your dog to become overweight! Some people like to put aside an entire day's worth of dog food and use it solely for training, never actually putting the dog bowl down on the floor. The choice of rewards is up to you and whatever works for your dog.

People sometimes wonder whether they always need to say their dog's name along with verbal cues. When you're first linking a cue with an action — the sections that follow show you how — just say the cue, such as "Sit" or "Come," without confusing your dog by adding her name. The shorter the cue, the easier it is for your dog to learn. However, once your dog knows the cue, adding her name can get her attention so she listens to you, like "George," (he looks at you), "Sit" (and he sits), or "Gracie," (she looks at you), "Come," and she trots right over. "Good dog!"

Come, and what it's good for

Come is the most important of all the cues, and it can save your dog's life by heading her off when she's headed for danger and bring her back when you can't find her. It can also help show your dog how to retrieve. ***Note:*** Never scold your dog when he comes to you, no matter what he may have just done, because remaining oblivious (at least in this circumstance) can help reinforce the Come cue. Always praise your dog for coming, no matter what. You want to send your dog the message that coming to you always is a good thing. Here's how to teach the Come cue:

- ✔ **Two-person method:** Each of you needs to have a few treats hidden in a pocket. Have the other person sit beside the dog, loosely holding her collar. Have the dog sit. Stand in front of your dog, and then back up about three feet. Say "Come," and then have the other person release the collar. If your dog comes, praise her and give her a treat. If she doesn't, keep encouraging her to come to you. If she won't, move closer. Get close enough that she can see and smell the treat. When she comes to you, even if it's only a few inches, praise her and give her the treat. Repeat this often, and then as your dog gets reliable at it, move farther away, a little at a time, until she comes to you on cue from another room.

- ✔ **One-person method:** Keep a pocket of treats, and throughout the day, whenever your dog is somewhere else in the house or yard, say "Come." If the dog comes to you, give her a treat. Practice this cue at random times and from random distances, but do it many times each day, even after your dog reliably comes when called.

- ✔ **Family affair:** Have everyone in the family carry treats. Gather everyone in a single room. Put the dog in the middle of the room. Have random family members call the dog's name to get her attention, then say "Come." If the dog comes to someone who did not issue the cue, the person needs to look away and ignore the dog. When the dog comes to the person calling her, that person then gives her a treat and lots of praise.

Sit, and what it's good for

Sit is one of the most useful and one of the easiest obedience cues you can teach your dog. Many dogs adopted from shelters know how to "Sit," even if they know no other obedience cues. But if your dog or puppy doesn't know how to sit, you probably can teach this cue in one or two training sessions. If it takes longer, that's fine, too. Just keep working on it.

The Sit cue is useful because you can teach your dog to sit whenever she tends to do something that you don't like, such as jumping on visitors who come to the door (the poor pizza guy). The Sit cue can show dominant dogs how not to be possessive of toys and food and otherwise can help children and dogs have good and safe relationships. Here are some ways to teach the Sit cue:

- ✔ **Lure and reward method:** Call the dog to you. Have a small treat in your hand. Hold the treat just over the top of the dog's nose. When she notices the treat, slowly move the treat up and over her head, so that she follows it with her nose (see Figure 7-1). You are luring the puppy into a sit. Puppies usually will sit to better keep an eye on the treat. When they do, say "Sit," and then immediately reward with a treat, praise, or favorite toy. You can also help guide your dog into a sit with your other hand.

- ✔ **Catch-'em-in-the-act method:** Most dogs sit on their own sometimes. Every time your dog sits, say "Sit," and give her a treat. Or, click a clicker the moment your dog sits and then offer a treat or other reward. (See the nearby "Clicker training magic" sidebar.) When your dog realizes she's getting a reward, she tries to figure out just what she did to deserve such a treat. Dogs often start volunteering behaviors just for a treat, so get ready to see plenty of hopeful sitting!

Figure 7-1:
Lure a puppy into a sit by drawing a treat back over her head so she follows the treat and sits on her own.

Stay, and what it's good for

Stay is a convenient cue for whenever you want your dog to stay put, but it's also an important safety measure. For escape artists, the Stay cue not only is a great tool for foiling attempts to bolt out the front door whenever anybody opens it but also for keeping a dog from heading toward a busy street or chasing a cat. Stay also keeps your dog in one place when you need him to stay out of the way. Here are some ways to teach the Stay cue:

- ✔ **Two-person method:** This method is an easy way to teach Stay, but you need a partner. Each of you needs to have a few treats hidden in a pocket. Have the other person sit beside the dog, loosely holding his collar, and have the dog sit. Standing in front of your dog, say "Stay" as you raise your hand up, palm facing the dog; keeping your palm up, back up about two feet. The person holding the dog needs to keep him from coming to you, if he tries. After just a few seconds, say "good dog!" and have the person holding the dog give him a treat.

  Repeat these steps a few times until the dog doesn't try to come to you at all. Then, you can try it with the other person still sitting next to the dog but not holding his collar. If the dog comes to you, the person with the dog need not try to stop him. Don't praise or say "No," just take the dog back and do it again. When the dog stays reliably, gradually practice moving a little farther away and holding the Stay a little longer each time. Always go to the dog to give him the treat, don't give him the treat if he comes to you. You don't want your dog confusing Stay with Come (see the earlier "Come, and what it's good for" section).

- ✔ **One-person method:** This method works the same as the two-person method, but it may take longer because nobody is holding the dog in place. Say "Stay" while holding your hand up, palm facing the dog, as in Figure 7-2. If the dog stays, go back to him and give him a treat, praising him. If he comes to you, just lead him back to where he was sitting and try again. Eventually he gets which behavior wins him the treat and which doesn't.

Down, and what it's good for

Down is a handy position in which to hold your dog during a long stay. This cue is called a *long down* in training circles. Put your dog into a long down during dinner to keep her from begging under the table while you don't want your dog bothering guests or just to help your dog relax. This behavior is challenging for energetic dogs, but other dogs take to it quickly.

Some active dogs will get almost all the way into a Down but want to hover just above the floor so they're ready to spring back into action as soon as you stop paying attention. Don't reward this pseudo-down with a treat, at least not after the first few times, because your dog is working out just what behavior you want from her.

Figure 7-2:
Practice the
Stay cue by
using a
hand signal,
palm facing
your dog.

Here's how to teach the Down cue:

- **Lure and reward method:** This method is similar to teaching Sit. Call the dog to you. Have a small treat in your hand. Hold the treat just in front of the dog's nose. When she notices the treat, slowly move the treat out and down toward the floor, so that she follows it with her nose. Go slowly, luring her into a Down position. Some dogs prefer to just walk toward the treat. If they do, take it back and start over. Don't offer the treat until the dog actually lies down. If she doesn't get it, guide her with your hand into a Down position. When she does it, say "Down," and then immediately reward her.

- **Catch-'em-in-the-act method:** Every dog lies down at some point. Every time your dog lies down on her own, say "Down," and give her a reward. Or, click a clicker the moment she lies down and then reward. (See the earlier "Clicker training magic" sidebar.) Again, when your dog realizes she's getting a reward, she tries to figure out just what she did to deserve such a treat. Dogs often volunteer behaviors just to get a treat, so pay attention. If your dog walks up to you, lies down, and looks up with a hopeful glance, reward her; she's being a good dog.

Heel, and what it's good for

Walking a dog is great exercise, but it isn't much fun if you're getting yanked down the street like a kite that can't seem to get airborne. Heeling can help. Heeling means the dog walks right next to you without pulling on the leash (see Figure 7-3). The *Heel* cue is difficult for exuberant dogs, especially when sights and smells are more interesting than the treat you're trying to use to reward your dog for a nice Heel. However, with some patience and practice, you can teach your dog to heel. Here's how:

✔ **Tree method:** Dogs like to move; they don't like to stand still. So, if you want your dog to walk nicely on a leash, simply stop moving every time he pulls. When he stops pulling, you walk. When he pulls again, you stop. Doing this takes a lot of patience on your part, but if your dog always gets to move when he isn't pulling, and never gets to move when he *is* pulling, he eventually figures out which scenario is more favorable to him.

✔ **Stop-and-go method:** Bring along a pocketful or bag of treats as you walk your dog. Walk with your dog just a short distance, maybe five feet, stop, say "Sit," and then give him a treat. Now, walk again, but just one step, stop, say "Sit, and then give the dog a treat. Keep this up, but keep changing the distance you walk, so that your dog never knows when the stop, sit, and treat are coming. He has to pay attention to you to see what you're going to do next.

Figure 7-3:
This dog is walking in a Heel position by staying beside his person without pulling on the leash.

Some dogs just pull no matter what you try. For these eager beavers, try a head harness or walking harness. These alternatives to collars work because they turn the dog's head when he pulls. It also helps to give your dog plenty of play excitement out in the backyard before going out on the walk, rather than after. Your dog may be a little calmer and less likely to pull.

Breaking Adopted Dogs of Bad Habits

Many of the things that people think of as doggy problems actually are perfectly normal dog behaviors. Dogs enjoy barking, digging, chewing up things, wrestling and nipping their littermates, and relieving themselves in the spot they think looks (or smells) best. However as much potential as they may have, many adopted dogs wind up in shelters because their owners didn't know how to manage their doggy behaviors. Although some dogs truly have behavioral *problems,* such as separation anxiety and aggression, they are much less common than are simple lack of management and training. The good news is that you can address these behaviors, turning your rambunctious new dog into a well-mannered companion.

One simple (and perhaps the best) way you can help correct most behavioral problems is to *give your dog more opportunities for exercise!* Many undesirable behaviors stem from boredom and restlessness, and many dogs — especially medium to large dogs — don't get nearly as much exercise as they need. Several long walks, plenty of active running games in the yard, hiking, swimming, whatever it takes . . . an exhausted dog is a happy, healthy, and well-behaved dog.

Exercise doesn't, however, solve every problem. Some basic tips to remember about managing your dog's behavior are

- ✔ **Praising good behavior.** People are so focused on behaviors they don't like that they forget to tell the dog when he's doing something they *do* like. Your dog is chewing his chew toy? *Good* dog! Your dog is using the yard to go potty? *Good* dog! Your dog sits to greet someone instead of jumping up? What a *good* dog! Reward good behavior often. It is an effective way to communicate positively with your dog.

- ✔ **Redirecting bad behavior.** Dogs love attention and hate to be ignored. If you get mad and yell at something your dog does, some dogs see it as better than no attention at all, especially if humans have neglected them in the past. Praise good behavior, and ignore bad behavior. However, if the behavior is something that has to stop — excessive barking, chewing on your shoe, or nipping, for example — redirect the behavior by distracting your dog into doing something completely different like come to you, chew a chew toy, or sit. When he changes direction and does something good, then praise him again.

- ✔ **Supervising your dog's behavior.** Supervision is an absolute key to managing dog behavior. Pay attention to and spend time interacting with your dog every day. If you aren't paying attention to your dog, you can't teach him where to go the bathroom, what to chew, when to stop barking, or when to sit rather than jump on someone. Pay attention! Be there! Participate, respond, and give your dog feedback, so he gets the attention he so desperately needs.

Don't give up on your chewing, digging, nipping, four-legged little wild child. Remind yourself that he is just being a dog and that together you can manage, redirect, and overcome almost all of your dog's so-called behavioral problems.

Managing Behavior Problems Common to Adopted Dogs

Although more serious behavior problems may require professional help, there is hope for many of the dogs with issues of distrust and mistaken interpretations of human behavior. Fixing these problems can take a lot of time and patience, but it often is possible. In each of the following sections on different behavioral issues, you get some information about how to handle dogs that inadvertently were trained to do something the wrong way or to mistrust humans who gave them a wrong impression. Don't forget to check out the "Managing the Mistreated Dog" section at the end of this chapter for more information about dealing with more serious behavioral issues.

Lassie come home: Keeping your dog from running away

Ah, the open road. The distant horizon. All those bunnies to chase, children to play with, scents to follow . . . some dogs simply can't resist exploration, so they tend to be skilled escape artists. Some breeds are more prone to wander than others. Beagles that catch a scent, Siberian Huskies with an itch to run for miles, or Greyhounds that spot a faraway squirrel may take off in a flash if given the opportunity. Any dog can run away, especially when it has nothing else to do.

Wandering is dangerous for dogs. Leash laws prohibit wandering in many areas, and dogs without leashes can be confiscated, and their owners can be fined. Wandering dogs often are hit by cars, get into scraps with other dogs or wildlife, and can even take up with dog packs, injuring livestock or even people. Many adopted dogs were found wandering, but nobody knows whether they ran away from their original homes or were dumped on the side of the road.

Adopted dogs may not be used to living inside or within a small fenced yard, so they may try to get out, because it's all they know. The risk of them wandering is too great, so pet owners must take precautions to avoid escapes. In most cases, dogs that have enough to do won't try to escape because their minds and bodies are occupied. Here are some tips for keeping your adopted dog safe and sound and under your control:

- ✔ Never let your dog outside unless he's within a fenced enclosure or on a leash.
- ✔ Bury fences a foot into the ground or line them with cinder blocks or cement to prevent digging.

✔ Don't rely on electronic fences for habitual runners. Many dogs run right through them, enduring the electric shock. Electronic fences also don't protect dogs from other animals.

✔ Don't leave dogs outside when you're not at home.

✔ Give dogs plenty to do in the yard: toys to play with, a digging box, another dog to play with, or you!

Oh the noise, noise, noise, noise, noise: Curtailing excessive barking

Adopted dogs that bark a lot may simply be barking breeds like Terriers, or they may have learned to bark to get attention from people who were neglecting them. They may've spent much of their lives chained in a yard alone with nothing else to do or felt compelled to guard their turf from people and cars constantly passing by. Dogs bark out of boredom or anxiety, but dogs that feel secure in their homes and that get enough exercise and attention are much less likely to bark inappropriately. You can help dogs that bark too much by using these strategies to calm them:

✔ When your dog barks outdoors in the yard, don't leave her unsupervised. Stay out there so you can distract her when she barks or take her inside.

✔ When your dog barks inside at things that are outside the window, close the curtain or otherwise block her access to the window.

✔ When your dog barks when people come to the door, have visitors bring treats that they can give to the dog as soon as she stops barking and sits. When she barks, ignore her. Don't yell — that just sounds like you are barking back at her — because doing so only encourages the loud behavior.

✔ When dogs simply can't seem to kick the habit, try using a *bark collar,* a collar that either vibrates or sprays a mist of citronella oil whenever the dog barks. This startling distraction can stop the bark — at which point you reward the dog for ceasing. Avoid shock collars that can be misused and are traumatic for some dogs.

✔ In extreme cases, where the dog's life is at risk or your landlord is threatening eviction, consider debarking the dog, a surgery that can be effective as a last resort but should not to be taken lightly. The surgery doesn't actually stop the barking; instead, it lowers the volume. If this extreme measure truly becomes necessary, ask your vet to do the surgery with a laser to minimize scarring across the opening of the larynx.

My dog is knocking me over: Teaching dogs to quit jumping up

Dogs sometimes are neglected for so long they grow frustrated when people walk past them in a shelter kennel and they can't make contact. When they get out of the kennel, they tend to jump wildly onto any human who gives them a sidelong glance. This bad habit can be difficult to break. Large dogs, in particular, can knock people over or cause injuries in their eagerness to get attention. Even well-adjusted dogs may jump just because they have learned that it works to get your attention.

The best way to prevent jumping is to play invisible dog. When the dog is wildly jumping around, completely ignore him. Doing so isn't easy. For some dogs, it can take weeks or even longer for them to settle down, but any attention you give them rewards the wild behavior. However, the moment your dog calms down, you can praise him and give him attention.

Another good way to cure a jumper is to teach the Sit cue in every situation in which the dog tends to jump. A dog can't jump up when he's sitting. (See the "Sit, and what it's good for" section earlier in this chapter.) When your dog knows the Sit cue, you can simulate situations in which your dog tends to jump, and say "Sit." Reward the sitting dog; ignore the jumping dog. Keep practicing!

Obsessive jumpers also can be managed with a collar and leash. If your dog always jumps on people whenever they visit, put the leash on him and don't let him do it! People too often expect dogs to control themselves without first teaching them how. Keep control of your dog, hold the leash, give him the Sit cue, and don't take the leash off in the house until your dog understands. Keep him with you. Pay attention. React to what he does, so he understands what you want. But don't forget to ignore, as much as possible, his jumping behavior and reward him when he calms down.

Didn't I have a couch here? Ending destructive chewing

Puppies need to chew, and many adult dogs like to chew throughout their lives, even if they don't do so with the same destructive energy as puppies. Adopted dogs often chew as a way to relieve stress and excess energy, so reducing the source of stress with more exercise, attention, interaction, and regular routine can make a big difference.

Dogs need to know what they're allowed to chew and what they're not allowed to chew (see Figure 7-4). Supervision is the key. Whenever your dog begins to chew something you don't want her to chew, say "No," immediately redirect her to a chew toy, and then praise and reward her when she chews the chew toy. If you don't see her chewing destructively, then you weren't paying attention. Remember, the key to managing behaviors like chewing, jumping up, digging, and barking, is to pay attention so you can react to what your dog is doing and give her a message: That's good, or that's not good.

Figure 7-4: Train dogs to chew their toys and only their toys, not your possessions or your fingers. Dog teeth never should touch human skin.

Other ways to minimize destructive chewing include:

- ✔ Keeping your dog in a kennel or crate — with a good chew toy — when you can't supervise.

- ✔ Providing your dog with easily accessible chew toys and rotating them frequently to keep her interested.

- ✔ Trying chew toys that you stuff with treats, so your dog has to work to get the treats out, keeping her mentally and physically stimulated.

- ✔ Discouraging your dog from chewing on items you don't want her to chew by spraying them with a foul-tasting but safe substance, such as Bitter Apple or a similar product available from your local pet store.

- ✔ Praising your dog whenever you see her chewing her chew toy, so she knows what you want.

Ouch! Nipping that annoying nipping and biting

Nipping gets attention, no doubt about that, and you need to remember that what dogs want more than anything else is attention, even if it's negative! Dogs that nip have not yet learned *bite inhibition,* or the lesson that doggy teeth never should touch human skin. This lesson is extremely important because dogs that are used to nipping are just one step away from biting. Even a playful puppy nip can draw blood or injure someone, and a nip to the face of a child can cause serious injury, so take nipping seriously and deal with it right away. It must not be tolerated!

You can always nip your dog's tendency to nip by reacting exactly the same way every time it happens: Pull back your hand or leg quickly, sharply yell "Ouch!" and then separate yourself from the dog. Go into another room and shut the door or just turn your back and don't look your dog in the eye. When he stops trying to nip, give him the Sit cue, and then reward the sit, as opposed to the nip. Do this every time. When your dog tries *not* nipping in a situation in which he'd normally nip, praise him and give him the attention he's craving.

Be careful not to inadvertently encourage nipping, and urge others not to do so either. People think letting a little puppy gnaw on their fingers or knuckles is cute, but doing so teaches the puppy that human hands are fair game and delectably chewable! Never allow a puppy's teeth to touch human skin without an immediate reaction. The sooner you teach your dog this lesson, the easier it will be. If your dog tends to nip visitors, guests, or children, do not allow him to get close to these people until the nipping is under control. The risk of injury is too great.

But this is my dinner! Stopping your dog from begging

Any dog can be obsessed with food, but many adopted dogs have food issues, particularly the ones that never knew where their food was coming from, whether they'd have enough, or whether some other dog or person might suddenly take their food away. When an adopted dog suddenly has enough food, she can be like a kid in a candy store who wants to try absolutely everything. And there you are, that nice, generous, food-providing human, sitting at the dinner table with a nice juicy piece of meat.

If you — or anyone else in your family, kids and adults alike — feed the dog from the table or even drop food on the floor that the dog eats, your dog learns that the table is a source of yummy things. That's an especially powerful message that can result in some serious begging from a formerly always-hungry adopted dog. If you don't mind your dog hanging out under the table gobbling up the kids' leftovers, no problem. But if begging really bugs you, the solution is simple. Feed the dog, and then give her a rest in her crate or kennel until family dinnertime is over.

Regardless of whether it's a bowl of popcorn in front of the television or a sandwich in the kitchen, you can use the Sit cue as a helpful motivator whenever your dog begs or gets pushy and obnoxious about food. Ignore all begging attempts, but ask your dog to sit, and when she does, give her a treat — maybe even some of your yummy food! Do this often, but only reward the Sit cue, never the pushy begging. Your dog soon learns to voluntarily sit, hoping for a treat. Reward her! A dog that sits to get what she wants is doing a good job of getting along with people. For more about teaching your dog to sit, see the "Sit, and what it's good for" section earlier in this chapter.

Where's the garden? Reclaiming your yard from a digger

A dog that loves to dig holes in the yard points to a lack of exercise. This bad habit is just simple good-time dog fun for Terriers and many other breeds and breed mixes. Some dogs dig to get somewhere, others love the resulting wonderfully cool dirt holes for resting on a hot summer day. Some adopted dogs got into the habit of digging during long hours alone in a yard at their previous homes and think that digging is what dogs do.

However, if you like having a lawn, flowers, pretty shrubs . . . *landscaping*, many trainers recommend creating a digging box for your dog. A sandbox surrounded by railroad ties or lumber makes a great spot for dogs to dig harmlessly. Tuck treats, bones, and other goodies under the sand and remember to supervise your dog. Whenever you see your dog starting to dig up your flowers or sod, take him over to his designated digging spot, point out the treats, and praise when he digs there. If your dog digs all over your yard and ignores the digging hole, then you're neither teaching him nor supervising him enough.

Comeback Kid: Coping with Separation Anxiety

Separation anxiety is a behavioral disorder in which dogs become severely anxious, destructive, or injure themselves when you leave them alone. Some adopted dogs are at risk for separation anxiety because they've been through trauma, multiple owners, and possibly even abuse. However, even dogs with happy pasts may be drastically affected by the loss of their former owners. They may fear that they'll lose you, too, which can result in anxiety. Puppies taken away from their mothers and littermates before 5 weeks of age also can be prone to separation anxiety.

Treat separation anxiety in partnership with your veterinarian, because only the vet can diagnose separation anxiety for certain. Behavior modification and medication can help, but you can also work with your dog at home by helping him practice enduring your absence for short periods to build his confidence. Leave for two, three, and four minutes at a time, and then come back in and greet your dog. When your dog manages even these super-short sessions without trouble, give him a reward. Dogs with separation anxiety need to learn independence, because they're desperately attached to you. Although this connection may seem flattering to you, it certainly isn't healthy for the dog.

Sensitive dogs can become more aggravated and upset by your absence whenever you make a big deal about leaving and coming back. Dogs pick up on the emotional cues of their humans, so minimizing the drama of your comings and goings can help. For instance, try putting your dog in his kennel or crate about 15 minutes before you leave, and then just leave without acknowledging your dog. Come back quickly, but don't acknowledge your dog at first. Go about your normal business a spell before letting him out of his crate a few minutes after you return, casually greeting him, and perhaps offering a treat. The less anxiety *you* experience during your transitions to and from home, the more your dog begins to feel confident that you *will* come back, and that your coming and going is no cause for alarm.

Who's the Boss? Managing Aggression

Aggression is serious business, and many pet owners downplay aggression until it's too late and their dogs bite someone. Shelter dogs that had to fight for their meals, take on other aggressive dogs, or suffered through teasing or other human abuse can be particularly vulnerable, on guard, and ready to defend themselves. Dogs that were never socialized to many different kinds of people and situations can also be aggressive out of fear of the unknown and a resistance to change.

Fearful, anxious dogs also become aggressive in situations when they think they need to protect themselves. Many dogs are so unsure of their resources — food, toys, bones — that they viciously guard these possessions. Unsocialized dogs are not good judges of people or situations that are safe versus those that are actually threatening.

Aggression is a problem that absolutely must be handled by a professional. A trainer or canine behaviorist specializing in aggression can give you individualized strategies for dealing with your dog. Every case of aggression is different, and general suggestions may not be helpful to your dog because what works depends on the cause of the aggression. Ask your veterinarian to recommend someone specializing in treatment of aggression.

As you work with a professional, however, you help minimize your dog's aggressive behavior by:

- ✔ Increasing exercise!

- ✔ Not allowing your dog to guard resources. Feed him by hand, not from a bowl. Let him chew toys only when you're holding them. Don't let him have anything to himself if he can't help from aggressively guarding the possession.

- ✔ Keeping your dog off the couch or bed whenever he growls as someone approaches. Sitting on the couch or bed is a privilege, not a right.

- ✔ Having your dog sit before giving him anything — treats, food, even petting or praise.

- ✔ Not letting your dog push ahead of you through doors. Keep him on a leash if necessary, even in the house.

- ✔ Never allowing your dog off leash around other people or animals until his aggression is under control.

Never try to fight with or manhandle an aggressive dog; he may bite you. Instead, completely ignore the aggressive behavior but don't give in to what he wants. For example, if your dog growls when you approach his food bowl, take away the food bowl.

If you are afraid of your dog, you absolutely must seek professional help, because you cannot effectively manage a dog you fear. Most important, don't ignore aggression. It does not go away. You must deal with it.

In many cases, aggressive behavior is a factor of fear and insecurity associated with being in a new home or with past experiences that can effectively be fixed. Only a few dogs are pathologically or incurably aggressive, but they should never be adopted out in the first place, and the shelter should have evaluated these dogs as unsuitable for adoption. Yet it can happen that an incurably aggressive dog gets adopted.

Even with curable aggression, however, the help of a professional makes all the difference, so at the risk of being repetitive, I will repeat: *Don't ignore any signs of aggressive behavior.* Deal with them immediately, rather than waiting until it is too late, and your dog has injured someone, or you're forced to have him put down.

Managing the Mistreated Dog

A dog that has been mistreated can be a wonderful pet, and may only need a little extra TLC. However, later on, problems can surface that are more serious and require medical and/or behavior treatment. Maybe you'll decide, with full knowledge, to adopt one of these special needs dogs, or, maybe you'll end up with one despite your best efforts to screen your new pet's behavior before adoption. Either way, consider what it means to adopt a mistreated dog, and be sure you're prepared to handle the task.

Dealing with a mistreated dog takes huge amounts of patience, tolerance, effort, and time, an experience for which not every pet owner is cut out. That's one reason it's so important to screen a shelter or rescue group carefully and to ask as many questions as possible about the potential adoptee and how much the shelter or rescue group knows about the animal. Aggression and anxiety sometimes indicate past mistreatment, but dogs can experience mistreatment without exhibiting these behaviors. Many dogs come to shelters and rescue groups with mysterious, hidden pasts. Shelter and rescue workers thus have no way of knowing what these dogs have experienced.

Remember that, just like an abused child, a mistreated animal has learned that humans can't be trusted, so show your pet that she has finally found a human who can be trusted. That, of course, means you must be trustworthy, kind, consistent, and a good provider of food, shelter, and — when your dog is ready — affection.

Lack of trust can be frustrating for a pet owner who desperately wants to hug, cuddle, pet, and comfort the dog. Some pet owners even report feeling hurt and rejected by their pets, but pets don't hide from, fear, or growl at their owners, or destroy the drywall, simply because they don't like them. They respond only to what they have learned in the past.

Deciding whether you can handle a problem

It takes a special kind of pet owner to deal with a special-needs dog with behavior problems. Sensitivity, patience, and a strong commitment to routine are paramount, but you must also be prepared to take on the responsibility of a pet's behavior. Consider the following questions:

- Are you prepared to watch over and manage your dog so thoroughly that he won't be able to injure other people or pets, or himself?

✔ Do you have the time to devote to a special-needs dog? You probably shouldn't adopt a special-needs dog if you:

- Work for extended periods

- Are away from home most of the day

- Have small children who need a lot of attention

- Are generally busy and distracted

✔ Will you get frustrated and angry at his fear and anxiety?

✔ Can you deal with the possibility that your dog may destroy your possessions when he's overcome with anxiety?

✔ Can you handle the occasional sleepless night, the worry, the extra veterinary bills if health issues are a factor?

✔ Are you willing to hire an animal behaviorist or trainer to help you?

If you're not prepared to deal with these issues, you shouldn't adopt a special-needs dog. If you are, then you may find that nurturing an abused dog back to physical and mental health is a highly gratifying, if not heart-rendingly rewarding, experience. These dogs desperately need someone who can take the time to help them, but you must decide whether that job is for you or someone else.

Getting professional help

It is so important to seek professional help from a trainer who has experience with mistreated dogs, an applied animal behaviorist who specializes in pet behavior problems, or a veterinary behaviorist who has a graduate degree in animal behavior. You may likewise want to seek help from a *behavioral consultant,* or someone — like a trainer, for example — who may not have an advanced degree but does have plenty of experience with animal behavior problems. Just remember to check out their references first, because they're not subject to the same professional regulations as vets and other behavioral specialists. That said, behavioral consultants can be helpful. For more help finding a canine behaviorist near you, check out the Animal Behavior Society's Web site at www.animalbehavior.org, ask your vet for a referral, or call your local university to see whether it has a department devoted to animal behavior.

Part III
Here Kitty Kitty: Rescuing a Cat

The 5th Wave   By Rich Tennant

"We'll adopt this one. I think that would be easier than trying to wean him off my husband's nose."

In this part . . .

Whether you're still searching for the perfect kitty or you've already fallen in love with a new cat — kitten or adult or senior — this part of *Adopting a Pet For Dummies* helps you find a good cat veterinarian and guides you toward resources that you need to provide the best care for your cat. You get help recognizing typical medical problems of adopted cats and explore how to manage behavioral issues common to adopted cats and to cats in general. From the best toys and cat trees to the safest cat-box filler and most nutritious diet, this part tells you what you need to know about the fantastic feline.

Chapter 8

Finding the Purrrfect Feline for You

- -

In This Chapter

▶ Deciding on a kitten or an adult cat

▶ Understanding the difference between feral and stray cats, and whether they make good pets

▶ Recognizing the signs of good cat health

▶ Analyzing your potential pet cat's temperament and personality

▶ Unraveling the mystery of mixed-breed kitties

▶ Getting clues about your cat's future behavior based on breed type

- -

America loves cats, and Americans own more pet cats than pet dogs — more than 77.6 million cats to only 65 million dogs. Cats make affectionate, loving, interactive pets. They may be independent, elusive, and they may insist that you pet them on *their* terms, but cats need, adore, and depend on people.

Unfortunately, through no fault of their own, thousands of pet cats are brought to animal shelters and pet rescue groups every year. Millions more exist as *feral* (wild — completely unsocialized with humans and probably incapable of ever living successfully in human homes) or stray cats, born in the wild with no homes or abandoned and living on their own without human owners. Why are so many cats and kittens without homes?

The reasons so many cats and kittens are without homes are numerous. Some people find themselves suddenly unable to keep or care for their cats. In many cases, people buy cats on an impulse but quickly regret the decision. Some people think cats don't require any maintenance, and when their kitties exhibit cat behaviors that humans find annoying, they give them up. Other people let their cats wander, and the cats get lost or injured and can't get back home. If these lost cats are not spayed or neutered, they contribute to the birth of more unwanted or feral kittens. Many homeless kittens are born each year and forced to fend for themselves.

According to the American Pet Product Manufacturer's Association, up to 49 percent of owned pet cats were found as strays. Some stray cats are incredibly friendly and crave attention, affection, and care, but others get nervous, anxious, or fearful of humans.

Yet, most of the cats in shelters and rescue groups have been screened for adoptability and are friendly felines that will make excellent pets for someone who's willing to learn about what cat ownership really entails — a cat lover. Yes, cats definitely require some maintenance and they require, and desire, your attention. Yes, cats need supervision, veterinary care, and high quality food. And yes, some strays can become excellent family pets . . . with some patience. Still interested? Then read on to find out more about how to bring a pretty kitty into your life, heart, and home.

Deciding between a Kitten and a Cat

If you've decided to adopt a cat from an animal shelter, you may need to choose between a tiny, fuzzy little kitten with big round eyes and a mischievous nature or an adult cat that has already matured past the kitten stage. Kittens can be fun and incredibly amusing, but they also involve more work than an adult cat that already is accustomed to life in a human household. Adopted adult cats frequently are fully litter-box–trained and have calmed down enough that they aren't perpetually climbing the curtains, scratching the couch cushions, or knocking over the teacup collection you thought was safe and sound on that way-up-high shelf. Kittens are not.

On the other hand, adopting a kitten enables you to bond with a cat from an early age, when a kitten's antics are more fun than a ball of yarn. The choice is a tough one: Is adopting a kitten worth the extra work? Or is adopting an adult cat without a home the better choice? Before you decide on one or the other, consider the factors that come with each choice.

Considering a kitten

Yep, kittens *are* cute. Who can argue? But is a kitten really the answer to your cat craving? Consider the following advantages and disadvantages to adopting a kitten.

A kitten may be the perfect fit for you because

- ✔ You control exactly how well the kitten is socialized and trained, so you can engineer productive and positive early experiences, improving your kitten's chance of developing a confident and friendly behavior.
- ✔ You can start showing your kitten right away, so she learns good behavior at a young age.
- ✔ Your kitten can bond with you from the beginning, and you can enjoy a longer time together.
- ✔ Kittens are fun to play with. They may even make you feel younger.

You may want to reconsider adopting a kitten if the following ideas concern you:

- ✔ Your kitten can grow up to be a lot of trouble if you don't bother to socialize or train her, and you'll have no one to blame but yourself.

- ✔ Kittens don't know that you want them to use the litter box. You have to train them to use it, and although some kittens willingly and easily accept the litter box, others can be more difficult to litter-box–train. In other words, you may need to clean up some kitty messes.

- ✔ Kittens scratch, claw, nip, and bounce, so you need to train yours not to do these things, if you'd prefer not living with an attack cat for the next 18 years.

- ✔ Kittens have plenty of energy, so they need exercise, interaction, and stimulation to grow up healthy, strong, and well-adjusted. These things must come from you!

- ✔ You won't know for sure how your kitten will look when she grows up. Her coat and its color, texture, length, and thickness can change. She may turn out to be a huge cat, or a teeny cat. Do you like surprises?

Acknowledging the advantages of an adult cat

Adult cats can be a real pleasure to adopt. Cats learn a lot by living with humans, and if the cat you adopt has a lot of experience with human households and human behavior, you may have a much easier job on your hands than raising a kitten. Adopting an adult cat has other benefits too. Adult cats:

- ✔ Are often completely litter-box–trained. Just show them the box, and then keep it clean for them.

- ✔ Are less likely to nip, pounce, and scratch you when they've already gotten over these kitten behaviors.

- ✔ May already understand about scratching posts, cat trees, dogs, and children. They're ready to purr and accept your happy strokes without destroying your furniture or scooting up the drapes at the first sign of your Golden Retriever.

- ✔ Are typically considerably mellower than wild, energetic little kittens.

- ✔ Are often adaptable and easily bond with their new owners. Feed them, pet them, love them, and they're yours forever.

- ✔ Are often easier to adopt. Shelters have a harder time placing adult cats, so by adopting one, you're saving an animal that may not otherwise have found a home.

But there are some disadvantages to consider, too. Adult cats:

- Can have serious behavioral problems if they've suffered past abuse or neglect or been roaming on their own for too long without human inter-action. They may not trust humans, and regaining their trust can take a long time. They may never be friendly with everyone.

- Can have some bad habits like scratching, biting, or pouncing, because they never were taught not to do these things as kittens. These bad habits can be difficult for cat and pet owner to correct.

- Can have difficulty adjusting to a new home and may need lots of extra patience, time, and training before they feel comfortable. They may even mourn the loss of their past owners or past animal friends.

- May have been exposed to diseases like feline leukemia. This disease can add expense to their care, result in a shorter life, and can affect other cats in the household — not to mention the grief of losing a close friend to an often fatal illness.

- May not have more than a few years left and may be in desperate need of a new home. Most cats live for 12 to 15 years or more.

Boy cat or girl cat?

People often wonder whether they should adopt a male or female cat, but the truth is that a cat's gender doesn't make any difference. Sure, some people like to speculate that male cats are more dominant or cuddlier, and female cats are more active or maternal, but individual personality and breed-related traits are much more influential than the sex of your cat. Because your cat will be spayed or neutered, health and behavior issues related to gender, such as spraying or roaming, aren't relevant. That frees you up to choose the cat you like the best, regardless of his or her particular anatomy.

What about feral and stray cats?

Feral cats are cats that have been roaming without homes for so long that they've become wild. In many cases, these cats are born from strays or other feral cats and never have any close contact with humans. These cats don't usually make good pets because they don't trust humans, aren't comfortable being touched by humans, and won't likely adapt to life in a human house-hold. They've missed that important window of socialization in the first three months of life, when cats learn what kind of interactions are acceptable.

Strays, on the other hand, are cats that used to live with humans, but for any number of reasons, they now are homeless. Strays may've been abandoned, neglected, or somehow lost, and in the process, they may have picked up some wild cat habits. However, because they were exposed to humans during kitten-hood, they often can be taught to trust humans again. Convincing a stray that you're more than just the person who puts the bowl of food out on the front porch may take time. Another stray may be so happy that he comes right in and makes himself right at home in your house. It all depends on the cat.

Feral cats are rarely, if ever, adopted as pets, because they make terrible candidates staying in shelters waiting for someone to take them home. Some people may choose to feed them or the colonies of feral cats they find living nearby. Similarly some humane societies strongly encourage people to capture feral cats one at a time in live traps and take them to a shelter or veterinarian to be spayed or neutered and then released. Other shelters, and some local governments, believe feral cats need to be captured and, in some cases, euthanized. The bottom line: A feral cat never would be happy or comfortable living indoors.

Strays are another story. If a stray cat adopts you, you may decide that the feeling is mutual. But before you decide to take in a stray, take it to the vet for a complete checkup. Stray cats may look perfectly healthy, but they can have serious diseases like feline leukemia or *feline immunodeficiency virus* (sometimes called feline AIDs). The cat may also have fleas and ticks and skin infections, or be malnourished. A vet can test, treat, and make recommendations about the cat's health. The vet also can spay or neuter the cat. After you know your cat is healthy, or at least not contagious, you can try integrating her into your household, but you need to be prepared to patiently endure this sometimes lengthy adjustment period.

Of course, you can always take your cat to a local shelter to have her behavior evaluated, her health problems treated, her reproductive organs — as some say — fixed, and then adopt her to a good home. If, on the other hand, you want the shelter to do these things for you but you're interested in adopting the cat, be sure to let the shelter workers know when you bring her in. Many shelters are willing to work with people who want to adopt a pet through them. Many also encourage people not to take in strays, but rather to bring stray cats to the shelter first.

Recognizing Signs of a Healthy Cat

Some cats clearly gleam with good health, but others look a little bit the worse for wear. Whether you're evaluating a stray or the cats in the shelter's cattery, look for the signs of good health that I describe in the sections that follow. Although an apparently healthy cat may still have some health problems, a cat with signs of certain bad health is a bad risk, unless you're willing and can afford to treat *all* of the health problems. Some people are willing to take on a special-needs cat, such as one that has feline leukemia, but you have to be prepared for this difficult job. A healthy cat has a much better chance at a long life as a rewarding and happy pet. Read on for signs of a healthy cat.

Silky coats and eyes like jewels

A cat with a soft, silky coat with no bare patches, parasites, or skin infections is a beauty to behold. Long coats need to be brushed and free of mats. Short coats need to be thick and plush, like velvet. A healthy cat's eyes are bright, clear, and free of discharge, although some flat-faced breeds like Persians tend to have tear stains that are especially visible on white or light-colored coats. Tear stains are not a sign of ill health, and they can be treated and removed with a special product available from your local pet store.

Itchy kitty? Signs of parasites and skin/coat problems

Whenever a cat is scratching, digging at his ears, or biting himself, he may have fleas or a skin infection. Many of these are easy to resolve and not a reason to reject a cat for adoption, but you may want to ask the shelter to have the cat treated before you take him home. A shiny, healthy coat is one sign of a healthy cat in general, although some cats with healthy looking coats could potentially have other health problems. Signs that your cat has a healthy skin and coat include:

- Shiny, thick fur.
- Clean fur and skin with no mats or dirt caught in the coat.
- No signs of fleas, such as black, brown, or reddish specks (flea dirt) or fleas themselves. Fleas are tiny, black or brown hard-shelled little bugs that jump . . . sometimes, right onto *you*.
- Supple skin free from sores, wounds, scratches, rashes, or other skin injuries or irritations.
- No sign of lumps, nodules, or other skin irregularities under the skin, when you feel the cat gently all over with your hands.

The tail end

A cat uses her tail for balance, but a tail also can cover up signs of health problems. The view from a cat's rear end needs to be clean, free of soil, and without any signs of infection, including redness, rashes, or irritation. Long-coated cats also need to be checked for mats around their tail area. A dirty or badly groomed rear end may be a sign of neglect or of a health problem, so ask the shelter about the problem and whether a vet has looked at the cat.

Curiosity quotient: How your cat interacts

Behavior is a big part of good health. Cats that are sick or injured can act fearful, aggressive, or depressed. Healthy cats are more likely to act interested in people and new surroundings and have energy and a lively personality.

Behavior also is also indicative of socialization. If a cat doesn't want to let any human anywhere near it, he may be feral and won't ever make a good pet. By evaluating your cat's behavior and the way he interacts with you, other people, and other animals, you can determine whether you have a healthy, well-adjusted kitty or a cat that needs medical or behavioral care.

Temperament Testing

Cats, like people, come with many different types of personalities. Some are shy; some are outgoing. Some are happy to help you type on the computer, turn the pages of your magazine, and tell you whether you've put enough tuna in the casserole. ("Meow," of course, means, "That's too much tuna. Put the rest in my bowl. Yes, down here.") Others prefer to do their own thing, pose on the windowsill, or slink behind the furniture hunting dust-bunnies. Activity levels and the desire for attention vary among different cats. Time spent in the wild, moving from owner to owner, or enduring long periods of neglect can have a negative influence on a cat's personality, or it can make the cat less likely to bond to people. However, some cats manage to secure human friends and are outgoing and well socialized wherever they go. It just depends on the cat.

Temperament testing isn't really a technical term, although some people use it that way, referring to particular tricks they've developed that can determine a cat's personality. Many animal shelters do some version of temperament testing on their cats, either using an established system or simply playing with the cat and testing the cat in certain situations, such as with other cats or dogs, to see how she reacts. Shelters do this to assess whether a cat is suitable for adoption and to help them find the right kind of home for an individual kitty. Unfortunately, these tests aren't always definitive because adopted cats may be on guard and insecure when they're tested, so they won't often reveal the full extent of their personalities until they've been in a home for a while and feel safer and more secure. A shy cat may be much more outgoing after a few calm, happy weeks in a good home. An aggressive cat may settle down into a confident and happy sweetheart. Or, issues like shyness and aggression can get worse. If only shelters had a cat crystal ball . . .

You can tell a lot from a cat, however, if you pay attention to a few key issues after an initial gut-check with your own temperament. Observation and interaction tell you plenty about your potential pet. Spending more than one visit with the cat before you decide is another key that can stave off impulse buying and give you a more realistic picture of the cat's personality.

Determining what traits suit your fancy

One important key to making a successful match is determining the kind of cat that you want and can live with. If you know an extremely active cat will irritate you, look for a mellower cat that prefers a warm spot of sun to a romp around the backs of the furniture. If a kitty's curiosity, acrobatics, and sense of adventure charm and amuse you, a sedentary cat may bore you. Maybe you think adopting a special-needs cat is worthwhile or that you have the extra patience and time needed to help a troubled cat learn to trust humans again. Or you may just prefer a cat that's already well-adjusted. Think about what you want, and then look for a cat that exhibits signs of the kind of temperament you prefer. Remind yourself that no matter how cute that kitten is, a personality clash ultimately is much more difficult to deal with.

When you have a good idea of what you want and need, then spend some time getting to know your potential pet. Maybe the chemistry will be instantaneous, or maybe you'll need a few visits to make sure, but tune in to your cat's personality to help ensure a great match-for-a-lifetime.

Profiling kitty companions

Personality can be influenced by many things, from past experiences to breed to genetics, but you can get some clues about your cat's personality without even knowing why your cat is shy or outgoing or has the heart of a hunter. Animal shelters and rescue groups want you to interact with and get to know a potential pet before you adopt, because they want to make sure the cat doesn't wind up right back in the shelter. On at least one occasion (preferably more than one), you need to set aside plenty of quality one-on-one time with the cat you are considering, before you sign on the dotted line. Use this time to help determine your cat's personality. When interacting with a potential pet, look for the following clues to the kind of pet you have in front of you:

- ✔ When you approach the cat or kitten, does she act curious about you? Does she approach you willingly seeking affection, or does she hide, cower, hiss, or act fearful? Cats are naturally curious, but some are more cautious than others. A well-adjusted cat needs to show interest in who you are and what you're all about.

- ✔ What does the cat do when you pet her? Some cats press against your hand, looking for more physical contact. Others want to be petted but have the curious ability to retract from hard petting so that you feel you're just barely brushing against them. Still others will permit you to touch them for a short period before they've had enough. Yes, and some cats simply can't get enough. Your cat's reaction to petting can indicate how much physical interaction she wants. If you want an interactive cat, look for one that enjoys petting and seeks out your physical attention.

✔ Will the cat let you pick her up? Some cats love petting but don't like to be held. Others let you hold them for a short time, but some cats want nothing to do with being dangled five feet above the ground by an unpredictable human. Although some cats may not let you hold them at first, they will warm up to it later. Consider how important holding a cat is to you. If you simply must hold your cat, or if you have children who want to carry the cat around, look for a cat that enjoys those activities. If you are happy letting your cat do her own thing, then you may be more satisfied with a cat that wants nothing to do with being cradled like a baby.

✔ Does the cat startle easily? Is she keenly aware of any loud noises or sudden movements you make? If you move your hand quickly, does she put herself on guard? Some cats naturally are skittish, and although a scaredy-cat's confidence may increase in a secure home, easily startled cats may not do well with active, loud households or families that include small children.

✔ Do you have children? Be sure to bring them along so they can get to know the new cat. Some cats are perfectly content with adults but don't like kids. Others think kids are the cat's meow and follow them around, doglike, looking for fun. Some cats willingly play dress-up and may even fetch a toy. Others consider such silly antics beneath them. The personality of every family member is relevant when choosing a cat.

✔ Do you have other pets — other cats or a dog? Ask shelter workers whether they know if the cat is good with other pets, and ask how they know. Seeing a cat free in a cattery and interacting with other cats is a good sign of how well she gets along with other cats, but it won't necessarily tell you how well she gets along with dogs or other pets.

In some shelters with limited space, cats may be housed near the dogs, and the loud barking of the dogs may be a constant stress for some of the more sensitive kitties. If a cat is cowering in the back of a cage, she may be absolutely sweet, lovable, and even self-confident in a mellower environment where she doesn't feel threatened or frightened.

Asking the experts: Shelter workers provide the skinny on your kitty

Face it, shelter and rescue foster-care workers spend more time than you can possibly spend, even in several visits, caring for the cat you're thinking about adopting. Depending on the shelter or rescue group, workers may spend a lot of time working with and playing with the cat. They may also know a history of the cat from the people who brought him to the shelter. Shelter workers may be able to tell you how good the cat is with children, other cats, dogs, other pets, in active households, or in quiet households. They may also know how active or mellow the cat is. Take advantage of this knowledge and remember that people who work for shelters and rescue groups often have a deep and abiding love of cats. They may be well tuned-in to your potential pet and want the best for that cat. They want to be sure the cat finds the right home, so let them help you.

Finding a Good Match: What to Expect from Different Breeds and Mixes

A cat's past experience is only one determining factor of its personality. Breed or breed mix also can influence a cat's temperament and its activity level and care needs. If you don't want to spend time brushing your cat every day, for example, then don't adopt a long-haired cat, regardless of how gorgeous he is. If you want a cat with a calm, tranquil personality, consider a Persian, but if you want a cat that acts like a dog, a classic American shorthair-type cat, or a Maine coon, may be best.

Knowing the classic profiles of some of the more common purebreds can give you insight into your cat's personality. Plus, it's fun to speculate just what kind of cat that *is.* You may also want to consider the color of your furniture and even of the clothes you like to wear. Cats shed. It's a simple fact of feline life. If you have white furniture and you can't stand the sight of cat hair, don't get a black cat. If you usually dress in black, you may want to avoid that snow-white Persian. Many cats have actually been surrendered to shelters simply because their cat hair was too disturbing to their owners. Come to think of it, if you can't stand the sight of cat hair, you probably should consider adopting a different sort of pet.

But assuming cat hair is okay with you, the breed or mix of breeds that make up your cat can give you some clues to her mysterious cat behavior. Take a good hard look at your cat. What ancient breeds are in your cat's genetic code? In most cases, until science progresses a little further, you won't know for sure what breeds contributed to a cat that has no pedigree. Yet, examining a cat's coat, size, and shape can give you some clues to its breed and behavior. Of course, for every generalization you make about cat breeds, you'll need to consider many exceptions, thus breed-based assumptions are merely one piece in a complex puzzle. Your Persian cat may be a dynamo! Your Siamese may be a couch potato. But in many cases, breed generalizations hold true. Read on to find out what these generalizations are.

Cats of undetermined origin: Mixed-breed cats

Most cats found in animal shelters are mixed-breed cats like the short-haired cat in Figure 8-1. Few purebred, pedigreed cats end up in shelters or rescues, but it can happen. Purebred cats are a small minority of all the cats living in the world today, but because these types are out there, you can see their echoes — their offspring. Heck, some purebreds actually were created from mixed breeds, blurring the lines dividing what is a purebred and what isn't.

Many of the cats in shelters, however, look like different versions of two basics: short-haired cats and long-haired cats. And many of these cats don't have the unique qualities of purebreds — the flat round races of Persians or the extreme skinny bodies of Siamese, for example. No, these cats are, for the most part, various versions of native cats that have existed in America for centuries. Most of the short-haired cats in shelters look much like the purebred American Shorthair, which is a pure strain of these native short-haired cats. Most of the long-haired cats in shelters look much like Maine coons, America's native long-haired breed. Put simply, they are domestic cats. 'Nuff said.

But, how do they act? Most short-haired and long-haired domestic cats are friendly, affectionate, relatively but not extremely active, healthy (unless they're exposed to disease), and most make great pets. They can adapt easily to living indoors but enjoy a nice prowl through the grass. (For safety, keep them on a leash or within a fence, so they can't or won't climb.) They are curious and can be mischievous but generally are content to settle down for a catnap. They are independent and don't require constant supervision but are always ready with a steady purr and a soft coat for petting. They are, generally, ultimately lovable.

Of course, mixed-breed cats vary widely in the finer points of personality, so look for an animal you can relate to that will fit into your household. Mixed breeds are just like they sound — a potpourri of ancient and modern felines, rolled up into one charming little furry bundle that may just be the perfect pet for you.

Figure 8-1:
Shelters are full of mixed-breed, short-haired cats just waiting for loving homes.

Perfectly stunning Persians (and their relatives)

Persians, like the one in Figure 8-2, are the most popular purebred cat breed, but these cherished beauties usually live indoors and rarely come in to animal shelters. Sometimes, however, a Persian loses her home, often because pet owners tire of all that grooming, or for many other reasons, from shedding to allergies. These Persians need a loving owner to care for them and keep their beautiful coats groomed. You may see a cat that looks like a Persian in an animal shelter, but without a pedigree, you can't know for sure whether the cat is a purebred. Nevertheless, cats with round heads, large luminous eyes, flat faces, long flowing coats, and plumed tails probably have some Persian in them, even if they aren't purebred.

Other similar breeds include the Himalayan, which is a type of Persian with Siamese-like points to its color pattern (color only on the face and extremities), and the Exotic. Exotics are increasingly popular because they have the face, shape, and personality of Persians, but they have short, plush coats so they don't require the heavy grooming that Persians do.

Persians — and their relatives — have a reputation for being calm cats. No racing madly about for these pretty kitties, although all cats, particularly kittens, get the "zoomies" once in awhile and may dash around the room for a minute or two. Persians love to sit, looking gorgeous and being admired. They love affection from the humans they know and adore but may shy away from strangers. Although some Persians undoubtedly are outgoing, many are reserved, elegant, sophisticated . . . aristocratic, even. They'll sit nicely for brushing and usually enjoy this gentle activity, especially if they've been groomed regularly since kittenhood.

Figure 8-2:
Purebred Persians are a popular breed with beautiful long coats that require regular maintenance.

Persians sometimes prefer people to other cats. Where many domestic cats would rather bat a catnip mouse around with a buddy, many Persians are happy to preside over a one-cat household. Of course, as always, there are exceptions. Grooming is the Persian's biggest challenge. Without a daily brushing and combing, Persians can develop mats and tangles that not only look bad but also can promote skin infections. Personality-wise, Persians are low-maintenance, and their long, flowing coats make them a pleasure to pet and beautiful to behold.

Clever Siamese . . . both types!

Siamese are another popular purebred that may occasionally land in a shelter. The Siamese is an incredibly active, vocal cat, and some pet owners tire of all the noise and activity when the Siamese doesn't meet their expectation of what a cat should be. Siamese need understanding owners who appreciate their sometimes high-strung qualities and communicative vocal style.

Siamese come in two types. The modern, "extreme" type has a long tubular body, wedge-shaped head, and large flared ears. They look like they would have been worshipped in ancient Egypt. The traditional apple-head style is less extreme with a heavier body and a more classic, blunter head shape. Although the modern style takes all the prizes at the cat shows, many pet owners have, and prefer, the traditional style of Siamese, because they were more popular, and perhaps even more memorable, in decades past. These types of Siamese are also more likely to show up in animal shelters and pet rescue groups.

Siamese cats have a winning curiosity and big personalities. They use their distinctive voices often, and they are one of those breeds that just might try to climb the Christmas tree or appear quite suddenly on top of the refrigerator. How the heck did they get up there? That's just a Siamese. They love to explore, play fetch, climb, get into things, and exercise their formidable intelligence. You have to stay one step ahead of these clever kitties! Siamese are perfect for people who want a highly interactive and vocal cat they can play with. Siamese may or may not be interested in snuggly cuddling, but they certainly keep you amused, and on your toes, 24/7.

The all-American shorthairs

American shorthair cats are a type of purebred, but they look much like most of the cats that you see in animal shelters, because they all basically came from the same origin — the domesticated street cats of early America. Sturdy and moderate, healthy and friendly, these beauties come in every conceivable color and pattern, from calico to tabby, from black to white, and everything in between. American shorthairs are known for being the quintessential cat-like cat — independent but affectionate, self-possessed but not snobbish. They love your lap and want to be with you but aren't so needy that they won't ever leave you alone. They *are* the cat lover's cat, pure and simple, and for centuries, they've been American-made.

Mellow Maine coons, America's native long-haired cat

Maine coons came over on the Mayflower and have taken over the hearts and minds of cat lovers in America. Rumored to have bred with wildcats — to explain their lynx-like ear tufts and large size — Maine cats have no wild cat blood and are more prone to act like friendly, agreeable dogs than fastidious, elusive, independent cats. Maine coons are great for cuddling, enjoy gentle children, and are truly impressive when they walk into a room. If your cat has long tufty ear hair, a thick shaggy coat, and is particularly large, she may just have a little Maine coon blood in her.

Chapter 9

Welcoming Home Your Adopted Cat

In This Chapter

▶ Cat-proofing your home

▶ Shopping for everything your new cat needs, from food to litter box to cat teasers and more

▶ Opening your home to your new cat the stress-free way

▶ Acquainting your cat with family members, including kids

▶ Introducing your new cat to other pets without causing a cat fight

Kitty alert, kitty alert, kitty alert! When you bring a cat into your home, you need to be ready. Kittens and adult cats can get into some real trouble if your home isn't cat-proofed. You need the right supplies to keep your cat well fed, safely housed, and happily managed. And you need to be ready to introduce your cat to her new environment: litter box, new cat bed, the family dog, children . . . the whole kit and caboodle. The way you introduce your cat to her new home can make a big difference in how quickly and confidently she adjusts. This chapter guides you through every step, from the preadoption preparation through the first day at home with your new feline friend.

Kitten-Proofing — Even For Adult Cats!

Curious cats of any age like to jump on, bat at, unravel, and chew on *things*. The problem with these playful behaviors is that cats and kittens can knock things over and break them, hurt themselves, get their paws or necks entangled, destroy things, choke on things, and even ingest harmful or poisonous substances. But you can make your house safe for a cat. You just need to do a little cat-proofing.

Cat-proofing is much like child-proofing but with a particular eye on things cats find compelling. To make your house safe for a cat or kitten, look around at all the potential hazards and then do the following:

✔ Tape down or hide all electrical cords.

✔ Tie up mini-blind cords, curtain ties, fringe, and tassels.

✔ Remove any toxic houseplants and other cat-specific toxins and poisons. Many common household plants, including dieffenbachia (dumb cane), aloe vera, amaryllis, geranium, philodendron, many bulb flowers, cacti, climbing vines, ivies, and ferns are bad for cats. Some of the more common poisonous plants and other cat-specific toxins and poisons include:

  • Fruit pits (like apricot and avocado) and seeds (like apple).

  • Many common flowering shrubs you may have in your yard, like azalea, honeysuckle, oleander, rhododendron, and holly.

  • Flea products or other pest-control products made for dogs or other animals besides cats.

  • Bleach, paint, household cleaners, or any other household chemicals.

  • Gasoline, oil, antifreeze, or any other chemicals that are stored in the garage or outside.

  • Over-the-counter or prescription medications or hygiene products like talcum powder or nail polish remover.

Signs of poisoning may include vomiting, diarrhea, burns or rashes around the mouth or paws, neurological symptoms like staggering or fainting, or any unexplained behavior change. If you suspect your cat has been poisoned, take her immediately to the vet or emergency clinic, or call the ASPCA Animal Poison Control Center at 888-4ANI-HELP (888-426-4435). For a $50 fee, you can talk to a veterinarian and get immediate advice over the phone.

✔ Keep nontoxic houseplants out of reach to prevent a big mess.

✔ Pick up all tiny choking hazards from the floor and other cat-accessible surfaces. String, yarn, dental floss, rubber bands, needles, pins, and tiny hard pieces of anything can all cause intestinal damage.

✔ Take all breakables off all accessible surfaces. Be sure you cover *all* surfaces your kitten may be able to reach.

✔ Enclose trash cans — send them into hiding, Coffee grounds and other food waste can be toxic or poisonous to cats.

✔ Place all household chemicals and medications out of reach.

✔ Cover the toilet paper rolls and tissue boxes, unless you don't mind waste or janitorial duty picking up shredded tissue.

✔ Block access to small spaces behind and under all major appliances like refrigerators and stoves and large moveable furniture like recliners. Cats can get stuck and even severely injured by these huge heavy objects.

✔ Keep the toilet seat down! Some kittens are curious about water, and can drown in an open toilet, unable to get out. (You were waiting for a reason to make everybody do that anyway, right?)

✔ Keep the doors closed. Make sure everybody in the family, kids included, is careful not to let the new cat scoot out the door when nobody's looking.

✔ Keep the doors to the garage closed. Never let your kitten in the garage. Climbing under or inside a car or finding hazardous chemical spills like antifreeze all put cats at great risk.

Stocking Up on Supplies

Prepare for your new cat by picking up some basic supplies that you need to keep your cat well-equipped and happy. Before you bring your new cat home, stock up on the right food, a good litter box, cat furniture, plenty of toys, and, of course, for those who so desire and can afford it, a few luxury items to make your new cat comfortable and happy to be home at long last.

Gathering the basics

Every cat needs a few basic supplies. You can get fancy with the basics or go for the bare-bones minimum. Cat supplies don't have to be expensive, but they can be if you choose the very best quality or fanciest brand names. Your cat probably won't care either way, but higher-quality products probably last longer — you be the judge. Shopping around and checking out all your options will pay off. Here's what you need.

Convenient cat carrier

You may not use a cat carrier every day. In fact, you probably won't. But a cat carrier is an essential item that enables you to take your cat anywhere in the car (or even on an airplane) safely. A cat that's loose inside the car can be a serious distraction to a driver, and the cat can sustain serious injuries in a car accident without the protection of a cat carrier. A cat carrier is the best and safest way to take your cat anywhere away from home.

Look for a carrier that has a handle, is easy to carry, and is easy to open and close — but not for the cat! Most pet stores stock a variety of plastic crates in different sizes. Put a soft cushion, fleece or faux fur pad, or flat pillow in the bottom of your carrier so it's ready to deliver your cat from the shelter to his new home.

For cats that resist entering a cat carrier, putting them in backwards sometimes helps. You can also put the cat into a pillowcase — without a zipper — and then put him in the carrier, which can calm down the cat because he can't see the carrier. Keeping the carrier out or at least occasionally allowing your cat to explore or play inside it also can help make the carrier more familiar and less difficult to get the cat into when necessary. Hide treats inside to make it even more rewarding.

The best cat food and food accessories

Your cat's health can be directly influenced by diet, so choose a high-quality premium cat food for your new friend. Cats can have sensitive digestive systems, though, so be sure to find out what your cat is eating before bringing him home. If you don't think the shelter food is good enough for your precious puss, or you can't buy it easily and you want to switch foods, introduce the new food slowly over the course of a few days to a week, gradually increasing the ratio of new food to old. Cat foods come in a vast variety, so consider your choice carefully. For more information about choosing the right food for your cat, see Chapter 10.

Cats also need good food and water bowls. Every cat in the house needs to have its own bowl. Basic metal or ceramic bowls are easy to clean and don't accumulate bacteria as easily as other materials. Cats love running water, so you may want to consider a cat fountain to provide a continuous supply of burbling, trickling water for your cat's drinking pleasure. If you choose to *free-feed* your cat — making food available at all times — you may want to consider an automatic feeder. Using an automatic feeder, however, isn't the best plan when your cat is overweight. For more about the appropriate way to feed your cat, see Chapter 10.

Litter boxes and filler

Because cats today are safest when living indoors, litter boxes have become a necessity. Fortunately, technological advances in litter boxes and litter-box fillers make this once-malodorous task less offensive.

Different cats like different kinds of litter boxes. If your cat used a litter box at the shelter or its rescue home, start by using that same kind of litter box and filler. You can try switching to a different type of litter box later, after your cat has adjusted to her new home. If you have a kitten, choose a litter box that is easy to climb into and out of (see Figure 9-1a). Some cats prefer a covered litter box for privacy (see Figure 9-1b), but they need to be cleaned at least once a day to minimize the odor that can become trapped inside the enclosure. Self-cleaning litter boxes (see Figure 9-1c) can be fun and interesting, and some cats enjoy them. They make some cats nervous, however. Check out the marvelous array of litter box choices at your pet store before choosing one.

If your house has two floors, you need two litter boxes, one on each floor. If you have more than one cat, you need at least one litter box per cat, and preferably an extra one. The more litter boxes you have, the less stinky each one is going to be, and the more privacy your cats will have if they need to use a litter box at the same time. Cats are territorial and like to use the bathroom *alone.* You know how they feel, right? It isn't exactly the time for a party.

Figure 9-1:
Three
popular
types of
litter boxes
include a
basic open
pan (a),
covered (b),
and self-
cleaning (c).

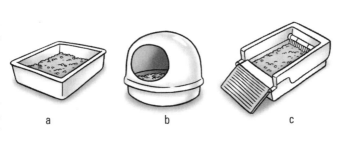

a   b   c

Some cats love to scratch and dig in clay litter. Others are happy to accept other litter media like recycled paper, corncob, or silica gel crystals. Again, it depends on the cat. Ask the shelter what kind of litter your new cat was using and start with that. Then, if you want to switch litter-box fillers, do so gradually, mixing new litter with old a little at a time. Cats don't like change.

You have a few good choices in litter-box fillers. Clumping litter makes waste easier to scoop. Crystal litter shines when it comes to odor control. Or, try one of the many paper-pelleted or other natural or recycled cat box fillers. Ask a pet store employee to show you the options and explain the benefits of each. For a new kitten that is just learning litter-box training, start with the kind of litter you think you want to use for the rest of the cat's life. After your kitten gets used to it, you shouldn't have any problems. In a few cases, cats reject a certain kind of litter. If your cat won't use the litter box, try switching types of litter to see whether that solves the problem.

As for showing your new cat how to use the litter box, see the "Getting acclimated" section later in this chapter for more information. For more about how to troubleshoot when your cat isn't crazy about the whole litter-box concept, turn to Chapter 11.

Sweet dreams, kitty

Some cats insist on sleeping with you in your bed, and many cat owners happily oblige their furry little bed warmers. Others, however, don't want their cats in their beds, don't have the space, or can't have cat hair in the bedroom. Some cats, by the way, would simply rather sleep alone. For all these reasons, preparing a comfortable, cozy cat bed that's ready and awaiting the arrival of your adopted cat is a good idea. You can buy a simple cat bed, or just place a pillow or a folded blanket or sheet either in your bedroom or wherever your cat likes to take catnaps — on a corner of the couch or in an armchair, or maybe on a special sunny spot on the carpet. Some cats like their beds near the action; others prefer secluded spots. You'll get a good idea of where your cat feels comfortable after she arrives in your home. Just make your best guess when placing the new cat bed beforehand. You can always move it later.

Collar and I.D. tags

A collar or harness with identification is a must for all pet cats. Your cat always needs to wear identification just in case he gets outside and someone finds him. Many shelters insert microchips in their cats, but this measure alone isn't enough, because many people who find cats don't have access to or know about microchip readers, and not every microchip reader reads every type of microchip. Today, many vets and shelters have universal microchip readers that are better able to get information off different brands of microchips, but even so, ID tags are an extra precaution. As for collars, a basic collar with a metal or plastic buckle works well for most cats, although cats that will walk on a leash may prefer the secure feeling of a harness.

Introducing a collar can be terrifying for some kittens or adult cats that have never worn one before. Some panic and thrash about until they get the collar under the chin and caught across the mouth. Some even get a front leg into the collar, if loose enough, and get stuck. In this panic state, getting the collar off can be difficult. So the first few times you put a collar on your new cat, make sure you supervise the cat for a while to monitor her reaction, and be sure the collar is fitted well, for your cat's safety.

Cat trees and scratching posts

Cats need to scratch, climb, prowl, and explore. This impulse is part of what cat lovers love about cats! But if you don't want that scratching and prowling to happen all over your good furniture, your cat needs some furniture of her own. Scratching posts and cat trees are perfect substitutes. Their carpeted surfaces beg to be scratched and usually are more appealing than that boring old leather sofa. Cat trees that enable your pet to climbing and have spaces in which your cat can hide are great for naps and the occasional mock hunting expeditions. Your local pet store likely has plenty of options, and you may consider placing scratching posts or cat trees in several different locations around your house, so your cat always has easily accessible cats-only territories to roam. Some people become creative building their own cat trees and scratching posts. Photos and even descriptions and directions for building many of these inspirational cat structures can be found on the Internet. Just search on "do it yourself cat trees" or "build your own cat tree," or other similar phrases.

Pretty kitty: Grooming supplies

Regardless of whether your cat's fur is long or short, it needs to be groomed. A daily brushing keeps your cat's coat in good condition and tangle-free, and it minimizes cat hair in the house. A flea comb not only helps you spot any invading pests before they get a foothold but also helps to remove tangles all the way down to the skin. You also need a nail clipper to trim the tips of your cat's nails. For more about grooming your cat, see Chapter 10.

Cats just wanna have fun: Cat toys

Toys aren't just a luxury for cats. Cats need them to stimulate and challenge their playful spirits, quick intellects, and agile bodies. Toys frankly help cats stay healthy.

Some cat toys, however, can be hazardous. Look for toys that don't have small pieces that can break off or get loose, becoming a choking hazard for your animal. String and yarn, if swallowed, can cause severe intestinal damage or get caught around paws or even necks. Instead, look for solid, rolling, wobbling, jingling, dangling, bouncing, squeaking, fuzzy, or catnip-scented toys. From balls cats can fetch to cat teasers, the options are endless. Even a tantalizingly dangling bathrobe tie or shoelace attached to a shoe can be fun.

One toy *not* to try: your hand. A common habit is to make your hand a toy for a playful kitten, moving your fingers around, and scooting your hand around. Using your hand as a toy may be fun at first, but when your cat is an adult with large sharp claws, it can become annoying. Don't let your cat get into the habit of thinking fingers are toys for batting and biting. If your adopted cat already is in this habit, try putting on a hand puppet and training her to play with that instead.

A favorite toy of some cats is a simple flashlight. Just train the beam on the wall and floor and move it around. Your cat may really enjoy "hunting" that elusive spot of light. Hours of fun!

Spoiling Fluffy with fancy supplies

Okay, you don't really need that purple velvet, jewel-encrusted, gold-tasseled sleigh bed for your cat. But if it exactly matches *your* purple velvet, jewel-encrusted, gold-tasseled sleigh bed, well . . . how can you possibly resist?

Although the majority of fru-fru fancy pet products still are designed for dogs, cats are claiming an increasing market share of the luxury pet-supply market. Plus, many of the pet supplies designed for tiny toy dogs work just great for cats. Some of the highest of the high-end products include:

- ✔ **Cat beds:** Available in a dizzying array of shapes, sizes, and price points, basic beds are pretty inexpensive, but you can spend hundreds of dollars on elegant to whimsical chaises, canopy beds, cat hammocks, and other furniture-quality cat beds.

- ✔ **Outdoor options:** Roaming cats are not safe cats, but that doesn't mean your cat never again gets a taste of the great outdoors. For cats that are accustomed to wandering, which often is the case with cats in animal shelters, the transition to indoor living can be difficult, but pet-product manufacturers have come up with some pretty ingenious ways to let cats enjoy the fresh air safely: mesh tunnels and towers that connect and provide a play space in the yard, mesh-covered kitty strollers for walks around the neighborhood, and leashes and walking harnesses for more willing cats.

✔ **Bling-bling:** Swarovski crystal collars, pretty pendants made of metal and rhinestones in the shapes of hearts, fish, birds, stars, and hundreds of other shapes, rhinestone letters that slip along a collar to spell the cat's name or a pithy comment ("Cats Rule," "Princess," "So Catty").

✔ **Kitty couture:** You can deck your kitty out in clothing from hats and sweaters to Halloween costumes, fancy holiday party-wear like feathery stoles shaped like collars, and whimsical jester collars with bells. Yes, some cats actually like wearing this stuff.

✔ **Technology:** You can indulge in high-tech variations of many of the products mentioned in previous sections in this chapter: fancy cat drinking fountains, automatic feeders, the fanciest self-cleaning litter boxes, to name just a few.

✔ **Cat trees extraordinaire:** Some people have elaborate room-sized cat trees and climbing apparatuses. Some people even devote entire rooms in their homes to their cats.

Of course, if money is an issue, you're better off spending it on a high-quality cat food, a good litter box with an effective cat-box filler, and proper veterinary care. But spoiling an adopted pet can be a lot of fun, especially when such pets never have had the opportunity to have attention lavished on them before. Why, a cat can get used to this kind of star treatment.

What to Expect When You Get Home

Any cat is going to be a little nervous when you first adopt him and bring him home. He doesn't know what to expect, and you probably don't, either! Every cat is different, and you, the cat, and everyone concerned have to figure out together how the newby fits into your household. When introducing a new cat into your home, don't be in a rush; take things slowly, gradually introducing your new cat to family members, pets, and surroundings.

Getting acclimated

Before you bring kitty home, set up a safe haven for your new friend — preferably a relatively secluded room such as a spare bedroom where you plan to keep the litter box.

Cats have a couple of requirements when it comes to their personal bathroom spot. They don't like it:

✔ Anywhere near their food

✔ Anywhere near their bed

You can keep the litter box and the cat's bed in the same room, especially at first, but put them on opposite sides of the room, or put the litter box behind something so it is at least partially hidden. The litter box needs to be placed where the cat can easily get to it without feeling anxious about a lot of nearby activity or loud noises from appliances, water heaters, or furnaces.

As soon as you get home, take your new cat to her special room and let her explore the space — including the litter box — and play with you. Showing your new cat this space is especially important when you have another cat or a dog. When that's the case, your new cat needs to stay in her small room for about a week. Although an entire week may seem like a long time to confine your new cat to one room, this adjustment period is important. Your new cat becomes familiar with her new home more quickly, thus minimizing an otherwise difficult adjustment. For more about safely introducing your new cat to other pets, see the section on "Meeting resident pets" later in his chapter.

If at first your cat doesn't seem inclined to use the litter box or know what it's for, don't worry. The concept may be new, even to an adult cat, and certainly to a young kitten (although many kittens take to the litter box immediately). Just be patient. Put the cat next to the litter box. If she steps in to explore, great! If not, try putting her in the litter box, repeating the process every hour or two. Scratch the litter a little. "See, isn't this fun, kitty?" If she steps right back out and wanders elsewhere, don't worry about it. You don't want her to associate the litter box with your anxiety! Eventually she will see the litter box as the best gig in town when it comes to her gastrointestinal needs. See Chapter 11 for help dealing with litter-box problems.

Meeting the family

Your new cat needs to meet every person who lives in your home and preferably relatives, friends, and other frequent visitors. Don't worry so much about doing this all at once; acquainting your new kitten with one or two people at a time is better.

On the first day home, each family member needs to approach the kitten or cat individually and spend some quality time interacting and playing together in the cat's special safe room. Small children must be instructed never to pick up a kitten, because if the kitten leaps out of their arms or they drop the kitten, he can be seriously injured. Instead, have family members sit on the floor and let the kitten explore them. Dangle tempting toys, offer tiny treats, and ply your new cat with praise and stroking. Most cats are quickly won over this way.

Some particularly shy adopted cats, however, may take a little longer to warm up to you. That's just fine. If your cat is shy, nervous, or traumatized, give him time alone in his small room (with litter box, cat bed, food and water dishes, and a few toys). If he hides for several hours, that's fine, too. Eventually he will grow braver and venture out. If your cat is shy or fearful, don't rush to touch him or pick him up. Let him come to you. Be slow, soft, gentle, and encouraging. Don't make sudden movements, yell, laugh loudly, or run around. Show your kitten that your home is a safe haven for him and that you're ready to be his friend when he's ready.

Children need to be particularly careful about how they act when they first meet a new cat. Although some outgoing cats are friendly and open to immediate, enthusiastic interaction with humans, children can startle a shy cat with loud voices and sudden, quick, and sporadic movements. Even if your cat takes a few weeks to really warm up to you, that's okay — all in good time. Patience brings you the best results, even when you're itching to interact with your new cat.

Meeting resident pets

When first bringing a new cat into a household where you already have another animal, you must be particularly careful and exercise caution with all such pet-to-pet introductions. Sometimes, resident pets are happy to accept a playmate, but in many cases, pets can get jealous, territorial, threatened, or just generally very unhappy about this unexpected change in their lives. Read on for some strategies on the best way to introduce pets to each other.

Introducing other cats and dogs

Some adopted cats have had bad experiences with dogs or other cats. In many cases, the resident cat feels slighted by you, territorial about the house, or threatened by the presence of another cat. Some dogs may not know *what* to make of a new cat, but the cat usually knows what to make of that dumb old dog. Caution and safe distances are in order.

The first thing to do is to keep your new cat with all her things in a room to which the resident cat or dog has no access. Don't let your resident cat or dog even *see* your new cat. Bring her into the house with the other animals in their own special place — put away. Leave your new cat in this room for a week, but, of course, be sure to visit and pay attention to your cat, frequently feeding, playing with, and grooming her. For now, though, let this room be her entire universe.

In the meantime, resident cats and dogs eventually figure out that there's another critter on the other side of that door. Cats may hiss or spit or simply be curious. If your dog barks at the door, take him away. Don't let him startle the new cat, but guide him calmly to the door for appropriate sniffing and talk to him about the new cat so he gets the feeling from you that whatever he's smelling and hearing on the other side is neither a threat nor an invader but rather a new family member.

Pets take their cues from you, so the more you act like the situation is entirely normal, not all that exciting, and one that requires good behavior, the faster your other pets understand.

As the week goes on, new and resident pets grow increasingly accustomed to the presence of the animal on the other side of the door. They may even stick their paws underneath the crack of the door to bat at each other (see Figure 9-2). When the cats or cat and dog seem more interested than frightened, try opening up the door just about an inch.

Figure 9-2: Introduce cats for the first time on opposite sides of a door. They can smell, hear, and even touch each other without feeling threatened.

The open door may engender a whole new series of hissing, spitting, scratching, barking, and clawing. If that happens, close the door. Be patient. Stay calm. Try it again in a few hours. Repeat this new exposure multiple times a day for as long as it takes the animals to react in a friendly — or at least neutral — way toward each other. When all parties understand that everybody else is A-okay, you can at long last let your new cat out of his little room.

But wait! Before you do that, you need to play the old switcheroo. Remember, the new cat hasn't explored the rest of your great big home yet and may be frightened by this experience. So, instead of letting all your pets mingle in a big free-for-all, pick up your new cat, have another family member pick up your resident cat or put your dog on a leash, and switch places. As your new cat gets to explore the rest of the house, resident pets can explore the room where the new cat has been staying. The room is full of interesting aromas and other signs of the new pet, and giving resident pets access to it further increases each pet's knowledge of and comfort level with the other.

Finally, gradually let the animals meet in the same room for the first time. Have someone to help you, and maintain control at all times so cats don't fight. Make sure each pet has an easy escape route if one happens to get away from you. Keep the dog on a leash until you're sure it and the new cat will interact in a friendly manner. Don't let the new cat pounce on or scratch the dog, and don't let the dog lunge or run toward the cat. If détente doesn't prevail so well at first, don't be discouraged. You can always return the cat to her familiar room. She won't mind, as long as she gets enough attention, food, water, a comfortable place to sleep, and a clean litter box. Going slow with introductions is better than rushing matters and having to repair a damaged relationship — or a damaged pet!

Introducing a new cat to the household may seem like an ordeal, but after your adopted cat and other pets accept each other's presence and work out their issues, you should have a happy household. In a few cases, pet combinations simply don't work, and you may have to enlist the shelter or rescue group's help in finding a new home for your adopted cat, but in most cases, with proper, slow, patient, calm introductions, that won't be necessary.

Introducing your cat to small animals, birds, and fish

And what about the other critters you may have in your household? If you have small animals like hamsters, rabbits, lizards, or pet birds, you must remember that cats are natural hunters, and these kinds of animals are their usual prey. Protecting these animals is your responsibility. You cannot expect a cat, no matter how well trained, to leave a small animal or bird alone if she has full access. Remember Sylvester and Tweety? Tom and Jerry? Your cat won't let Tweety's or Jerry's quick thinking (or Granny, for that matter) get in the way of a good meal.

Small animals must be kept in cages or tanks that are secure enough to keep a clever, curious cat from lifting off or pray opening the lid with her paws or nose. Keep small animals in a room to which the cat has no access, unless you're directly supervising to make sure your cat doesn't get a little *too* curious. Birds also need to be kept in a separate space unless your cat absolutely cannot reach the cage. Never, however, underestimate the cleverness and agility of your average cat. Adopted cats that have lived on the streets and had to find their own food may be particularly adept at hunting, so be on your guard at all times to protect your small animals.

If you have a fish tank, be sure that it has a strong, secure glass top or other covering that won't permit your cat *any* access. Many cats try to bat at or catch fish and are fascinated by their movements in the water. Conversely a small kitten can even fall into a fish tank and not be able to get back out, so exercising caution is a two-way street: Keep your fish tank covered. If you have a resident cat and you're considering a small animal, perhaps you need to reconsider. Some cats won't bother small animals, but if you're not sure, or you're not sure about your ability to keep the two separate, there's no reason to put a small animal at risk.

Run of the house

After a week or so, your cat should be feeling happy and confident. She may have even given you the slip and popped out of her safe room to have a look around the house. If so, that's great. That means she's feeling self-possessed enough to explore. Some cats are ready for a look around more quickly than others. If your cat hasn't yet ventured out, you can begin leaving the door to the cat room open. Sit outside the room doing something fun and irresistible, like dangling a cat teaser or brandishing a yummy treat. Don't put pressure on kitty but instead, act relaxed, calm, happy, and as if you're having the time of your life out there in the big old world. Most cats — being curious — are happy to come out and have a look around. Always leave the cat room door open, however, so your cat can return to her safe room if she feels the need. You can move the litter box at this point if you want to, but do it gradually, moving it just two or three feet every day until it's where you want it. Remember that the litter box and water dish always need to be accessible. Most cats can't open doors.

Recognizing Adjustment Problems

Most cats adjust quickly to their new homes but some — particularly adopted cats that have been shuttled around to multiple homes, spent a long time wandering, or were abused — may have a harder time settling in. While shelters or rescue groups should not offer cats with serious behavior problems for adoption, cats sometimes don't display these qualities until you get them home. If your cat refuses to use the litter box, hides constantly, or behaves aggressively, you may be able to resolve these problems using the training strategies in Chapter 11. In most cases, with a little patience, a regular routine, and daily training, you can help your cat to adjust nicely. Chapter 11 also tells you how and where to find a feline behavioral consultant, if you can't seem to resolve the issue and aren't sure what to do.

All cats crave a regular routine, whether they are adjusting nicely to their home or having some problems, so establish one right away to make your new cat feel comfortable. Feed your cat at the same time every day and have a play and/or training session or two at the same time every day. Let your cat look forward to the morning grooming session, the after-work cuddle time, and the evening television/lap-cat hour. If your cat knows what to expect from you and her new life, she gains confidence faster.

The first few weeks with a new kitten can be the most challenging, but after everyone gets to know one another and settles into a new routine, life should get back to normal . . . or even better than normal, because now you have a new adopted cat, and cats make life a little nicer. Purrrrr . . . fect.

Chapter 10

Kitty Care

. . . .

In This Chapter

▶ Deciding what, when, and how to feed your cat

▶ Choosing a vet and preparing for your first and subsequent visits to the veterinarian

▶ Protecting your cat against diseases and pests with vaccinations and pest-control products

▶ Grooming your cat for spectacular beauty and good health

. . . .

*A*dopted cats may not be accustomed to premium food, regular vet visits, and daily grooming sessions, but these amenities are important for cats. Independent though your adopted cat may be, she nevertheless needs you to take good care of her. Some adopted cats may have nutritional or health problems that need to be resolved right off the bat. Others may have serious grooming issues, or maybe your cat is the picture of glowing health. Regardless of the shape and condition your cat is in *today,* paying attention to nutritional, health, and grooming needs can help bring your new cat back to a healthy state.

In this chapter, you find out about your cat's nutritional needs, how to choose a good cat food and whether your cat is at a healthy weight. You also discover how to choose a good cat vet and provide basic cat health maintenance, kitten vaccinations, annual exams, and pest control. And you'll explore how to groom your beautiful kitty, from the top of her silky head to the tip of her twitching tail, making the most of that pretty coat and those hypnotizing eyes.

Keeping Your Cat Healthy

Your cat's good health depends on many factors, but the number-one defense against poor health is your friendly neighborhood veterinarian. Your vet provides you with information about keeping your cat healthy, from recommending a food to reminding you when your cat is due for her next vaccination, working with you from the first visit to all the follow-ups thereafter. Your vet also answers your questions, helps you choose a good flea-control product, advises you about spaying or neutering, and even recommends a trainer, so don't neglect this valuable resource.

You're also a key player in providing for your cat's good health, because you're the one who:

- Knows your cat best
- Watches your cat grow, change, and age
- Spots physical changes in your cat that can be the first signs of disease
- Notices changes in behavior, eating and drinking habits, or any limping, skin bumps, eye or teeth problems, or other problems your cat may exhibit

What you do about the changes you witness throughout your cat's life can make all the difference, so pay attention to your cat. Her health is in your hands.

Choosing a great cat vet

A great cat vet is worth his weight in catnip. Some vets really love cats, and even specialize in them, working in cats-only clinics and hospitals, but others see all types of pets. Your job is to find a vet with whom you feel comfortable, who communicates well and generally seems to like and appreciate *your* cat.

Other factors that you need to consider are office location, friendliness of the staff, how long you have to wait in the waiting room, how often the vet's office is open, whether you have access to an associated emergency clinic, and how qualified and experienced your vet is with cats. Don't be afraid to interview a few vets if you aren't comfortable with the first vet you find. The relationship between you, your vet, and your cat is long-term and not something you want to rush into!

The first exam

When you find a vet that you love, you need to schedule a first exam before taking your new cat home. Even though shelters sometimes have a vet examine animals before adoption, you may still want to take your new cat to the vet — your vet. The first visit with a vet is the beginning of your relationship and your joint effort to promote your new cat's health.

During the first visit, your vet asks you for information about your new cat, such as:

- ✔ Where you got your cat
- ✔ Whether you know your cat's age and breed
- ✔ How much you know about your cat's health and previous vaccination history
- ✔ Whether your cat is spayed or neutered
- ✔ Whether you have any specific concerns

If you notice anything unusual about your cat, such as a lump, a problem with her coat, itching, head shaking, limping, or other strange behavior, the first visit with the vet is the time to mention it.

After these preliminary inquiries, your vet probably will give your cat a physical examination on the exam table, poking and prodding virtually every part of your cat's body to make sure everything feels healthy. During an exam, the vet also:

- ✔ Looks at your cat's eyes, ears, mouth, teeth, and skin
- ✔ Checks for skin and internal abnormalities
- ✔ Listens to your cat's heart and breath sounds
- ✔ Watches your cat walk to make sure everything is moving correctly

If the exam points to anything unusual, from signs of an ear or skin infection to a crooked gait or a heart murmur, your vet may recommend conducting some tests.

Your vet probably will give your new kitten a deworming product, because most kittens are born with worms, and will give your kitten or cat her next (or first!) set of vaccinations before discussing other health-care issues with you, such as ongoing parasite prevention to protect against fleas and heartworms and when to have your cat spayed or neutered.

Spaying or neutering your cat

Considering the hundreds of thousands of unwanted cats in the world today, spaying or neutering your new cat as soon as possible makes sense. Spaying or neutering your cat not only prevents an accidental litter of kittens, but it also proves to be good for your cat's overall health. Not only are female cats spared the health risks of pregnancy and delivering a litter of kittens, they no longer run the risk of developing uterine or ovarian cancer — because those organs have been removed. Spayed cats also have a lower risk of breast cancer. Male cats, on the other hand, won't develop testicular cancer, won't go wandering off looking for female cats, and are less likely to spray in the house to mark territory. Female and male cats alike may be calmer and more affectionate after they're spayed or neutered.

Although sterilization surgery can be relatively expensive, many shelters and rescue groups have partnered with local vets to offer deep discounts or even free surgeries. Some shelters have promotional events during which the service is free. Ask your shelter how you can pay less for this important procedure.

Vaccines and deworming

Vaccinations are a controversial subject. Not everyone agrees how often older cats need to be vaccinated, particularly because cats sometimes develop cancerous tumors near the sites of their vaccinations. On the other hand, vaccinations can prevent some very serious, even fatal diseases. Clearly vaccinations have a place. The question simply is how often they're needed.

The law dictates how often cats must be treated with a rabies vaccine. The rabies vaccine is important, especially for cats. More cats get rabies than do dogs, because cats are more likely to wander around outside and come into contact with wildlife. However, even inside cats need to get a rabies vaccination. You never know when your cat may sneak outside or when a raccoon may get into your house — it happens more often than you may think.

Most vets agree that a series of vaccinations during the first year of life are important for building up your kitten's immune system between weaning and maturity. The typical vaccination schedule for a kitten varies somewhat according to the vet's preference, your cat's exposure and age, and where you live. Table 10-1 shows a fairly common vaccination schedule, including a series of FVRCP vaccinations. The FVRCP stands for: *feline viral rhinotracheitis* (an upper respiratory infection), *calicivirus* (an upper respiratory infection), and *panleukopenia* (an intestinal virus). Kittens also need a feline leukemia vaccination, if they test negative for the disease, and a rabies vaccination, which is required by law. If you adopt an adult cat, and you don't know anything about his vaccination history, he needs to have an FVRCP vaccination and a feline leukemia vaccination (if the test for the disease is negative) and then another of each vaccination two or three weeks later. Your cat also needs to have a rabies vaccination.

Table 10-1	Kitten Vaccination Schedule		
Kitten's Age	**FVRCP**	**FeLV**	**Rabies**
6–8 weeks	1st	—	—
12 weeks	2nd	1st	—

Kitten's Age	FVRCP	FeLV	Rabies
14 weeks	—	2nd	—
16 weeks	3rd	—	1st
from 18 months	yearly	yearly	yearly (or as required)

The real controversy comes after the first year. Talk to your vet about how often you need to vaccinate your cat, which vaccinations are important for your cat, and whether your cat may be prone to vaccination-site sarcoma. Some vets recommend annual booster vaccinations for the FVRCP, feline leukemia virus, and rabies, but other vets prefer a less frequent vaccination schedule, depending to some extent on your cat's health and how often he is outside.

Dealing with fleas, ticks, and mosquitoes

Your new friend may have picked up a few unwanted friends without knowing it while wandering the streets on her own or living with other strays at the shelter. Fleas, ticks, mites, flies, and even worms transmitted by mosquitoes can all afflict adopted cats. Your vet will examine your new cat for these pests and recommend treatment and/or prevention strategies, especially for cats that spend any time outside, even on a leash or in a fenced yard. Even indoor cats can get fleas. These pests show up just about anywhere, and often live in carpets and furniture. Your vet may recommend heartworm preventive and monthly spot-on flea control even for outside cats, and may have additional recommendations for cats that spend time outdoors.

Many convenient products exist to control pests, but the best and safest come from your veterinarian, so get your pest control products there. Although they may cost a little more, the extra pennies are worth the additional product effectiveness for the health of your cat. Some people choose to buy these products online at reduced prices, although most vets don't recommend that practice because they prefer to see your cat and be involved in what medications and products you're using on the cat.

Never ever use a pest control product that's intended for a dog on your cat! Many such products are toxic to cats and can even kill them. Even products made for cats can be toxic if used incorrectly, so follow the directions to the letter.

Remaining on the lookout for health problems

Every cat can be injured, develop a chronic disease, and catch fleas, but adopted cats are particularly susceptible to these problems. If a cat was injured in the past — in a fight or struck by a car — he may have a particularly vulnerable spot you don't know about. Sudden limping or pain can be a flare-up of a past injury. Cats new to the shelter may still be recovering from injuries, skin rashes, hair loss, heartworms, or flea infestations. These conditions range from mild to life-threatening.

Older adopted cats also are susceptible to diseases of aging, and the cats that didn't receive good healthcare in their younger years may be more susceptible than healthy cats that were fed well and were under a vet's care. These diseases and conditions include diabetes, kidney disease, urinary tract problems, thyroid problems, heart disease, and cancer. Animal shelters and pet rescue groups check their cats for serious problems, but some adopted cats may not show signs of these chronic conditions. You may discover them later, which is why taking note of any physical or behavioral changes in your adopted cat is so important — so you can alert your vet. The sooner your vet diagnoses a health problem, the easier it can be resolved or managed.

Adopted cats that haven't been vaccinated but have been exposed to wildlife and other cats as they wandered as strays may have contracted serious diseases like feline leukemia (FeLV) or feline immunodeficiency virus (FIV, sometimes called feline AIDs).

✔ **Feline leukemia (FeLV):** FeLV is the most common cause of illness and death in pet cats today. This dangerous retrovirus suppresses your cat's immune system so he cannot fight off infection. FeLV is easy to contract, not only through wounds but also by sharing a food or water dish with another cat. Humans and dogs are not at risk for contracting this disease, but other cats are at a high risk. Signs of FeLV include weight loss and lack of appetite, low energy and weakness, diarrhea, excessive thirst, and strange behavior. Some cats show no signs.

The test for feline leukemia is simple, but sometimes it can give a false positive, so retest in two months if you can, or test twice if you're trying to decide about adopting the cat. For FeLV-free cats, a vaccine exists that is usually successful in preventing this disease. Indoor cats that are never exposed to other cats may not require this vaccine. Ask your vet for advice about whether your cat needs this vaccine.

If you discover your new adopted cat has FeLV and you have no other cats, you may decide to keep the cat anyway. Adult cats with FeLV have about a 33 percent chance of actually mounting an immune response to the virus and getting rid of it. About half the cats with FeLV never get sick from it, although they should not interact with other cats, because they can pass the disease along. Half of the cats with FeLV die within three years from related complications, but because humans aren't at risk, you still can give your FeLV-positive cat a good, happy, fulfilling life for a few years, or if your cat is one of the lucky ones, for many years to come.

Some vets may not want to deal with FeLV patients, but if you're willing to keep a cat with this virus and your vet recommends euthanasia when your cat shows any symptoms, consider looking for a different vet who is more open to the option of caring for FeLV-positive cats.

✔ **Feline immunodeficiency virus (FIV) — feline AIDs:** Feline AIDs is similar to the AIDs virus in humans, but it is not the same and is not transmissible to humans. Cats transmit it to each other, usually through blood and saliva exchanged during fights, so outdoor cats — especially unneutered cats that are likely to fight — are at high risk. Signs of FIV include wounds and sores that won't heal, gum infections, respiratory infections, weight loss, gastrointestinal problems, and a messy-looking coat.

Feline AIDs has no cure. A vaccine is available, but it causes subsequent FIV tests to show up positive, which can be problematic, because vaccinated cats look no different to a vet than cats with the virus. Some vets tattoo the cat's ear with "FIV vacc'd," but many vets don't recommend the vaccine because of this problem.

An easy test determines whether your new adopted cat has FIV. Although cats can live for many years with FIV, they usually eventually contract fatal secondary infections caused by their compromised immune function. Even so, the years they do have are often happy, and the cats do not suffer. At one point, vets thought FIV was as contagious as feline leukemia, but they now realize it isn't. FIV-positive cats can live safely with other cats, as long as they don't fight. Playing, grooming, and sharing food and water dishes do not transmit the virus. If you decide to keep an FIV cat, you can enjoy many happy years together until the cat finally starts to show signs of ill health.

You may not always know whether a limp, a twitch, or a strange cry warrants a call or a trip to the vet. The better and longer you know your cat, the more you'll develop a good sense of what is and is not normal for him, but in general, a few signs point to cats that may have serious conditions.

In an emergency, you may not have time to figure out what to do, so before that emergency strikes, post your veterinarian's phone number, the number for the ASPCA Poison Control Center — 888-426-4435 (a $50 consultation fee may apply) — and phone number and address of the nearest 24-hour emergency veterinary clinic in an accessible spot. Even if everything turns out to be just fine, give your vet a call whenever your cat displays any of the following possible symptoms of an emergency condition:

✔ **Signs of a seizure:** These signs include loss of consciousness, uncontrolled jerky movements, stiffened body, glazed stare, or nonresponsiveness.

✔ **Uncontrolled bleeding:** If your cat is injured beyond a little scratch and you can't stop the bleeding, see the vet right away. If you can stop the bleeding but the wound looks serious or infected with pus or redness and swelling, call your vet.

✔ **Continual vomiting, vomiting blood:** Cats with hairballs will cough and gag and upchuck a hairball, but repeated vomiting and any sign of blood in the vomit warrant immediate veterinary attention.

✔ **Signs of extreme pain:** These signs may include yowling, hiding, shaking, or dramatic behavioral changes.

✔ **Uncontrolled movement:** The signs include staggering, falling over, or loss of consciousness.

✔ **Evidence that your cat ingested a poisonous substance:** Any of the above symptoms can be signs of poisoning.

✔ **Evidence of serious injury:** Your cat shows signs of serious injury if he is struck by a car, falls from a high perch, or is struck hard by some other object.

✔ **Frequent visits to the litter box, or sitting or lying in the litter box.** Frequent potty stops can be a sign of urinary blockage. Total blockage is a true emergency and requires immediate medical attention.

Making time for an annual exam

Even though your adult cat isn't going to need a vaccine booster every year, taking her to the vet for an annual checkup is important. Yes, even though she's perfectly healthy! No, this isn't a waste of money. Cats are susceptible to many of the same diseases of aging as humans — cancer, heart disease, diabetes, and arthritis, to name a few. Regular vet checkups keep you and your vet in close touch with your cat's health. They enable your vet to keep an eye and two hands on your cat once a year to check for early warning signs of chronic diseases in addition to general symptoms of aging.

Veterinarians have plenty of resources at their disposal for reducing suffering, including pain and discomfort. They also rely on therapies that can actually cure diseases, or at least slow down their progression, giving your cat a longer, healthier, happier life and more time with you. Don't neglect these important checkups. Remember, your cat's life is in your hands.

Chow Time!

Some adopted cats came from homes where they received good nutrition, but many were fed low-quality diets or had to fend for themselves while wandering. Your adopted cat now has a permanent home and the opportunity to thrive, so feed her the best diet possible to give her a better chance at having a strong, healthy body. The sections that follow provide the nutritional information you need to know.

Choosing the right food for your cat

Cats are carnivores, and their unique biology results in some specific nutritional requirements. Cats need:

- ✔ Meat protein.

- ✔ The amino acid *taurine,* which is found in muscle meat. Insufficient taurine in a cat's diet can result in blindness and/or heart disease.

- ✔ Vitamin A from organ meat sources (because they can't digest vitamin A from plants).

- ✔ More niacin from meat sources than other pets because of unique feline enzyme activity.

- ✔ Certain essential fatty acids that are found only in animal fat. Insufficient amounts of fatty acids can result in skin and coat problems.

Vitamin and nutritional deficiencies can cause problems that range from sores in the mouth and a poor, pathetically ragged coat to a suppressed immune system. Kittens born to malnourished mothers may have birth defects.

No, your cat should not eat a vegetarian diet, unless your vet recommends it for a specific health problem. No, your cat should not eat dog food, which contains more plant matter than cat food. Cats need cat food, or an extremely carefully constructed, supervised homemade diet. If you're like most pet owners, commercial cat food is the easiest and most convenient choice.

Every adopted cat needs to be checked by a vet for health problems. (For more information, see the earlier sections on "Choosing a great cat vet" and "The first exam.") If your vet has specific nutritional recommendations for your cat, by all means, follow them. To address chronic disease, your vet may even write a prescription for a specific kind of food that's only available through the vet. For a healthy cat with issues that can be easily resolved with treatment, however, all you need to do is switch your cat to a high-quality premium cat food.

The first thing you need to know about choosing a food for your new cat is what your cat was eating before you adopted her, how much she was eating, and whether she had any particular eating habits, preferences, or finicky mealtime behaviors. The shelter or rescue group should be able to provide some insight into your new pet's eating habits. From that information, you can decide whether to continue your cat's feeding regimen or try a different one.

If you decide to change your cat's food, don't be overwhelmed by the many pet foods available today. Keep the following simple tips in mind when choosing the best quality food you can afford:

- ✔ **Read the label.** Cats need real meat protein in their diets. Cat foods that meet nutritional requirements for cats and are approved by the American Association of Feed Control Officials (AAFCO) are packaged with an official statement on their labels that confirms these factors. All premium foods have this statement.

- ✔ **Price often *is* an indicator of quality.** The cheapest foods don't contain the same high-quality ingredients as the most expensive foods. Generic or store brands usually are lower in quality, while premium brands made by companies like Purina, Iams (Eukanuba), Hills (Science Diet), Nutro, and Waltham usually use better ingredients in the form of more digestible proteins and denser nutrients.

- ✔ **Dry kibble is fine for many cats.** Dry kibble is cheaper and lasts longer than canned cat food. Other cats prefer canned food because they like the taste (and it looks more like real meat). Many pet owners like to moisten dry kibble with a little tasty canned food for the best of both worlds. The choice is up to you.

- ✔ **Organic, natural, holistic foods generally are pricier and contain ingredients that manufacturers believe are the highest quality and closest to what cats would eat in the wild.** Some of these terms are regulated (like "organic"), and others aren't (like "holistic"), so buyer beware. Nevertheless people who choose organic food for themselves often prefer these foods and believe them to be well worth the price for their cats.

- ✔ **Raw diets — either homemade or frozen and packaged — are controversial.** These diets consist of raw meat along with other components like ground vegetables and bone meal, which some people believe mimics what a cat would eat in the wild. Others believe this kind of diet can put a cat at risk for infection from pathogens from the raw meat or incomplete nutrition. Talk to your vet if you're curious whether a raw diet is best for your cat.

Avoiding harmful foods

The occasional bit of boiled chicken, grilled salmon, or filet mignon will probably make your cat happy (not to mention motivated to follow your training cues), but cats cannot and should not eat all the food people eat. Food that isn't good for humans certainly isn't good for pets. Fried foods, high-fat foods, and foods containing sugar like cookies and candy are not only void of any helpful nutrition, but they also can fill up your cat so he doesn't eat his nutritious food, thus resulting in malnutrition. These foods also contribute to obesity and digestive upset. If you thought your table scraps looked relatively tasty when you gave them to your cat, you probably won't feel the same about them when they come back up — or run right through.

Some foods do more than disagree with your cat; they can be toxic. For the sake of your cat's good health and safety, never feed your cat:

- ✔ Onions or garlic, which can cause anemia.

- ✔ Green, or unripe, tomatoes or their leaves and stems, or the green parts of potatoes, which contain a poison.

- ✔ Chocolate, which contains theobromine, a stimulant to which some cats are extremely sensitive.

- ✔ Coffee, coffee beans, coffee grounds, tea bags, or anything containing caffeine (including chocolate, see above).

- ✔ Grapes or raisins, which have been proven poisonous so far only to dogs but which may also be poisonous to cats. No point in risking it.

- ✔ Alcohol, which can poison any pet.

- ✔ The seeds or stones in apples, peaches, apricots, and plums.

Switching foods

If you decide to switch your cat's food from the brand she was eating at the shelter, buy a small bag of the old food and a small bag of the new food, and then gradually phase in the new food. At first, combine new and old food at a ratio of about one part new to three parts old. After a few days, feed about half new and half old. After a few more days, feed three parts new to one part old, and then after a few more days, feed your cat the new food exclusively. If your cat starts having digestive problems like vomiting or diarrhea, slow down the transition, gradually increasing the amount of new food over the course of a week or two.

Deciding between free feeding and meal feeding

Some cats can be *free-fed,* meaning their food dish sits out all day and they can nibble on their kibble whenever they choose. This feeding arrangement works well for cats at a healthy weight that are not food-obsessed, but it isn't usually a good idea for overweight cats. They may eat their entire daily allowance of food at once and then beg for more. Free feeding is an especially bad choice if you're likely to give in to that begging and overfeed your cat. It also doesn't work well when you have a dog (or another cat) that eats the cat food. You won't be able to tell how much each cat is eating, and one cat (or the dog) may be scoring all the chow.

The other option is feeding your cat at appointed mealtimes and then taking up any food that remains after she walks away from her bowl. Young kittens need to eat three or four times a day, with their daily allowance of food divided among these feedings. Adult cats may be able to get by with being fed just once a day, but most prefer two daily meals, an approach that keeps your cat from getting too hungry.

Don't give in to the beggar, or you risk contributing to a weight problem. Feed your cat according to her weight. The cat-food package (can or bag) tells you how much to feed. Then, if your cat starts looking too heavy, you can decrease the amount slightly. If she looks too thin, increase the amount slightly. Many pet-food companies overestimate the amount of food a pet really needs to stay healthy, so start by feeding your cat in the lower range suggested on the pet-food label or ask your vet how much you should feed you cat.

Do you have a fat cat or a scrawny kitty?

Because so many adopted cats are either too thin or too fat, you need to get a clear picture of whether your cat needs to eat a little more than usual until he reaches a healthy weight, or whether you need to limit your cat's meals and treats to help him get back *down* to a healthy weight — no matter how much he begs.

Adopted cats may have additional nutritional issues. Many cats in animal shelters were picked up off the streets where they were living on their own or in substandard conditions. These cats can be underweight and malnourished and may be suffering from problems caused by nutritional deficiencies (see earlier section on "Choosing the right food for your cat").

Some adopted cats have the opposite problem. They've been in a home where they were overfed and now are overweight or obese. In fact, so many pet cats in America are obese that many vets consider the problem an epidemic. They get that way because their owners feed them too much, leave food out all day and don't monitor their intake, and because they don't get very much exercise. Obesity puts extra stress on all your cat's internal organs and can aggravate arthritis in senior cats.

Pet owners tend to be in denial about weight problems their pets may have; they don't want to admit their cats are too fat. They are, however, more willing, in general, to admit their cats are too thin. However, many people who have cats of a normal, healthy weight believe their cats are too thin. Well-meaning pet owners tend to want to nurture their new pets with food and treats, but doing so can quickly backfire when an underweight cat blows right past normal to become an overweight cat.

If you have any doubts whether your cat is overweight or underweight, your vet can make the call for you and advise you about how to correct the problem. You can also tell by looking at Figure 10-1. How does your cat look? What's the verdict?

Administering the body evaluation test

Take a good hard look at your cat. Look at her from the top and from the side, and feel her ribs. Can you feel those ribs, or are they so covered with flesh that you can't even tell where they are? What about the top view? Your cat should show a graceful waist tuck. From the side, her abdomen should tuck up slightly.

If you not only feel but also see your cat's ribs — if her bones protrude sharply, and she looks like the first picture in Figure 10-1 — your cat is underweight. If your cat looks like the last picture, with a belly hanging pendulously toward the floor — if you can feel no sign whatsoever of ribs, and if her torso looks more like a beach ball than a slender hourglass — your cat is too heavy. Many adult cats have pendulous skin on their bellies with just a small amount of subcutaneous fat, so even a too-thin cat looks fat from the side, and you need to check other criteria to be sure.

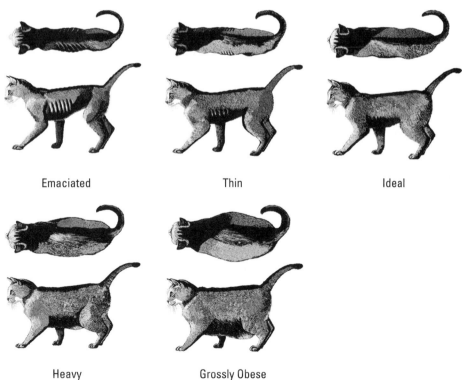

Figure 10-1: Is your cat too thin? Too fat? Just right? Use these pictures to help determine whether your cat needs to cut back on calories, put on a few pounds, or stay just the way she is.

Emaciated   Thin   Ideal

Heavy   Grossly Obese

Courtesy of Nestle Purina PetCare Co.

Correcting a weight problem

If your cat has a weight problem, work in cooperation with your vet to solve the problem. Underweight cats need to eat a nutrient-dense diet in the form of a premium food — dry, canned, or a combination of both — and can probably be free-fed, so they have access to food whenever they need it, unless, of course, you have other cats (or a dog) that have access to the food bowl (see the section on "Deciding between free feeding and meal feeding" earlier in this chapter).

Treats for training or good behavior can be rich and nutrient dense, such as small chunks of boiled chicken or fish, or healthy treats made just for cats, but they shouldn't be full of processed ingredients and sugar.

If your cat is overweight, cut back slightly on meal portions. To keep your cat from getting too hungry, you may want to divide the daily allowance of food into several small meals, and/or switch (gradually) to a reduced-calorie food. Reduce or eliminate food treats, replacing them with the treat of your attention and affection. Moreover, help your cat get more exercise. Put the food bowl and the litter box on different floors of your house, play active games with your cat, or take her outside on a leash for a stroll around the yard.

Helping Your Cat Practice Good Feline Hygiene

Grooming is important to cats. You can tell by the way they're always cleaning themselves so fastidiously. In spite of all that effort, your cat needs help keeping herself healthy and beautiful, even if she won't quite admit it. All cats need to be brushed and combed and have their nails clipped. Long-haired cats also need a bath every month or two.

The trick to grooming a cat is getting her used to the process from the beginning. Brush and comb your kitten every day, and clip just the tips of her nails off at least once a week. Bathe long-haired kittens within about a month of bringing them home, and keep bathing them monthly. Pretty soon your kitty just assumes that this kind of personal hygiene is part of the normal routine . . . and indeed, it is.

Grooming disguised as a health-care checkup

Grooming does more than make your cat look pretty. Every grooming session gives you an opportunity to feel all over your cat's body for anything unusual.

Look at her eyes, ears, nose, mouth, teeth, and under her tail for signs of infection, parasites, or anything unusual. You may be the first one to catch the first signs of a health problem, and the sooner you catch it, the better your cat's chances for effective treatment. Be observant about your cat's body and behavior, and you'll be acting as an advocate for her good health and long life.

Brushing and combing basics

Brushing and combing your cat every day not only minimizes the amount of cat hair in the house and keeps long coats tangle-free, it also affords you a better chance of noticing any fleas that decided to hitch a ride. A small, soft, natural-bristle brush works for almost any cat. Brush the cat all over from head to tail, paying special attention to areas where the coat is longer and can become tangled. Then, using a small, fine-toothed steel comb, go through the entire coat, combing all the way down to the skin. As you comb, look for any signs of fleas or skin problems like rashes, sores, discoloration, or lumps. Cats with extremely short coats can even be rubbed down with a chamois cloth, instead of a brush, for a lustrous finish.

Most cats enjoy the feeling of being brushed and combed, but if yours doesn't, don't give in and quit. Your cat needs to find out that brushing is an important part of the regular routine. Just start out brushing a tiny bit each day for just a minute or so. As your cat learns to tolerate brushing more easily, you can increase the time.

Whenever your cat has a tangle or a mat, she may enjoy the grooming process even less. Don't cut out tangles or mats with scissors — it's easy to slip and cut your cat's delicate, thin skin. Besides, you'll leave an ugly hole in your cat's coat. Instead, work the tangle out a tiny bit at a time with a steel comb, starting at the outer edge. If you can't untangle the matted fur, take your cat to a groomer. If you insist on doing it yourself, cut tiny slits in the tangle, using extreme caution, and then work out each tiny piece. The slits should be parallel to the hair but perpendicular to your cat's body.

Some owners of long-haired cats have them shaved or cut down every summer. This option is warranted especially when the cat's fur is extremely matted — but you won't let it get to that point, will you? Some cats enjoy this newfound short-haired freedom, but others act embarrassed or seem to feel naked. Part of the joy of owning a long-haired cat is that the cat has, well . . . long hair, and not a buzz cut! Keeping that long coat tangle-free means your cat can stay looking the way she was meant to look.

Clipping nails down to size, not the quick

Cats don't usually like to have their nails clipped. Yet, keeping the tips of your cat's claws blunt is important, so they don't pierce your skin when they knead your lap or pat your cheek. Clipping nails also minimizes damage to carpets and furniture whenever your cat sneaks in a few scratches on these non-scratching-post items. If you adopt an adult cat that resists having his nails done, you may want to have a professional groomer or the vet do the job. However, doing it yourself is much easier and cheaper, so get your kitten used to this simple task right away.

You can use the same nail clipper for your cat that you use on yourself, but for cats who aren't used to having their nails trimmed, don't wield those clippers right away. First you need to be able to touch her paws. While brushing and combing your cat, pick them up, squeeze the paw pads gently, and touch her nails. Do this paw exercise only a little bit at a time if she's resistant. When she accepts these actions, let her sniff and examine the nail clipper. Then, while acting calm and cheerful, clip off just the tip of one nail. Don't act anxious or worried. Your cat will pick up on your emotions and think something is wrong!

If you have to clip just one nail every few days at first, that's fine. Slow progress is more likely to result in your cat's eventual acceptance of this grooming ritual. After your cat is willing to let you proceed, here's what you do:

1. **Take your cat's paw in your hand, gently pressing the paw pad under the first nail with your index finger and just above the nail on the top of the toe with your thumb.**

   Doing so makes the nail pop out. See Figure 10-2 for an example of how to do this.

2. **Look for the pink vein that runs down the center of the nail, called the** *quick.*

   You do not want to clip into the quick because it hurts, and you may turn your cat off of nail clipping forever. If your cat has black nails, and you can't see the quick, just clip right at where the nail starts to curve down, or slightly past that point (toward the nail's tip) if you are nervous about cutting too much off.

3. **Clip off only the sharp tip.**

   If you clip your cat's nails every week, you'll never have to clip off much, and that's easier and safer for everyone.

   If you accidentally cut too far and the kitty bleeds, just use firm pressure at the area for a few minutes. You can also pack cornstarch at the tip, use a powder product you can buy at the pet store for this purpose, or just wait. No normal cat has ever died from a bleeding nail.

4. **Praise your cat for being so patient.**

   Don't forget to offer him a reward, like a small yummy treat or lots of attention.

Figure 10-2:
Press on
both sides
of your cat's
toe to push
out the
claw; clip
off just the
sharp tip,
being
careful not
to cut the
quick.

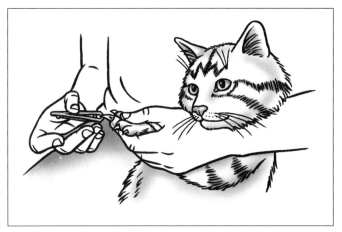

Figure 10-2: Press on both sides of your cat's toe to push out the claw; clip off just the sharp tip, being careful not to cut the quick.

Giving a cat a bath

If your cat has a long coat, bathing is an important part of grooming. Long coats can pick up dirt and bacteria, and they can hide skin problems. Keep your cat's coat and skin clean and healthy. Here's what to do:

1. **Thoroughly brush and comb your cat's coat.**

   Any remaining tangles will tighten if they get wet, so be sure to get out all the tangles.

2. **Gather all your supplies together and have them ready, because you won't be able to let go of your cat during the bathing process.**

   Shampoo and conditioner made for cats, a sprayer or cup for rinsing, and a big soft towel are the essentials.

3. **Run warm but not hot water in the bathtub or sink.**

   Using a sink may be easier because it's smaller, less intimidating, and you don't have to bend down or stand on your knees to bathe your cat.

4. **Put a collar on your cat (if she doesn't already have one), so you can hold on to her.**

   Holding on is made even easier when you enlist someone to help you.

5. **Gently wet down your cat's fur, all the way to the skin, and then work in the shampoo and rinse thoroughly before applying conditioner. Rinse again.**

   Always rinse longer than you think you need to, because shampoo residue can cause tangles and attract dirt.

6. **Scoop up your cat in that big soft towel after she's completely rinsed and gently dry her.**

   By this time, your cat probably looks pretty pathetic, all wet and bedraggled. Funny how cats just don't look like they were meant to be wet, isn't it? Keep her out of drafts and cold until she's completely dry.

7. **Blow-dry the coat on the cool setting while brushing it.**

   This step is essential for long-haired cats, but it also works for short-haired cats. In only a few minutes, you'll have your clean, soft, fluffy beauty back again.

Chapter 11

You Really *Can* Train a Cat

In This Chapter

▶ Discovering the secrets of successful litter-box training

▶ Dealing with your cat's hunting instincts: scratching, climbing, attacking, hiding, running wild, and talking too much

▶ Helping your next cat coexist with resident pets

▶ Finding a feline behavioral consultant

▶ Teaching your cat useful basic obedience cues

*E*verybody knows you can't train a cat. A dog, sure. But not a cat! Cats are independent. They do what *they* want to do. If you say "Sit," they're likely to respond with some feline version of, "Why should I?" Isn't that true?

Actually, no, that isn't true. Yes, cats are independent, and they prefer to do what they want to do (Don't we all?), but cats also like rewards. (Don't we all?) If you ask them to do something, and they decide they actually *want* to do it because they know they'll get something good — a tiny piece of tuna, perhaps, or lots of fond attention — then yes, cats will respond to your cues. You *can* train a cat.

In this chapter, you'll find out how to get your cat litter-box–trained and even — if you so desire — how to toilet train your cat! You discover how to redirect scratching to the scratching post rather than the bedpost, and you find out why clicker training is one of the easiest methods around for training your cat. Are you ready to get started? How about getting the matter of your kitty's daily constitution out of the way first?

Not Going Outside the Box

The first order of training business for you and your adopted cat is making sure your cat understands that the litter box — and not your carpet, couch, or pile of fresh laundry — is her personal toilet. Most cats are easily trained to go in the litter box (for information on how to introduce your cat to the litter box, see Chapter 9). For some adopted cats, however, the litter box presents a particular challenge. Here's what to do about it.

Kitty, meet litter

Many adopted cats, especially older ones, already are trained to do their business in the litter box. But some cats seem particularly resistant to litter-box training, and you may not understand why. Perhaps they weren't provided with a litter box, or a clean litter box, in their former homes. Perhaps fear, insecurity, or a medical problem is causing a problem. Luckily, because cats like to use soil or sand for a bathroom, because they can scratch it loose and cover up their waste, most surfaces in your home won't be as appealing a spot as the litter box (except maybe that basket of laundry). However, if your cat is having a litter-box problem, don't despair. You can help reorient or teach your cat that the litter box really is the best place to go by reading on for strategies to help correct litter-box aversion.

Dealing with litter-box aversion

For unknown reasons, some cats simply do not find the litter box appealing. Perhaps your cat never was trained to use the litter box, just doesn't have that bury-the-waste gene in her body, or is having another health problem that makes her unable to control her natural elimination process. In that case, the best thing to do is start from square one by following these six steps:

1. **Have your cat checked by a veterinarian for any urinary tract or other health problem.**

   Sometimes, the problem really is as simple as an infection that needs medication or a switch in diet.

2. **Consider the type of litter box and filler you're using, and the placement of the litter box.**

   Different cats have different preferences, so the problem may be as simple as changing the type of litter box or filler or moving the litter box to a different location. If your cat always has accidents in a particular place, put the litter box in that place. Or, try a less busy area of the house, or maybe an area where you're around more often. Maybe your cat prefers a covered litter box for some privacy, or maybe that self-cleaning litter box is startling and scary. Some cats are even picky about how deep the litter is. Try putting in a little more litter, or a little less.

3. **Start litter-box training as though your cat doesn't know anything about the concept of a litter box — as if she were a brand new kitten no matter how old she is.**

   Just keep taking her to the litter box and showing her how fun it is. If she insists on not using it, confine her to one room for a while with her food, water, bed, and the litter box, placing it as far from the food and bed as possible. For more about litter- box training, see Chapter 9.

4. **Institute a more regular routine for the cat in your household.**

   Cats feel more secure and safe when they have a clear and consistent routine. Routine reduces stress and anxiety in pets, and sometimes litter-box issues are resolved when problems with stress are resolved. Establishing a routine is particularly important for adopted cats that have endured multiple changes in their environment.

5. **Practice kitty stress-relief.**

   Litter-box–training setbacks can be the result of your cat recently losing a home, being taken from the streets, having a litter of kittens, being abused, or suddenly being made to live with another cat, dog, small child, or other creatures. These all are obviously issues for adopted cats, and they're big sources of stress that can be the cause of litter-box–training problems. Being patient with your cat as it adjusts, doing your best to minimize stressful situations at home, and interacting gently and positively with your cat takes you further toward resolving these issues than becoming frustrated and angry. When your cat relaxes into her new home and gains confidence, she may feel perfectly happy about using that litter box.

Your cat can learn to use the litter box, but you need to be patient. Don't give up on her. Remember, some adopted cats learn quickly, but others need a little extra patience and gentle encouragement before they feel well enough, safe enough, and confident enough to do things your way. If your cat still refuses to use the litter box, and you've tried all of the strategies above, consider consulting a feline behavior consultant for help with your individual situation. Someone who interviews you and interacts with your cat may be able to come up with some ideas that are tailor-made for you. Later in this chapter, you'll find information about how to find a feline behavioral consultant.

Your Cat: Mighty Hunter

Many feline behaviors are related to a cat's natural hunting instinct. Some of these behaviors may seem like problems when a cat comes to live inside a human house: scratching, pouncing, biting, yowling, hyperactivity, prowling around at night, and of course, bringing you those little furry or feathered "presents" freshly killed from the great outdoors. Rather than yell or swat at your cat for doing these things, you need to (against your own natural instinct, perhaps) praise him.

Come again? Yes, that's right. You need to praise your cat for being a good cat. But you also need to redirect the behavior that doesn't work for you by showing your cat the ways he can exercise his natural instincts that are socially acceptable in a human world. Keeping you up at night or drawing blood are obviously not acceptable situations, even if they are natural for your cat. You can, however, do something about those issues. You just need to work within your cat's instinctual framework. This strategy will leave your cat fulfilled but still leave plenty of time for purring and petting.

Letting your cat sleep all day means that at night he's more than likely going to be awake. If, on the other hand, you spend several active play sessions engaged in hunting-like activities with your cat during the day, he more than likely will adjust his natural schedule, sleep during the night, and consider his toys (and not your fingers and toes) as his prey.

During play, don't let your cat pounce on you, but instead encourage him to pounce on his toys and praise him when he does. Good kitty! Good mighty hunter! And if he does bring you back a dead rodent or other small animal that he's proudly slain in quest of being the mighty cat of your household, then yes . . . take a deep breath, look the other way, and praise him. "Thank you kitty." Then, when he isn't looking, dispose of the victim.

Don't bother trying to train the hunter out of your cat. Cats need to fulfill a natural impulse to hunt, and adopted cats that have spent plenty of time outdoors can be quite good at it. Just remember that with the right direction, he can fulfill his natural impulses harmlessly. That's what all those great cat toys are for.

And if you don't want your cat killing small animals, keep him inside, which is the safest option for everyone — your cat and the local wildlife.

Scratch Zone

Scratching and clawing are instinctual behaviors for cats. They truly can't help it. In the wild, cats mark their territory by leaving scratch marks on trees, and this scratching also conditions their muscles and tendons and helps them keep their claws in top condition. Scratching helps shed the outer, old layers of cat claw. Cats also scratch to mark their territory, releasing pheromones from glands in their paws. Although humans can't smell these subtle aromas, other cats can. The pheromones are unique to each cat, telling other cats who is hanging out where, who is ready for breeding, and who is in charge. Even if you have no other cats in the house, your cat can't help doing it. It's instinct, pure and simple.

So how do you deal with your scratching cat? Some people automatically assume that the best option is to have a cat declawed. However, this painful and invasive surgery puts cats at a disadvantage if they ever need to climb a tree to escape a predator or defend themselves. Many vets are opposed to declawing, while others are willing to perform this surgery. The subject is controversial, so do some reading about it before you decide to take the drastic step of having part of your cat surgically removed.

A better option (in my opinion) is to teach your cat to use her claws responsibly. The best way to do that is to give cats plenty of acceptable scratching options and train them to scratch where you want them to scratch, rather than wherever they may decide (without any guidance) to scratch on their own. Your cat needs at least one, but preferably several, good scratching posts (see Figure 11-1). Carpeted cat trees, boards tightly wrapped in rough twine, and heavy corrugated cardboard make good scratching options; some of them you can construct for practically nothing. Your local pet store has many options if you don't want to build your own, or browse the stores to get ideas. Whenever you catch your kitty scratching somewhere you don't like, immediately take the cat to one of his scratching posts. You can even help guide his paws along the acceptable surface.

Be sure to praise your cat when she scratches the right place, and if she approaches the scratching post or cat tree and starts scratching on her own, give her a healthy cat treat such as a tiny bit of chicken or tuna, a commercially made premium cat treat, or just an affectionate stroking. Reward good behavior whenever you see it, instead of focusing only on the behavior you don't like.

Figure 11-1:
A scratching post provides an acceptable place for your cat to exercise his natural instinct to scratch.

All about catnip

She purrs, rolls, kicks her legs in ecstasy, tries to bury her head in the carpet and wobbles and weaves. Is your cat drunk? Is she sick? Is something very, very wrong? A cat's normal reaction to catnip may look pretty strange, and many pet owners worry that catnip is somehow harmful or addictive. However, this member of the mint family is a harmless herb that won't cause your cat any health problems and isn't addictive. Cats just seem to love it. You can buy catnip or its spray form in the store, or you can grow it in your garden. Catnip is hearty and easy to grow in most climates. Not all cats react to catnip, and those exposed to it too often tend to lose interest; however, catnip can't be beat for an occasional treat or as a way to attract your cat to a scratching post, cat bed, or toy.

Sometimes, providing attractive scratching alternatives is enough, but other times your cat insists on scratching the carpet, the back of the recliner, or the doorframes. When that happens, you need to redirect your cat's behavior. Supervise your cat carefully, and every time you see her scratch in an unacceptable location, say "No!" and move her to an acceptable location. Respond the same way if your cat tries to dig those claws into *you*. Help her put her paws on the scratching post surface and move them in a downward direction. If she scratches there, praise her or even offer her a tiny treat. Cats respond well to positive reinforcement, so consistently redirecting her to the right spot *and* rewarding her for using it work quickly with most cats.

You can also make scratching posts more attractive by rubbing or spraying catnip scent on them. Always reward scratching done in the right places and redirect scratching in the wrong places. Pretty soon your adopted cat happily scratches the scratching post as though she never dreamed of scratching anywhere else.

If a cat/kitten is absolutely set on scratching, and you want a temporary fix while you're trying to train her, check your local pet store for a set of "soft paws." These plastic sticky claw covers, applied to each sharp claw, keep cats from ripping and tearing furniture, carpets, and even skin. They can be a bit tricky to put on the first time, but they are a harmless and non-invasive way to cap your cat's nails for a few weeks while trying to get a handle on the situation. I haven't met a cat that reacted violently to them, just crabby for a day or so because they probably feel a little strange.

Foiling the Climbing Cat

Some cats never would think of scaling the drapes or shinnying up the Christmas tree, but others — especially kittens — think this kind of high-flying action is pretty darned amusing. You won't think it amusing, however, if you end up with snagged and tattered window treatments or a tipped-over Christmas tree surrounded by shattered ornaments.

In nature, cats climb, and they like to be up high so they can see what's going on — potential prey, potential hazards, potential bowl full of Fancy Feast. You can enact two basic, simple strategies to keep cats from climbing:

✔ Block access to spots where you don't want your cat to climb.

✔ Provide your cat with alternative climbing spots where he's allowed to climb.

Unless you're constantly supervising your cat, some other strategies you can employ are

✔ Tying back your draperies so they're out of the way and your kitten can't get to them.

✔ Keeping your cat out of the room where the Christmas tree or other climbable plants are in place.

✔ Removing or blocking access to all potentially scaleable surfaces.

After you take these preventive measures, you still need to fulfill your cat's need to perch on high. Cat trees are perfect for this purpose. They enable your cat plenty of places to climb, crawl through, hide in, explore, or perch upon in a kingly fashion. A house with a cat can't have too many cat trees. Whenever your cat tries to climb something unacceptable, simply place him on the cat tree and then praise him. He soon gets the picture.

If obsessive climbing seems to be related to fear or anxiety, talk to your vet and consider consulting a feline behaviorist.

Attack Cat: Biting, Scratching, and Pouncing

You thought you adopted a sweet little kitty but now you've got a wildcat on your hands — biting, scratching and pouncing on your hand, your foot, your head. This common problem is evident especially with kittens, but also with some adult cats that remain particularly active and playful or that never were taught not to engage in this type of mock hunting behavior. Yes, that's what your cat is doing. She plays like this with her siblings early in life and continues to pretend to hunt by attacking you.

But some attack behaviors are more serious. Some research suggests that attack behavior is more common in kittens that were raised or fostered apart from their littermates, perhaps because they never learned about appropriate interaction with other cats, an important part of a cat's social development.

Cats can also attack owners because of transferred aggression. For example, they may see a stray cat outside and feel threatened, but can't attack the cat so they channel that aggression onto you. Some cats also attack out of boredom or frustration at not having another cat to play with.

This behavior isn't malicious. In most cases, it's natural cat behavior or a perfectly understandable behavioral response to unnatural conditions of living inside with humans. But, you protest, your socks are all snagged, and your ankles are bloody! Understandable. Certainly, nobody wants to be attacked, and you can redirect your kitten's hunting instinct, prey drive, or play drive. Here's how:

- ✔ When your cat tries to attack you, freeze. Do not move. Prey animals do this, too. Cats are attracted to moving, fleeing things. If you stand perfectly still or hold your hands perfectly still, your cat may just lose interest.

- ✔ Recognize the signs when your cat is about to pounce so you can quickly redirect her to something other than your flesh. You know the hunting and/or attack mode is engaged when your cat's

  - Tail is twitching or swishing quickly back and forth.

  - Eyes are dilated.

  - Posture is in a crouching position.

- ✔ When your cat is in the mood for a hunt, provide her with things to hunt. Small stuffed mice, toy birds or feathers on a "fishing pole" or elastic string, squeaky toys, sparkly balls, wind-up toys . . . all can provide her with hours of pouncing fun, with nary a scratch or puncture wound. Just be careful to select toys that are safe for cats and won't come apart or present a choking hazard.

- ✔ When your cat is enjoying an ecstatic catnip-toy play session, keep your hands and feet away. She's more likely to nip and scratch when in the throes of catnip euphoria.

- ✔ When your cat bites you, immediately separate yourself from her. Immediately! Your cat is motivated to get your attention, and if biting causes her to lose your attention, she will stop doing it. Remember to reward her when she plays with you nicely.

If these diversions don't do the trick, you probably need to consult a feline behaviorist if:

- ✔ Your cat's biting and scratching seem truly defensive or aggressive.
- ✔ You think your cat is truly attacking rather than playing.
- ✔ You can't seem to effectively redirect your cat.
- ✔ You or other family members are becoming afraid of the cat. Consulting a feline behaviorist is especially important when you or family members are afraid of the cat.

The Amazing Disappearing Kitty: Shyness and Hiding

Some cats, like some people, are naturally shy. Some adopted cats, however, may be unusually shy, even to the point that fear impedes their ability to function normally. Fear is, of course, a survival instinct that protects cats from danger. However, if your adopted cat had traumatic or frightening experiences as kitten between 3 and 7 weeks of age (a time perhaps long before you ever met your cat), she can retain the effects of this experience throughout her life.

Obviously you can't go back in time, but you can help your cat overcome her fear and shyness with extra patience and sensitivity. When you first bring your cat home, don't worry too much or become irritated if she hides from you. You can try to coax her out, but give her as much time as she needs and be patient. Speak in a soft voice, offer her treats, and keep the household quiet, calm, and nonthreatening. Help build her confidence in you and in herself by providing her with a routine, punctuated by plenty of encouraging but gentle talk and frequent rewards for even the tiniest progression toward trust. So she finally stuck one paw out from under the bed, eh? Well now, that deserves a treat. It may take a long time for a troubled cat, but eventually you can show her that she has nothing to fear from you.

After you've gained her trust, you can desensitize or help her to get used to other more stimulating noises and people in tiny doses. If your cat always hides whenever company comes over, that's fine. Let her come out in her own time.

As long as she gets plenty of interaction time with the people she knows and trusts, you don't need to force a shy cat to change her personality. However, if your adopted cat remains frightened even of you, or if she refuses to come out or to eat after a week or two of trying to help her adjust, talk to your vet and/or a feline behaviorist. Either should be able to provide you with specific advice about strategies to help your cat regain her confidence.

Harry Hou-Kitty: The Escape Artist Cat

Adopted cats that spent a lot of time wandering outside may actually enjoy that kind of life and may not be happy about suddenly becoming an indoor cat. Although living indoors certainly is much safer for cats, your outdoor cat is likely try to slip back outside through cracked doors, loose screens, and open windows. Remember, cats have the compulsion to hunt. They want to be outside where all the prey animals are hiding.

If your cat truly needs to be outside, you can leash-train your cat, or let him out in a fenced area as long as you can supervise him and know that he can't get over the fence. You can also (with supervision) attach a long lead from his collar to a stake or tree in the yard so he can explore. Never leave your cat alone while he's tied up outside. Many unsupervised cats have been attacked by other animals or were strangled by their leashes or collars! Cats that are trained to walk on a leash happily explore the neighborhood with you in tow, but don't expect them to heel. Do, however, expect to get comments from interested neighbors.

Meanwhile, be careful not to let your cat out by mistake or accident. Instruct other family members, especially children, to latch doors to the outside. Get in the habit of watching to be sure that the cat isn't getting ready to slip out the door unobserved under your feet when you open it. Keep screens over open windows and patio doors, and keep those screens well patched.

Keeping ID tags on your cat and/or making sure your cat is microchipped (many shelters and rescue groups require this) gives you peace of mind, in the event your cat does escape. You're much easier to find if your information is clearly displayed on your cat's collar. And if the collar is lost, a microchip may be the clue that leads to you and your cat being reunited.

Roaming is dangerous for cats. People often feel guilty that they don't allow their cats to wander freely outside, especially when they've adopted cats that formerly lived in the great outdoors. Wandering cats are frequently killed by cars, chased and attacked by dogs, wounded or killed in cat fights, or picked up and kept by people who don't take good care of them. The world outside simply isn't safe for wandering pets, so do the right, safe, and responsible thing as a good loving pet owner and keep your cat inside.

Cat Talk: When Your Cat Just Won't Be Quiet

Meow. Murrr. Mau. Meeeoo. Some cats keep quiet, but others just can't seem to stop talking. Communicative cats talk to get your attention, express their needs and desire, or make their displeasure clear to all. If your cat is a talker be glad she's so willing to try to speak to you. And yet sometimes all that noise gets a little irritating.

Never punish your cat for talking! Instead, try to distract her into doing something else. If she's talking at night, she needs more exercise during the day. If she's following you around, talking, give her some focused attention and play-time, even if only for a few minutes. If she talks to be fed, don't fall into the trap of rewarding her with a treat every time she talks. True, she can't meow if she is eating, but rewards like these reinforce her talkative nature. Plus, too many treats can lead to a weight problem. For a beggar, get in the habit of giving her rewards that aren't always food treats — a toy, some petting, a round of "catch the feathers," or whatever she enjoys.

Cat on Cat: Sibling Rivalry and Other-Pet Issues

Bringing an adopted cat into your home when you already have another cat or dog can be particularly challenging. In some cases, resident pets and new cats get along just fine after a few initial hisses and swats to establish dominance. In other cases, however, you can run into some pretty serious issues. Resident cats may feel extremely neglected and may behave aggressively toward a new cat or even become depressed and stop eating. Cats are extremely territorial, so the resident cat may feel comfortably established in your home and wonder, "What's with this new interloper?"

An adopted cat, on the other hand, may feel ill-at-ease about coming into a home with a resident cat or a dog, especially if he has never lived with other pets before. He may feel fearful, insecure, or even aggressive, emotions that have serious consequences and can result in cat fights and injury. As the pet owner, you must create a balance between the resident cat's need to feel special and appreciated and not neglected, and the new cat's need to feel he has a place in his new home and that he's loved and cared for. Both cats need their own litter boxes, food and water bowls, their own space, and their own escape routes whenever they interact, just in case one or the other suddenly feels the need to leave the situation.

In Chapter 9, you find detailed information about introducing two cats or a cat and a dog with the best results. If you've done everything right, and you're still experiencing problems, seek advice from a feline behaviorist. Aggression is the second most common reason (after litter-box issues) that people visit animal behaviorists, and it often is caused by problems between pets. A professional can take a detailed history of your pets, find out about your setup at home, and give you some targeted advice relevant to your individual situation. In most cases, with informed strategies, pets can learn to coexist peacefully.

Calming Kitten Chaos

If you have adopted a kitten, you may be shocked to realize how energetic they are: like little furry bullets of destruction! Kittens have a lot of energy, just like human children, puppies, or youngsters of any species. You can no more expect a kitten to sit still and behave than you can a toddler. Kittens need outlets for that energy, and if you don't provide them, your kitten will amuse herself in her own way, which, of course, can mean total chaos.

Instead of letting your kitten race wildly around unchecked and unchanneled, schedule regular play sessions for her so you can interact in an active and stimulating way. Many cats quickly learn to fetch a small ball if you throw it and figure out that you'll do it again if they bring it back. Kittens love to leap after cat teasers, bat at feathers, or chase a flashlight beam around the room. This active kind of play not only tones and conditions a kitten's body but also helps develop her mind, her natural intelligence, and her bond with you.

Preoccupied though she may seem with birds outside the window or dust bunnies under the bed, your kitten craves your attention. If she can be all-kitten and have your attention too, she'll be in kitty heaven. Wear her out at least twice a day with nice long play sessions, and she'll be much less likely to make mischief when you turn your attention elsewhere.

If your cat seems truly hyperactive, and no matter how much you play with her, she seems unable to settle down, or if she behaves nervously or seems anxious, fearful, or skittish, have your vet check her out to make sure she's healthy. If she's okay, then, consult a feline behaviorist or cat trainer for advice.

Finding a Feline Behaviorist

Cat owners may feel frustrated when they have training or behavior issues. The world may seem chock-full of dog trainers, but seriously lacking in cat obedience classes and behavioral consultants. True, more people consult professionals about behavioral problems in dogs than in cats, and some less-experienced or less-educated behavioral consultants may mistakenly apply the same theories and practices to cats that they use on dogs. That's why finding someone who specializes in, has considerable experience with, and understands the unique personality and nature of cats is so important.

Applied feline behaviorists (the term for a behaviorist specializing in problems with pet cats) can help you to address issues of anxiety, fear, aggression, and failure to bond with humans in ways that may never have occurred to you by evaluating your individual situation, pet, home life, and interactions. They can help with seeming simpler litter-box training and multipet household issues, and if qualified, even prescribe medication to help with severe problems.

Although your local cat club may not offer basic obedience classes, its members may be able to help you find a specialist in feline behavior, but you need to know what you're looking for. Anyone can call himself a behavioral consultant, but veterinary behaviorists must have a veterinary degree, and many applied animal behaviorists have advanced degrees in animal behavior in addition to training experience, so you should always ask for references and credentials. Even if you can't find an applied feline behaviorist in your area, many of these professionals do consultations over the phone. Some of the places you can look for a professional who can help you with the behavioral issues you and your cat can't seem to work out on your own are

- ✔ Your veterinarian. Ask your vet to refer you to a feline behaviorist.

- ✔ The online directory of certified applied animal behaviorists on the Web site for the Animal Behavior Society at `www.animalbehavior.org/Applied/CAAB_directory.html`.

- ✔ The Internet. Search "animal behaviorist" or "feline behaviorist" on your favorite search engine and check out the Web sites of the many professionals to find one who has a practice near you or one who does phone consultations.

Training Your Cat the Easy Way

Many cats already have excellent manners, thank you very much. However, cats can learn some additional behaviors you may not believe. You can teach a cat cues to Sit, lie Down, Stay, Come, and other basic obedience commands. Some people want to train their cat so he learns to:

- ✔ Sit and won't escape when you open the front door.

- ✔ Walk nicely on a leash so he can enjoy the great outdoors safely.

- ✔ Come to you when you call him for grooming or cuddling.

- ✔ Stay when staying is in his best interest and safety.

Okay, the truth is some cats don't have any interest in learning verbal cues, or they learn them but do what you say only if they darn well feel like it. But many other cats think that following cues is great fun, and they enjoy the bonding and time you spend together in training sessions.

Training a cat is exactly the same as it is for training a dog. Rather than repeat that information here, just turn to Chapter 7 and read the sections about training the "Sit," "Heel," "Come," and "Stay" cues for dogs and do the same things for your cat. Yes, the cat has to think the effort to be trained is worth it, but many cats are highly motivated to achieve rewards and attention. ***Remember:*** Just because most people don't bother to obedience train a cat doesn't mean that it can't be done. Plenty of people have done it, and you can, too.

Clicker training, or another similar training method that marks a particular behavior with a quick sound or signal and then rewards for it, is the best way to motivate a cat, so read about clicker training in Chapter 7 and give it a try. Clicker training works quickly and is a highly effective method for training cats.

Part IV
Befriending a Little Critter

The 5th Wave   By Rich Tennant

"Oh, it was so cute. He looked at me with those big ears, his nose twitching, and he started hopping up and down. That's when I said, 'Arthur, stop hopping up and down! We'll go pick out a rabbit this afternoon.'"

In this part . . .

They may be mammals, but they aren't your ordinary run-of-the-mill dogs or cats, no-sir-ee. This part of the book is passionately devoted to the little critters that are so popular as pets but so often abandoned when kids get tired of feeding the bunny or the hamster bites out of self-defense and nobody wants to touch him again. If a critter is your speed, don't go to the pet store! Instead use this part of the book to find out how to find an adopted critter that needs a new home, to discover more about the needs, personalities, care, and feeding of different kinds of critters, and how to track down a veterinarian who specializes in small-animal care. Heck, you even discover that you can actually train a rat or a bunny or a ferret, and I tell you how in this part of the book.

Chapter 12

Choosing Your Critter

In This Chapter

▶ Determining whether an adopted small animal is the best pet for you

▶ Choosing the perfect critter to adopt

▶ Finding a critter through a shelter or small-animal-specific rescue group

You adopt dogs and cats at animal shelters, right? Actually, animal shelters take in more than just your standard-issue canines and felines. Many people relinquish their smaller critters to shelters when they can't care for them anymore, so shelters often have ferrets, rabbits, guinea pigs, hamsters, rats, and other small furry little creatures that desperately need homes. Adopting a small animal from a shelter or small-animal rescue group is a great way to do something nice for an animal in need. A small animal may just fit *your* needs better than a needy, barking dog or a prowling, yowling cat.

In this chapter, you find out what it means to adopt a small animal and what owning a small animal entails. Small animals are perfect for certain kinds of pet owners but not such a great choice for others. You get a quick overview of the variety of small animals that frequently are available for adoption and what each is like, so you can decide whether a small animal — and which one — is right for you. You also get information about where to find small animals to adopt and how to go about adopting one from a shelter or rescue group.

Considering a Little Critter

Adopting a small animal may seem like a no-brainer, yet, small animals are pets, too, and they require veterinary care, maintenance, attention, stimulation, and interaction, just like any other pet. Before you decide that a small animal is an easier alternative to a more traditional pet, check out the following facts about little critters (for details about specific small animals, see "Finding the Critter That's Right For You" later in this chapter):

✔ Most small animals are nocturnal and thus are busy, active, and sometimes loud and distracting at night. Although they probably won't vocalize, they will be busy running in their wheels and moving around.

✔ Many small animals live surprisingly long lives, so caring for a critter can be a long-term commitment.

✔ Because most small animals live in enclosures, they need to be kept fastidiously clean and well fed with a constant supply of fresh clean water to prevent starvation or dehydration that can quickly occur. When an animal is tiny, it needs to eat and drink often.

On the other hand, small animals can make rewarding pets for people who aren't so sure they want to walk a dog every day or spend their evenings vacuuming up cat hair. Small animals are undeniably adorable, cuddly, and tactile, with their soft fur and wiggly ways. Some love to be held, and others prefer to interact with you in other ways. Most of them can be hand-tamed and even trained to come when called or perform tricks for treats.

The short version is just this: Small animals take a different kind of work than dogs and cats, but caring for them provides many of the same rewards and benefits. Is this the pet for you? Read on to find out.

Exploring the appeal of small-animal pets

Small animals make great pets . . . for some people. They can be fun and interesting to observe in their habitats or just the cutest creatures that you can imagine. Consider adopting a small animal if any of the following apply to you:

✔ You want a pet, but you're away from home most of the day and can't come home in the middle of the day to walk a dog or stroke a cat.

✔ You travel frequently and can't take a pet with you, but you have a willing friend, neighbor, or pet sitter who can tend to your pet's needs while you're away.

✔ You don't want to exercise a dog every day.

✔ You like to have life and movement in your home but aren't crazy about a big furry pet following you around all day or getting on your lap all the time.

✔ You don't mind cleaning out a cage and changing litter once a week. Little bits of animal waste are fine, as long as they don't resemble your own.

✔ You think it makes perfect sense to pay a veterinarian for the care of any critter, no matter how small.

✔ You feel sorry for all the little prey animals out there that are subject to the hungers of animal predators and the dangers of traps — you want to save them all.

✔ You think common pets are boring. Exotic mammals like ferrets and chinchillas fascinate you, and you want to learn their ways and take care of their needs.

Deciding you and small critters aren't a fit

Small animal ownership isn't for everyone or every situation. Even if you like the idea of adopting a small animal, you probably need to avoid doing so if any of the following apply to you:

✔ You have prey-oriented dogs or cats (or snakes) that are clever at solving problems — like how to get to that gerbil — and good at getting into things you thought you'd safely put away.

✔ You tend to be forgetful and may neglect to feed and water a small animal every day. Small animals can't last very long without food and water, and they can't bark or meow or get in your way to remind you to feed them.

✔ You don't like cleaning out a small animal cage every week.

✔ You fear getting bitten, nipped, or scratched. Small animals are prey animals with strong instincts to protect themselves when they're fearful.

✔ You want a pet that, like a baby, will interact frequently with you in a rewarding way, making you feel truly cherished and special. Although many people obtain these benefits from small animals, small animals don't interact with people in the same way dogs and cats do, and thus they may not provide you with the kind of bonding and total adoration you seek.

✔ You have kids who — charming as they surely are — can't keep their hands off things and haven't yet developed a sense of self-control.

Pairing kids with critters: Perfect pet or potential problem?

When considering a child's first pet, people often think first of small animals. Although small animals can indeed make great pets for responsible, gentle children, they're not the default perfect pet for all kids. Consider that small animals:

✔ Don't bond with children in the same way that dogs or even cats do.

✔ Are delicate. If a child wants to poke, prod, and carry around — or even drop — a small pet, tragedy can result.

Many small animals have been severely injured or killed unintentionally by the careless or clumsy handling of a small child, and many small children have been bitten and scratched by small animals trying to defend themselves. There is no quicker way to turn a child off of pet ownership like a sharp bite from a hamster or a sound scratching from a rabbit scrambling for safety.

✔ Are not more disposable than dogs or cats. However, many people see them that way, which is why so many small animals are abandoned in shelters and with rescue groups. Please don't adopt a small animal to test a child's readiness for a better pet and then abandon the animal (or worse, allow it to perish) just to prove the child isn't ready for pet ownership. This kind of thing happens all too often and is exactly the kind of thing that shelters and rescue groups are trying to prevent when they place small animals with people they hope are responsible caretakers. Don't forget: Small animals are pets, too!

On the other hand, kids who are responsible and mature enough to understand how to handle a small animal with safety and care actually can get a great deal of enjoyment and even education from a small pet animal. I have two little boys, so don't be offended by the following evaluations of childhood maturity and responsibility. I know what it's like to recognize when my own kids weren't yet ready for the temptation of a small pet to play with — neither could be reliably trusted to hold our hamster until about 8 years of age. When deciding whether your child can be mature and responsible enough to handle and help care for a small animal, consider the following:

✔ **Age:** Any child can live with a small animal, but children younger than 7 may not be able to *handle* a small animal. Let them look but not touch, unless you're holding the animal and allowing the child to pet it while you maintain control.

✔ **Maturity level:** Is your child a little grown-up in miniature? Or, does your child tend to lose control, have tantrums, try daredevil stunts? Is your child coordinated or prone to dropping things or losing track of what he's doing? Evaluate whether your child makes smart decisions on his own, or whether she has a good sense of what is safe for herself and others. Please be realistic about your child's maturity level before giving him or her that little gerbil or bunny as a pet.

✔ **Responsible nature:** Does your child play quietly, act calm, and have empathy for small creatures? If so, your child may be a good match for a small animal. But if your child isn't responsible for his own actions yet, is likely to take a small animal out without asking, or may just want to see what happens if she pushes the guinea pig down the driveway on a skateboard, please spare the poor creature and wait until your child is willing and able to maintain self-control and follow the rules.

Any pet in any household is the responsibility of the adult, and the adult must be the ultimate caretaker. Children can learn plenty about responsibility by taking care of a small animal, but if they forget to clean the cage or change the water, the adult must be vigilant enough to intervene and make sure these important jobs are accomplished, one way or another.

Finding the Critter That's Right for You

If you think you're the small-animal type, take the next step; check out the following sections, which briefly describe the joys and challenges associated with specific small animals. Look for aspects you can't live with and the ones that sound particularly appealing. Your answer — the particular pet you have been waiting for all along — may be obvious.

After getting tired of caring for small animals, many owners either release their rabbits, mice, or other domesticated small animals into the wild where they rarely survive, or they give them to a shelter where many end up being euthanized. Reading the following sections is vital to ensuring that your new pet doesn't end up as a statistic.

By the way, keeping gerbils, ferrets, certain kinds of birds, and hedgehogs as pets is illegal in California. Some of these pets also are illegal in other areas, so check your local ordinances to make sure the pet you want is on the up-and-up.

Ferret facts

Ferrets (see Figure 12-1) are adorable but challenging little creatures with high energy levels that don't really ease up much as they age, so consider the following before you decide whether you're up for the challenge of owning a ferret:

- **Time commitment:** Ferrets are a commitment — they can live up to ten years or even longer. They also need a few hours every day out of their cages for supervised play time, and plenty of attention, interaction, and even training from you. Ferrets are *not* a low-maintenance pet.

- **Attention requirements:** Ferrets require plenty of exercise, interaction, and training. They can, however, be taught to walk on a leash and use a litter box, and most of them enjoy a good (leashed) romp in the snow.

- **Tendency for trouble:** Ferrets are good at getting themselves into trouble or getting into things you didn't think they could possibly find, reach, or fit inside. They can climb, leap, and knock things over, fall, or get stuck inside furniture, walls, toilets, and other "how the heck did he get in there" places. They also love to chew and eat things that you really wished they hadn't gotten their teeth around, especially sponge or foam rubber, which can get stuck in their intestines, causing a blockage and requiring expensive emergency veterinary care.

- **Housing:** Ferrets don't tolerate heat well, so they must be kept inside under temperate conditions. In addition, because of their tendency to get into trouble (see previous bullet) when not supervised, ferrets need to live in a roomy, comfortable enclosure — typically a ferret cage — with plenty of places to climb, explore, sleep, eat, and play.

✔ **Cost:** The ferret cages I describe in the previous bullet can be expensive and so can ferret care. Ferrets need a premium ferret food (if you absolutely can't find ferret food, you can use Iams kitten food — many other brands of kitten food are not nutritionally appropriate for ferrets), regular vet visits, and they must be spayed or neutered to prevent serious behavior and health problems and control odor. Spaying is a must, because females can get a life-threatening anemia if they're neither spayed nor bred. Ferrets also need regular vaccinations, just like dogs and cats.

✔ **Odor:** Neutering the male ferret helps a lot with odor control, but even a neutered and descented ferret has a unique musky odor that ferret owners must be willing to tolerate. Although most ferrets are spayed or castrated and descented before they leave the breeding farm (most end up with a "dot dot" tattoo in the ear to indicate their status), ferret clubs and associations are beginning to discourage descenting because they think it isn't necessary — ferrets rarely use their scent glands and with or without the glands, the body odor stays the same.

✔ **Special considerations:** Some ferrets in need of rescue actually are deaf — usually the white ones. This condition is hereditary and is common in many white animals, including dogs and cats. But a deaf ferret still can make an excellent pet. Hearing-impaired ferrets require extra patience and training, however. For more information about deaf ferrets, see the section on ferret health in Chapter 14.

Be aware that some states, cities, and local areas require permits for ferrets, and some don't allow ferrets as pets at all. For example, it is illegal (although this law always is being contested) to own a ferret in California. Please don't adopt a ferret if you live in an area where they are not legal. You risk having the animal taken away, and your adopted ferret doesn't need to lose yet another home.

Figure 12-1:
Ferrets are related to weasels, minks, and otters, and they resemble their long-bodied, bright-eyed cousins. The ferret's long skinny torso enables him to squeeze through tiny spaces.

Rabbit run-down

Who doesn't love an Easter bunny? The following may help you decide whether you do:

✔ Rabbits may look cuddly and cute, but many of them do not enjoy being handled or held. Rabbits are the quintessential prey animal, and they exhibit strong instincts to protect themselves by fleeing in fear at the slightest hint that they may be in danger.

✔ Rabbits need regular vet care, and they need to be spayed or neutered to prevent the extremely high risk of cancer of the reproductive organs in females and unpleasant behavioral changes related to hormone surges in males, including aggressive behavior like lunging and nipping, and destructive behavior.

Of course, if you have two bunnies of opposite sexes, altering them prevents reproduction — something that's otherwise nearly impossible to prevent in rabbits (you've heard that story).

Guinea-pig guide

Guinea pigs, or *cavies* as their fans and devotees call them — their actual Latin name is *Cavia porcellus* — are winning little critters originally hailing from New Guinea. They come in several different types, with short, wavy, or long hair (see Figure 12-2). The following considerations give you an idea of what to expect from raising a cavy:

✔ **Vocal creatures:** Guinea pigs talk a lot with many different sounds: squeaks, wheeks, whinnies, snorts, grunts, purrs, and more. Many of these sounds are reserved for communication with humans. If your pigs see you opening the refrigerator door, prepare for a chorus of excited wheek-wheek-wheeks.

✔ **Attention requirements:** Guinea pigs are social and much happier with other cavies around, particularly in a so-called *harem* with one male and several females. They also like plenty of attention from humans, particularly the ones bearing food. Although they need regular attention, guinea pigs are lower maintenance than some small animals. As long as they have food, water, a clean cage, and other cavies to cavort with, they won't mind if your attention is elsewhere.

✔ **Care and maintenance requirements:** Guinea pigs need vet care if they are injured or sick. Females need to be spayed, or you should be prepared never to let them mingle with males when they're fully mature, because the pelvic bones fuse with only a narrow opening if they're not bred while young. Breeding attempts can subsequently injure the mature female. Their cages need frequent thorough cleaning and frequent fresh water changes, and guinea pigs require extra vitamin C added to their diets, preferably in the form of supplements and fresh fruits and vegetables. The long-haired pigs need regular grooming to keep their coats in good condition.

✔ **Housing:** Because they can get foot injuries from wire-bottomed cages, guinea pigs need to be housed in cages with solid bottoms. They need plenty of room so they should have a spacious enclosure.

✔ **Tendency for trouble:** Guinea pigs are relatively docile, tending not to bite and scratch, so they make good pets for gentle kids whose parents are willing to take the responsibility to ensure they're kept clean, watered, and fed.

Figure 12-2: Guinea pigs like to talk to you and sit on your lap, but they can be nervous about being held high above the floor unless you get them used to it at a young age.

Rats rule

Rats are among the most sociable and arguably the most intelligent of the small mammals. With good cleanliness practices and lots of interaction, rats also are among the most rewarding of the small animals because they are so interactive and interested in you. They are also very easy to train and can live five to seven years in captivity. Just check out the following to see whether rat-human bonding is the kind of pet experience you seek:

✔ **Attention requirements:** Rats want and need plenty of attention and can actually interact with humans in a fairly sophisticated way, compared to some small animals. Rats also prefer to live with other rats, so get at least two same-sex rats (you don't want to contribute to an unwanted litter and more unwanted rats!).

✔ **Tendency for trouble:** Rats enjoy supervised play time outside their cages, but free-roaming rats can get stuck in some pretty weird places and just won't be safe — not to mention the chewing damage they can cause to your home — if you let them do their own thing.

✔ **Housing:** Rats have particularly delicate respiratory systems and never should be kept in bedding made from wood shavings with phenols in them, particularly cedar and pine. (Some wood shavings are marked "phenol-free" and those are fine.) Most rats have a pathogen in their lungs called *microplasma* that is almost impossible to get rid of. If aggravated by phenols, bad ventilation, or a dirty cage, it can cause pneumonia and other serious respiratory problems and even death. Antibiotics administered by a vet can control the condition but usually won't cure it. Therefore, their cages need to be well ventilated — no glass tanks please — and kept very clean, with recycled paper bedding. Rats also can develop a foot infection called *bumblefoot,* which may be caused by wire cage floors.

Hamster and gerbil handbook

Hamsters and gerbils sure are cute little critters, and they are the ubiquitous child's first pet. See if they work for you by considering the following:

✔ **Attention requirements:** Gerbils are sociable, but be sure any small animals housed together are properly sexed! It can be hard to tell what sex a dwarf hamster or gerbil is, and you don't want to make more unwanted babies. That's how many hamsters and gerbils wind up in shelters. Hamsters and gerbils require less interaction than some small animals, although many are happily hand-tame. If nobody ever handles these small mammals, they'd probably be perfectly happy with their hamster or gerbil friends and appropriate housing (see the upcoming bullet in this list).

✔ **Tendency for trouble:** Small children always need to be supervised when handling hamsters and gerbils. One quick jump and these little critters can plummet to the ground, injuring themselves or scampering off and getting lost.

✔ **Housing:** Appropriate housing includes a large clean cage with a wheel for exercise, multiple levels for exploring, and fresh food and water.

✔ **Special considerations:** Golden hamsters are larger than dwarf hamsters, but both have similar care needs. Golden hamsters, however, need to be kept singly to prevent fighting. Same-sex dwarf hamsters, on the other hand, get along just fine together and enjoy the company.

Always be sure the hamster or gerbil you adopt has dry fur, particularly a dry tail, and bright clear eyes. Otherwise, you may be adopting a sick pet that needs veterinary care.

Backing away from that wild baby bunny

Don't even think about taking in that seemingly abandoned baby bunny in the yard. Okay, you may not be able to keep from thinking about it, or even moving it out of the way of the dogs in your backyard, but here's the truth: Wild baby bunnies almost always die in captivity. That nest of bunnies you found probably isn't abandoned, anyway. Mother rabbits usually make their nests out in the open, and come to nurse their babies about five minutes during the middle of the night, then leave for the rest of the time. The mother probably is coming back, but if you move the bunnies, she will be extremely distressed trying to find them. If you disturb the nest, try as best you can to cover it back up the way it was and then *leave the baby bunnies alone.* Leaving them alone gives the bunnies their best chance for survival. If you know for a fact the mother has been killed — for instance, if your dog or cat killed the mother — or if the baby bunny is injured, immediately contact the humane society to find a skilled wildlife rehabilitator. Rehabilitating a baby bunny is extremely tricky, and most people won't be successful trying to do it themselves. For more information about this subject, see the House Rabbit Society's Web page at www.rabbit.org.

Mouse manifesto

Mice are tiny guys that are pretty much the same as the wild mice you may find running around under your sink or in your basement. Although pet-store mice are more likely to be white, mice come in many colors and even some patterns. They also multiply with astounding frequency, leading to too many mice for too few homes. Use the following considerations to decide whether a mouse can work for you:

- ✔ **Attention requirements:** Mice are tiny, quick, and good at hiding, so of all the small animals, they're the ones that are least in need of human handling. Some mice can become tame and really enjoy being handled, but as long as they have cage buddies, their social needs are fulfilled.

- ✔ **Tendency for trouble:** Small children, in particular, may not be able to handle a mouse without letting it escape. Male mice tend to fight, but females generally get along just fine. Mice are hard to sex, so be sure you aren't putting males and females together.

- ✔ **Housing:** Mice need a well-ventilated cage with a solid bottom and paper bedding rather than wood shavings containing phenols that can cause them respiratory distress.

- ✔ **Special considerations:** Mice also need careful monitoring for signs of disease. If a mouse gets sick, it needs to be taken to the veterinarian. Yes, even though it's "just a mouse." Vets have seen it all, so don't be embarrassed to take in your tiny little friend for care.

Exotics: Chinchillas and hedgehogs

Exotic animals can be rewarding pets, particularly when you provide a home for a critter in need, but they also require a little extra know-how. Each exotic small animal has some specific, unique care, feeding, and socialization needs, so if you adopt one, be sure you get all the information necessary to care for the animal appropriately.

✔ **Chinchillas** (see Figure 12-3) are gorgeous, cuddly, extremely shy little critters with beautiful coats that are sometimes used to make wearable fur. But you won't use *your* chinchilla that way! Then again, be sure you really want a chinchilla. Consider:

- **Attention requirements:** Chinchillas can live between 10 and 20 years, so a chinchilla is a big commitment. They're also sensitive and easily frightened, but you need to spend time interacting gently with them and providing good food, fresh water, a clean environment, and of course, veterinary care.

- **Tendency for trouble:** A baby chinchilla can be socialized to accept handling, but physical contact between humans and adult chinchillas that haven't been trained to interact this way can be extremely stressful for the chinchilla. An adult chinchilla may never be comfortable with being handled.

- **Housing:** Appropriate housing includes a large clean cage with vertical space for climbing and jumping. Chinchillas bathe in dust rather than in water and need plenty of room, especially if they're not hand-tame.

- **Special considerations:** Chinchillas are easily stressed and can take weeks, even months not to be fearful at your approach. These guys need plenty of patience and a consistent routine to feel confident and free of fear in a pet home.

Figure 12-3:
A chinchilla is a small furry creature that can usually learn to be hand-tame only if taught from a young age.

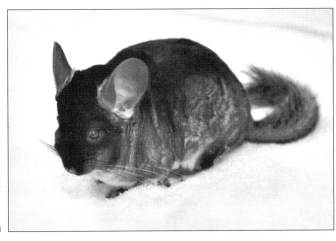

✔ **Hedgehogs** (see Figure 12-4) come from Africa and are small spiny critters that roll up in a ball when frightened. Their spines are sharp and hard, and they feel a little like plastic toothpicks. Interested? First think about the following:

- **Attention requirements:** Hedgehogs live about five to eight years in captivity. Most hedgehogs prefer to live alone, although a few get along fine with a hedgehog buddy. They require a proper diet, attention to their expressions of fear or contentment through body language, and veterinary care whenever they get sick.

- **Tendency for trouble:** Be sure hedgehogs are legal where you live.

- **Housing requirements:** Hedgehogs must be securely enclosed because they're good climbers, fast runners, and great escape artists. They also need plenty of space to move around.

Figure 12-4:
A hedgehog is a small spiny animal from Africa that has become more popular as an exotic pet during the last decade.

Save a Critter Today! Finding Adoptable Critters

If you love the idea of adopting a small critter, take the time to look around. Although many critters may need homes, your best bet for finding one is a shelter or rescue group that's devoted to assessing the health and adoptability of the animals they take in. Unless you're willing to devote the amount of time and money necessary to curing a small animal's health problems, work with a shelter or rescue group that can ensure the small animals they adopt out are in good health and simply in need of a little TLC.

But how do you find such a place? Chances are, your local animal shelter occasionally gets critters, and may be looking for a home for some small animals right now. Check there. If the shelter doesn't have the critter you believe will work best in your home and life, then seek out local or regional all-animal rescue groups or critter-specific groups. Here are some places to start looking, beginning with general links to rescue groups and shelters with many different animals, followed by critter-specific organizations:

- ✔ 1-800-Save-a-Pet (800-728-3273), a database where you can search pets in need of adoption by your zip code and the kind of pet you seek, including small animals. Call for automated service or check the Web site: `www.1-800-save-a-pet.com`.

- ✔ Petfinder, a nationwide database of pets in need of adoption, including small animals: `www.petfinder.org`.

- ✔ Pets911, another nationwide database of pets in need of adoption, including small animals: `www.1888pets911.org`.

- ✔ The American Ferret Association Web site includes links to shelters with ferrets all across the United States: `www.ferret.org/index.htm`.

- ✔ The House Rabbit Society has many local chapters across the United States. Find these, plus links to independent rabbit rescue organizations in areas without local chapters, at the House Rabbit Society's Web site: `www.rabbit.org`. Some chapters also rescue other small animals.

- ✔ Guinea Pig Adoption is an international rescue group resource list: `www.cavyrescue.com`.

- ✔ Rat Rescue Association offers rat information and rat adoption: `www.ratrescue.org`.

- ✔ Southern California Rabbit and Small Animal Rescue Association has a page devoted to hamsters in need of rescue, in southern California and elsewhere in the United States: `www.rabbitadoption.org/hamster.html`.

- ✔ This Chinchilla Rescue group is based in the San Francisco Bay area, but its Web site also includes a list of Chinchilla rescue groups across the United States, Canada, and England: `www.chinchillarescue.org`.

- ✔ Flash and Thelma Memorial Hedgehog Rescue is based in Colorado: `hedgieflash.org`.

Chapter 13

Getting Ready for Your Critter

In This Chapter

▶ Critter-proofing your home

▶ Buying the supplies you need

▶ Introducing your critter to his new home

*B*efore bringing your small animal home, you need to prepare. If you plan to give your small animal free time outside the cage — most small animals benefit from this treatment, and some require it for good physical and mental health — you have to pet-proof the areas in which your pet will play. You need to consider what kind of enclosure best suits your pet but still fits in with your lifestyle. You also need food, treats, toys, and grooming supplies all ready to go before you introduce your new pet to your home.

If you prepare for healthy introductions and potential adjustment problems, you can welcome your new pet into your home a little easier. Use this chapter to navigate through everything from pet-proofing safety considerations to introducing your pocket pet to the entire family.

Preparing Your Home for Critter Conditions

Small animals can fit into some incredible — and dangerous — places, so before you bring home your pet, you need to make sure your home is secure. Be on the lookout for any holes in the walls or around pipes or other fixtures, open heating vents, or other openings that are attractive to small animals that burrow, tunnel, and hide in dark spaces by nature.

Small animals like to explore, seek out food, chew on things, and get inside furniture and other small places. If you lose track of them or stop watching, they can be injured, poisoned, or lost. Although you can train some small animals to come when you call them or when you shake the treat box, you can't always rely on any animal to come all the time. Even if you aren't planning to let your small animal out to roam, consider what can happen if your pet accidentally escapes. Better to secure the premises, just in case. Here's how.

Making your home critterproof

Critter-proofing your home, particularly the room or rooms where your critter probably will live, means taking these precautions:

- Patching, filling, or blocking all holes into the walls and floors or that lead outside. Small animals are just that — small. They can squeeze through anything that can accommodate the size of their skull.

- Taping, covering, or otherwise hiding all exposed electrical cords.

- Relocating (if possible) furniture with moving parts that your small animal can get inside or under — recliners, sleeper sofas, and rocking chairs for example.

- Moving chewable objects off the floor as much as possible.

- Choosing a room that is easy to clean for your critter's free-roaming activities.

- Keeping your critter well out of reach and preferably in a room and a location where your other pets won't ever see or at least cannot get to him. Most cats and dogs see small animals more as dinner than as a buddy, unless you have a ferret or rabbit that's about the same size as the cat or dog.

- Keeping your critter's cage out of direct sunlight and chilly drafts when necessary. Many critters can become overheated and get heatstroke quickly, so be sure your critter stays cool, preferably (for most critters) at a temperature of between 65 and 75°F (18 to 24°C).

Considering the free-roaming route

You may be wondering about this whole free-roaming business. Well, it's a controversial subject among critter owners. Some people dedicate entire rooms, series of rooms, or even their entire houses to their critters so they have a place to roam free. In most cases, these critters have cages that serve as safe havens, in and out of which they can wander whenever they choose. Many such pets, however, spend much of their time hanging out with their people. The most common critters that are allowed to roam freely are ferrets, rabbits, rats, and guinea pigs. These critters do need time outside their cages to stretch their legs and appease their curious minds. They want to explore, to interact with people, to frolic, and to dash and climb.

However, in most cases, letting critters roam free *all* the time is not a good idea because they can

- Easily get lost or stuck in small spaces, especially critters like ferrets, rats, and mice.

✔ Demolish a carpet, a molding, or a sizeable chunk of drywall in a short period of time, if they're left unsupervised and not redirected. Rats and rabbits, in particular, can be incredibly destructive chewers.

✔ Leave waste spread far and wide. Believe me, cleaning it up is no picnic. *Note:* Ferrets and rabbits sometimes can be litter-box trained.

✔ Sustain injuries. Critters at large risk being stepped on, sat on, or hurt in myriad other ways.

In almost every case, critters are safest in a roomy, clean enclosure with plenty of space to move around, coupled with daily free time outside of the cage, carefully supervised by you, the vigilant pet owner.

For small quick animals like hamsters and mice, a hamster ball is the safest option when you aren't holding your pocket pet. Hamster balls are plastic balls inside of which your tiny pet can run all over the place. They get plenty of exercise and can move around wherever they want, but they won't get lost or destroy your house.

Never allow a pet in a rolling hamster ball access to stairs, open doors, or to a dog or cat. The dog or cat may be able to open the ball and get to your little critter. Similarly, don't forget and leave your tiny animal inside the ball for extended periods of time. He needs to eat and drink frequently, and if you forget about him for too long, he can become ill, or worse, stuck in that hamster ball without any nourishment. Limit your small animal's stay in one of these balls to no more than an hour.

Stocking Crucial Critter Supplies

Before you bring home your new critter, pay a visit to your friendly neighborhood pet store to stock up on the necessary supplies. This trip to the store is your chance to really think about the best enclosure for your pet, compare different foods, and consider the kinds of toys and exercise equipment your critter needs.

Settling into a new enclosure

Your first order of business, and your most expensive purchase, is your pet's enclosure. A spacious, well-ventilated enclosure with a solid floor is best. Your pet's enclosure needs differ according to what kind of pet you have, but the two most important factors to remember are the size of the enclosure and how easy it is to clean.

In most cases, your critter benefits from the largest enclosure you can afford, even if it's larger than the minimum sizes I recommend in the following list.

Most of these little critters need room to enjoy a little burrowing or tunneling (see Figure 13-1), so keep that in mind when making your selection. Likewise, because small animals require clean enclosures to stay healthy, you must clean the enclosure at least once a week for your small animal to thrive. The easier it is to clean, the better. The basic enclosure requirements for the most popular small animals are described in the following list:

- **Ferret enclosures:** Ferrets need clean, spacious, and safe wire cages that are at least 24 x 24 x 18 inches in size and full of interesting things to do. The larger the enclosure, the better. Glass tanks are out for ferrets, because they don't have sufficient ventilation. Ferrets need their cages stocked with furniture, including:

  - Hammocks for sleeping

  - Rags or hats for nesting

  - Toys to play with

  - Tubes for tunneling (PVC tubes work fine — choose those sized to fit your ferret, usually 3 or 4 inches in diameter)

  - Paper litter for burrowing

  - A litter box

  Ferrets like to relieve themselves in corners, so put the litter box in the corner of the cage, filled with recycled paper litter or wood pellets. Clay litter is bad for your ferret's respiratory system, so avoid clay cat box fillers. Place several litter boxes in corners of rooms in which your ferret is allowed to roam, so he can relieve himself neatly wherever he is. Ferrets don't like to hold it until they get back into their cages, so be ready. For more about litter training your ferret, see Chapter 15.

- **Rabbit hutches and cages:** Rabbits need plenty of space, so a wire cage of at least 24 x 24 x 48 inches is best. If possible, choose a cage with a solid floor; otherwise, cover the wire floor of your rabbit's cage with a solid mat. Rabbits can develop foot infections from spending too much time on wire. Place a litter box in the corner of your rabbit's cage and in the rooms where your rabbit is allowed to roam. Fill the litter boxes with recycled paper or pelleted grass litter to attract your rabbit. Clay cat box fillers aren't good for your rabbit. For more on litter training your rabbit, see Chapter 15.

- **Rat pads:** Rats need plenty of space, because they're active, athletic, and want to climb and move around. One rat needs a minimum enclosure of 24 x 24 x 24 inches, with plenty of time outside of the cage to explore and get exercise. Rats like things to climb on, swing from, and crawl through. For each additional rat, you need to add at least one square foot of space, but the bigger the enclosure for rats, the better.

- **Guinea pig digs:** Guinea pigs need space to move around, but they don't do a lot of climbing. If they have ramps, they'll move around on more than one level, but they're also fine in a spacious one-level enclosure with plenty of things to do and places to burrow. Guinea pigs need a solid floor at dimensions of at least 24 x 24 x 24 inches per pig, but the bigger the guinea pig enclosure, the better.

✔ **Securing your hamsters, gerbils, and mice:** Hamsters, gerbils, and mice need well-ventilated cages that are safe from other pets and won't allow them to squeeze out and escape. These little critters can squeeze through some pretty small spaces, so keep that in mind when choosing an enclosure. Mesh or wire cages work if the wires are close enough together. A glass tank also works for a few of these little guys — particularly gerbils and mice — but put too many in one, and you'll have ventilation problems. A 10-gallon tank is the absolute smallest tank you can use for two gerbils or two mice. Bigger is better. Cover tanks with secure, closely fitting wire tops that you can buy at the pet store.

Hamsters need a minimum of about 18 x 18 inches of space; dwarf hamsters need about one square foot each. More space is better. Golden hamsters should never be housed together. Solitary creatures, they fight when put together. On the other hand, dwarf hamsters, gerbils, and mice prefer company . . . same-sex only please!

✔ **Exotic critter enclosures:** Enclosures for exotic critters need to be tailored to their specific needs. Because hedgehogs are such efficient climbers, for example, they're likely to escape from a wire cage. Provide them with a minimum 20-gallon glass tank with a securely fitting wire mesh top, plenty of fresh bedding, and a big bowl of water for drinking and swimming. Chinchillas, on the other hand, need plenty of vertical climbing space, so wire mesh cages with solid floors, branches for climbing, and boxes off the ground for nesting are best. For one chinchilla, provide an absolute minimum of 2 x 2 x 3 feet, with the largest dimension being height.

Figure 13-1:
Small animals like this hamster need plenty of room to explore, preferably on multiple levels.

If you choose a wire cage, make sure the bars are close enough together that your pet can't squeeze out. If you choose a glass aquarium, buy a matching wire top that fits securely and tightly.

Getting the supplies your pet needs

If you have a larger small critter like a ferret or rabbit, you may need supplies for litter-box training or even for taking your pet on a walk; however, every critter needs the following supplies:

- ✔ **Bedding:** Get the kind made from recycled paper, aspen wood shavings (not pine or cedar) or pellets, or grass pellets (see previous section about enclosures). Avoid wood shavings made from pine or cedar, because they contain phenols, natural compounds found in woods that smell good but can damage a small animal's respiratory system. Recycled paper litter is an excellent substrate for all small animals. Carefresh is one that vets frequently recommend.

- ✔ **High-quality food:** Get the kind made for the kind of animal you have. Different animals have different nutritional needs, so don't feed one pocket pet the food designed for another. Some foods state that they are appropriate for more than one kind of pet. Supplementing your critter's diet with healthy produce is a good idea. For more about feeding your small animal, see Chapter 14.

- ✔ **A heavy ceramic food bowl:** This kind of bowl is less likely to tip, and your critter can even stand on the rim and enjoy his food. Purchase one that is small enough for your critter to eat from without climbing completely into it.

- ✔ **A water bottle:** Get the kind of water bottle that attaches to the side of your critter's enclosure with the little metal ball in the tip so the water doesn't leak out when your pet isn't drinking. Some critters like to chew plastic bottles, so look for the kind that installs on the outside of the wire cage with the nozzle poking through. For aquariums, look for glass water bottles, but handle them with care to prevent breakage. A water bottle keeps your critter from messing up his water with litter or using it for a toilet. However, you still need to give your critter fresh water every day, and clean out the water bottle every few days.

- ✔ **Food supplements:** Supplement your critter's diet as recommended for your particular animal. For instance, guinea pigs need extra vitamin C. For more about supplements, see Chapter 14.

- ✔ **Exercise equipment:** Your critter's gym can include ladders and ramps for cage climbing, ropes and hanging toys for swinging, and of course, the ubiquitous small animal wheel for running — appropriate for hamsters, gerbils, mice, and some rats. Some of the newer wheels don't make as much noise as the old-fashioned metal kind.

> ✔ **Shelters and tunnels:** Your pet's cage needs plenty of places in which to hide and burrow. You can buy shelters and tunnels, or make them yourself out of cardboard boxes and tubes, rags, and PVC pipes. Most small animals also need nesting material — clean paper towels or toilet paper for shredding, pieces of soft cloth, or nesting boxes.

Ferrets and rabbits need litter boxes (if you plan to box-train them) with high sides and a low front so they can easily climb in and out and do their business without spraying outside of the box. Triangular-shaped litter boxes are available for ferrets, because they prefer going in the corner, but square litter boxes work just fine. You may also want to pick up a leash and harness to be able to walk your ferrets or rabbits, and a bell is a necessity for your ferret's or rat's harness. The sound helps you keep track of your pet when he's roaming.

Helping Your New Critter Settle In

When you first bring your new critter home, keep in mind how your tiny pet must feel, taken from his familiar environment and put in an entirely new world. Give your critter some time to adjust by following these tips.

Understand the limits of handling

Although handling is a good way to tame and get to know your critter, take it easy for the first day or two. Give your new pet time to explore his new home, try his new food, and test his new water bottle. Let him look around or sleep or hide, whatever he needs to do to adjust. You can begin taking your critter out of his cage for short periods, handling him gently the second day — just don't overdo it. Most critters sleep most of the day and are more active and open to handling in the evening. Let your critter get his rest when he needs it. Unless it's necessary, don't handle a critter while he is sleeping. You can startle him and get a nip, or stress him out and make him afraid of you.

Give him space

Some critters act scared when you first bring them home, and others don't. If your critter seems frightened by too many people, small children, or other pets, put him in an area where he won't be exposed to so many stimuli right away. Give him time and introduce these loud noisy creatures one at a time over the course of a week. Give your critter time outside his cage to explore, too, but do so in a quiet critter-proofed room and supervise vigilantly so your critter doesn't get lost or injured.

Ferrets and rabbits often spend considerable amounts of time hiding at first, or they may bound out and be ready to play from the get-go. Respect your individual pet's pace, protect him vigilantly from children and other pets that may be a little too interested in exuberant interaction before your new pet is ready, and keep him in his cage when you can't supervise — until everyone is adjusted to the new situation.

Supervise your children

If you have children, supervise their interactions with your new pet until you know your child understands how to handle the critter carefully and responsibly.

An adult always is ultimately responsible for a small animal's care, even if the animal ostensibly belongs to the child.

Know when to get help and when to back off

If your critter doesn't seem to be adjusting well, you may need to take additional measures. Talk to your vet if you're giving your critter space and a calm, quiet environment, and your critter is:

- ✔ Not eating or drinking
- ✔ Panting constantly or acting severely stressed
- ✔ Refusing to let you touch him
- ✔ Behaving aggressively or constantly trying to bite you

Your pet may have a medical problem. If your critter checks out just fine, back off and let your critter adjust. Adopted small animals sometimes have been through many changes, and some rarely were handled by humans, so their new homes may seem strange and frightening to them. Be patient and progress at your critter's own pace. Some critters may never be entirely comfortable with all humans, but with some extra work, gentle handling, and plenty of space, your critter probably can learn to accept interactions with you on some level. For more about training your small animal, see Chapter 15.

Chapter 14

Taking Charge of Your Critter's Care

In This Chapter

▶ Understanding your critter's health-care needs

▶ Feeding your critter

▶ Discovering how to groom your critter

A well-housed critter in a clean environment receiving healthy food has a good chance of staying healthy and living out its expected life span, whether that's 2 years or 20. Every critter is a little bit different, and different pets have different requirements for sound health, social interaction, and nutrition. In this chapter, you find out how to keep your critter healthy by discovering how to choose a good critter vet, what health issues you need to look out for, and how to recognize signs your critter needs a vet's help. Plus, you can find out what kind of diet, nutritional supplements, and grooming your critter needs to be at his bright-eyed, bushy-tailed best.

Keeping Your Critter Healthy

Even if the critter you adopt looks healthy, you'll want to take him to the vet before agreeing to adopt him or at least make sure your adoption agreement has a provision that says the shelter will take the critter back if a vet finds that your new pet has a health problem. You may opt to treat the problem instead, but knowing you have the option is best. Because critters are prey animals, they tend to hide illness until it is advanced, and a vet may be able to spot signs you didn't notice.

An initial vet visit is particularly important for ferrets and rabbits, but it's also a good idea for smaller critters like guinea pigs and hamsters, because your vet can get to know your critter and form a good idea of what your critter looks and acts like when healthy. After the first vet visit, even healthy critters need to visit the vet once every year for a checkup.

Sometimes, even under the best conditions, critters get sick and need additional veterinary care. Adopted critters, in particular, need at least one or two initial vet visits to resolve problems related to past neglect. All small animals deserve and occasionally require veterinary care, so please consider the vet bill part of your commitment to caring for your critter, even if it costs a lot more than the critter itself.

Finding a good critter vet

Veterinarians have many different specialties, personal favorite pets, and skill levels. Some are great with cats or dogs, some prefer birds and reptiles, and some specialize in critters. Many general vets have considerable experience with small animals, but others have had little. Experience can make a big difference when your critter has a critical health issue.

Most towns and cities have many vets to choose from, so check around and don't assume the first vet you visit is necessarily the best one for you and your critter. Many highly qualified veterinarians have plenty of experience with small animals, and it pays to seek them out.

You can find good vets simply by asking other critter hobbyists about who they like and dislike among vets and about what kind of experiences they've had. You can also check out the House Rabbit Society's Web page (www.rabbit.org) to find veterinarians who treat rabbits (listed by state). Many vets who treat rabbits are likely to treat other small animals, but ask first, just to be sure.

After you've found a potential vet, call the clinic and ask:

- ✔ How many small animal patients the vet or vet clinic sees each year, particularly your type of small animal.

- ✔ How much the vet is willing to talk about small-animal care, training, and maintenance.

- ✔ What kind of equipment the vet or vet clinic has for treating small animals.

- ✔ What emergency services the vet has if you need to schedule an after-hours issue.

- ✔ What kind of diseases and other health problems the vet has treated in small animals.

- ✔ What prices the vet charges for office visits and what tests or other services that vet typically performs on small animals.

  Be sure to mention what kind of small animal you have, because tests for a ferret may not apply to a hamster. Veterinary costs can vary widely, but higher costs aren't always associated with better care.

If the vet's location and prices seem reasonable to you, schedule an appointment and observe how the vet checks out your little critter. You want to be sure that the vet:

- ✔ **Seems familiar with the animal.** The vet should be able to answer your questions about typical problems common to your small animal and give you a sense that he or she keeps up on the current literature about small-animal care. If you aren't sure, ask the vet how many small-animal patients he or she currently has. If the vet has at least a few critter clients, that is better than none. Having many critter clients is, of course, an even better sign.

- ✔ **Handles your critter confidently yet gently, with the kind of care that makes you comfortable.** If the vet seems uncomfortable handling a ferret or a hedgehog, for example, then you may want to look for a different vet.

- ✔ **Acts like critters are just as important as *you* think they are.** Does the vet dismiss your pet's problem, or does he or she seem just as committed to helping your critter as any other kind of pet?

These are essential considerations — if you don't like the way the vet handles your critter, keep looking.

Understanding potential health problems

Small animals tend to have specific health issues the same as other pets. Adopted small animals may be even more likely to suffer from some of these issues, particularly the ones related to trauma, malnutrition, and unhealthy environment, because an inability or unwillingness to care for the animal properly may have been what led its owners to give it up. Any small animal may have several of these common health issues, which you need to discuss with your vet on your pet's first visit. If you notice any of the following at any time during your small animal's life, please give your vet a call:

- ✔ Injuries related to broken bones or other structural injuries related to fights or accidents such as mishandling, dropping, or being stepped on. Signs include any limb or tail or any other part of the animal that looks misshapen.

- ✔ Wounds from fighting or infection caused by unsanitary living conditions.

- ✔ Lumps, bumps, and other skin cysts and tumors.

- ✔ Overgrown teeth.

✔ Heatstroke, which is common when the animal is left in direct sunlight or too near a heater. Most small animals are extremely sensitive to heat and must be kept at moderate temperatures, never higher than 80°F (27°C), and always need to have fresh water and shade. Signs include panting, refusing to eat, or refusing to move. Never keep a small animal in direct sunlight.

Beyond these conditions, each small animal is a different species and likely has its own unique problems. When you first visit the veterinarian, ask specifically about species-specific conditions (bring this book with you if necessary) so the vet can check for them. Some conditions may not show up until your animal is older, but that first visit helps your vet track your animal's progress and note any initial symptoms that may signal a problem later on. Here are some of the most common health problems to ask your vet about, organized according to your type of critter:

✔ Ferrets can be born deaf in one or both ears, which can make them a little more difficult — but certainly not impossible — to train. Some ferrets also suffer from a gastrointestinal condition called *epizootic catarrhal enteritis* (or green slime disease), adrenal disease, insulin gland tumors, a potentially fatal and contagious virus called Aleutian disease that's similar to parvovirus in dogs, lymphoma, and influenza, which your ferret actually can catch from *you* (and you from him).

✔ Rabbits have sensitive respiratory systems and can suffer toxic reactions to cedar and pine shavings and liver damage if the rabbit ingests these wood shavings. A common bacterial infection is *pasteurella,* which infects a rabbit's lungs. Rabbits may suffer from hairballs; however, because they can't vomit them up the way cats do, hairballs can be fatal for bunnies. So rabbits need regular brushing when they're shedding and plenty of fresh hay to help them pass hairballs, and some may need regular hairball medication. Ask your vet about it.

Rabbits also can have misaligned teeth and gastrointestinal infections. Some rabbits are extremely sensitive to penicillin and similar antibiotics like amoxicillin. If your rabbit needs antibiotics, make sure your vet has experience with rabbits and prescribes an antibiotic that is bunny-safe. Normal rabbit urine often is orange or even almost red, and sometimes cloudy, but if you see a thick white sediment in your rabbit's urine, be sure that you're not feeding alfalfa hay, which isn't good for bunnies and be sure you're not feeding too many pellets, because excess calcium can cause sand or even stones in the urine.

✔ Guinea pigs can suffer from respiratory problems like lung infections that turn into pneumonia. The Bordatella bacterium that also infects humans, dogs, cats, and rabbits also infects cavies, but this infection — mild in some animals — can be very serious for guinea pigs. For that reason, never house them with rabbits. Some guinea pigs suffer from cervical lymphadenitis (bacterial-infected lumps), misaligned teeth that can cause starvation when your guinea pig can't chew his food, gastrointestinal problems, skin fungus, foot infections, heatstroke, and eye infections.

✔ Rats are extremely sensitive to respiratory problems, and the most common ones are highly contagious: coronavirus and the Mycoplasma pulmonis bacteria. These viruses can develop into fatal infections and are easily aggravated by unsanitary conditions and other irritants like pine and cedar litter. Rats also may suffer from skin tumors and infections, mites or fungal infections causing hair loss, eye infections and tear stains, misaligned teeth, ear infections, pituitary gland tumors, swollen salivary glands, and chronic kidney disease.

✔ Hamsters, gerbils, and mice can develop many of the same problems: skin infections and cysts, tumors, diabetes, hair loss, respiratory problems, ear infections, teeth problems, dehydration, and heatstroke. Gerbils can lose their delicate tails, a protective mechanism to help them escape predators. These tiny mammals often won't show they're sick until it's too late, so don't delay in taking them to the vet.

✔ Hedgehogs are not sociable, and unlike many other small animals, need to be housed alone. Pine and cedar wood shavings can irritate their respiratory systems and feet. Temperatures below 75°F (24°C) can send a hedgehog into hibernation, but domesticated hedgehogs are not really meant to hibernate and can actually die if they try it. On the other hand, temperatures higher than 85°F (30°C) can cause your hedgehog to suffer a form of heatstroke, so keep your hedgehog in a tank with a constant temperature. Hedgehogs also are prone to obesity and liver disease, mites, several forms of cancer, and a neurological condition called Wobbly Hedgehog Syndrome that can lead to wobbling and paralysis.

✔ Chinchillas are prone to diarrhea or constipation, and they need a constant source of hay so they can digest the hair they're constantly licking when they groom themselves. Chinchillas also are prone to seizures, liver disease, skin problems, and hair loss — when frightened, chinchillas can drop big patches of hair. Temperatures of 75°F (24°C) and above (even lower when the humidity is high) can be fatal to chinchilla, so they absolutely must be kept in a cool dry environment. Chinchillas also need to take regular dust baths, so provide them with *chinchilla dust* (a dry bath product you can buy in the pet store). They roll and shake in it and have a jolly old time — a necessary aspect of chinchilla self-grooming. For more about the chinchilla dust bath, see the section on grooming, later in this chapter.

Keeping your critters from breeding!

One of the most important preventive health practices you can do for your critter is to make sure you don't allow your small animal to produce any more unwanted critters. For ferrets and rabbits, spaying or neutering has the added benefit of improving behavior and helping the animals calm down and not be so driven by their, um . . . urges. Spaying or neutering can help these pets be less destructive and aggressive when they hit adolescence.

As for small animals, it doesn't take much to wind up with an accidental litter of gerbils, mice, or hamsters, but most critters can be spayed or neutered to prevent breeding — even mice can be spayed or castrated, although most vets won't spay a female because of the risks to such a small animal. If you've discovered you have both sexes and want to house them together, finding a vet willing to castrate a male small animal shouldn't be too hard, because it's a simpler and less invasive surgery than spaying the female. The procedure requires gas anesthesia and is quick.

If you can't or don't want to spay or neuter your critter, never keep same-sex critters together and be certain about the sex of your critters before putting them in the same enclosure. Too many people thought they knew they had two females, only to be surprised with a litter of tiny hamsters or mice and no resources to take care of so many pets. Remember that critter overpopulation is one of the reasons so many critters are homeless, waiting in shelters, or abandoned to the wild. Do your part by refusing to make the problem worse. Talk to your vet about what is appropriate for your critter.

Chinchillas are particularly sensitive to anesthesia, and a spay/neuter can be too risky for your adopted pet. Instead, don't house too opposite-sex chinchillas together. If you aren't sure whether an adopted female may be pregnant, and you have a choice, consider adopting a male.

Knowing when to see a vet

Critters are sensitive to things that may not make as much of a health impact on larger animals, and many critters — being prey animals that can't afford to appear weak — hide signs of illness until they are extremely sick. If you notice any of the following signs of illness in your critter, see a vet right away:

✔ Wheezing, panting, difficulty breathing, a runny nose, watery eyes, lack of energy, loss of weight, looking shriveled or dehydrated, or non-responsiveness. These symptoms can all signal a respiratory infection, a common but potentially fatal problem in many small animals.

✔ Swelling in any body part or a large lump that can signal a lymph node infected by bacteria or a tumor. Even if the lump bursts and seems to heal, see a vet. If the lump is caused by a bacterial infection, it is contagious to other small animals. If the lump is a tumor, your vet can advise you about the best course of action for your pet. Some people mistake the heavily-filled cheek pouches of hamsters as tumors, but hamsters just like to fill up their cheeks — it's perfectly normal.

✔ Noticeable weight loss or weight gain, which can signal many things, from misaligned teeth to chronic disease.

✔ Diarrhea, constipation, or any change in your pet's feces. Bunnies sometimes make softer droppings at night.

✔ Sores or ulcers on feet, often caused by wire-bottomed cages.

✔ Hair loss or skin changes.

✔ Listless behavior, nonresponsiveness, or any obvious change in behavior with no apparent cause.

✔ Changes in eating or drinking patterns, such as suddenly eating less or drinking more. A poor appetite and drooling can signal tooth overgrowth and an inability to eat correctly. Excessive drinking can signal diabetes.

✔ Wobbling, dragging rear legs, disorientation, falling over.

✔ Signs of heatstroke, a common problem in many small animals: shallow rapid breathing, panting, drooling, stretched out on the ground refusing to move, weakness, shriveled body from dehydration, pale gums, nonresponsiveness/coma.

Feeding Your Critter

Every critter has different dietary needs. Some eat meat (like ferrets), some prefer seeds, nuts, and grains (like hamsters), some prefer leafy greens and fruit (like rabbits), and some critters like a little bit of everything. Without the right nutrients, your critter can quickly develop nutritional deficiencies, diseases, and improper growth. One rule of thumb: Always feed your critter a commercial food made specifically for that kind of critter. Most critters also benefit from fresh foods added to their commercial diet, but beware that the wrong foods can be dangerous for your critter, so be sure you know which foods are healthy for your critter and which are not.

Many critters, particularly bunnies, hamsters, guinea pigs, and rats, are prone to overgrown teeth, but providing wood for gnawing can help keep this problem in check. You can buy wooden chew sticks in pet stores, or use fruit tree branches you collect on your own, a great choice for small animals. Preventing tooth overgrowth is much easier than fixing it, so keep it in check.

All critters need to have a constant supply of fresh water in a clean container. Other than that, here is what you need to know about your critter's nutritional needs:

✔ Ferrets need to eat a premium food made for them, or if you can't find it, a few premium brands of kitten food (such as Iams) can be used as substitute. Ferret diets are much easier to find than they used to be, so choose one if possible. Ferrets are carnivorous. They need lots of protein and no vegetables. They can't digest fiber very well so they shouldn't eat starchy foods like bread or grains. They can eat very small amounts of fruit if it's mashed well or pureed. A nice treat for ferrets is the occasional tiny bit of cooked meat. Fatty acid supplements contribute to a soft shiny coat, and laxative supplements made for ferrets during shedding season help hairballs pass easily.

✔ Rabbits need lots of fiber and vegetables. Limit bunny pellet food to about ¼ cup per day after your rabbit is full-grown, because too much can cause urinary sand and stones. Even more important is a constant supply of fresh timothy hay (not alfalfa) and a little bit of fresh pineapple or papaya, which (along with the hay) helps rabbits process and pass hairballs. Give your rabbit fresh vegetables, particularly dark leafy greens like Romaine lettuce, collard greens, and beet greens, carrots and their tops, radish leaves, clover, dandelion greens, parsley, watercress, and crisp green peppers. Avoid iceberg lettuce and fruit, with the exception of small amounts of high-fiber berries like raspberries and blueberries. Rabbits fed a proper diet don't need supplements, but they do eat their own droppings, which actually is healthy for them because the droppings are high in nutrients. Consider those rabbit droppings to be multi-vitamins for your bunny!

✔ Guinea pigs are vegetarians and can't digest meat or fat. Feed them fresh guinea pig pellets, plenty of timothy hay, and vegetables and fruits high in vitamin C, an important vitamin guinea pigs (like humans) can't manufacture on their own. Without it, they can develop scurvy. Every day, give your piggy vitamin-C-rich produce, even if his guinea pig food has added vitamin C. Choose foods such as citrus peel, broccoli, Brussels sprouts, parsley, collard greens, kale, and red bell peppers. Pigs also like lettuce mixes (not iceberg lettuce), carrots, and other fresh veggies. Some pigs nibble on vitamin C chewable tablets as a treat.

✔ Rats thrive on a high-carb diet. They need plenty of healthy grains. Feed them a premium rat kibble or lab blocks supplemented with leafy greens, corn, oats, and the occasional cooked bone with meat on it for chewing and protein. Even though rats eat just about anything, avoid giving your rat high-fat junk food and sweets. Rats also need chew sticks to keep their ever-growing teeth worn down.

✔ Hamsters need a premium hamster mix with grains and corn and a little seed. Hamsters love sunflower seeds, but reserve these as a special treat. Supplement your hamster's diet with plenty of dark leafy greens and fruit like chunks of apples, carrots, berries, and orange wedges.

✔ Gerbils are omnivorous and need a gerbil mix but also a little animal protein. Gerbils need to have some fresh vegetables and the occasional feeder cricket or dog bone for animal protein. Reserve fattening sunflower seeds for a special treat.

✔ Feed mice a premium mouse kibble such as mouse lab blocks, some grains like corn, rice, and oatmeal, and small amounts of leafy greens and fresh fruit.

✔ Hedgehogs do well on a premium hedgehog diet (L'Avian makes a good one), or if you can't find commercial hedgehog food, try a premium ferret or kitten food with some meal worms, crickets, or earthworms mixed in. Yum! Add a small amount of leafy greens and fruits, but no high-fat foods. Hedgehogs quickly become obese, which is a serious health threat to them.

✔ Chinchillas require a constant supply of grassy hay like timothy (not alfalfa) and a premium chinchilla commercial diet plus small amounts of fresh leafy greens. Like rabbits, chinchillas eat their own droppings, which are an important source of vitamins for them.

Critter Grooming

Little critters generally groom themselves — or each other — but a few critters need some special help from you, particularly long-haired guinea pigs, ferrets, rabbits, and chinchillas. Unless they get into something yucky, most critters don't need to be bathed. Regular brushing with a soft brush and combing with a fine-toothed comb can remove dead hair and prevent tangles and mats in long coats. Trim your critter's nails if they get too long, give them chewy wood to keep their teeth short, and that's about it.

If your critter gets fleas or mites, you need to get rid of these pests before they do serious damage to your critter's skin or transmit diseases. However, never use a pest control product on your critter that is designed or intended for a dog! Some products for cats are safe for ferrets and rabbits, but always consult your vet before putting any pest control product on your critter. Your vet can advise you about toxicity issues and the safest way to eliminate pests from your beloved little pal.

A few critters need some extra help in the grooming department. Here's what to know about critter-specific grooming:

✔ Ferrets don't need to be bathed very often — only every few months — unless they get extremely dirty. In fact, too-frequent bathing dries out ferret skin and makes the ferret produce even more musky oil, making it smell worse. Bathe your ferret the same way you'd bathe a cat (see Chapter 10). Ferrets like to be brushed, and they tend to accumulate a dark waxy debris in their ears that you can clean with a simple ear wash available at the pet store. Brush your ferret's teeth about once a week and get ferrets accustomed to nail trimming right from the start, so they tolerate it. Be sure to wash cage bedding at least weekly to help keep your ferret clean.

✔ Long-haired guinea pigs need their hair trimmed about every other month; otherwise, it keeps growing and gets in your pig's way. Comb daily to prevent tangles and mats, which can attract dirt and bacteria, leading to skin infections. Guinea pigs don't need baths, but they may need their nails trimmed. Keep an eye on those piggy paws.

✔ Rabbits need daily brushing to prevent hairballs, which can be very dangerous for them, causing intestinal obstruction. *Never bathe your rabbit!* Bathing can actually be fatal for your rabbit because it lowers his body temperature too much and causes so much stress that he can collapse.

Bunnies groom themselves fastidiously, so with a little help from you and a hairbrush, your bunny should stay perfectly clean. Prepare for seasonal heavy sheds requiring extravigorous brushing to remove large amounts of shedding fur. Trim your bunny's nails with a nail trimmer made for pets and, if necessary, trim his teeth. Ask your vet to show you how. If your rabbit's ears get dirty, you may also want to clean out visible wax — don't go into the ear canal, just clean up the wax that you can see in the exposed part of your bunny's ear — with a moist cotton swab.

✔ Rats, hamsters, gerbils, and mice don't need grooming, with the possible exception of trimming off just the tips of their nails if they're getting too long and scratching you. These smallest of the pocket pets are good at keeping themselves well groomed, as long as they have a clean environment. If your critter begins to look ungroomed, he may be sick. Visit the vet.

✔ Hedgehogs love to swim, so provide them with a swimming hole they can easily get in and out of, and they will keep themselves clean. Change the water every day. Anything that looks like bad grooming — broken quills, weepy eyes, ragged claws — may be a sign of a health problem. See your vet.

✔ Chinchillas need daily brushing to help prevent dangerous hairballs. They also need to take dust baths, rather than water baths. Purchase chinchilla dust at your local pet store and put it in a large shallow dish. Put this in your chinchilla's cage every day for 30 to 60 minutes, so your chinchilla can roll around and get clean in his chinchilla way. Then remove the dust so your chinchilla doesn't use it as a litter box or get too much dust in her sensitive eyes.

Chapter 15

Critter Behavior and Training

- -

In This Chapter

▶ Understanding why adopted small animals act the way they do

▶ Correcting and managing behaviors and recognizing inherent small-animal qualities

▶ Dealing with physical and behavioral problems requiring training or management

▶ Training your critter to use the litter box, to be held, and to come

▶ Figuring out what those funny critter noises and movements probably mean

- -

*Y*our sweet little critter may look like a fuzzy angel, bashful and sweet and even a little cuddly in a trembling sort of way. But what happens when you get home, your little darling gets comfortable, and suddenly, you have a big problem on your hands? Your critter may be trying to bite or attack you, shredding your carpet, eating your walls, or refusing to come out of hiding.

These scenarios are quite common for small animal owners, and they're a big reason so many small animals are abandoned to animal shelters. What you call a problem, however, in many cases is just normal small-animal behavior. It doesn't require fixing, but it does require management. In other cases, small animals may truly have behavior problems that are caused by past neglect or abuse. You can also address them with some targeted strategies. This chapter shows you how to tell the difference between normal small animal behaviors and true behavior problems, and it gives you helpful tips for dealing with both. I also explain how to train your small animals in ways that make them much easier to keep as pets. The key to bringing out the best in your small animal is frequent, positive, nonthreatening, rewarding interaction. Here's how to go about it.

Adopted Small Animal Issues

Adopting an adult critter gives you a big advantage over adopting a younger one. Many critters, such as ferrets and rabbits, are calm and cuddly as babies but after they hit adolescence, they develop some undesirable behaviors. That's when people throw in the towel and abandon the critter to the wild or an animal shelter. But adolescence passes, and the critter becomes a much more docile adult, especially after it's spayed or neutered. What *you* see when adopting an adult critter is much more likely to be what you get. Someone else went through the difficult part. Now you get to reap the benefits of maturity.

Even so, many adopted small animals (adults included) need to learn a few lessons about living with humans. Previous owners who purchased an adorable ferret kit or baby Easter bunny may not have researched nor realized these pets need to be trained from the get-go. Worse yet, many of these animals were abused. You may not want to think about someone slapping your ferret or kicking your bunny, but unfortunately, it happens all too often when a pet owner gets angry about being bitten or scratched.

Animals remember fearful experiences, and they remember them for a long time. Your small animal may be suspicious and afraid of a human hand, a foot, or the mere presence of people. As a new critter owner, your big job is teaching your new pet slowly but surely that her life now is different and that humans mean good things: petting, stroking, playing, and treats. She must be taught that nipping, scratching, and biting won't be tolerated but never slapped, flicked, kicked, or otherwise hurt for doing these things.

To find out how you're supposed to train a small animal not to do the things you can't tolerate without making her even more afraid of humans consider which behaviors are fixable, manageable, or simply incorrigible.

Many behaviors that seem abnormal actually are sexual behaviors related to the onset of adolescence. These behaviors can occur at a young age in small animals, as young as 4 or 5 months. Sexual behaviors include biting, mounting, spraying urine on other pets or you, circling you, and general wild destructive behavior. Spaying or neutering your pet usually resolves these behaviors, which really aren't abnormal at all but can seem startling to pet owners.

Fixing what you can

Small animals do things that they think are perfectly normal. In this list, I explain some of these behaviors that you can fix:

- ✔ **Biting:** Ferrets nip while playing because the skin of other ferrets is pretty tough. It hurts sensitive human skin, however, and ferrets can (and need to) learn not to nip people. Whenever your ferret nips you (playfully or otherwise to engage your attention), immediately put him in his cage and ignore him for five minutes. Then try to play again. If he nips you again, back in he goes. If he doesn't nip, reward him with a treat and play with him in the way he enjoys. He soon gets the message that nipping doesn't benefit him.

If your ferret refuses to calm down, you can safely *scruff* him by lifting him gently by the loose skin on the back of his neck. This isn't painful nor does it psychologically threaten the ferret. Adult ferrets are okay with scruffing, if you hold them up with one hand and support their lower bodies with the other hand, just long enough for the ferret to calm down.

Never give in to a nipping or biting ferret. If he nips you to make you put him down, don't do it; don't send him a signal that the nipping works and that he can control you. Instead, keep petting and offering treats. You may need to try handling a nipper with thick gloves until he's trained. Although he can nip your glove, it won't have any effect on you, and he soon discovers nipping won't have the desired effect. The trick is to make sure you always show him that your hands are helpful, a source of good things, and not hurtful.

Rabbits, rats, and hamsters that nip, bite, or scratch probably are doing so out of fear. They may have been abused in the past by human hands. Go slowly with these critters and touch them in a soft, gentle, nonpredatory way, just a little at a time, until they learn to trust you. Be patient. Your little critter may vividly remember bad experiences from the past.

Many small animals bite out of fear at an approaching hand or after being startled, moved while sleeping, or cornered. Ferrets, rabbits, rats, and hamsters are quite likely to react that way, but any small animal can bite if it's afraid. If you figure out what causes your small-animal's fear, stop doing it. Approaching your pet from a different angle or in a different way may keep you from frightening him.

✔ **Hiding:** If your small animal hides all the time, you can almost always (with time) gently coax her out of hiding with companionship, gentle words, a calm environment, a regular routine, and tempting treats. Coaxing out critters like chinchillas sometimes can take many weeks, but with patience, you can prevail.

Hiding is normal for small animals; however, if your usually friendly pet suddenly starts hiding, contact your vet to rule out any physical issues. If nothing is wrong physically, fear of some event, noise, interaction, or infraction may have traumatized your pet. If so, you may have to start back at the beginning to regain your pet's trust, even if you never find out what caused the fear.

✔ **Aggressive behavior:** In some cases, aggression is really just play, as with ferrets (see earlier section about biting). What you see as aggressive, your small animal may see as interaction or communication. True aggression is never normal but in most cases, it is a sign of fear, not a sign that something is inherently wrong with your pet. You can fix fearful aggression by eliminating the sources of fear. Although doing so takes a lot of time and patience, it's necessary for your animal to thrive and be healthy. If your pet is afraid of you, slow down, back off, and continue interacting in a less threatening way. If the animal is afraid of children or pets, keep these enthusiastic family members away until the pet is better adjusted.

One of the most effective ways to manage aggressive and destructive behavior in ferrets and rabbits is to have them neutered. Many ferrets are neutered at a young age, but people are less likely to neuter their rabbits, especially when they have only a single rabbit and no risk of pregnancy. Neutering does much more than prevent pregnancy; it makes rabbits calmer, more docile pets, because they no longer are driven to distraction by raging hormones. Other small animals can also be neutered, so talk to your vet about whether spaying or neutering is a possibility for your pet.

✔ **Litter-box–training problems:** If your ferret or rabbit stops using the litter box or just can't seem to get the concept of litter-box training in the first place, you can almost always train or retrain your pet using the methods I describe later in this chapter.

Managing what you can

Managing an undesirable behavior that your pet can't realistically give up is just a matter of rechanneling it in an acceptable way. Many undesirable behaviors can be managed successfully with a little patience, such as the following:

✔ **Excess energy:** Channel excess energy with plenty of play activities and training. Take your active ferret or bunny for a walk on a leash with a harness and train him to do some tricks.

✔ **Frequent elimination:** You can manage behaviors such as frequent elim-ination by placing more litter boxes around the house in spots your pet thinks of as critter restrooms.

✔ **Chewing and digging:** Small animals chew and dig. It's simply part of what they are. Chewing and digging can be easily managed by providing plenty of opportunities for appropriate kinds of chewing and digging. Chew sticks, crunchy carrots, and cardboard to shred can tempt your gnawing bunny or rat away from the baseboards. Carpet squares for dig-ging can satisfy energetic rabbits. If you can't supervise your small animal, you need to put him safely in his cage so he can't destroy things — and don't forget to put his chewable objects inside with him.

Accepting what you can't change

As a successful small-animal owner, you recognize your pet simply has some traits that you can't change. Don't forget that you're dealing with a drastically different critter, so why would you want to change your little pet? After all some of your critter's qualities, especially the ones in the list that follows, are what make small animals so interesting. Accepting your little pal for what he is, rather than expecting him to behave like a tiny version of a dog or cat, makes all the difference. *Vive la difference!*

- ✔ Your adult small animal is not a dog or a cat, may never be cuddly, and may never want to sit on your lap or be carried around like a baby. This trait actually is similar in humans. You once were cuddly as a baby, but as an adult, you probably don't make a habit of snuggling up in your mommy's lap. (And if you do, well, that's really none of my business.)

- ✔ Your small animal has plenty of energy and is likely to be more energetic at night when you'd prefer to be sleeping. Nocturnal or *crepuscular* (active at dawn and dusk) behavior is innate; you can't change it, so you have to be prepared to deal with it. Move that hamster cage into another room if the sound of your pet incessantly running on her wheel drives you batty. Even if she's awake during the day — the way ferrets and mice often are — your pet sleeps and plays on her own internal clock. You and your pet get along best when you respect her schedule, which she really can't control anyway.

- ✔ Your small animal needs attention and interaction, either from you, a cage mate, or both. Small animals get bored! You can't just adopt small animals and then ignore them. They become antisocial or can even die without attention. Small animal owners must accept responsibility for this interaction. Rabbits do get bored more easily than folks think — get them some toys like balls they can chew up or roll around. They also like toys that make noise. Bird toys sometimes work well, with chewy wood and jingly bells. Ferrets tend to get bored, too, and that can cause behavior problems. Let ferrets go crazy attacking their toys, chasing and wrestling stuffed animals and bouncy balls instead of your hand. Sometimes ferrets interact wonderfully with small dogs or cats, which can make great playmates for ferrets.

- ✔ Prey animals breed like, well . . . rabbits, to continually replenish their populations. Have your small animals neutered or don't house males and females together. You can't keep an unneutered opposite-sex pair from breeding when you put them in the same enclosure. You just can't.

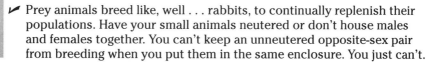

Knowing when it's a physical problem

In some cases, behavior problems really are warning signs that your pet is in pain or ill. Talk to your vet if your small animal

- Tries to bite every time you touch a certain part of his body, snarls or nips when you try to move him, or acts uncharacteristically vicious. These reactions can be signs of pain.

- Pulls out his fur or chews on his skin. Doing so can be a sign of a skin irritation or other discomfort that is causing generalized anxiety.

- Stops eating or starts drinking much more than normal, which can point to any number of diseases, including diabetes, a thyroid problem, or cancer.

- Urinates much more than normal or suddenly has lapses in litter-box training when he was well trained before, which may signal a urinary tract, bladder, or kidney problem. More frequent urination can also be a temporary reaction to a spay/neuter surgery and will resolve on its own.

- Refuses to play, shivers, or whines and cries, which can mean pain or discomfort.

Understanding What Small Animals Can and Should Learn

Sure, you can train a dog. You can even train a cat. But a rabbit? A rat? A guinea pig? A tiny little mouse? Actually, most critters can be trained at least to some degree. Ferrets and rabbits can learn to use a litter box; rats and guinea pigs can learn to come when you call; and even the tiniest of the pocket pets can learn a few useful skills, like when dinner is coming and how to feel comfortable in the palm of your hand.

Some adopted small animals don't need to know too much. They just need healthy living conditions and proper care. However, others can learn quite a bit. Ferrets, rabbits, and rats, in particular, are interactive creatures that can be trained with good results. Training these pets can make them much easier to live with. With the right direction, even the smallest of the small animals can make a great pet. It just takes a little know-how. In the sections that follow, I tell you what you can and should teach your small animal . . . and what, conversely, may be expecting a little too much of your pet.

The easiest and best way to train a small animal is to work with their natural instincts. Understanding the way your small animal thinks explains plenty about how to communicate with him, and really, that's all training is: intraspecies communication.

Litter-box training your ferret

Young ferrets are the easiest to train to use the litter box, but if you have adopted an older ferret that never was litter-box trained, with a little patience and persistence, you probably can train him to use the box. Adopted ferrets that absolutely will not use the litter box may have a medical problem and need to be checked by a vet.

For a healthy ferret, successful litter-box training is a snap, as long as you remember that ferrets:

- ✔ Like to eliminate in corners
- ✔ Won't eliminate where they eat or sleep
- ✔ Won't hold it or wait long to find a good spot to do their business

Understanding these three principles makes litter-box training relatively easy if you put a litter box, a food bowl, or a bed in opposite corners of areas to which your ferret has access and have several litter boxes at convenient locations so your ferret never has to go far to get to one.

Litter boxes with high sides are best for ferrets, to avoid *overspraying,* or tinkling in a spray that overreaches the sides of the litter box. Some boxes are made just for ferrets. They fit nicely in corners and have extrahigh sides. The front part needs to have a low side so the ferret can climb in easily.

Follow these tips, and you can have your ferret litter-box trained in about a week (younger ferrets may learn more quickly, older adopted ferrets may take longer):

- ✔ Put a litter box filled with recycled paper filler or wood pellet filler in a corner of your ferret's cage, and place food bowls or bedding in the other corners. Ferrets don't like to use their eating or sleeping quarters as a bathroom.
- ✔ Leave a little bit of waste in the litter boxes at first, so your ferret smells where the proper spot is.
- ✔ Praise your ferret with great exuberance for going in his litter box — even offer him a treat, even if he doesn't do anything in there. When he

eliminates in the litter box, praise him even more. Ferrets like your attention and try to repeat the things that make you focus on them, so be sure to give them your attention when they eliminate in the right spot; punishing a ferret for making a mistake may make him repeat the wrong behavior because to a ferret, attention may be desirable, even if it is negative. Ignore mistakes completely, except to clean them up.

✔ Move your ferret to the litter box immediately whenever you see him backing into a corner, a sure sign that he's preparing to do his business.

Try schedule-training your ferret by putting him in his litter box every time he wakes up from a nap, comes out to play, or finishes eating or drinking.

✔ Try putting a couple of drops of vanilla extract in all your ferret's litter boxes. Some ferrets are attracted to the smell of vanilla.

Litter-box training your rabbit

Rabbits don't have to leave those little *pills,* or round pellets of poop, everywhere they go. They can easily be litter-box trained, even as adults. In fact, adult rabbits actually are easier to train to the litter box than young rabbits.

Unlike ferrets, dogs, and cats, rabbits sleep and use the bathroom in the same spot. And if your rabbit urinates or defecates in her food or water bowl, that just means she's marking her territory — don't expect her never to mark her territory elsewhere in her cage — once in awhile — especially if you have other pets

A large cat-sized litter box works great for a rabbit, but you need to fill it with recycled paper filler or grass pellets rather than cat-box filler, which can be dangerous to a rabbit if she accidentally eats some of it.

You can enjoy success with litter-box training your adult rabbit in just a few days and your younger rabbit in a few weeks (some rabbits learn more quickly or take much longer, depending on the rabbit), if you follow these tips:

✔ Rabbits like a clean environment, so you need to clean out the litter box at least twice a day to encourage them to go in the box.

✔ Put some timothy or oat hay in the box to attract your rabbit.

✔ Keep a litter box in the corner of your rabbit's cage and in every room or area where your rabbit spends free time, is allowed to roam, or tends to use for a bathroom.

✔ Put newspapers in your rabbit's cage while you're training, instead of letting your rabbit walk on the wire bottom and excrete through the mesh. Besides, wire is bad for your rabbit's feet, and the newspaper gives you a chance to clean up any messes immediately.

Try putting just a little piece of the soiled newspaper into the litter box to direct your rabbit to the right location. The rabbit will smell her own scent from the soiled newspaper in the litter box and be more likely to choose that spot as her future personal toilet.

✔ Put your rabbit in her litter box often to encourage her to recognize the pleasant experience the litter box provides.

✔ Keep the food bowls scrupulously clean and keep just a little scent of waste in the litter box. As long as you do, your rabbit soon catches on.

✔ Avoid punishing your rabbit for mistakes. Instead, shower him with gentle cheerful praise when he does what you want.

✔ Having your rabbit spayed or neutered makes litter-box training even easier.

Hand-taming pocket pets

Smaller animals — being prey animals — are shy and aren't likely to leap into your hand the first time they meet you. When you weigh only a few ounces, you have to protect yourself. However, small animals can quickly learn that you indeed are trustworthy. You just need to be patient, calm, and gentle.

Some small animals are easier to hand-tame than others. Ferrets, rats, hamsters, gerbils, and mice may be happy to let you pick them up upon first meeting. These social critters want to play! Guinea pigs probably won't take long to trust you, but they aren't much for being carried around. They'd probably prefer exploring you on the floor to having you pick them up. Guinea pigs also can learn to purr happily in your lap while you pet them. Rabbits and chinchillas tend to be a little more skittish, and so are pets that have been neglected, not socialized with humans into adulthood, or even abused. The latter may be particularly shy about letting you hold them. To hand-tame a shy critter, use these steps to build trust and confidence:

1. **Let your critter adjust to his new home.**

   Allow a day or two to pass before you attempt to handle him.

2. **Interact with your critter in the evening to get him used to your presence.**

   Most critters are nocturnal, so visiting your critter at the same time every evening is best. Try sitting next to the cage and quietly talking to your critter every day for a few days before ever trying to touch him. Approach the cage slowly and quietly, but head-on so you don't look like you're a predator sneaking up on its prey.

3. **Start to touch your new critter slowly.**

   Open the cage, put your hand in, and put a treat on your palm. Let your critter do all the work to start out, sniffing and exploring your hand. A shy critter may not even approach your hand for a few days, but keep trying once or twice a day when your critter is awake.

4. **Let your critter crawl into your palm to get the treat several times without trying to lift him out right away.**

   As he gains confidence crawling into your palm, you then can begin moving your hand a little at a time. If he runs away at first, that's fine. Just do it again the next day. Baby steps!

5. **Allow your critter a few weeks to warm up to being held and petted.**

   Most critters are happy to let you hold and pet them after a few weeks; however, remember that any sudden movement, a scare, a loud noise, or grabbing at your critter can truly terrify him, and like some critters, he may not soon forget the experience. You may have to start all over again, and it can take even longer the second time.

Children (and maybe even adults) need to wear long pants when holding a rabbit on their laps because a startled bunny can leap off and accidentally scratch the child with his claws.

Keep these ideas in mind while hand-taming your critter:

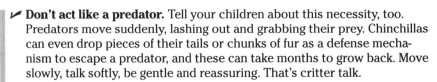

- **Don't act like a predator.** Tell your children about this necessity, too. Predators move suddenly, lashing out and grabbing their prey. Chinchillas can even drop pieces of their tails or chunks of fur as a defense mechanism to escape a predator, and these can take months to grow back. Move slowly, talk softly, be gentle and reassuring. That's critter talk.

- **Spend more time next to the cage, talking and offering treats.** If your critter is aggressive and tries to bite you, he may be responding to past traumatic events, or simple basic fear, and you may need to slow down. Don't touch your critter. When he starts coming out often to see you and score those yummy treats, you can gradually try to touch him again. Be patient!

- **Understand that some adopted critters may never trust humans.** If they've had traumatic experiences in the past, you may never get to hold your critter, but you can still spend plenty of time watching and talking to him, feeding him, and learning about him. If that's enough for you, you can feel good about having rescued a critter, even if you can't cuddle with him.

Teaching small animals to come

Some small animals quickly learn to come on cue, because for critters, life is all about finding good things to eat. If a sound from you always means a treat, your critter learns to come a'runnin'. For any critter this kind of training is simple. Decide on the sound you want to mean "Come." Sounds that are clearly different than other sounds are best. For instance, a whistle, a click, or shaking the treat box are better sounds than just a word, which may sound to your critter like every other word you say. Critters also respond well to clicker training (see Chapter 7), so try this method to precisely reinforce behaviors you want your critter to repeat, like coming when called.

All you have to do is make the sound — whistle, treat-box shake, click from the clicker — and immediately give your critter a treat, and do so often, many times a day. The treat can be a piece of your critter's regular food, maybe his favorite kind of seed or piece of fruit, or whatever is healthy for your critter but motivating enough to get his attention. It won't take long for your critter to associate that sound with a reward, and when you make the sound, your critter probably comes to you quickly. This training is handy for when you want to round up free-roaming critters to go back in their cages or to coax hiding critters out of their nests or dens to play. Repeat, repeat, repeat: sound and treat. Simple!

Interpreting Your Small Animal's Sounds and Movements

Small animals are fascinating to watch, and each individual species has its own unique sounds, movements, and behaviors. Although humans don't always know everything a critter is thinking or conveying by its actions and sounds, behavioral scientists have figured out some basic truths about critter communication. Here's what to look for — and what it probably means — when your critter sends you those curious critter communiqués.

Understanding ferret sounds and behavior

Ferrets make many interesting sounds. The ones that sound like laughing, hissing, or squeaking generally are signs of happy play behavior. Crying and whining usually are signs that your ferret is uncomfortable or needs something. Ferrets are acrobatic and active, particularly when they're young, and they love to explore, hunching about like little weasels and snaking into small spaces just to see what may be in there.

Ferrets need several hours every day to play outside of their cages so they can exercise and vent their high energy.

Ferrets tend to play actively for short periods and then take long naps. However, if your ferret shows no energy at all, is shy, hiding, crying, or refuses to play, he may be sick. Talk to your vet.

Hearing what your rabbit is saying

Rabbits may be the ultimate prey animal; even domesticated rabbits often behave as if they're constantly afraid of being gobbled up. Rabbits have long ears to hear any sign of impending danger, ever-twitching noses to catch a wiff of any scents of predators, and an ever-alert behavior. Rabbits often look nervous . . . and they are! They don't like to be held off the ground, and most rabbits don't enjoy being carried around, perhaps because they feel they can't make a quick escape. Rabbits hate to be chased, and fast-moving people and other pets make them extremely nervous — never let anybody chase your bunny. Children need to be taught to slow down and approach rabbits calmly, quietly, and as unlike a predator as possible. Some rabbits do like to sit in laps for petting, but preferably while you sit on the floor.

If your rabbit leaps into the air or screams, you know he's truly terrified. Remedy the unsettling situation immediately!

Rabbits generally are quiet, but sometimes they make:

- ✔ Purring and clicking sounds that usually signal contentment
- ✔ Teeth chattering and growling that can mean fear, anger, or pain
- ✔ Screams that signal terror

If you can't find any reason for your rabbit's unhappy noises, talk to your vet.

A rabbit that is relaxed and happy in his home environment relaxes fully onto the floor with legs lazily outstretched, ears relaxed, and belly exposed. Now that's trust. If your rabbit rubs his chin on you, feel justifiably flattered. Your rabbit is rubbing his scent glands on his territory, marking you as inexorably *his*. Congratulations! Your bunny loves you.

Rabbits need plenty of time outside of their cages to hop around the house, interact with you, or just explore their surroundings. Never let a day pass without free-bunny time.

Figuring out your rat's behavior

Rats are truly sociable little creatures that can develop fairly complex relationships with humans. You can teach rats tricks, basic commands, and they're happy to hang around with you, riding on your shoulder, sitting on your lap, or even playing a game of fetch. Really! Rats are smart little critters, and the more you interact with them, the more you give them an opportunity to exercise their formidable intelligence.

Just because your rat has a buddy doesn't mean he doesn't need time with you. Rats do best with at least a few hours of cage-free interactive time every day.

When rats grind their teeth, they're usually contented, but teeth chattering with hackles raised usually means they're upset. Rats are more outgoing and naturally less cautious than mice and other small animals, because they're larger and better at defending themselves against predators. Rats nevertheless can be startled or frightened by a careless child or a too-curious dog or cat, so protect your rattie from harm and fear. Rats are social creatures that prefer the company of other rats (same-sex-only please). Wrestling is a normal interactive behavior for two rats, but if two male rats actually start fighting — and wounding each other — try housing three together to break up the tension.

Listening to your guinea pig

Guinea pigs generally are *not* fond of being carried around, and picking them up incorrectly can damage their spines. However, guinea pigs need and crave interaction with their fellow pigs and with you. Just keep them on the floor, lifting them out of their cages carefully with one hand over their backs and one hand under their bellies and keeping them level.

Guinea pigs make a wide range of interesting noises. Chuts and chutters, wheeks and whistles, squeals and purrs and drrs and chirrups . . . you may feel like you need a translation guide! In general, however, soft grunting, purring, or muttering sounds mean your guinea pig is happily going about his business, but loud teeth chattering, squealing, or screaming are signs your guinea pig isn't having a good time. Guinea pigs are pretty mellow and sociable, so if a guinea pig screams, bites, or scratches, you can be assured he's extremely frightened. Back off and let him calm down.

Guinea pigs are so food motivated that they can be pretty vocal, wheeking for all they're worth, when they see you heading toward the refrigerator or the box of yogurt drops. This kind of noise is all about anticipation. Hand-feeding your guinea — healthy treats only, please — is the quickest way to the heart of your little pig.

Don't keep your pigs in the pen *all* the time. Guinea pigs need to spend some time outside of their cages each day to wander around and check out the wide world beyond their cage walls.

Checking out hamster, gerbil, and mouse behaviors

Hamsters, gerbils, and mice are tiny pets that can be shy but generally are easy to hand-tame and enjoy socializing with humans and each other (with the notable exceptions of Golden hamsters and male mice, which need to be housed alone or they fight). These little critters all like to have plenty of bedding for digging and burrowing, and they enjoy shredding paper towels and cardboard. They are good escape artists but enjoy romping around the room inside a hamster ball or running on a wheel inside their cages to expend energy and get exercise. Hamsters tend to hide their food away, storing it up for the winter — just in case. Hamsters and gerbils tend to be more active at night, while mice are active about any time. All these animals may occasionally make tiny little noises, but the only time they will really squeak is if they are in pain or frightened. When your tiny guy speaks up, you'd best pay attention!

How smart is your critter?

Assuming a rat is smarter than a mouse or a ferret is smarter than a hamster is easy, but how intelligence in small animals is determined can be tricky. If a small animal is good at reproducing and avoiding predators, well, that's pretty smart in small-animal terms. If a small animal is good at interacting with humans on a more sophisticated level, like rats and ferrets, that seems to us to be pretty smart, in human terms. It's all a matter of perspective, but most animal behaviorists agree that the more you interact with and stimulate your small animal — physically and mentally — the more you give that animal's natural intelligence a chance to develop fully.

Part V
Bringing Home a Feathered Friend

The 5th Wave By Rich Tennant

"I really don't think there's anything funny about adopting a parrot just because it sings the theme from 'Mission Impossible' whenever I use my Ab-Cruncher."

In this part . . .

*I*f you're really for the birds, this part of the book is for you. Birds can make excellent companions for the right people, but pair them with the wrong people and disaster is bound to result. That's why so many birds need new homes. But before you decide on a feathered friend, read this part of the book to be sure bird ownership really is for you. Birds — especially large parrots — can be a real challenge, but these chapters prepare you for what living with a pet bird is really like. And you discover how to find a bird veterinarian, what birds must eat (hint: it isn't just seeds), and the kind of personal and veterinary care birds require. You also find out how to recognize and apply sensible strategies when dealing with common problems of adopted birds.

Chapter 16

From Macaws to Budgies: Choosing Your Feathered Friend

In This Chapter

▶ Understanding the special needs of pet birds and the extraspecial needs of adopted birds

▶ Deciding whether you can accept the noise, the mess, and the high care needs of birds

▶ Meeting the different types of birds and what they're like

▶ Finding bird rescue groups and shelters with birds that need homes

*Y*ou've seen them in pet stores, in friends' homes, maybe in zoos or while visiting the tropics: beautiful, brightly colored birds singing, talking, fluttering their plumage, and even doing tricks. The idea of a bird as a pet can be compelling, but a bird in reality can be a real handful, depending on what kind you choose to adopt.

People don't often realize just how difficult birds — particularly large parrots — are to keep, maintain, and tolerate. The noise level alone is daunting, let alone the constant care, cleanup, and social interaction that large birds can require. For that reason, many, large parrots and other birds have been abandoned to bird rescues and animal shelters. Even smaller birds, which have fewer aggressive care needs than larger birds, wait in shelters to be recycled into new homes.

But of course, adopting a bird doesn't do any good if like the original owner(s) you end up having to abandon the bird yet again because *you* can't handle the required living arrangements either. In that spirit, this chapter tells you the good, the bad, and the ugly of what it means to adopt a bird and explains the characteristics of many different kinds of parrots and other birds, so you can determine whether bird ownership really is for you. If you decide that it indeed is, then check out the last part of this chapter for information about tracking down national, regional, and local shelters and rescue groups that have birds waiting for new homes with humans who understand what they really need.

Understanding Your Adopted Bird

"SQQQUUUUUU*AAAAAAAAAAA*WWWWWWKK!!!!" Yikes, what was that horrifically loud, piercing noise? Oh, nothing, just the cockatoo.

That noise, however may be indicative of your spending only four hours with him today, and he doesn't think that's enough. He probably wants you to deliver another snack, and watch out, because he just may decide to try to nip off the tip of your finger — he wouldn't be the first cockatoo to remove a sizeable chunk of human flesh.

No, this loud, demanding, and sometimes bloody scenario isn't an attempt to send you shrieking in the opposite direction . . . well, not exactly.

Birds, unlike many of the other animals I talk about in *Adopting a Pet For Dummies,* essentially are neither domesticated nor cut out for confinement. To be successful as pets, birds require very clean, spacious conditions and specialized training from the get-go. They need lots of handling, interaction, hands-on treatment, training, a regular schedule . . . and even then, after they hit adolescence, they become difficult anyway. Like small animals, birds often are affectionate only during their baby years, but when they grow up, they won't have patience for cuddling, stroking, and other such biped nonsense. A sexually mature bird may consider you his mate, but beware the large parrot who fancies to you. Male parrots aren't exactly romantic with their mates. Many adult women are chased around the proverbial desk by amorous parrots, and if one catches you, watch out. He can bite, and hard. You've seen those big beaks.

Adopted birds of all shapes and sizes more than likely have aged past the cuddly baby stage, and in most cases, were relinquished because people couldn't live with their seeming rude behavior. Adopted birds experience many behavioral issues related to neglect, too much confinement, and improper care. Some start pulling out all their feathers until they're virtually naked. Others injure their own skin, fight incessantly, or try to bite any human body part that gets within striking distance. And yes, some make noises louder than any human can make.

By adopting a bird that has been relinquished, you're agreeing not only to acknowledge that bird's behavior issues but to do your best to resolve them, so your bird and the humans with whom he lives can be healthy, happy, and sane.

When birds don't get the attention they need, they become even more difficult. Some people argue that birds aren't meant to live in cages, but rescuing a pet bird in need of a home is an act of kindness — as long as you can give the bird a good life — because once treated as a pet, birds have little chance of survival if returned to the wild.

Some adopted birds are difficult to hand tame, especially if they've never been hand tamed before or they've had bad experiences with human interaction. Some prefer the company of other birds, as long as they have plenty of room to move around, claim their own space, and interact with plenty of room to flee when necessary. Other birds prefer to be alone. Personality clashes and fights can lead to unhappy results, including injury and even death. In other words, adopted birds need you to provide the appropriate, safe living and social environment for them.

Knowing What Adopted Birds Need

Birds *need.* They need a lot. And if you don't have the time, the patience, and a high tolerance for loud noises and an occasional painful bite, you may want to reconsider your dreams of owning a great big parrot to add a tropical flare to your living room. When they're well managed and they get plenty of exercise, stimulation, interesting toys, positive structured social interaction, and a varied nutritious diet, many birds make fine — if loud — pets. The larger birds can work well in a home where people work at home or for businesses where activity exists during the day and the night is peaceful, assuming noise isn't a problem. But birds also are messy, scattering their food, splashing in their water, spreading dust and feathers far and wide. And the more unhappy, unsatisfied, or bored they are, the louder and more destructive they become.

In short, here's what most pet birds need from their pet owners (that's you). Adopted birds need all these things (see list that follows), perhaps even more urgently than a bird that has always had all its needs met, for them to adjust to their new homes and to learn that humans are sources of good things and a safe environment:

✔ Freshly prepared food, including fruits and vegetables, raw and cooked, and a prepared diet with complete nutrition, according to your particular bird's needs (for more on what your bird needs to eat, see Chapter 18).

✔ Fresh pure water — replenished at least daily or when it becomes dirty or your bird uses it as a toilet, which can mean more frequently.

✔ A clean cage that sometimes requires daily cleanup. If *you* also want a clean environment, add to the daily cage-cleaning, sweeping up or vacuuming the area surrounding the cage — even if you have a cage with a seed-catcher.

Feathers float and seed husks and messy fruits and vegetables will be flung.

✔ Things to chew. Constantly replenish chew toys as they're destroyed or become old news and boring. *Note:* Bird toys are expensive, and in some cases, you need to replace them weekly.

So happy together (or not)

Assuming adequate cage space is provided (and potential exceptions are noted), bird expert Nikki Moustaki in *Parrots For Dummies* (published by Wiley), indicates the following birds are most likely to get along with each other:

✔ Cockatiels

✔ Budgies

✔ Hanging parrots

✔ Conures

Moustaki says the birds least likely to get along well with other birds (and prone to fighting) are:

✔ Cockatoos

✔ Caiques

✔ Lovebirds (ironically)

✔ Some macaws

✔ Lories

✔ Things to climb on, swing from, and play with. Adopted birds may have a lot of excess energy, and they need an outlet so they don't get anxious and stressed.

✔ A cage . . . a big cage. The bird needs to have plenty of room to flap around, climb around, and have different areas to hang out in.

✔ Time out of the cage, including perches and a play area outside of the cage large enough to climb around on.

✔ A whole lot of attention, interaction, training, and even discipline. Parrots spend much of their lives doing a darned good imitation of a child in the throes of the terrible 2's, and they need at least a few visits from you for training and talking every day. The more time you can spend with your bird, the better. A large parrot would probably prefer to hang out on your shoulder all day long, if you'd let him, but even small birds need you to pay attention to them for at least two or three 15-minute sessions every day. Adopted birds may need an extra degree of patience during this integration time because they might not trust humans.

Finding a Breed that Suits You

If meeting all of the needs birds have sounds doable and you still think you want to adopt one, the next step is considering what kind of bird best fits your lifestyle. Challenging as they may be, some birds are easier deal with than others, and some people and situations are better suited to some birds than others. Larger birds are louder, messier (only because they eat more), can do more damage when they bite, and thus are not normally good pets for homes with children. Smaller birds still make a mess and often spend much of the day twittering away, a sound that you either enjoy because it's so lovely or hate because it irritates the heck out of you. Small birds are easier to care for, however, and make better pets for beginning bird owners. Although every bird is an individual and generalizations always come with exceptions, here's what to consider about different types of birds.

Choosing for health and temperament

The type of bird you choose (see the sections that follow) has a great deal to do with how you and your bird get along and interact, but if the bird you choose is unhealthy or has an undesirable temperament, the particular kind of bird hardly matters. Before you whisk that pretty bird home, take a good hard look for signs of health problems and temperament problems. With birds, the two often are related. A bird with an anxious, aggressive, or fearful temperament may look unhealthy because he's plucked his own feathers or bashed himself around in the cage. A bird with a health problem may be nippy, aggressive, or fearful, because he doesn't feel good.

Some people are willing to adopt birds with health and temperament problems, but because of the added veterinary expenses involved and the even greater time commitment special-needs birds require, you had better know what you're getting into. You always need to take your bird to the veterinarian before making an adoption official (for more about this process, see Chapter 18). Only a vet can truly tell you whether your bird is healthy, but as a first step toward finding a healthy bird with a good personality, here are the signs that your bird is in good health and has a suitable or at least trainable temperament:

✔ The bird needs to have bright full plumage with no bare spots or missing or broken feathers. Cockatoos have a bald spot under their crests, which is normal, but bare patches on the chest, cracked quills, and raggedy-looking feathers can be signs of ill health or a behavior problem.

✔ The bird needs to have clear, clean eyes and a clean shiny beak. Cloudy eyes or any discharge from eyes or nostrils can indicate a health problem. If you can get a look in the bird's mouth, you should see a clean dry tongue without white spots or ulcers.

✔ The bird's vent, or rear end, needs to be clean and dry.

✔ The bird needs to act alert and react to you. A tired or listless bird may be a sign of a health problem.

✔ When you interact with the bird, he should seem interested in you, not frightened half to death or aggressively trying to attack you. Even birds with good temperaments can be loud and needy, but you want to avoid extremely fearful or aggressive birds, which can be difficult to manage.

Go large: Macaws and cockatoos

Large parrots — fluffy white cockatoos with their dramatic crests and brightly colored macaws with their huge hooked bills and superior talking ability — are the most challenging birds to keep as pets. They can live 80 years or longer and produce the most incredibly loud sounds. When they bite, it really hurts. That said, some people nevertheless are willing to put up with the less attractive aspects of owning large parrots and provide them with what they need.

Cockatoos come in 18 different species and many more subspecies, ranging from just over a foot in height to more that two feet. When cockatoos are babies, they're famous for being cuddly and adoring. As adults, however, that kind of behavior rarely continues, and people find themselves dealing with an emotionally sensitive bird with huge care needs that emits a dust to which many people find themselves very allergic. Sensitive and needy, cockatoos require plenty of interaction and tolerance to noise. Some of the more common types of cockatoos that you may find in need of adoption are

- ✔ **Moluccan cockatoos** are the most common type of cockatoo, and they're one of the loudest of the large parrots. They require constant social activity. If they don't get it, they become neurotic and can turn to self-mutilation.

- ✔ **Sulfur-crested cockatoos** are another common type of cockatoo, which actually refers to several different kinds of cockatoos with yellow crests.

- ✔ **Umbrella cockatoos** are slightly smaller and all white. Charming and affectionate, umbrella cockatoos also are incredibly loud and easily displeased.

Rescue groups are overflowing with cockatoos, because they're so incredibly difficult to keep. Please be sure that you're really ready for the noise, mess, time, expense, and emotional commitment cockatoos require.

Macaws come in 17 different species and range from one foot to more than three feet in length. These birds are smart, good at talking, and can develop interesting and complex relationships with people, but they're also incredibly loud and can easily dismantle an entire fancy wooden ($30) bird toy in 20 minutes. Macaws are prone to periods of all-out shrieking and screaming, usually around sunrise or sunset. Your neighbors probably won't be fond of these times of day. Some common types of macaws that are likely to be up for adoption include:

- ✔ **Blue-and-gold macaws** are the most common type of macaw. Because there are so many of them and because they tend to be moody and sometimes unpredictable, many are abandoned to rescue groups.

✔ **Military macaws,** another common type, are a little smaller than the blue and gold. They're green and tend to be very outgoing, but they're also easier to train and socialize than other macaws — not easy, mind you, just eas-*ier.*

✔ **Greenwing macaws** are among the largest of the macaws. Greenwings are about 35-inches long with a huge beak. They're less prone to nipping and unpredictable mood swings.

✔ **Scarlet macaws** are a brilliant scarlet red and can reach 39 inches in length. Scarlet macaws are smart, feisty, and they bite hard and are prone to random nips for no apparent reason.

✔ **Hyacinth macaws** are the largest of the macaws. Bright blue, they sometimes exceed 40 inches in length. Although very sociable birds, they can play rough with their formidable beaks, which are capable of easily biting off a human finger. These birds are not for novice bird owners.

Talking about Amazon parrots and African greys

Amazon parrots and African greys are medium-to-large birds that are the enthusiastic talkers of the parrot world. However, because of their long life spans, social needs, occasional tendency to nip, and high-volume method of voicing their displeasure, many of these intelligent and beautiful birds are abandoned to rescue groups and shelters.

Amazon parrots are the pretty green ones, but different species have different splashes of color here and there. The yellow-naped and yellow-headed Amazons are the most common. They talk well, are smart, but they're unpredictable and moody. You may be getting along just fine, then out of nowhere, your Amazon decides to chomp on your ear. Ouch! Nevertheless, they like to be out and about, hanging with you on your shoulder and checking out what you're doing. The blue-fronted, orange-winged, and lilac-crowned Amazons are less common but still are frequently kept as pets, so you may sometimes see them with rescue groups.

The Congo and Timneh African greys are the two types of parrots with grey feathers of varying shades. The Congo has a scarlet tail, and the Timneh has a maroon to black tail. The African grey arguably is the smartest and most verbal of the parrots, and it can develop intense and interactive relationships with humans. Some even learn words in context and are happiest with plenty of communicating and interacting. Greys are among the easier parrots to train because of their intelligence and willingness to engage in activities with you.

Conures, Quakers, toucans, and other medium-sized birds

Many medium-sized birds seem like smart and interactive pets without the size of the larger parrots, but watch out. You may be surprised how loud these medium-sized guys can be. A conure can blast your eardrums with his exuberant screeching! Quaker parakeets can scare you out of your skin with their sudden cries. Here's what you need to know before deciding on any of these medium-sized birds:

- ✔ **Conures** come in 42 species from across South and Central America and range from about 8 to 18 inches in length. Conures are outgoing and affectionate but l-o-u-d! You may be amazed by how much noise such a little bird can make. Not only are they loud, they also make a lot of noise. Conures also enjoy having another conure, of any species, as a cage buddy, as long as they have enough room to share. (Did I mention they're *loud?*)

- ✔ **Quaker parakeets** are docile-looking birds with big mouths. They're sometimes called monk parrots and they're good talkers that can acquire large vocabularies. Some states consider Quakers illegal, because they're so prolific in the wild, including in the United States, from Florida to the Northeast and even into the Midwest. Quaker parakeets are so named because they actually shake and quake, bobbing their heads and looking a little like they're having a seizure. Not to worry, it's simply the Quaker parakeet's way. Quaker parakeets are affectionate and like to be handled, but they're very loud and make noise for much of the day.

- ✔ **Lovebirds** come in nine species, all from Africa. The most common pet Lovebirds are the peachfaced, masked, and Fischer's. The *peachfaced* is the most common and is quieter than most medium-sized birds, but they will whistle and sing. They don't usually talk. Lovebirds may sound made for each other, but they often fight with each other, unless you find a matched pair that have good chemistry. Lovebirds must be handled daily, or they become nippy and antisocial.

- ✔ **Lories** are happy, busy, vocal birds that require a special diet of soft fruits and flowers, because they can't crush or digest seeds like many other birds. They require a nectar powder mixed with juice made just for lories and the occasional inset treat (mealworms and grubs).They also have messy wet droppings. If you've heard Lories don't need water, don't believe it. They don't get along well with other birds but they need a lot of attention and supervision from you, because they're likely to get into mischief. Watch your fingers, though, lories can be biters. Oddly, they like to sleep on their backs, so don't be surprised if your lorie looks dead. He's probably just snoozing.

✔ **Eclectus parrots** come in nine subspecies and are notorious for being loud. One of the few parrots that are easy to sex, the green eclectus are the males, and the red are the females. Their soft small feathers look almost like fur. Eclectus are real talkers and can learn many words and say them often, loudly, and interspersed with shrieking, just for fun.

✔ Other less common birds that occasionally pop up with rescue groups are **caiques** (pronounced *kai*-EKES), **toucans, mynah birds, vasa parrots, brotogeris parrots, hanging parrots, hawkhead parrots, parrotlets, pionus,** and rarer species of some of the more common birds listed above. Each has unique care needs, and any rescue group worth working with can give you detailed care information and make sure you're prepared for a rare bird's individual needs.

What about doves?

Doves or pigeons come in more than 300 species. They populate our urban areas, but some people keep them as pets, breed them, show them, or raise them as homing pigeons. Domestic doves or pigeons all are descended from the Rock Dove. Doves are calm, quiet birds, but they don't talk and they aren't very interactive. They may learn to sit on your finger, but you probably won't develop the kind of intricate social bond you can develop with louder, messier parrots.

Parakeets and cockatiels: Pros and cons

American parakeets — also called budgies — and cockatiels are the easiest birds to own and generally are much easier to adopt from rescue groups. Because they are easier to handle, rescue groups will consider homes for these little guys that they wouldn't consider appropriate for a larger bird. Friendly, sociable, and interactive, they're also not as loud or messy as larger birds, simply because of their smaller size (see Figure 16-1). But they still scatter seed and feathers, bite if they're displeased or frightened, demand attention, and require good nutrition, a clean spacious cage, and fresh water. They won't, however, blast out your eardrums, preferring, instead, to sing and whistle happily quite often throughout the day.

If you clip their wings to keep them from hurting themselves, budgies and cockatiels can be trained to spend time out of the cage, riding around on your shoulder, hopping around on the table, eating from your hand, and generally being a good little buddy.

Parakeets and cockatiels can bite; they can injure or frighten a small child if they're treated roughly and feel forced to defend themselves. They're delicate and easily injured if squeezed, dropped, or handled roughly. If they're loose, they can fly into ceiling fans, boiling pots of water, or out the window. An adult must be ultimately responsible for the care, feeding, cleaning, and safety of these small, happy birds.

Figure 16-1:
Parakeets (left) and cockatiels (right) make friendly and vocal pets.

After you've decided that rescuing a bird is indeed your destiny, and you've figured out which kinds of birds may suit your needs, you're ready to locate the bird of your dreams. You have a few options. Although you can find a bird in the newspaper ("free to good home"), this option is not the most desirable option, because although such birds may well need good homes, you may not get the full story about the bird's health, behavioral issues, or care needs. An animal shelter or bird rescue group is much more likely to have:

✓ Evaluated the bird for suitability in a pet home

✓ Enlisted the services of a vet to check the bird for health problems

✓ Worked with the bird to determine its personality and other relevant information a pet owner wants to know before making a choice

First, be sure check with your local animal shelter and rescue group to find out whether they have birds. Don't rush to buy the first bird you see. Remember your limitations, your abilities, and what you're willing to handle. Think about the kind of bird that works for you, and then visit birds as they become available, using your head — and not your heart — when making a decision. Let the experts at the shelter advise and help you decide about adopting a bird.

If you aren't sure where to find a shelter or perhaps want to look beyond your immediate region, use the shelter-finder resources on the Internet. Many of the animal-shelter resources can help you search for birds, so I've listed them here again, for your convenience.

✓ Search by type of bird and your zip code at Petfinder: www.petfinder.com

✓ Find local shelters at Pets911: www.pets911.com

✓ The ASPCA maintains a list of animal shelters: www.aspca.org

To find a bird through a bird rescue group, search the following sites. You'll find lots of information about bird care, deciding what kind of bird is right for you, and where to find birds in need of homes. These sites do not promote bird breeding but rather rescuing birds that were saved from unhealthy, neglectful, or abusive situations or whose owners can no longer keep them. Don't be offended if these groups screen potential adopters carefully. They don't want to see their precious feathered rescues endure any more loss or abuse. It's all about the birds:

✔ Foster Parrots is a parrot rescue, adoption, and sanctuary: www.foster parrots.com

✔ Bird Adoption.org lists bird rescue groups by state: www.birdadoption. org/groups.htm

✔ Bird Placement Program, Inc.: www.birdrescue.com

✔ Avian rescue: www.avianrescue.org

Chapter 17

Creating a Bird-Friendly Home

- -

In This Chapter

▶ Making your home safe for a new bird

▶ Buying and building the supplies you need

▶ Introducing your bird to his new home and family, including kids and pets

▶ Recognizing adjustment and potential health problems

- -

*B*efore you bring your beautiful new adopted bird into your home, you have a few important jobs to do. Your home can be hazardous for a bird in ways you had not considered. You want to think about how much access you want to give your bird to your home, whether you want him to fly, and where to keep his cage. You also want to be fully stocked with the best bird supplies so your new bird has everything he needs from day one.

In this chapter, you discover how to prepare your home, including safety considerations and supply checklists. You also get a quick tutorial on how to introduce your bird to his new environment and on potential problems you may encounter along with some simple solutions. Let's take wing!

Getting Ready for a Bird in the House

Your bird may have already been around the block, transferring from place to place as various owners haven't been able to care for him. He may have already encountered some hazardous situations or even been injured for lack of a bird-proofed environment in the past. But that's all over now! You're committed to providing your bird with a safe, healthy home. Here's what to do.

Bird-proofing

Birds are clever, acrobatic, curious, mischievous, and great climbers. They can get into places you never imagined they could. Even with clipped wings (for more on wing clipping, see the section later in the chapter, "To fly free or not to fly free?"), they sometimes fly for short distances, especially small birds like budgies and cockatiels. Whenever you let your bird out of his cage, you need to be sure the environment that your bird explores is safe for him, especially if he happens to be a large parrot. Here's what to do:

- ✔ Block any open spaces, such as open vents, chimney flues, or holes in furniture.

- ✔ Cover or hide all electrical cords.

- ✔ Remove all zinc or lead items from the room, including galvanized metal food and water bowls. Exposure to these metals can kill your bird. Use nonreactive stainless steel instead, for your bird and for your other pets. Other common household items that can contain zinc are staples and paperclips, zippers and snaps, padlocks and keys, jewelry, hardware like nails and bolts, and coins. Some old-fashioned curtains may contain lead weights at the base. Never let your bird play with these objects, and never leave them lying around where your bird may find them.

- ✔ Trade in your nonstick cookware. When heated, nonstick chemicals release fumes that can quickly kill a bird. Switch to cast iron, stainless steel, or porcelain-coated cookware.

- ✔ Put household cleaners, medications, and personal hygiene items in a different room. Many chemicals that are harmless to humans can kill birds.

  Whenever you use household cleaners, run your self-cleaning oven, or spray perfume or hairspray, or even smoke, put your bird outside for a while. The chemicals in these fumes can kill your bird, and they can travel through your air vents, so even if your bird is in a different room, he still may be exposed.

- ✔ Put all houseplants in a different room.

- ✔ Close curtains or blinds to keep your bird from banging into glass windows. Cover or put removable decals on mirrors.

- ✔ Remove all candles. Not only is a lighted candle a hazard to a bird, but scented candles — potpourri, incense, and essential oils, too — can be hazardous to your bird.

- ✔ Always keep oven and dishwasher doors closed. A curious bird can mistake those racks in the oven or dishwasher for perches and go exploring. You may not see your bird inside these appliances when you close the door and use them. Be safe! Close the doors, and always take a peek inside before turning on any appliances . . . just in case.

- ✔ Close all windows and doors and toilet lids and fish tanks, turn off ceiling fans and appliances like stoves and ovens, put away sharp objects, and place other pets in another room whenever you plan to take your bird out of his cage.

Even within his cage, your bird needs a safe environment that's free of toxins, choking hazards, bacteria, and other dangers. Before you bring home your bird, here is what to consider when bird-proofing the location of your bird's cage:

- ✔ Place the cage out of direct sunlight and away from the drafts of air-conditioning and heating vents.

- ✔ Keep the cage in a well-lit room that never gets below about 55 to 60°F (13 to 16°C). Remember, most birds are from the tropics.

- ✔ Keep the cage away from curtains, miniblinds, household plants, or other materials your bird may be able to grab through the bars of his cage.

- ✔ Place the cage in an area where your dogs or cats cannot get to it and bother or stress your bird.

- ✔ Use newspaper or pelleted paper as a litter in the bottom of your bird's cage, but never use corncob bedding, cat litter, hay, or anything else containing dust or that may foster the growth of mold and fungus. Dust and mold spores are dangerous for birds.

After they become acclimated to their new surroundings, birds often enjoy being in a room where people hang out, so they can watch the action; however, make sure the cage is left out of the direct path of high traffic areas to prevent your bird from frequently being startled.

To fly free or not to fly free?

Maybe you feel just a little guilty not allowing your bird to fly freely. After all, in their natural environments, isn't that what birds are supposed to do? Sure, but in the same way that domesticated cats are safer inside, pet birds also are safer if they are not allowed to fly recklessly around your house. Birds that fly free in homes not only drop their droppings anywhere they please and scatter feathers far and wide, but they also are at greater risk for injury. One whack with a ceiling fan blade, one test bath in the toilet bowl, one collision with a window or mirror, and your bird can suffer serious injury or death.

However, birds with their wings clipped can explore more safely and can be supervise more easily when they can't fly away from you. Do not, however, underestimate how fast your bird can flutter-hop out of sight! Like any other pet, birds need plenty of room to exercise, interesting things to stimulate them, interaction with you, and an ever-watchful eye. No substitute for supervision exists when your bird roams, flutters, or even flies free — you realize a few minutes too late that those flight feathers have grown back in. When you can't watch your bird, let him play inside his spacious cage.

Wing clipping may sound to you like a punishment that humans exact on their pet birds to keep them in place. But in reality, it's merely trimming back a bird's flight feathers (they grow back), so the bird can't take off and freely fly around the house. Birds with clipped wings don't lose the ability to fly forever. Wing clipping thus is considered a safety measure that prevents pet birds from bashing into unseen windows, whirling ceiling fans, hot appliances, and other birdy hazards.

Some people choose not to clip their birds' wings. As a result, some small birds — parakeets, cockatiels, lovebirds — can safely fly around a bird-proofed household; however, most larger parrots need to be clipped to prevent injury and possible escape, not to mention helping you get them back into their cages when they'd rather take off to explore the house. Some people recommend clipping only one wing, but doing so only makes a bird feel unsteady and uneven. Even minor flapping from perch to cage or floor can be off-kilter.

Clipping a bird's wings is a delicate operation, and not being sure about it can result in a traumatized bird and an injured pet owner. To avoid injuring or traumatizing your bird (or yourself), have an experienced and knowledgeable avian veterinarian or bird hobbyist show you exactly how to clip your bird's wing, so you're sure you know which of your bird's feathers are the flight feathers, and which not to trim. No matter what you decide — to trim or not to trim — keeping your bird safe is your responsibility.

The Best Bird Supplies

Your bird needs some basic supplies, such as clean water, good food, and a great big roomy cage, to be healthy and well adjusted. Be sure you're well stocked before bringing home your bird. The sections that follow describe what you need.

Cage considerations

When it comes to birdcages, bigger always is better, but the cage needs to be at least as wide as two full wingspans of the bird you're housing. When you think about how much space birds use in the wild, you'll want to go big, even for small birds. Your bird will use all the space and still be ready to come out for playtime. A large, high-quality cage is a good investment. A huge outdoor aviary — in a temperate climate or for use during nice weather — is pure bird heaven.

For small birds, a large cage may even enable them to fly a little bit, from perch to perch. For a large bird, a huge cage big enough to allow climbing exercise goes a long way toward averting bad behavior. The cage needs to be large enough for the bird to do some full-out wing flapping without hitting the sides, and preferably big enough to do some serious climbing and fluttering from perch to perch.

Other things you need to consider when selecting a cage include the following:

- ✔ Cages are expensive so you may want to consider buying a used cage. If you do, though, be sure the cage is free of rust and not made from lead or zinc, heavy metals that are poison to birds.
- ✔ Make sure the bars on any cage you select are close enough together that your bird can't get his head stuck between them.
- ✔ Hang perches on which your bird can climb and toys to play with inside the cage, rotating them with other ones frequently to keep your bird interested. Don't, however, fill the cage with so many toys that your bird has no room to climb around.
- ✔ Your cage needs to be equipped with secure, nontippable water and food bowls.

Food for the birds

Birds need a high-quality premium diet made specifically for them, but mere birdseed isn't enough to keep a bird healthy. Although some birds do fine on fortified seed or pellet diets designed to provide complete nutrition, many vets think that for maximum health, birds also need fresh food, cleaned, chopped, and sometimes cooked, by you. Some adopted birds that are used to eating only seed may resist eating other fresh foods, so buy the best premium bird diet that you can find for your type of bird, and then supplement with healthy food suitable for your bird. Introduce this extra food a little at a time to help your bird adjust. For more about what your individual bird needs to thrive, see Chapter 18.

Perches

Birds can't stand comfortably or easily on flat surfaces so they need perches for comfortable standing, sitting, sleeping, and climbing. Perches help exercise a bird's feet and naturally help wear down nails and beaks. Provide your bird with a variety of perch sizes in untreated wood, and put in one cement perch to help wear down nails. Avoid slippery — although attractively natural-looking — manzanita branch perches and sandpaper perches. Your bird may have a hard time getting a good grip on the manzanita perches, and he can chew up sandpaper and ingest it. Make sure you leave plenty of space for climbing and wing flapping; you don't need to fill up the entire cage with perches!

Bird stimulation: Toys and climbing devices

Birds get bored. They want to play, climb, ring bells, scale ropes, swing on swings, and chew, chew, chew. Birds need plenty of toys and objects on which to exercise, but their cages don't need to be filled so full of toys that your bird has no room to stretch his wings. Instead, purchase or build a wide variety of toys, climbing implements, and things to chew, and then rotate them every few days or at least weekly so your bird always gets to discover something new.

You can purchase many bird accessories, but they can be expensive. You can make bird toys out of untreated ropes, untreated wood, and other items, but if you have a bird that pulls apart his toys, avoid anything that your bird can dismantle and end up choking on — such as a clapper on a bell. Look at the pet store and examine the toys to get an idea about toys that you can make yourself. With the right basic materials and a drill, you can get pretty creative.

Travel carrier or small travel cage

Use a travel carrier or small cage for transporting your bird to and from your home whenever you need to take your bird to the vet or elsewhere. You can buy a small crate, such as one you'd use to transport a cat or small dog to the vet, for medium and large parrots. A small cage with one secure perch and a cover also will work. Your bird's regular cage needs to be too large to transport conveniently, so having a travel cage is very important.

Cage cover

Sometimes birds need downtime, and you need an occasional break from screeching. A cage cover is the answer. Although you should never keep your bird covered all the time, some birds enjoy naps under wraps or prefer to be covered at night. You can spend a large amount for a custom-fitted cage cover or just use a blanket or sheet that you already have at home.

Perch cleaner

Perch cleaner is a product that dissolves cemented-on bird waste from perches and comes with a little brush. Use it, or get a steel brush to scrub perches by hand. Cleanliness is next to birdiness! If you don't want to buy a product, just scrub the perches with a steel brush and some soap and water, and rinse well. Spray them with a bleach/water solution (one part bleach to ten parts water) and let them dry completely before returning the perch to the cage.

Cuttlebone

Birds like to gnaw on *cuttlebone* (a porous crunchy fish bone), which you can buy at pet stores with a clip attached for so you can easily secure them to the side of the cage. These bones are a good source of calcium for your bird.

Nontoxic cage bedding

Newspaper or recycled paper litter make good bedding for the bottom of the bird cage. This bedding will catch the bird's droppings and control odor, and it will also make the cage look more attractive. Avoid wood shavings made from pine or cedar.

Spray bottle, grooming spray, or a bird bath

Birds like to stay clean, and some love to splash around in a wide and shallow birdbath. Others prefer you to mist them with lukewarm (never hot!) or cool water from a spray bottle. You can also spray your bird with grooming spray that's available at pet stores. For more about grooming your bird, see Chapter 18.

Nail trimmers or cement perch

Some birds keep their nails worn down nicely on a cement perch. Others occasionally need to have theirs trimmed. Ask your vet to demonstrate, so you can trim your bird's nails at home. The more hand-tame your bird, the easier trimming its nails is. If nail trimming traumatizes your bird, have your vet do it when you have your bird's wing feathers clipped, if necessary. For more about nail trimming and wing clipping as part of a regular grooming routine, see Chapter 18.

Bringing Home Birdie

Before you bring your bird home, you need to pay a visit to your avian veterinarian to make sure your bird is healthy and doesn't need to be quarantined first from other pets. Ask the vet to show you how to clip your bird's wings, so you can keep them safely shorn for out-of-cage explorations. Chapter 18 provides pointers on choosing a good bird vet and explains what to expect during that first visit. After your bird's health clearance is approved by the vet, you can bring your new friend home.

When you first bring your new bird home, you can imagine that he's a little nervous and maybe even terrified. Although some birds are so used to a changing environment that they seem unphased by their new homes, many others are shy and even fearful for at least a few days. Your bird needs a little extra sensitivity during this time. In the following sections, I explain what you need to know to help make your new adopted bird feel right at home.

Introducing your new bird to its new home

By the time you bring home your bird, you should have his new cage ready to go. The cage in which you bring your bird probably is not going to be his permanent home, because travel cages usually are too small to serve as a permanent home, unless your bird is very small. Put a blanket or towel over the back half of the cage so your bird has a spot to feel safe and be sure that it's located out of direct sunlight and drafts. Keep a blanket handy to cover the entire cage when your bird needs some down time, but never keep it covered all day just to stop your bird from squawking. Deal with the squawking instead. (See Chapter 19 for more about dealing with bird noise.)

Try to pick up your new bird first thing in the morning, because nighttime can be scary for a new bird. When you pick up your bird in the morning, he has an entire day to get used to a new cage, new house, and new sights, sounds, and movements in your home.

When you arrive at home, your first big challenge is moving your new bird from the travel cage into his new home cage without letting him fly away, injure himself, or bite off your finger. A sensible goal, right? If your bird already is hand-tame with clipped wings, getting him into his new cage is easy. If not, you have to be ready for just about anything.

When handling your bird initially, wear thick leather gloves. If your adopted bird has had bad experiences with human hands, he may not associate gloves with those past experiences. And if your bird bites you (or the glove, that is), it won't hurt, and you'll be able to continue handling him without losing control or composure or scaring your bird.

Try opening the door of the travel cage and holding it against the open door of the residence cage. Make sure the opening is the largest one of the cage. Your bird may explore and climb right into the new cage. If your bird isn't inclined to do this, reach your gloved hand in and try to coax him into the new cage. If necessary, you can gently grasp your bird around his body with both hands and put him in the new cage. Close the door.

Now you can step back and give your bird some time alone. Let him calm down. Talk to him in a soft voice. Don't look him in the eye, like a prey animal would, and don't make sudden movements. Leave the room for awhile, or stay nearby but don't pay attention to your bird. Acting in this way gives your bird time to work things out on his own. If possible, leave a nightlight or other dim source of light on during the evenings for at least the first few weeks. Some birds — particularly cockatiels — are prone to night frights and flap wildly around in fear if something startles them in the darkness, even something as harmless as the beam from the headlight of a car passing outside.

For the first few weeks, spend plenty of time next to your bird's cage talking in a low, reassuring voice. If your bird seems eager to come out, let him out — as long as his wings are clipped. If he is eager to interact with you, let him. Keep those gloves on until you're sure that he won't bite you, or at least not hard enough to hurt. Be patient and give your bird time to adjust.

Getting to know the family

Everyone in the family — including dogs and cats — may be very interested in seeing what the new feathered family member is all about when you first bring your bird home. Interest is good, but don't let everyone mob the cage at once, poke fingers through the bars, or jump wildly around — the way kids often do — in front of the cage. Remember, your bird probably is extremely nervous and fearful about this new transition. Let family members approach the cage one at a time, slowly, with eyes averted. Have them talk in a soft, gentle voices and keep hands out of the birdcage.

Everyone in the family needs to feel welcome to visit the bird as often as they like during the day. This kind of interaction is good for your bird and helps him adjust and get to know everyone in the house. Just remember to take it slow and try not to startle your bird. As your bird becomes more comfortable, you can begin the process of training and hand-taming him, if he isn't already tame. For more on how to hand-tame your bird, see Chapter 19.

Child-bird relations

Most children younger than the age of 6 never should handle a bird. Older children can learn to handle a bird responsibly, if they're capable of staying calm and not hurting the bird — even if the bird happens to give them a nip. Small birds like cockatiels and parakeets are particularly good for small children because their bites aren't damaging, but children always need to be supervised whenever they handle a bird, because these small birds are so easily injured or lost if they are outside of the cage and wandering around. A child can become distracted and stop paying attention, and the bird can be lost or injured.

Some children successfully handle very tame larger birds with direct adult supervision, but be aware of the risks and keep your child and your bird safe. Never put any of your dependents in a situation that can harm them! Birds are wild creatures, and they can be unpredictable. So can children. Children can get a great deal of enjoyment from a bird, even if they never are allowed to hold it.

Other pets: The Tweety and Sylvester syndrome

If you have other birds, you first and foremost want to be sure your new bird is in good health and not carrying any contagious diseases that can affect your resident birds. If you have dogs or cats, you have to be extra careful to keep your yummy bird safe. Some birds — particularly larger parrots — get along just fine with gentle dogs and those few cats that have somehow lost their natural instinct to hunt birds. However, even when you think you know how your pets will interact, mistakes happen. Many birds have been killed by other family pets.

Your bird needs to be housed well out of reach of other pets. Pets must not be able to climb up and stare at the bird, bark at the bird, or swipe a paw through the bars of the cage. Don't put your bird through Tweety's daily trauma with Sylvester. Your bird has enough stress adjusting to yet another home. Keep your bird well protected, and you'll be doing all your resident pets a big favor.

Chapter 18

Caring for Your Adopted Bird

In This Chapter

▶ Finding a good bird vet and scheduling regular well-bird checkups

▶ Exploring two important and easy ways to keep your bird healthy

▶ Recognizing symptoms of common health issues adopted birds can experience

▶ Improving your bird's health and behavior through proper feeding and grooming

*P*roviding good diets and healthcare for pet birds is crucial, because malnutrition and other health problems can be at the root of behaviors that cause people to relinquish their birds to shelters and rescue groups. The bulk of health problems that pet birds tend to develop come from just two highly preventable conditions: poor diet and poor — dirty, cramped — living conditions. You can change those conditions for your new bird with a little knowledge.

That's why this chapter helps you sort through what you need to know about bird diets and healthcare — how to keep your bird healthy, how to find an avian veterinarian to support your bird's health, how to feed your bird in the best way possible to prevent diseases and nutritional deficiencies, and how to keep your bird well groomed and clean.

Keeping Your Bird Healthy

When you adopt a bird from a shelter or a rescue group, your bird has probably already been carefully checked out by a veterinarian and is — if the shelter or rescue is doing a good job — being fed a healthy diet. However, some birds in need don't receive this kind of screening and care; some are so used to a seed-only diet that they resist healthy food; and some may have never once in their long lives visited a veterinarian.

Birds tend to be stoic, which in this context means they don't quickly show signs that they're sick. Birds that exhibit obvious symptoms of poor health probably have been sick for a long time or have very serious health problems. Birds don't show their illnesses for good reason. In the wild, a bird that appears sick, or shows other signs of weakness, is the first one plucked from the flock by a predator. Appearing fine and not standing out in a crowd essentially are wired into a bird's instinctive behavior.

But as a pet owner, your task is seeing beyond the obvious, knowing your bird's personal habits and patterns, and keeping a vigilant eye on your pet. As you feed your bird the right way and keep his cage clean, you also need to spend some time just observing him every day. If you notice any changes in behavior, such as strange movements, agitation, or lethargy, or any change in his droppings or eating habits, then you need to act fast. The first step is to call your veterinarian.

Finding a good bird vet

Even before you bring your bird home — especially if you have other birds that can be affected by a contagious birdborne disease — you need to take your new bird to the vet for a health checkup. Of course, before you do, you need to find a good vet who knows about birds.

For most pets, the first level of care is the family veterinarian, who sometimes must refer you to a specialist for an advanced problem. If you already have other pets and a vet you like to use, you may assume that vet is the right one for your new adopted bird. The trouble is many veterinarians have little experience with birds. Sure, they may see the occasional budgie or cockatiel, but rarer birds, such as large parrots, and rarer conditions or species-specific conditions probably are not your local vet's area of expertise.

On the other hand, some veterinarians actually specialize in caring for birds. When you're looking for the right vet for your bird, don't just default to the vet who's so wonderful with your dog or cat. Ask the family vet how much experience she has with birds and whether she knows of another vet who specializes in birds. Even if you have to drive a little farther, you may find the visit well worth your trouble. Avian veterinarians know about diseases and conditions unique to birds and the best course of treatment for bird-specific problems. They may also be able to give you some great insight into your bird's individual behavior problems.

Before choosing an avian vet, try to find out the answers to these questions:

- ✔ Is the veterinarian a member of the Association of Avian Veterinarians (AAV)?
- ✔ Is the veterinarian board certified in avian veterinary medicine?
- ✔ How long has the vet been treating birds?
- ✔ Does the vet keep birds at home (or even in the office)? If so, which types?

✔ How much does the vet charge for avian services?

✔ Does the vet offer emergency services, if your bird happens to require immediate after-hours care and attention?

The answers you get for these questions will give you insight into how much experience the vet actually has with birds.

Before you decide for sure on an avian vet, schedule an appointment for your bird to have a checkup so you can see how you like the office, whether the location is convenient, whether the staff is friendly and professional, and most important, how you like the way the vet handles your bird and talks to you. Good communication is important, and you trust that the vet will handle your bird gently, safely, and appropriately.

In some cases, your local family vet may be just fine for routine care, and for that matter, may even be a bird owner, too! But seeking out and at least meeting with a nearby avian veterinarian is worth the effort. Most large cities and many smaller ones have them.

If you can't track down a great bird vet, the Association of Avian Veterinarians can help. It can provide you with a list of bird vets near you. Call the AAV at 561-393-8901 or visit its Web site at www.aav.org, where you can search for avian vets by area.

The first vet visit

When visit your vet for the first time with your new bird, you can expect a few standard procedures. The vet will ask you about your bird, where you got him, how long you've had him, what you know about his past health history, whether you know his gender, what kind of cage you're keeping him in, and what you're feeding him. Some vets also ask about other pets in your household, whether you plan to let your bird spend time outside of the cage, and other questions about your lifestyle and bird-care knowledge. Your vet may give you a care sheet with information about diet, bird safety, and basic training, and can even help you with behavior problems and preventive care and point you to other informational resources.

If your vet finds a problem with your bird, he will recommend a course of treatment. Some problems are easy to resolve, such as a skin infection that requires antibiotics or an overgrown beak that requires trimming. Others may require the services of a specialist. Take your vet's advice in pursuing treatment.

Don't neglect this initial vet visit. It gives your vet a baseline upon which to compare your bird's health status at all future visits or when problems arise. Schedule a well-bird vet visit about once every six months after that, just to make sure everything is A-okay or to follow up on prescribed treatment.

One last word about the vet visit: You need a travel carrier, similar to a crate you'd use to bring a cat or small dog to the vet or a small travel cage that you can cover with a cage cover or blanket so your bird doesn't become frightened by being on the move and out of control. Make sure your bird can't escape from this travel carrier or cage. If you use a crate, put a blanket on the bottom so your bird has something to grip. If you use a travel cage, be sure the perches are tightly secured and remove hanging toys inside that otherwise can bounce around and hit your bird. During winter months, when it is cold, be sure the car is already warm before taking the bird out. A heavy quilt over the carrier for going between car and buildings is good. Better yet, ask if the vet will make a special house call.

Common health problems in adopted birds

Most bird health problems are the result of poor nutrition and an unclean environment. As a pet owner, you can drastically reduce your adopted bird's chances of becoming ill by feeding your bird a proper diet and keeping your bird's cage, including food and water bowls, perches, and toys, clean and dry. And still, you also need to remain vigilant, keeping an eye out for signs and symptoms of poor health. If you notice any symptoms of the conditions described in the list that follows, call your vet and schedule an appointment.

- **Injuries:** Many adopted birds are injured, or were injured in the past, before they came to you and never were treated. Adopted birds can become injured from abuse, being loose and flying into something, tangling with another pet, or even from self-mutilation caused by neglect or poor environmental conditions. Injuries are dangerous for birds. Broken bones can prevent your bird from breathing. Bacteria from infected wounds can enter the bloodstream. If your parrot gets a wound — including the self-inflicted kind — or shows any signs of injury, go to the vet immediately.

- **Parasites:** Birds that live in unclean conditions occasionally develop feather mites or red mites. See the vet to treat mites, because trying to treat them yourself is difficult, and some of the mite products for sale in pet stores may not be safe for your bird. Other parasites include worms and intestinal parasites, the signs of which include diarrhea and weight loss. *Note:* On your first visit, your vet should examine your bird for mites and test for worms.

- **Bacterial infections:** When they live in filthy conditions, birds can acquire a bacteria that causes tuberculosis. Humans with weakened immune systems can catch the same infection, which is airborne. In birds, tuberculosis is a digestive disorder. Signs include weight loss and other digestive problems like diarrhea. Birds with this kind of bacteria, called *mycobacterium avium,* can't be cured of it, but a superclean environment and low stress keep symptoms to a minimum. Another common bird bacterial infection is *psittacosis,* sometimes called *chlamydiosis* or *parrot fever.* It is also contagious to humans; however, it's a respiratory bacteria that your vet can treat effectively, especially if it is caught early. Signs include yellowish or light greenish droppings, lethargy, discharge from the nostrils, and difficulty breathing.

✔ **Viral infections:** Viruses in birds can be mild or deadly. Three of the most serious include *psitticine beak and feather disease,* a contagious and fatal disease causing feather loss and lesions on the beak; *polyomavirus,* an incurable fatal virus for which there is a vaccine (so ask your vet if your bird is at risk); and *Pacheco's disease,* a type of viral hepatitis that is highly contagious and often fatal.

✔ **Fungal infections:** Fungal infections can afflict adopted birds that aren't healthy and have been eating a poor diet, because their weakened immune systems fall prey to infections that a healthy bird's body otherwise would resist. Birds can get yeast infections after being treated with antibiotics or if they're not eating a healthy diet. Signs include white sticky goo on your bird's tongue and in his mouth and sometimes digestive upset. Your vet can treat a yeast infection with medication and a vitamin A-rich diet. Yeast infections aren't serious unless they go untreated, in which case they can eventually prove fatal. Another common fungal infection that can be fatal is *aspergillosis,* which causes respiratory distress and can be caused by dirty, moldy bedding. Black hairy-looking mold can produce this kind of fungus.

✔ **Gout:** You may think of gout as a rich human's disease of overindulgence, but malnourished birds can get it, too. If your bird's leg gets swollen or he stops using one leg, suspect gout.

✔ **Obesity:** Can a malnourished bird also be fat? Certainly. Birds fed a high-fat, low-nutrient diet can quickly become overweight, especially when they're never let out of their cages to exercise. Obesity is hard on your bird and compromises his health in many ways. He can develop a food infection called *bumblefoot,* and all his internal organs have to work harder to function. A low-fat, nutrient-dense diet can help correct obesity in your adopted bird. For more about how to feed your bird a healthy diet, see "Feeding Your Adopted Bird: A Mixed Bag" later in this chapter.

✔ **Feather plucking, chewing, and self-mutilation:** People often think of feather plucking and other forms of self-mutilation as behavioral problems, and indeed, they often are. Birds that are bored, neglected, abused, or under a lot of stress often develop these behaviors, some more often than others. Cockatoos are famous for being prone to feather plucking, but it also occurs with other birds like Macaws, Amazons, and African greys. But behavior isn't always the root cause, so if your bird is plucking or chewing his feathers, has bald patches or wounds, see your vet to make sure the cause isn't physical. If everything checks out, treat these symptoms as a behavioral problem. For more about dealing with this common problem of adopted birds, see Chapter 19.

✔ **Egg binding:** Even without a mate, a female may go into a nesting mode and lay eggs, but in malnourished females, eggs sometimes get stuck. This problem also can occur when a female has been laying too many eggs. Weakness, a tumor, a deformed egg, or other problems likewise can cause egg binding. If your bird pants, squats, or stops walking, suspect egg binding and consider it an emergency. See your vet immediately. Don't try to pull out the egg yourself. Doing so can fatally injure your bird.

✔ **Respiratory distress from environmental causes:** Birds have extremely sensitive respiratory systems, and many regular household appliances can produce fumes that are deadly to birds. Common offenders include any heated nonstick surface (such as nonstick cookware and appliances with nonstick surfaces), household cleaners, self-cleaning ovens, scented candles, garden chemicals, insecticides, gasoline or kerosene, charcoal or lighter fluid, and even crayons and markers. If your bird begins vomiting, bleeding from the face, or becomes paralyzed, unconscious, has seizures, or seems unresponsive — a sign of shock — rush your bird to the emergency clinic immediately.

Respiratory distress from chemicals is a form of poisoning in birds, but birds can also be poisoned if they ingest something poisonous. Houseplants or toxic food also can poison your bird. If you even suspect your bird has been poisoned, call your vet immediately. If your bird shows any sign of poisoning, such as vomiting, paralysis, loss of consciousness, seizures, or unresponsiveness, and you can't get to a clinic right away, call the National Animal Poison Control Center's 24-hour Poison Hotline at 900-548-2423.

You can find out more about these and other bird health conditions, including symptoms and treatment, by consulting Wiley Publishing's *Parrots For Dummies* by Nikki Moustaki.

Bird breeding: Why — and how — not to

Think of the hundreds and thousands of birds in shelters and rescues, waiting for new homes because their former owners bought a cute little baby bird on impulse and then couldn't handle it when it grew up. The fact that so few qualified bird owners are out there is, in itself, a good reason not to breed your birds, unless you plan to keep, care for, and properly manage and train all the resulting babies. Even if you decide to try to breed your birds, you may not have any luck. Bird breeding is a relatively unpredictable art, and birds need specific conditions and an acceptable mate to be able to breed. Breeding also can be dangerous for birds. Eggs can get stuck in the female — a condition called egg binding, see the previous section, causing severe complications. Even a single bird going into breeding mode can cause severe stress.

Unlike dogs and cats, birds cannot be spayed or neutered. This surgery is far too risky on the avian anatomy. However, preventing breeding in your birds is simple. If you have more than one bird, or even if you have just one female (or if you aren't sure of the sex), you can keep your birds healthy, calm, and safe from producing new baby birds. Just follow these three rules:

✔ Do not provide a nesting box or anything resembling a nesting box, such as little wooden or plastic houses, shelters, or cardboard boxes.

✔ Do not provide nesting material or anything resembling nesting material. Your bird should not have access to shredded paper, litter, newspaper, soft cloth, straw, or anything else that looks like it can go into the construction of a nest.

✔ Do not expose your birds to light for more than 12 hours per day. Too much light can launch a bird into reproductive mode, which not only is stressful to the bird but also can lead to all sorts of behavior problems. Birds need light, so don't keep them in the dark all the time, for goodness sake. But if your bird starts desperately trying to build a nest out of something, anything, or starts laying eggs (even in the absence of a partner), reduce her daylight hours by only a few, with curtains or shades in the room or a cover over the cage.

Feeding Your Adopted Bird: A Mixed Bag

In the wild, birds fly around looking for things to eat, and they get a huge variety of fruits, plant matter, nuts, and seeds. That canister of bird seed from the grocery store may say it has added nutrients and makes a complete diet for birds, and the bird pellets in the pet store — the ones that look suspiciously like cat food but in prettier colors — say they are superior to seed in providing a complete nutrient profile in every bite. But what fun can a bowl full of kibble be to a curious and intelligent parrot?

Giving your bird a balanced diet

I've never subscribed to the theory that any pet — or human, for that matter — should eat just one thing at every meal, every day. Although some people still insist such a diet is good for dogs, most people agree that for birds, variety is indeed the spice of a healthy avian existence — and not just the spice, but rather the core of a sound and complete diet. So, feed your bird:

✔ **Seed:** Birds need seed, but not too much. No more than 50 percent of your bird's diet should consist of seed because seed is very fattening and not their sole diet in the wild. Choose seed that is fortified to be nutritionally complete, but remember that pet birds don't get nearly as much exercise as wild birds, either, and too many high-fat seeds turn into a high-fat bird.

Seed gets stale and rancid quickly, so keep it in an airtight container and don't buy more at one time than your bird will eat in about a month or two. And that jar of seed your neighbor gave you because she gave away her bird last year . . . toss it.

✔ **Fresh foods:** Fifty percent of your bird's diet needs to be fresh foods. (See the section, "Giving your bird the best and worst foods," later in the chapter for a list of the best fresh foods for your bird.)

✔ **Nutritionally complete pellets:** Some people are big advocates of the pelleted diet because it provides complete nutrition. However, it is processed and not at all like the food birds eat in their natural habitat. Pellets can be a great portion of a healthy diet, but if you intend to use pellets, feed about 25 percent seed, 25 percent pellets, and 50 percent fresh food. Be sure to buy pellets that are appropriate for your kind of bird.

✔ **Fresh water:** Without a constant supply of clean fresh water, your bird can quickly become dehydrated and die, and drinking dirty water can introduce bacteria into your bird's system. Birds need to drink a lot, so thoroughly wash your bird's water dish every day and refill it at least once a day, or more often if it gets dirty.

This kind of varied diet is not only healthy for birds but also essential for mental stimulation. Birds are interested in what goes into their bowls. If they always have a selection — a few pellets, a few seeds, a few nuts, a few grains, a mini green salad and a few pieces of fruits and veggies — they get more satisfaction out of their meals, are less bored, and in some cases, their behavior is even improved, partially because improved nutrition and partially because of improved mealtime satisfaction.

Giving your bird the best and worst foods

If your avian veterinarian suggests specific foods for your individual bird, you should, of course, be sure to heed that advice. If your bird is healthy, here are some of the best foods to offer him in addition to his processed food:

✔ Sprouted and/or cooked legumes like lentils, black beans, lima beans, kidney beans, garbanzo beans, and black-eyed peas.

✔ Cooked grains, such as brown rice, quinoa, couscous, whole-grain pasta, and corn.

- Root vegetables and their leafy tops, such as carrots, radishes, turnips, and cooked potatoes — skip the potato tops — including white and sweet potatoes.

- Broccoli, including the stems and leaves, and cauliflower.

- Other veggies like zucchini, yellow squash, asparagus, Brussels sprouts, tomatoes, artichoke, and eggplant.

- Leafy greens like Romaine lettuce, collards, radicchio, mustard, endive, dandelion, Swiss chard, kale, parsley, and the greens from beets and turnips.

- Peas, especially fresh sugar snap peas or snow peas — large parrots enjoy getting the peas out of the pod.

- Sweet and spicy peppers, both red and green.

- Tropical fruits like papaya, mango, kiwi, pineapple, and melons, including watermelon, cantaloupe, and honeydew.

- Orchard fruits like apples, pears, peaches, plums, and apricots, but don't offer the pits or seeds; they're toxic!

- Citrus fruits, like grapefruit, oranges, and tangerines.

- Dried fruit like raisins, figs, and dried apricots.

- All berries, including strawberries, blueberries, blackberries, raspberries, and gooseberries.

You can also share your healthy cooked dishes, like cornbread, scrambled eggs, and oatmeal with dried fruit and nuts, with larger parrots.

Birds *don't* need to eat any of the food items in the list that follows, because they can, in fact, be dangerous for them. So you should *never feed your bird:*

- Onions, including green onions or scallions, leeks, or shallots, especially raw. If you have a delicious vegetable soup with a few cooked onions in it, you can probably give your bird a bite or two without a problem, but don't hand off a raw chunk or bouquet of scallions for munching.

- Avocado, including guacamole. You may think avocado, with its suggestion of the steamy tropics, is a perfect food for birds. Think again. It is poisonous to birds, and they don't eat it in the wild.

- Rhubarb. The leaves are toxic to humans, but even the sour stalks can be toxic to birds, so avoid them.

- Persimmons.

- Nonorganic apples, grapes, and strawberries that are extremely pesticide-ridden. You may as well skip eating them, too, and go for the organic versions.

- The pits of fruits like peaches, nectarines, apricots, and plums can be toxic for birds, so cut out the pits before serving these fruits. The fruit itself, however, is just fine.

✔ Apple seeds, which can be toxic to birds. Core those apples first. And remember to buy organic!

✔ Mushrooms.

✔ Salt, which is bad for birds. (Pepper is okay.)

✔ Chocolate, in any form.

✔ Anything with caffeine, including coffee, tea, and cola.

✔ Anything containing alcohol. It isn't funny to give your parrot beer or wine. You're poisoning him.

✔ Junk food. If it's fried, high fat, high sugar, and generally bad for humans, then you can bet that it's bad for birds.

Understanding the diets of specific species

Beyond general dietary rules, individual species have certain differing diets in the wild. Knowing what your species eats can help guide you in choosing what foods to add to your bird's diet:

✔ Budgies, cockatiels, and hyacinth macaws eat mostly grains and seeds. Grains need to be more dominant in the diets of these birds, when kept as pets, because pet birds don't get enough exercise to burn the fat that they'd burn off in the wild. Likewise, be sure to supplement these diets with healthy vegetables like leafy greens, small bits of fruit and nuts, and some nutritionally complete, species-specific pelleted food.

✔ Some macaws, namely military macaws and blue-and-gold macaws — two of the more common macaws — eat lots of fruit, nuts, roots, berries, and seeds in the wild. Make sure your macaw has a lot of variety, including pellets. Hyacinth macaws eat mostly palm nuts in the wild and benefit from more nuts than seeds.

✔ Blue-throated and green-winged macaws exist mostly on fruit and flowers, with only a few nuts and seeds. Give them plenty of fresh fruits, cooked sprouted vegetables, grains like corn and oats, and just a few seeds and nuts for a treat.

✔ Cockatoos and some Amazons eat seeds, fruit, and the occasional insect. Cricket anyone? These birds need plenty of variety, and they thrive on sprouted beans and legumes, grains like corn and oats, and cooked vegetables like green beans, carrots, and bell peppers.

✔ Pigeons in the city may eat just about anything, but your pet dove does better on fresh fruits and a seed mix made for doves.

✔ Lories and lorikeets have special brush-like tongues for sipping nectar and scooping up bugs. Lories need a commercially prepared nectar-like diet made just for them.

Fruit and yeast infections

If your parrot is diagnosed with yeast, or *candida,* take a break from feeding fruit and anything with sweetener. Sugars, even the natural kind, provide the ideal breeding ground for yeasts, so let your bird's body recover form this persistent and sometimes chronic problem before resuming fruit treats. Instead, focus on leafy green and other nonsweet vegetables. Avoid sweet potatoes, yams, and carrots, too.

Knowing how often to feed your bird

In the wild, most birds eat at dawn and at dusk. Although many bird owners keep food in their bird's cage all day long so the bird can nibble at will, be sure your bird has fresh, clean, nonmoldy, nonrotten food in the morning and in the evening, when he normally is prompted to eat. Also be sure to clean out the food bowl thoroughly at least once a day. Don't let food or water sit for more than a day, or it can attract bacteria and mold.

If your bird is overweight, feed him only twice a day, and take food away during other times of the day, or just provide fresh vegetables and no seed between meals. Seed is fattening, and a bored bird with nothing else to do is likely to overeat.

Converting your bird to the proper diet

One common problem with adopted birds is that they've spent their entire lives, up until they came to live with you, being fed a substandard diet. Birds are creatures of habit, and if they're used to eating seed and only seed, they often shun any other new foods. They may not even recognize pellets and other foods as food! What is a well-meaning bird owner to do?

You don't want to change your bird's diet too quickly, so start by mixing about 75 percent of your bird's original diet with fresh foods and pellets. Mix them together so the seeds are sticking to the fresh food. If your bird just picks out the seeds, don't worry. He's slowly learning that in his new home, dinnertime has a slightly different look and taste.

Every few days, slightly decrease the amount of seed and increase the pellets and fresh food until seed is a mere 25 to 50 percent of the diet. If your bird continues to shun the other food, offer seed only in the mornings and leave grains, veggies, and pellets in the bowl for midday free-feeding. Be patient and experiment to find the fresh foods that your bird suddenly realizes he actually likes! Habits are hard to break, and birds tend to stick with their favorites, but teaching your bird to eat a more varied diet is good for him in many ways. For some severely malnourished birds — and that includes all too many of the birds waiting to be adopted — the change in health, appearance, and behavior is dramatic when real nutrition finally becomes a part of your bird's life.

Grooming Your Bird

Birds love to groom themselves and each other, so you may think you don't have much to do about grooming your bird. And you'd be right, except that life in a cage is much different than life in the wild, where bark, rocks, hard-shelled nuts, and other rough surfaces naturally wear down a bird's nails and beak, keeping them trim and healthy. In a pet environment with so many smooth perches, slick metal cage bars, and carpet or tile floors, birds often get overgrown nails and beaks. Sandpaper perches, touted as an easy way to keep nails trimmed, actually can damage your bird's feet, and yet they don't do much for his nails. The sandpaper also is dangerous if your bird eats it. Some birds wear down their nails on a cement perch, but just because you provide one in the cage — only one, they should not all be cement — is no guarantee that your bird will use it.

Some experienced bird owners learn to trim their bird's nails with a nail trimmer, but don't attempt to trim your bird's nails until you get a personalized, face-to-face lesson on nail trimming from your vet. One false move and you can clip a nail too far, causing bleeding, and that can be dangerous, not to mention extremely stressful, for your bird. If your bird isn't used to having his nails clipped, he may protest vigorously and scratch, claw, and bite you, and thus cause an accident with the clippers, an escape, or worse. Let a professional demonstrate, and if you're never comfortable doing this chore, take your bird to the vet for regular nail trimming.

Regular trimming of your bird's flight feathers can also be a part of regular grooming if you know how to do it and your bird is tame enough for you to do it. Have your vet demonstrate this procedure for you, to be sure you understand how to do it without injuring your bird.

Beak trimming sometimes is necessary for pet birds. Beaks can become overgrown and deformed, actually injuring the bird or making it impossible for the bird to eat, but you should *never do this yourself.* A mistake in beak trimming can be fatal, not just cosmetic. Let your avian vet handle this chore, if it becomes necessary.

Finally, birds are clean animals, and they love to take baths and showers. Provide an open shallow birdbath for your bird, or mist him daily with lukewarm water from a spray bottle or plant mister. Many large parrots really enjoy taking a shower with you. Don't put shampoo on them! But do enjoy their enthusiastic flapping as they tap ancestral memories of rainforest downpours and leafy jungle foliage dripping with rain.

Chapter 19

Training Your Bird

In This Chapter

▶ Distinguishing between normal bird behaviors and real behavioral problems

▶ Calming, quieting, and taming your bird

▶ Getting to the root of feather plucking, picking, chewing, and self-mutilation

▶ Socializing and training your bird

▶ Bonding with your bird, even through avian adolescence

*Y*ou love your new bird, of course you do. But sometimes, yes, go ahead and admit it . . . he's driving you absolutely batty! Birds are wild creatures, not domesticated over thousands of years like dogs and cats, so they have certain behaviors that are undeniably difficult for humans to put up with. They aren't being bad; they're being birds. But that's exactly why so many of them end up in shelters and with rescue groups, waiting for new homes. Add to that a few daunting behavior problems resulting from neglect, abuse, poor nutrition, and unsanitary conditions that many birds develop, and you have yourself a pretty difficult housemate on your hands.

In this chapter, I explain how you can deal with some of the more common behavior problems in adopted birds and parrots, including the ones that aren't problems at all but rather are perfectly natural bird and parrot traits. From screaming and biting to feather plucking and fearfulness, this chapter helps you recognize these behaviors and determine when to visit a vet. It also offers you strategies for altering or redirecting these behaviors and helps you determine whether you need extra professional help in the form of an avian behavior consultant. Are you ready to tackle those baffling bird behaviors?

Understanding Bird Behavior

If you purchase a hand-fed baby bird, you start — for the most part — with a clean slate. An adopted bird, however, already has plenty of notations on that proverbial slate, and whatever that writing says determines, to a large extent, how your new bird behaves in your home. Unfortunately, many parrots have some bad habits already ingrained. Or, I should say, they have *habits* ingrained that aren't so much bad as they are birdlike and incompatible with life in a human household. But luckily for you, birds are smart, and they can learn from you and adjust some of their behaviors with a little guidance.

But first, consider what so-called behavior problems actually are merely bird behaviors: In the wild, birds squawk. Loudly. They interact with other birds, mate, climb around a lot, and fly a lot. They're cautious and hyperaware of anything that resembles a predator. And, they have to find their own food.

What they do *not* typically do in the wild is fight, bite each other, scream nonstop, pluck out their own feathers, injure themselves, or — and this is a big one — live in cages.

In other words, if your pet bird makes noise, get used to it. If she's a little cautious, flighty (so to speak), or nervous when people stare at her or approach her quickly, she is just being a careful and cautious bird with an intact survival instinct. But if your bird is behaving aggressively, attacking people, screaming all the time, or plucking out her own feathers, you can bet something is wrong.

Think about the unnatural situation that your wild friend is in, even if she was born in captivity, as most pet parrots are today. If your bird is in a cage all the time, especially in a cage that is too small to really stretch out, flap around, and get exercise, she probably will develop some neurotic behaviors. When birds don't get enough exercise, social interaction, or mental challenges, they make noise and complain about it. Can you blame them?

A bird in a cage can't fly, climb all around the trees, or work for her dinner. A bird in a cage is largely limited in her movements and has food provided in a little cup, all ready to eat aside from some minor seed husking. That's hardly challenging. If your bird isn't challenged by her environment, you need to provide her with other challenges to keep her healthy and well adjusted. Training, interaction, a varied diet, all can help your parrot adjust to her relatively unnatural caged environment — because if your bird is driving you batty, you can probably assume that something is driving *her* batty, too.

Solving Bird Behavior Problems

So how do you tackle these problems? You can put a Band-Aid on problems by covering the cage of a squawking bird, refusing to interact with a biter, or leaving a fearful bird alone, but these reactions don't help your bird overcome boredom, unhappiness, or fear. Instead, get to the root of the problem, and you'll address the issue from the inside out.

The first thing to do with a bird that is exhibiting problem behaviors is visit with the vet. Your veterinarian can check out your bird and run tests to make sure she is not experiencing any health problems. Many bad behaviors from aggression to feather plucking sometimes have a medical cause, so resolve any physical problems first. Once your bird is declared physically healthy, you can begin tackling your bird's issues with behavioral strategies and training techniques. The following sections explain how.

In some cases, if a bird becomes impossible to handle or dangerous, you may — as a last resort — have to consider rehoming your bird. If you do, please contact the shelter or rescue group where you originally got your bird, so they can find him a new home and a good owner. If you can't care properly for your parrot, she's probably better off with someone who can, but please remember how many birds are waiting for good homes. If you can work out your problems and provide your troubled bird with a forever home, you'll find your bird is a challenging but rewarding and engaging companion for life.

The bird that won't adjust: Fear and anxiety

Because birds have to be ever alert for predators in the wild, a certain degree of caution just makes sense. However, a well-adjusted bird that's socialized to humans shouldn't normally be fearful or anxious all the time, and should adjust after a few days to a new environment. Adopted birds that are not accustomed to humans or have bad memories of human interactions can take much longer to adjust. If your bird constantly cowers, flutters madly around the cage whenever anyone approaches, refuses to let you touch him, or begins neurotic self-destructive behaviors like feather plucking and chewing, you may have a fear and/or anxiety problem on your hands.

The following list gives you steps to overcome this problem, so your bird grows accustomed to the idea that you exist in the house and you're not a predator or abuser:

1. **Consider where your bird is located.**

   If she's against a wall, she'll be more secure than when she's against a window or in the middle of a room, where she may feel like danger can approach from all sides and she has nowhere safe to roost. Move her to a wall or corner, and be sure your bird is in a place that isn't directly in the middle of all the household activity, but likewise isn't completely isolated from it, either. Birds like to see what's going on and are interested in what humans are doing, even if it makes them nervous. You don't want kids barreling by the cage all the time, bumping into it, and poking their fingers in, but the bird needs to be in a central living area where she gradually gets used to the normal level of activity in your home.

2. **Start spending some scheduled periods of time in the room with your bird.**

Don't sit right next to the cage and don't stare at your bird, which is what a predator might do. Instead, sit nearby doing something other than paying attention to your bird. Read, work on your computer, pay bills, watch television, hum to yourself. Do something that makes little soft noises, rather than something completely silent or startlingly loud. Spend time in the room with your bird every day, preferably at the same time.

Your bird may cower or act nervous at first, but as you do your thing every day without directly interacting with your bird, she should gradually get used to your presence. Depending on the severity of the problem, this bonding can take weeks, months . . . or even longer. But be patient. You're rehabilitating a troubled bird, and that takes time.

You can tell when your bird is comfortable in your presence. She sits relaxed on her perch rather than flitting nervously around the cage. She may close her eyes and doze, sing or twitter happily, stretch her feet or flap her wings for exercise, and she may eat with her head down in the bowl where she can't see you. If she does these things in your presence, you can feel confidant that she's getting used to you.

3. **Gradually move a little bit closer to the cage a day or two at a time.**

   Look at your bird briefly now and then, say a few soft gentle words to her, but don't stare or move suddenly.

At each step in this process, stop or go back to the previous step whenever your bird starts getting nervous again. Don't get closer or interact more until your bird obviously is comfortable with your current level of interaction. Eventually, your bird should get used to your presence and the inevitable presence of others in the home.

4. **Continue working slowly but surely with your bird, one step at a time, from getting comfortable with you in the room to getting comfortable with your hand inside her cage and getting comfortable stepping onto a stick that you hold in your hand.**

   For more information about how to train your bird to react to the step-up cue, see "Bird Basic Training" later in this chapter. Adopted birds may or may not ever be able to be hand-tame, but even if your bird never wants to ride around on your hand or sit on your shoulder, she needs to be trustworthy outside of her cage and trained to step up onto a handheld perch so you can put her back in her cage when necessary.

If your bird shows no progress at all, seems profoundly frightened, or is injuring herself despite your best efforts, please consult an avian behavioral specialist who can get information about you and your individual bird and work with you to help your frightened bird.

Noise solutions

Probably the chief complaint from all parrot owners — particularly the ones who live with large parrots or the more vocal medium-sized parrots like conures and Quaker parakeets — is the noise, The Noise, THE NOISE! Adopted birds, hand-fed babies, pet-shop birds, the simple fact of their existence is that they all make noise. Noise primarily is a problem with the louder parrots. Small birds like parakeets and cockatiels don't make loud noises, although they may twitter contentedly throughout the day, which is perfectly normal.

But when it comes to larger parrots, the volume can be pretty high. Although screaming is normal for large parrots, particularly in the morning and at dusk, adopted parrots sometimes may have a particular issue with making noise, simply because they never were taught not to squawk and scream, and/or they've gotten used to making a lot of noise until their needs are met. If your adopted bird came from a home where he was not getting enough attention, was covered up all the time whenever he made normal parrot noises, or was inadvertently rewarded with attention — such as people screaming "Shut up!" — for screaming, he may have a bad habit.

If you have a bird that's a screamer, the first step is to consider exactly what makes your bird scream. After you've ruled out any health problem, ask yourself:

- ✔ **Am I paying enough attention to my bird?** Birds often shriek out of boredom or to get your attention. Try spending more time with your bird, and letting her out of her cage more often.

- ✔ **Am I rewarding her screaming?** When your bird screams, think about what you're doing at that express moment. Do you go to the cage and yell at your bird? Doing so may sound to your bird like you're joining in on the screaming fun. Do you take your bird out of her cage and give her plenty attention when she screams? Attention is great, but if your bird discovers that screaming is the fastest way to get the attention she wants, then she'll learn how to do it and she'll do it often.

One simple but concrete concept can keep you from reinforcing your bird's screaming: Reward your bird only when she's quiet, not when she's screaming. Take your bird out of her cage and pay attention to her frequently, but *never when she is screaming*. Ignore screaming completely. Leave the room. Don't yell; don't even look at your bird. But, the minute she stops, praise her, give her a treat, take her out to play. Birds are smart, and yours will get the idea quickly if you *don't reward screaming*.

If you aren't able to get a handle on your bird's noise level, please talk to an avian behavioral consultant who can provide you with information about your individual situation and give you customized strategies for reducing the noise level. But remember that all parrots make noise some of the time, so to some degree, you just have to get used to it, if you're committed to living with a parrot.

Biting and aggression

Despite Alfred Hitchcock's portrayal to the contrary, birds in the wild generally are not aggressive. They don't exist in groups with a pecking order, they don't try to challenge the dominant bird, and although they sometimes squabble over mates or territory, fighting and biting each other are not a normal part of life as a bird.

In captivity, however, things can be a little different. Here are some reasons that adopted birds may bite:

- ✔ Sexually mature birds may bite the object of their affection, which often is a human, when feeling threatened by a change in the environment or a stranger in the room. Sometimes an adolescent bird, for no apparent reason at all, may try to bite her partner. One theory indicates that such partner biting may be a protective mechanism intended to prompt the beloved to fly away.

- ✔ Some birds that are stuck in a cage all day may grow overly territorial and suddenly bite anyone who gets near their territory. Birds can be protective of their territories and will try to nip and bite anyone who gets near it. And sometimes, birds turn on the person they most enjoy for no apparent reason.

- ✔ Adopted birds that have been abused may bite out of fear or because they've had bad experiences with human hands in the past. Some birds can become extremely aggressive. These biters should never ride on anyone's shoulder or be held near the face, because they can cause severe permanent damage. Cockatoos in particular have been known to rip off parts of ears, noses, cheeks, and even fingers.

The solution to biting is not to stop handling or paying attention to your bird. Instead, the solution is just the opposite. Don a pair of leather gloves and handle your bird more often, but in a gentle, calm way. Putting your bird in the cage — in essence, removing your attention from the bird — is a good way to keep from reinforcing bad behavior. But when it comes to biting, do not reinforce biting by yelling or putting the bird back in her cage. In this case, you teach her that biting gives her the power to make you do whatever she wants. Instead, if she bites you when you're holding her, ignore her. But when she stops, praise her good behavior. Meanwhile, keep the bird away from your face, bare skin, and certainly away from children.

When your bird discovers that biting gets her nothing and that when she stops biting, she gets rewarded, she learns not to bite. However, if her biting is caused by extreme fear or anxiety, deal with this problem first (see "The bird that won't adjust: Fear and anxiety" section earlier in this chapter). Don't be too eager to handle your bird if she's afraid of you.

Large birds can bite extremely hard and can injure you severely, so please check with an avian behavioral consultant whenever you have an aggressive biter and you find that:

✔ You're afraid of or unable to handle your bird at all, including getting her back into her cage when she's out.

✔ You feel your bird has control over you.

Feather picking and chewing

Feather picking and chewing are tragic behaviors that happen when a bird is so bored, upset, fearful, disturbed, or in such discomfort that she plucks and chews her own feathers. Some birds even give themselves wounds. If your bird is exhibiting these symptoms, get to the root of the problem. Sometimes the solution is easy. Consider your answers to the following questions:

✔ **Is your bird healthy, or is he having a skin problem?** Something as simple as itchy skin or mites can cause plucking. Check with your vet and get a health clearance first.

✔ **Is your bird eating a healthy, complete, and varied diet?** Nutritional deficiencies often are a cause of plucking, picking, and self-mutilation. See Chapter 18 to be sure you're feeding your bird a high-quality, complete diet.

✔ **Is your bird's cage large enough?** Is she getting enough exercise? Birds that are stuck in claustrophobic conditions with little to no time spent outside of the cage and no opportunities to exercise and expend their formidable energy stores sometimes turn that energy against themselves. Take your bird out more often or get him a bigger cage with plenty of toys to play with and room to climb around.

✔ **Is your bird getting enough mental stimulation?** Birds have plenty of opportunities to solve problems and interact socially in the wild. A large parrot has the I.Q. of a young child, and you probably know what happens when a toddler has nothing to engage his curious brain. If all your bird does is sit in a cage all day with nothing to engage her, she may develop the neurotic behavior of self-mutilation. Give your bird more things to do — things to chew, interactive toys, swings, and of course, attention. Turn on a television or a radio for your bird, or move her cage to an area of the house with more activity.

> ✓ **Speaking of attention, is your bird getting enough?** Maybe she is pining away with loneliness. Praise her and play with her and tell her she is beautiful, even if she's plucked like a chicken, poor thing.
>
> ✓ **Is your bird fearful or anxious?** If so, be patient and work on helping your bird overcome these anxieties as described in "The bird that won't adjust: Fear and anxiety" earlier in this chapter.

If you can't determine a cause and a vet has proclaimed your bird in perfect health, please check with an experienced avian behavioral consultant for help determining the nature of the problem and developing customized strategies for dealing with it.

Finding an Avian Behavior Consultant

Many pet bird owners are relatively inexperienced and can use a little help from someone who has been around the block when it comes to birds. People who have kept, dealt with, and trained birds or who have advanced educations in bird behavior and training frequently offer consulting services to pet owners who are having problems dealing with behavioral issues.

Sometimes a solution to the problem you and your bird are experiencing is simpler than you think, and when you explain your situation to someone with experience and an objective eye, he or she can advise you about exactly what to try. Sometimes, even with more advanced problems, an avian behavior consultant works closely with you and your bird to come to a workable solution.

These trained professionals are devoted to the welfare of birds and the people who are committed to keeping them responsibly, so don't hesitate to contact them for help. The more advanced a problem, the harder it may be to solve, so even if your bird behavior issues seem small, give a professional a call. To find one, ask your veterinarian or call a nearby vet school for information about avian behavior consultants in your area. Or, ask friends with birds or local bird breeders who they recommend.

Bird Bonding: Bringing Out Your Bird's Best

Your adopted bird is a social creature and wants to interact with the environment. Birds need socialization so they gain self-confidence and can take human interaction in stride. Birds also are smart, and they like rewards, attention, treats, and praise. That's great for you because that means you can train your bird with relative ease.

Animals — even the human kind — get smarter and better behaved with attention, interaction, and physical and mental challenges. That goes for any pet, and it certainly applies to your adopted bird. Spending time with your bird and training him every day brings out his best side — his intelligence, his affectionate nature, his health, and his innate beauty. Praise your vain and lovely friend, keep him healthy, and teach him about interacting in the human world. Punishment doesn't work well with birds, because they usually see any kind of attention as positive, and besides, physical punishment can severely injure and traumatize a bird. Focus, instead, on rewarding the good, ignoring the bad, and refusing to let your bird run the show. Remember, it's your house. You're in charge, and you're a benevolent dictator when it comes to managing your adopted avian pet. Rule with a firm but gentle hand, and you nurture your new pet's confidence and outgoing — if a little bit wild — nature.

Bird Basic Training

What can you train your bird to do? The answer may surprise you. Birds can learn to sit on your finger, hand, arm, shoulder, or even on your head. Many birds talk, and some often groom you, follow you around, and do tricks like waving on command or even using the toilet. Training a bird is similar to training any other animal, including a dog, cat, or rat. Birds even respond well to clicker training. (For more information about clicker training, see Chapter 6.)

Treats or rewards are another means to good bird training. Just remember that too many fatty treats can make anybody fat, regardless of your species, and keeping the treats that you give your bird small also is a good idea, especially if you're giving your bird a lot of them. In fact, to avoid overfeeding your bird, you may even want to decrease the seed content of his dinner. Smaller, healthier treats not only keep birds in good shape, they also can be consumed more quickly. When your bird is in training, the last thing you need is to have to wait for your avian wonder to munch through a huge treat. Depending on your bird's size, a sunflower seed, or even a half of a seed, is a fine treat. Another good option is half or even a quarter of a Cheerio.

Birds are prone to stress, and too much of it when you're trying to train your bird can make him act up, shriek, pull out his feathers, or even get sick. With that in mind, you need to keep a close eye on your bird as you interact with and train him. If he becomes agitated, pull back a step or two and just sit with him, talking gently. Making your bird happy about his new memories of humans and his new home, in turn, makes your bird happy and well adjusted overall.

Socializing with your bird

Socialization isn't a complicated process. It's simply getting birds accustomed to interaction with and handling by humans. To socialize your adopted bird, start slowly and progress according to your bird's comfort level. Every bird is an individual that learns at a different rate. Different birds have different barriers to learning based on past experiences and personality. Therefore, much of training a bird is a matter of gauging your individual bird's reaction to what you do. Start by simply sitting next to the cage.

Some birds are not stressed out much by the presence of humans. They may be used to people and happy for the company. Others may be fearful, shy, or even angry when you approach them. During your initial encounters with your bird, move slowly, speak softly, and behave calmly. Try to relax and enjoy the experience yourself. You may try reading a book out loud while sitting in a chair beside your bird or offering him a treat through the bar. Don't be surprised if he's afraid to take it from your hand at first. Spend time with your bird each day, and pay attention to how he reacts to your presence. If he's scared or aggressive, don't be in a rush to touch him. Just bide your time every single day beside his cage, calmly and quietly going about your business. Maybe that means working on your computer, reading the newspaper, or talking on the phone.

After a few days or so, depending on the type of bird you have, your bird may seem comfortable and interested in your presence. Some birds may take a few weeks, or even longer, but you can tell that comfort level has been reached when your bird:

✔ Comes forward to see you as you approach

✔ Hops over to the side of the cage nearest you

✔ Looks at you and makes chirping — rather than shrieking — sounds that seem to be directed toward you

✔ Pokes his beak through the bars of his cage as if trying to play with you

For some calm, collected birds, acceptance may simply come in the form of relaxed sitting on a perch, looking at you with interest.

Hand-training

Start hand-training after you find that your bird is comfortable with your presence (see the previous "Socializing with your bird" section). Begin by opening the door and putting your hand inside the cage. Start slowly. Don't try to persuade your bird to step on your finger, just get him used to the non-threatening presence of your hand in his cage. Do this step a few times every day for just a few minutes.

When your bird is used to this process — after a few days, weeks, or longer; don't rush the process — you can start encouraging him to explore your hand. He may or may not step up on your finger, but continue to move slowly and watch your bird for stress and progress as he grows more comfortable with your hand. If you scare your bird, you may need to back up a step and just sit by the cage for a few days again.

When your bird voluntarily steps onto your finger, hand, or arm, don't move at first. Let him explore you. If he nips at you, say "No!" firmly and loudly but don't flinch. When he explores you without biting, see whether he will take a treat from your other hand. If you're afraid of being bitten, wear a leather glove when you put your hand in the cage and keep progressing a step at a time, until your bird is ready to learn the step-up cue (see the next section), or voluntarily steps onto your hand or finger.

The step-up cue

The step-up is the most basic bird cue. Its purpose is getting the bird to step onto your hand or a perch on cue. After birds know how to do this simple move, you can build on it, teaching your bird many different tricks and behaviors.

Some birds need virtually no training to learn this move, because birds naturally step onto branches — or perches — that are put in front of them. When your bird is comfortable with your hand, practice putting your finger or hand (or a hand-held wooden dowel or bird perch) directly in front of him, touching his chest). If your bird steps right up, say the words "step up" as he's doing so and then praise him and give him a treat (see Figure 19-1). Repeat this process many times each day, and your bird quickly learns what the cue "step up" means. If stepping up means he gets treats and attention from you, your bird is motivated to do it as often as he can. Remember, your bird wants to be with you.

Figure 19-1:
Train your
bird to
step up.

If your bird doesn't automatically step up, he may need a little practice. Watch him closely, looking for opportunities to put a perch in front of him. If he is climbing around in his cage, perhaps toward his food bowl or otherwise on the move, put your hand-held perch in front of the one he is trying to step onto, and then say "step up" and praise him when he steps onto your perch instead. This exercise may take some practice. Try not to become frustrated if your bird isn't getting it or won't step on the perch or your hand. For some birds, step-up training takes a long time, even though others do it right away. Remember, every bird is an individual, and your adopted bird needs your patience and regular training to understand and thrive. Even if you work on the step-up cue for only a few minutes a day, do it every day. You'll feel so proud of your feathered friend — and yourself — when he finally steps up consistently.

Teaching your bird to behave on your shoulder

When your bird gets used to hanging out with you, he may enjoy riding around on your shoulder. Many birds think doing so is great fun. They can groom you, play with your earlobe or earring, get a good view of your world, be by your side, and generally feel like they're communing in a social way with the leader of the flock. However, you don't want your parrot on your shoulder if he's going to gnaw violently on your earlobe, rip out your earring, pull your hair, climb onto your head, or squawk with a deafening volume directly into your ear.

Birds love rewards. When your bird is on your shoulder, give him many rewards of attention, praise, and tiny treats when he's behaving himself. If, on the other hand, he bites you, squawks, or otherwise misbehaves, put him back in his cage immediately. Leave him there for five to ten minutes. Then you can take him back out and give him another chance. If he bites you right away, back into the cage he goes. If he's good, reward, reward, reward. Figuring out what kind of behavior lets him stay up there on his very favorite human perch won't take your bird very long.

Cage-free manners

Most birds enjoy spending time outside of their cages, but if your bird isn't behaving while enjoying his free time, then you must show him which kinds of behaviors are acceptable and which are not. When you let your bird out, play with him for at least the first few minutes. Talk to him, give him toys and treats, and generally interact. Then, step back and do something else. See how your bird behaves. If he squawks, jumps down on the floor to follow you around, nips at your ankles, or tries to dismantle the woodwork, say "No!" and immediately put him back in his cage. Let him stew in there for five minutes. When he's quiet, take him back out and try again. Every time he misbehaves, back in his cage he goes for five minutes. When he is quiet and good, let him out again. He will quickly understand what kind of behavior warrants freedom.

Parrots can learn tricks — even very complicated ones — with relative ease. Simply break the trick down into steps and teach the steps one at a time, rewarding as you go. Read the chapters on training dogs (Chapter 7) and training cats (Chapter 11). The same strategies apply beautifully to birds. For more about training parrots, check out *Parrots For Dummies* (Wiley) by Nikki Moustaki.

Mating Season and Avian Adolescence

Oh no, suddenly your adorable juvenile bird is a teenager. Birds go through adolescence at varying ages, depending on the species, and adolescent birds, like adolescent children, sometimes can be a real challenge. If your bird doesn't have a cagemate love interest, he may consider you his — or her — mate. Some birds are lovey-dovey, but some birds aren't always sweetly romantic to the ones they love. Instead, a bird that thinks you're his life partner may behave aggressively, nipping and biting you, preening you a little too roughly, even upchucking on you — a huge compliment in bird terms but not particularly appreciated by humans.

Adolescents also become territorial, guarding their cages or perches and nipping intruders. This common behavior nevertheless should not be tolerated in pet birds. Wear gloves and don't let your bird intimidate you. A territorial bird needs to be handled and shown that he may not be aggressive in guarding his cage, which is, after all, *your* cage, too. You paid for it, right? A misbehaving free bird needs a timeout in his cage. An aggressively amorous bird also needs to be shown that biting and terrorizing his beloved is unacceptable. Keep those gloves on, and keep your bird away from your face.

For birds with cagemates, mating season can be a disturbing time for onlookers. Whenever birds are fighting or being too rough, they may need to be separated, but affectionate birds, or even those that are quite blatantly getting it on, don't need be separated. Unlike dogs and cats, birds can't be neutered because avian anatomy makes the surgery much riskier. Many birds bond well with same-sex cagemates, but even in mated pairs, birds won't reproduce if you don't provide a nesting box or any nesting material. Even if they get amorous, they won't produce any baby birds. In a few rare cases, birds may go into a superbreeding mode, trying desperately to nest. If that happens (suspect this if your bird tries to build a nest out of anything she can find, squats or sits on a corner on the bottom of the cage, or acts very agitated), just decrease the amount of light to which your bird is exposed every day to less than 12 hours. Doing so impedes the nesting instinct. For more about this topic, see Chapter 18.

Birds thrive on companionship, so fear of breeding is no reason to keep birds alone in a cage. Just maintain regular contact, training, and gentle discipline with birds during the difficult breeding stage. If you're the object of your bird's affection, don't be bullied, but don't ignore your bird, either. It's a little like raising teenagers — sometimes it isn't fun, but it's worth it when you behave like a responsible and caring parent.

Part VI
Giving an Exotic a Second Chance

The 5th Wave   By Rich Tennant

"Hey! I think you've found a friend!"

In this part . . .

They're scaly or slimy or hairy, and many of them need new homes. If you're interested in adopting a snake, lizard, turtle, frog, salamander, tarantula, or other creepy-crawly, this part helps you choose the one that matches your lifestyle. In it, you also discover how big of an enclosure your exotic pet needs — bigger is almost always better — and what kind of environment is right, whether desert terrarium, rainforest replica, or something in between. You also find out about choosing the right foods, providing the right care, finding an exotic pet vet, determining how much handling your exotic pet wants and needs, and taming your pet so he doesn't stress every time you get near his cage. Exotic pet ownership isn't for everyone, but for herps, and herpers who adore them, this is your part of the book.

Chapter 20

Choosing a Creepy Crawler

In This Chapter

▶ Deciding whether you're really suited for an exotic pet

▶ Choosing the right exotic pet

▶ Finding exotic pets in need of new homes

*W*hen you visit an animal shelter, you're likely to see dogs and cats, some small animals, and maybe a few birds. Dedicated rescue groups also tend to specialize in the furred and feathered, but what about animals with scales or shells, wet slimy skin, or eight hairy legs?

The shelter system doesn't typically take in abandoned reptiles, amphibians, arachnids, and other creepy crawlies — although I have seen some turtles in animal shelters, but plenty of exotics still are in need of good homes. Tracking down these exotics is just a little bit trickier. If you're willing to look, you can find a few rescue groups devoted to this subcategory of pets, and most of the groups that do rescue them are comprised of hobbyists who informally take in animals. You don't have the organized system of foster homes and placement interviews you usually encounter with other, more traditional pets. Why you may ask?

Far fewer people *want* an exotic pet than a furry mammal. Yet, reptiles, amphibians, and arachnids are actually far easier to care for than their warm-blooded counterparts. If you find one that appeals to you, if you get the right supplies and proper housing, and if you meet the animal's nutritional needs, you can find yourself in a relationship with an easygoing pet.

On the other hand, creepy-crawly pet ownership isn't for everybody. In this chapter, I help you find out whether you're suited for exotics, and if so, which exotic pet is right for you. This chapter is your primer on all things creepy-crawly, and your guide to finding an eight-legged, four-legged, or no-legged pet in need of a new caretaker.

Determining Whether Exotic Herps and "Bugs" Are Right for You

Reptiles and amphibians, or exotic *herps* according to many hobbyists, and other "bugs" — an even more informal hobbyist term for exotic pets such as tarantulas, hissing cockroaches, and scorpions — have some particular pros and cons. Deciding if you really would make a good caretaker for this unusual pet category isn't difficult, as long as you know exactly what you're getting into. Are you willing to find out about and meet your pet's specific care requirements? Or are you just hoping for a pet that takes no work? Are you hoping to use your pet to frighten your friends or shock your parents? Or are you truly fascinated by the world of herps, arachnids, and insects?

Although an abandoned dog or cat may have developed some behavior problems and needs training, you usually don't have to worry about the same problems with reptiles. However, if a reptile is no longer a baby and hasn't been handled regularly, that cool iguana may never be interested in riding around on your shoulder, and that nervous rat snake may be nippy for the rest of his life. Are you willing to care for a pet even if you can't touch it? Adopted exotics also sometimes have health problems — such as mites and skin infections — caused by neglect or unclean living conditions, or even skeletal deformities caused by poor nutrition.

Ask yourself these questions to be sure you really want an exotic pet:

- ✔ **Why do I want a herp or bug?** Enjoying the exotic pet's shock value is fine as long as you're also genuinely interested in finding out about and caring properly for your pet.

- ✔ **Am I prepared to make a long-term commitment?** Many exotics such as most large snakes, medium-to-large lizards, tortoises, and female tarantulas can easily outlive a dog or a cat. For more on life spans of individual exotics, see Chapter 1.

- ✔ **Is anyone in my home going to be severely bothered by the presence of a creepy crawler?** Some people truly are frightened by spiders, snakes, or other exotic pets, even if you don't think such fears are rational. If people in your home are bothered so much by these pets that keeping one long term isn't actually realistic, please don't adopt an exotic pet.

- ✔ **Do I have other pets that may try to prey on my small exotics?** Lizards, frogs, and other small pets that move fascinate cats and some dogs. On the flip side, a giant python can swallow a kitten or a puppy. Can you keep all your pets safe?

✔ **Do I really have time for an exotic pet?** Exotics may be low-maintenance, but they certainly are not *no*-maintenance. Some take less time, but others actually take more time than other pets, and they all take *some* time for feeding, basic observation for health and other problems, and cage cleaning and maintenance. Most exotics need their enclosures cleaned about once a week.

✔ **Am I squeamish about feeding bugs and small rodents to reptiles?** Most exotics require a diet of live food of some sort, whether crickets and mealworms or mice and rats. If you're squeamish about touching those critters or don't want to see them periodically devoured, consider a vegetarian exotic like a green iguana.

✔ **Do I have a good and affordable source for the food my exotic needs to eat?** You need time, patience, space, noise tolerance, and the stomach to breed your own crickets or pinkie mice as a source of food for your exotic.

✔ **Do large reptiles intimidate me?** Some reptiles, such as large iguanas or giant snakes, grow so big that you won't easily be able to handle them. If a reptile that large intimidates you, consider an exotic that stays relatively small, such as a water dragon or a corn snake.

✔ **Deep down, do I want a fluffy pet?** Few exotics provide the same hands-on fluffy-lovey feeling of a dog or cat. Are you sure scales, shells, or exoskeletons will fulfill your pet owning needs?

✔ **Are exotic pets legal in my area?** Many cities and regions don't allow certain exotic pets, so make sure your pet is legal before adopting and recognize that poor care and irresponsible management of exotics often contributes to legislation against them.

✔ **Am I willing to pay for veterinary care if my exotic gets sick or injured?** Are you willing to pay and work to resolve health and nutrition issues your adopted pet may already have? Do you have access to a vet who is comfortable and experienced with exotic pets?

Picking Your Exotic Pet

If you think you want an exotic pet, but aren't sure which one exotic is right for you, consider the time commitment required of different exotics. According to *Reptiles & Amphibians For Dummies* by Patricia Bartlett (Wiley), some of the lowest-effort exotics are corn snakes, king snakes, horned frogs, White's tree frogs, and Tiger salamanders. Painted turtles, Greek tortoises, and Eastern newts fall in the middle of the spectrum, and green iguanas are among the most time-consuming.

If you consider cage cleaning a marker of high maintenance — in other words, how much daily time you have to spend to take care of your pet — then amphibians are high on the list, because their moist cage environments need more vigilance in cleaning and water changes to keep them bacteria free.

Most arachnids, such as tarantulas, are relatively low maintenance, and most lizards generally are somewhere in the middle- to high-maintenance range.

The following sections list the most popular exotic pets and what you must consider before adopting one.

Constrictors: Pythons, boas, and other huggable snakes

Snakes that squeeze are the most popular types of pet snakes. However many people give up their constrictors because they get too big, they get mites or some other unpleasant health problem, or they just get tired of feeding mice and rats to their pets. Consider the following before you decide whether to adopt a constrictor or similar type of snake:

✔ **Time commitment:** Most snakes, including the popular ball python, are relatively low maintenance. Larger snakes such as pythons like Burmese pythons, reticulated pythons, red-tailed boa constrictors, or anacondas can grow to more than 15 feet in length and may require more than one person if you need to handle them. Giant snakes don't require frequent care but when they need their large cages cleaned, it's more of an effort. Some constrictors can live 20 to 30 years, or even longer.

✔ **Housing:** Constrictors require spacious enclosures (see Chapter 21 for recommended dimensions relative to the snake's size). Your snake's tank needs to include a source of heat, such as an under-tank heating pad, so the snake can regulate its own body temperature.

✔ **Special considerations:** Constrictors eat whole rodents, from baby pinky mice to large rats, and some larger snakes need larger animals than rodents, such as rabbits or chickens. All these are best fed to the snake prekilled. For a large snake, feeding can be costly, depending on your source of food, and some people don't like feeding these animals to reptiles. Pay attention to your constrictor's health and watch for signs of mites, tiny flea-like parasitic creatures that feed on blood and can cause snakes severe skin irritation. Finally, keep in mind that frequent handling helps keep snakes tame, but they don't require handling for their own well-being the way domesticated mammals do. For more on handling snakes, see Chapter 23.

Small slitherers: Garter snakes, king snakes, corn snakes, and other Colubrids

Most small snakes fall under the family *Colubridae.* In other words, they're called Colubrids. These snakes include the common garter snakes, king snakes, and rat snakes including rat-snake sub-types like corn snakes and milk snakes. Colubrids are — with the possible exception of the ball python — the most popular snakes kept as pets and the most common nonpoisonous snakes you're likely to see while tromping around in the wilderness in the United States.

Because so many Colubrids are bred in captivity and sold in pet stores, many of them also are abandoned to pet stores, reptile societies, and hobbyists when their owners get tired of feeding them and cleaning their cages. See if adopting one of these small slitherers is right for you:

✔ **Time commitment:** Small snakes are easier to care for than big snakes, but they still can live for 7 to 20 years or even longer. They need regular cage cleaning and feeding, and regular handling if you want them to be tame.

✔ **Housing:** Although some rat snakes can grow to more than 8 feet long, most types are smaller and stay less than 5 or 6 feet. Garter snakes and some ball pythons may only reach 3 feet. Despite their smaller size, cold-blooded Colubrids need spacious cages with a source of heat and an unheated side for cooling off.

✔ **Special considerations:** A few Colubrids have venom, but not the more common ones. They also move faster and are good at escaping, so they need tightly fitting lids on their tanks and must be handled with care. These small snakes, when handled frequently, can behave in a tame and responsive manner. They make good pets for people who like hands-on interactions. For more on how to handle snakes, see Chapter 23.

Green iguanas

Life with an iguana isn't the maintenance-free existence that you might imagine comes with owning a reptile. In fact, it's far from it. Actually, the green iguana is high maintenance, even though it's among the most popular of the reptiles. Yet, tame, healthy iguanas can be incredibly rewarding pets if they're lucky enough to find caretakers who understand how much and exactly what they need in the way of environment, nutrition, and training. Here's what's involved in living with an iguana:

- ✔ **Time commitment:** Iguanas are vegetarians. They require freshly prepared raw vegetables every single day. Rotting food matter needs to be cleaned from their cages often. Iguanas also need daily handling if you expect them to be tame and daily interaction of some kind if you don't want them to fear you or act aggressive. Iguanas also have a long life span, living up to 20 years or even longer when well cared-for.

- ✔ **Housing:** The super-popular green iguana looks unassuming in a small cage in a pet store when it's less than a foot long, but green iguanas live for a long time and grow big — some up to 6 feet long! So when buying an iguana cage, you can't get one that is *too* big. Some people devote entire screened-in porches or rooms to their iguanas, or even let their iguanas roam free in their homes so they get plenty of exercise.

- ✔ **Special considerations:** Iguanas have sharp claws and strong jaws, and if they aren't tame — because of a lack of handling and training — they can be very skittish and even aggressive. Iguanas can claw and bite you, and these injuries can be severe if you aren't careful.

Turtle time

Turtles are amusing, fun companions. The most common pet turtles — and the ones most likely to be in need of a new home — are red-eared sliders and box turtles, although in many states it is illegal to take these pets from the wild. Turtles have individual care needs depending on what kind of turtle you have. Find out whether turtles work for you by considering the following:

- ✔ **Time commitment:** Turtles have incredibly long life spans. Some box turtles can live up to 100 years. Even the tiny aquatic red-eared sliders can live 40 years with proper care. They eat fruits and vegetables, which can be time consuming to prepare and must be offered fresh every day. Box turtles enjoy supervised time outside in temperate weather in a protected area where they're safe from predators, including your own dogs and cats.

- ✔ **Housing:** Both the small aquatic red-eared slider and the box turtle need spacious tanks with room for swimming and for resting out of the water. Their tanks must be kept clean.

- ✔ **Special considerations:** Turtles need vitamin supplementation (available in the pet store) and aren't usually very interested in interacting with humans. They do best with people who are interested in observing their turtles but who don't crave constant interaction or feel the constant need to touch them.

Turtles can be a source of salmonella, so anyone handling a turtle needs to be particularly careful to wash his or her hands thoroughly afterward. Infants and people with low-functioning immune systems shouldn't handle turtles at all.

If you want to know more about turtles as pets, check out *Turtles & Tortoises For Dummies* by Liz Palika (Wiley).

Other reptiles of the tropics and the deserts

Many different lizards find their way in and out of pet homes. Some of the more common include anoles, chameleons, leopard geckos, bearded dragons, water dragons, blue-tongued skinks, monitor lizards, Gila monsters, caimans, and alligators. Some of these reptiles are easy keepers. Anoles, chameleons, leopard geckos, bearded dragons, water dragons, and skinks can be fun and interesting pets as long as you keep their cages clean, give them enough space, and find out about their specific nutritional, temperature, lighting, and other care needs.

- ✔ **Time commitment:** Lizards can live for just a few years or as long as 20 years or more. If you want your lizard to be tame, you need to handle it regularly, but many lizards don't particularly enjoy being handled.

- ✔ **Housing:** Different lizards have specific housing needs, but they all need plenty of space to move around, bask under a heat lamp, or cool off as necessary to regulate their own body temperature. Their tanks must be kept very clean.

- ✔ **Special considerations:** Each species of lizard has its own unique care needs so you need to take the time to learn as much as possible about the lizard you adopt. Many pet lizards die in captivity because they were missing some nutrient or environmental condition their owners could easily have provided had they been aware of it, so please do your research.

These reptiles, in general, can be interactive, sometimes are tame enough to handle — depending on their past history — and are relatively easy to feed and keep healthy, as long as you know what you're doing.

If you're interested in more information about leopard geckos — one of the most popular pet lizards — check out *Leopard Geckos For Dummies* by Liz Palika (Wiley).

Other reptiles, such as monitor lizards, Gila monsters, caimans, and alligators, can be quite dangerous. Gila monsters are venomous, and monitors, caimans, and alligators become large and aggressive, with jaws and bodies strong enough to seriously injure a human. Owning them often is illegal, so think three times and check the local laws before attempting to adopt one of these formidable fellows.

Whatever reptile you choose, do plenty of research before committing yourself to keeping and caring for that animal. For more information on specific care needs of different reptiles, see Chapters 21 and 23, and read *Reptiles & Amphibians For Dummies* by Patricia Bartlett (Wiley).

The slime factor: Frogs, salamanders, and newts

Amphibians, such as common frogs, tree frogs, exotic frogs, salamanders, and newts, are long-lived, mellow pets. Some have brilliant colors and amazing patterns.

- ✔ **Time commitment:** Because bacteria, algae, mold, and other nasty things grow quickly and easily in moist environments, amphibians need to have their homes cleaned — including their water changed and plants rinsed down — about once a week, and may need a complete overhaul of their tank environments with new substrate and complete water change every few months.

- ✔ **Housing:** Different amphibians need different types of environments. Some, such as certain tree frogs and salamanders, prefer drier environments and enjoy a terrarium with plants, moss, and a small shallow swimming area. Some, such as aquatic frogs and newts, do best in tanks that are half water and half rocks with areas to climb out of the water and bask. Some frogs, salamanders, and newts are aquatic and live in fish tanks, cohabitating with or without fish. Some arboreal species, like various tree frogs, prefer an environment with tall tree-like places to climb and hang out.

- ✔ **Special considerations:** All amphibians need constant access to sufficient moisture, whether in the form of a swimming area or a misting system, which can be as simple as you spraying a plant sprayer into the cage. Amphibians have porous skin and they breathe through their skin, so this moisture is important to keep them healthy.

Don't expect cuddles from your amphibian, but they're beautiful and interesting pets to watch.

Shell chic: All about hermit crabs

Hermit crabs may seem like the world's easiest pet after the pet rock. After all, they're hermits, right? But hermit crabs need care, too.

- ✔ **Time commitment:** Hermit crabs need fresh food and clean water every day, and they need a clean environment so you have to spend time cleaning their enclosures at least weekly. No, you don't have to walk or train them, but they still require some time and attention, especially if you want them to be tame.

- ✔ **Housing:** Hermit crabs do well in large aquariums on sand with a salt-water pond, stocked with a selection of clean, sterilized shells to choose from as they grow and molt.

- ✔ **Special considerations:** Forget those shells decorated with potentially toxic paint. Hermit crabs need respect and attention to their health and safety, just like any other pet. Hermit crabs make good pets for kids as long as kids understand how to handle them carefully and responsibly.

If you're interested in a hermit crab, check out *Hermit Crabs For Dummies* by Kelli A. Wilkins (Wiley).

Bugs: Tarantulas and beyond

Tarantulas can be docile companions and can even be hand-tamed. Other bugs people sometimes keep as pets include hissing cockroaches, scorpions, and giant centipedes. Most rescued tarantulas are the common Chilean Rose Hair, everybody's favorite first spider.

The more common pet tarantulas are less likely to bite because their first line of defense is to flick or kick tiny barbed hairs at you, which can be very irritating to your skin and can even be dangerous to you if they come into contact with your throat or in your eyes or nose. They are preferable to getting chomped by a pair of arachnid fangs, but getting shot with those little hairs is no picnic, either.

- ✔ **Time commitment:** Arachnid or insect caretaking isn't for everyone, but if you love the six-to-eight-legged set and are willing to get to know them, they're easy keepers. Just keep their cages clean and provide them with food and water. They don't need attention, but you may want to spend time staring at them in admiration.

- ✔ **Housing:** Arachnids and other bugs need clean cages and a place to hide. Their enclosures depend on their individual needs, so do your research, but most need higher temperatures than room temperature so they will need to have a heat source. They need close-fitting tops to prevent escape. Some have additional needs like branches for arboreal spiders to climb in and mulch for ground-dwelling spiders to burrow under.

✔ **Special considerations:** Most spiders, centipedes, and scorpions eat bugs or *pinkies* — a term for baby mice before they get their fur — and may or may not need vitamin supplementation in the form of dusting or gut-loading crickets and pinkies. (For more about feeding these creatures, see Chapter 22.) To keep them healthy, you must be willing to give them these necessary dietary items. Pet cockroaches mostly eat dry grains, fruit, vegetables, and even dry dog food. Scorpions and giant centipedes are venomous, and beginning hobbyists shouldn't ever handle them. They are for advanced hobbyists only.

Some people think tarantula bites are deadly, but most are more akin to a bad bee sting. Unless you're allergic, don't worry; a bite won't kill you. But it certainly won't be an enjoyable experience either, so be careful! Spiders favored by more advanced hobbyists have more potent venom.

Seeking Out Secondhand Snakes, Lizards, and Spiders

If your local shelter doesn't have any exotics, you aren't necessarily out of luck. You can still look at the following places to find the exotic of your dreams:

✔ **Pet stores:** Many people who decide they can no longer keep their exotic pets take them to pet stores, which often take them in and sell them, enclosure and all, on the cheap. These "recycled" exotics may have health problems caused by neglect and/or malnutrition, and they may be in inappropriate enclosures. Or, they may be healthy and well housed.

✔ **Local enthusiast groups:** Another place to find exotics that need homes is through local enthusiast groups such as reptile clubs or societies. They may know of in-need herps or bugs and can probably offer you helpful care advice.

✔ **Veterinarians and breeders:** Local vets may know of people who are looking for new homes for their exotic pets, and local herp and bug breeders may also be fostering pets they can't keep long term as they look for good permanent homes.

✔ **The Internet:** The Net has some resources for national, regional, and local organizations that handle rescued herps and bugs, although don't expect to find as many organizations for these exotics as you can for mammalian pets. Search these on the Internet by typing "Reptile rescue" or "Amphibian rescue" and the name of your state.

Chapter 21

Preparing for Your Exotic Pet

In This Chapter

▶ Preparing your home for your new pet

▶ Figuring out what kind of home and environment your new pet needs

▶ Helping your new herp adjust to his new home, family, and life

*T*his chapter can help you get everything ready for your exotic before you come home. You also discover exactly what to expect during the first few days as your new creepy-crawly creature gets used to his new environment. Is he settling in, and does he have everything he needs? For exotics, environment is everything. This chapter is your guide to doing it correctly.

Herp-Proofing Your Home

You probably aren't planning on giving your new ball python, green iguana, or tarantula the run of the house, but before you bring home your exotic pet, you nevertheless want to herp-proof your home. Small, flexible, creeping, and crawling exotics are good at escaping, and you may find yourself with a herp on the loose, despite your best efforts.

Your home can be a hotbed of hazards to an escaped or free-roaming reptile, amphibian, or tarantula. If your pet escapes, you may never find him again, and he probably won't last long considering natural predators, fearful humans wielding shovels, and the probability that your climate doesn't match his natural climate. Even if he doesn't get outside, he can also be injured or killed in many ways. Some herps are extrasensitive to environmental toxins.

But even before you bring home your exotic pet, take the following precautions:

✔ Make sure that your doors or screens don't have any cracks and that they close securely. Remind everyone to keep doors and windows shut to prevent escape.

✔ Keep curtains and miniblind cords out of reach. Lizards can snag and tear their toes in fabric or get entangled in cords.

✔ Pick up all potential choking hazards. A loose herp can choke on coins, buttons, pins, or small bits of fabric, causing intestinal impaction. Ingesting cat litter can also be deadly.

✔ Store all chemicals away from your herps. Furthermore, don't use any chemicals around your herps, especially sensitive amphibians with their porous skin. That includes pesticides, flea spray or powder made for dogs and cats, scented candles or potpourri, air fresheners, tobacco smoke, paint or paint remover, perfume, nail polish remover, markers, glue, mothballs, bleach, ammonia, or any cleaning chemicals.

✔ Make sure you keep your herp out of the kitchen and bathrooms because of the risk of salmonella contamination to humans. Herps can also drown or get injured in many other ways in these hazard-rich rooms.

✔ Remove all houseplants your herp can conceivably access, to prevent possible poisoning.

✔ Keep all hygiene products and medications for humans or other pets well out of reach and inaccessible to any loose herp that can accidentally ingest them.

✔ Store foods considered toxic for herps, including salt, coffee or tea, cola or anything with caffeine including chocolate, and anything containing alcohol, out of reach. For more on what to feed — and not to feed — your exotic pet, see Chapter 22.

✔ Be sure all family members understand how to handle your new herp correctly — or not to handle him at all. Children must understand that they should never take an exotic pet out of its enclosure without direct supervision from an adult. Never allow kids to handle reptiles unsupervised or pass reptiles around to their friends. If you aren't sure whether your child will obey this rule, do not keep the reptile in his or her room. Supervision is the key to safety.

According to the Centers for Disease Control (CDC), no child younger than 5 should handle a reptile, and no household with a child younger than 1 year old should even own a reptile because of the risk of salmonella contamination. That also goes for households with people who have compromised immune systems. When children do handle reptiles, they must wash their hands thoroughly with soap afterward. Most reptiles carry salmonella in their systems.

If you believe your exotic has been injured or poisoned, rush him to your vet or emergency vet clinic. For possible poisoning, if you absolutely can't get to the vet, call the National Animal Poison Control Center at 888-426-4435, which charges $50 for a professional consultation over the telephone — well worth the price to save your pet's life.

Tracking a herp-on-the-lam

If your exotic pet gets loose — whether on purpose or by mistake — and you can't find him, these clues may help:

✔ Most herps naturally hide to avoid predators, or to hide from potential prey. Look in dark places, such as cupboards, closets, under furniture, in piles of clothes or towels, or even inside shoes.

✔ Most herps are from tropical or desert environments so they like heat. Look in warm places, such as potted plants in the sun, lamps with warm bulbs, laundry baskets filled with laundry fresh from the dryer, heating vents, or sunny window ledges.

✔ Herps like to squeeze into tight spaces so look inside nooks and crannies such as behind baseboards or moldings, under furniture cushions, or inside furniture. Watch for moving parts, such as with recliners. You don't want to squish anybody!

✔ Check the washing machine, dryer, oven, toaster, microwave, dishwasher, or any other appliance before turning it on . . . just in case!

Exotic Equipment and Supplies

Exotics need some supplies to stay safe, healthy, and clean. Before you bring home your exotic, make sure you stock up on these provisions. Most important, be sure your exotic's new enclosure is all set up, secure, and ready to go so you have somewhere to put your new pet as soon as you bring him home.

Exotic enclosures

Because your herp can't go wherever he pleases, the size, condition, and cleanliness of his enclosure is extremely important for his health and well-being. Herps and other exotic pets need enough room to move around, and no animal, including herps, wants to live in a bare cage in full view of predators.

Your exotic's enclosure should mimic as closely as possible that animal's natural environment, be it desert, swamp, forest, woodland stream, prairie, or ocean beach. The temperature, humidity, and access to water, sand, rock, moss, or whatever substrate is appropriate, can all dramatically impact your herp's health and longevity.

REMEMBER

Where you place your herp's enclosure is equally important. Your herp can't move to another room if he gets uncomfortably hot or cold, so keep your herp's home out of direct sunlight, drafts from fans or vents, and extremes of hot or cold areas of the house. And as with any pet that lives inside a cage or tank, size really does matter, and in most cases, the bigger, the better. If your herp will live in an aquarium with a screened top, buy the biggest one you can comfortably afford. If your pet will live in a wooden box or a wire mesh cage, also go large, or build your own, if you can do a good job of building a safe and escape-proof enclosure. For arboreal herps like iguanas, tree frogs, and tree-dwelling snakes and spiders, cages need to be tall with things to climb on (see Figure 21-1). For land-dwellers like bearded dragons and geckos, floor space is more important than vertical space. For amphibians, depending on what type, plenty of room to stretch out and swim plus spaces to dry off a bit are important.

Figure 21-1:
The active iguana needs plenty of room to move around, climb, and explore.

For each type of reptile, Table 21-1 shows you the *minimum* size of enclosure your herp needs, based on your animal's length from the tip of his nose to the tip of his tail. For turtles, measure the shell in its longest dimension. Add 50 percent to each amount for each additional animal kept in the enclosure.

Table 21-1	Minimum Cage Dimensions/Volume for Reptiles and Amphibians		
Animal	*Enclosure Length or Gallons*	*Enclosure Depth*	*Enclosure Height*
Large snake	¾ pet length	⅓ pet length	¾ pet length
Small snake	1 pet length	½ pet length	¾ pet length
Tree snake	¾ pet length	⅓ pet length	1 pet length

Animal	Enclosure Length or Gallons	Enclosure Depth	Enclosure Height
Iguana, monitor lizard	4–5 pet lengths	2–3 pet lengths	2–3 pet lengths
Other lizard	2 pet lengths	1 pet length	1 pet length
Aquatic turtle	4 pet lengths	2 pet lengths	3 pet lengths
Land turtle	5 pet lengths	3 pet lengths	2 pet lengths
Small tree or dart frog	10-gallon tank for one animal, 5 additional gallons for each additional animal	—	—
Large frog, newt, or salamander	20-gallon tank for one animal, 10 additional gallons for each additional animal	—	—
Ground-dwelling arachnids and bugs	3 pet lengths	1½ pet lengths	1½ pet lengths
Arboreal (tree-dwelling) arachnids	1½ pet lengths	1½ pet lengths	2–3 pet lengths
Hermit crabs	1 to 3 hermit crabs in 15- to 20-gallon tank	—	—

Light, heat, bedding, and water

Every herp, arachnid, or insect has its own heating and light requirements, as well as some more complex considerations like humidity and water chemistry.

✔ Reptiles need heat to move, eat, and digest food properly. The best way to provide it is to provide a basking spot consisting of a heat source and a basking platform. Ceramic heat emitters, heat lamps, and heating pads that attach beneath the tank are good heat-source options, but avoid so-called "hot rocks," because they can get too hot and burn your pet. Most vets don't recommend them. A regular rock or even a brick under a heat lamp or heat emitter makes a good platform for basking, because the rock holds in the heat. However, in the wild, turtles such as red-eared sliders often choose a downed tree trunk or a grassy or dirt spot on the shore rather than a rock, so a flat piece of wood makes a better basking site for a turtle. It is harder to clean, but worth it for the turtle.

Having a temperature gradient in the tank — a hot side and a cool side — is extremely important for cold-blooded reptiles that have to self-regulate their body temperatures. A true gradient is difficult to achieve in smaller tanks, especially when you're using a high-wattage bulb for a basking light. The whole tank gets hot, and many turtles and lizards end up getting dangerously overheated — a common cause of reptile death and just one more good reason to have as large a tank as possible.

✔ Many types of lizards need light not only to see but also for the ultraviolet rays that help their bodies manufacture vitamin D3, so they can utilize the calcium they get in their diets. You have to provide calcium, but you can read more about that in Chapter 22. Look for a light for lizards that includes UVB (ultraviolet B) light. Most snakes and nocturnal reptiles and amphibians don't require UVB light.

✔ Reptiles need a substrate, or bedding, in their cages that mimics their natural environment — sand for desert types, cypress or sphagnum moss for burrowers, wood shavings — but not pine or cedar, which emits phenols that can harm your snake — or plain old newspaper are possible choices.

✔ Amphibians aren't quite so picky about heat and light because they thrive in cool moist climates and are happier and more active when the sun sets. Light your amphibian with a regular fluorescent light so *you* can admire his gorgeousness, but don't worry about his lighting needs. In general, creatures that are nocturnal have evolved to manufacture their own vitamin D-3, so they don't need to get it from light the way daytime-active reptiles do. Amphibians require constant pervasive moisture in both substrate and the air of the enclosure, as well as cool temperatures. Sphagnum moss and cypress mulch make good substrates for amphibians. Amphibians also need dechlorinated water — chemicals easily enter their systems through their superpermeable skins.

✔ Frogs need terrariums designed to mimic their particular natural environment. Tree frogs thrive in woodland terrariums with branches to climb and cool green foliage. Tiny colorful dart frogs need superwet rainforest tanks with plenty of places to hide and lush tropical plants. Horned frogs like a woodland environment, but floor space is more important than vertical space, and they like to burrow into the substrate.

✔ Salamanders and newts also require either a woodland-type aquarium or an aquatic setup, depending on their natural environment. If you aren't sure what you've got, ask your vet for advice on what your particular pet needs. For instance, an axolotl is entirely aquatic, an eastern newt is aquatic except for during its intermediate life stage as an *eft* in which it's terrestrial, and fire salamanders are mostly terrestrial.

✔ Spiders, scorpions, cockroaches, and centipedes like moist humid environments similar to what amphibians favor, but without the lagoon. Give these creepy crawlers places to burrow and hide, and plenty of room to move around. Arboreal spiders need something to climb on and crouch upon. Mist spider enclosures with a spray bottle filled with dechlorinated water every day, and you don't need to provide drinking water. Peat moss, vermiculite, or even potting soil makes a good substrate for spiders, scorpions, cockroaches, and centipedes.

✔ Hermit crabs move around, and they need a tank that gives them some horizontal space. They need clean shells to swap out for the ones they outgrow, and they do best in groups with other crabs, because these little guys are social. Always provide a shallow dish of saltwater — hermit crabs drink seawater in their natural environments and need to ingest some salt for good health — and clean, fresh dechlorinated drinking water with a wet clean sea sponge in the water dish. Don't let any water stand too deep in your hermit crab's cage, or he can drown. Sand makes a good substrate for hermit crabs. Hermit crabs enjoy warm tropical temperatures.

Exotic supply list

Before you bring home your herp or bug, be sure you have the appropriate supplies:

✔ An enclosure of appropriate size with a secure access. Some cages open from the front or sides, and often appropriately so, because a frightened arborial spider or a lizard making a break for it often dashes upward rather than trying to run in a straight line. A side-opening cage can therefore help foil any escape attempts.

✔ An appropriate substrate (litter or lining) for the bottom of the cage.

✔ Spray bottle to keep humid environments moist. Label your spray bottle so you don't mix it up with the spray bottle of bleach-water solution you probably use for cage cleaning.

✔ Pump, filter, and water conditioner for aquatic areas.

✔ Food and water bowls of appropriate size and depth.

✔ A place to hide.

✔ For reptiles, an under-tank heating pad, incandescent bulb, or ceramic heat emitter as a source of heat.

✔ A full-spectrum fluorescent light and a light timer to ensure appropriate amount of exposure to light. For reptiles, include a UVB light. Write the date on the bulb — it's common for pet owners to use bulbs past their prime, and although older bulbs emit plenty of visible light, the UVB emission is considerably reduced.

✔ A thermometer and humidity gauge, so you can monitor the conditions in your herp's enclosure.

✔ Vitamin/mineral supplement, as appropriate (see Chapter 22).

✔ The right food, such as crickets, fresh vegetables, mice, or a commercially prepared diet (see Chapter 22).

Everything under the sun: Outdoor housing

Not every herp does well in an outdoor enclosure, but if your herp is a local, hailing from the environment where you live, you may be able to keep him in an appropriately large enclosure outdoors. The easiest pets to keep outdoors are large terrestrial turtles and iguanas, which need space and do well in outdoor enclosures during warm weather. Some iguanas live most of the year in screened-in porches, and some turtles have their own turtle pens where they spend most of their time. Places to hide and cool shady spots are important for animals living outside. The biggest outdoor concern of tortoises and box turtles isn't where to get warm but rather where to go to keep from overheating.

You can build wood-and-mesh enclosures for iguanas, and large turtles can plod around a fenced-in pen as long as they have a big dish of water and a big dish of fresh salad and fruit. Just be sure to bring these pets inside, into a safe and clean, appropriate enclosure when the weather gets colder than tropical. How cold is too cold? That depends on the animal in question and where it lives. If the temperature and/or humidity changes a few degrees or points beyond what it would be in that animal's natural environment, head inside. Beware of the box turtle's amazing escape-artist abilities. They can scale some fairly steep inclines.

Exotic Homecoming: What to Expect

You may have purchased your new pet's enclosure, but before you bring your new pet home, you need to take him to the vet. (See Chapter 22 for more information about finding a good exotic pet veterinarian and what to expect on the first visit.) Your vet can ensure your pet is healthy and ready for his new home.

This section focuses on ensuring that your pet's homecoming is safe and secure, including transporting him home and welcoming him with open arms by allowing him to settle into his new digs.

Traveling with your exotic — bringing him home

Transporting your new pet safely home for the first time, to the vet, or anywhere else for that matter, is important in maintaining your creepy crawlers' health and well-being.

For large exotics such as an adult iguana or a large snake, whose home enclosures are too big to shove into the back of the minivan, your pet needs a separate travel carrier like the kind you use for a cat or dog, with enclosed plastic sides and a wire door on the front. You need to be able to securely close the carrier, and make sure it doesn't have any spaces through which your pet can escape.

For smaller animals, you may want a travel cage so you don't have to move a heavy tank or mess up your exotic's lovely decor. Most pet stores sell small, medium, and large plastic tanks with ventilated tops and handles, perfect for transporting a pet. Put a little of your pet's bedding in the bottom and take him to the vet in this lightweight carrier. Keep it well ventilated, but cover it with a cloth if being moved stresses or startles your pet.

Welcoming your pet home — making him comfortable

When you first bring your new exotic pet home with you, place him in his new enclosure, and step back to have a look. Have you remembered to provide him with a good place to hide? The stress of moving into a new enclosure or being transported to a new location is hard on any pet, and without a place to hide and feel safe, your new lizard, snake, amphibian, or tarantula can suffer from severe stress.

How your animal adapts depends on what kind of animal you have, how old it is, and how it has been treated in the past. If your new pet skitters, scampers, or slithers off to hide, don't worry. Some animals take some time to get used to new surroundings. However, some exotics show no sign of stress or fear when moved to a new home. They just continue to go about their business, building webs, scaling branches, or sitting on the warm side of the tank waiting for a tasty rodent.

Letting your exotic settle in

Because most exotics aren't particularly interactive, all you have to do is stand back and watch. With exotics that you plan to handle, however, don't be in a rush to reach in, grab them, and start hand-taming the minute you get home. Let your pet hang out and adjust to his new surroundings for a day or two, unless, of course, he seems to be adjusting just fine. In that case, try picking him up gently and handling him carefully. With a small or larger tamed iguana or other sociable lizard, or with a baby or larger mellow snake, you may be able to start training in the first few days. For more about training your reptile, see Chapter 23.

Your other family members are likely to be interested in the new pet, but hold off on passing your new pet around to every family member on the first day. Respect your pet's stress level and take it slowly. Be patient, let different family members come up to the tank or cage one at a time to say hello, and wait until your exotic pet seems ready and willing to be sociable.

Always supervise a child's handling of the new pet, and have children hold exotics while sitting on the floor so the pet doesn't get hurt if the child gets startled and drops him on the floor. And of course, put all other curious pets behind closed doors when handling your exotic pets.

Calling a vet

If your adopted pet hides constantly, refuses to come out or eat, or anything seems wrong to you, phone your vet. Don't worry if your reptile doesn't eat for a few weeks or even a month or so, if you know he had a recent large meal before you brought him home. Even tortoises may skip eating for a few days once in awhile. But if your animal looks like he is losing weight, changes his behavior, seems to be having trouble breathing, looks bloated or injured in any way, or acts listless and unresponsive as if unaware that you're even there, a vet probably needs to get involved, so give him or her a call. Your pet may have a health problem that can be easily remedied, and until your pet is healthy, you can't expect him to adjust well to his new home.

Exotics and other pets: Can they interact?

Some people think it's hilarious when their cat plays with their iguana or the dog curls up with the Burmese python. However it isn't so hilarious when the cat decides to eat the iguana, the iguana decides to bite the cat's nose, or the Burmese python or the dog decide that one or the other looks like a good wrestling partner.

Exotics sometimes can interact under carefully supervised conditions with other pets, but for the safety of everyone involved, never leave an exotic unsupervised with another pet, never put a pet in an exotic's cage, never put an exotic in a pet's bed, and never throw them together in the middle of the yard just to see what happens. Too many pets have been severely injured or killed this way. Some species just aren't made to mix, and if they get along, you're lucky, but you don't need to tempt fate.

Chapter 22

Exotic Care and Feeding

In This Chapter

▶ Identifying the health problems exotic pets may experience

▶ Making sure your exotic pet stays healthy

▶ Taking care of and feeding the most common reptiles, amphibians, and other exotics

Caring for an exotic pet can be a challenge, and many exotic pets suffer severe health problems just because their owners don't understand what kind of care and nutrition they need. But today is your lucky day because this chapter provides you with the basics of exotic pet care. Be sure to enhance your knowledge by reading books and magazines about your new pet and surfing reputable Internet sites such as Melissa Kaplan's Herp and Green Iguana Information collection at www.anapsid.org and the care sheets on the Colorado Herpetological Society Web page at coloherp.org/careshts/index.php. You can also consult an exotic pet vet for additional tips on caring for your exotic pet.

In this chapter, you find out what health problems are serious for your adopted exotic, how to track down the elusive but essential qualified exotic pet vet, what to expect when you take your pet in for a checkup, and the basic care and feeding requirements for the most common exotic pets likely to find themselves in need of second homes. Bone up on these basics, and you can give your new exotic pet a second chance at a healthy life with everything he needs to grow, thrive, and be his unique and beautiful — because beauty is a relative term — scaled, slimy, or hairy self.

Bright Eyes and Scaly Tails

Adopted exotics can thrive in captivity if they are given the opportunity to get or stay healthy, but some adopted exotics have some health hurdles to overcome, right from the start. For that reason, visiting an exotic pet vet as soon as you adopt your exotic is important — or even before you decide for sure on the exotic pet for you.

As for what *you* can do at home to keep your exotic healthy, remember that for exotic pets that live most of their lives in cages or tanks, environment really is everything. A dirty home, poor food, filthy water, the wrong temperature, the wrong humidity, and the wrong lighting — all these factors can make an exotic pet sick.

Fortunately, you have the power to control your exotic pet's environment, so you have the power to help him regain or maintain good health. Feed your exotic an appropriate, fresh, nutritionally complete diet. Correct nutritional deficiencies with vitamin supplementation. Give him a large and appropriately furnished space and keep it at the right temperature, humidity, and with the right lighting for your pet's needs. Provide plenty of fresh clean water, and keep his home scrupulously clean. That's all you have to do!

That's all, you ask? Well, sure that's a lot, but keeping any pet is a big responsibility, and it does take time. In this next section, you find out what to do to provide your exotic pet with an environment that gives him the best chance at vibrant health and a long life.

Finding a good exotic pet vet

Some vets don't see exotics, so it can be a challenge to find a good and qualified exotic pet veterinarian. But it is a great idea to find an exotic pet vet, even before you adopt your pet. That way, as soon as you know when you're bringing your exotic home, you can set up an appointment with your vet to get your new animal checked out.

Although the vet who has always treated your dogs and cats *may* know something about exotics, chances are, she probably doesn't specialize in this area. Your vet may know other vets in the area that do treat exotics, however. Ask for a recommendation, or ask other local vets, reptile clubs, or local hobbyists what vet or vets they recommend for the type of exotic you're adopting.

You can also search for exotic vets in the phonebook, looking for vets with ads that say they treat exotic pets. If you can't find a vet with such an advertisement, call a vet and ask whether he or she treats exotics or knows a vet who does. You can also call a nearby veterinary school to find an exotic vet. The school may have some on staff.

Or, check out the Association of Reptilian and Amphibian Veterinarians (ARAV) Web site at www.arav.org. You can search the site by state for ARAV members, many of whom are exotic pet vets or who know how to refer you to one. The Herp Vet Connection also allows you to search for member-recommended herp vets by state at www.herpvetconnection.com. A good exotic pet vet is worth driving a little extra distance.

If you are a long distance from an exotic vet, you can still be served well by a vet who has little experience but is open to learning. Because many exotics have many needs that are not yet known, and data on bloodwork, radiograph techniques, and other aspects of disease treatment and diagnoses still are limited, a true expert in exotic pet medicine is rare. Many vets are willing to acknowledge they still are learning and will investigate the information that's available and talk to experts on the vet Web sites to find the answers. Those vets who feel they know it all may not be the best in this situation. As long as your vet can perform a general exam safely on your exotic and is open to discussing a plan of action and learning together, that is a great start.

When you're checking out vets, you can find out a lot just by asking. Before you make an appointment, call and talk to the vet's office. Ask the vet a few questions, such as:

- ✔ How much experience they have with your specific kind of exotic
- ✔ How many exotic pet clients they have in the practice
- ✔ How long they have been treating exotics
- ✔ Whether the vet is an ARAV member
- ✔ Whether the vet owns any exotic pets

Depending on where you live, you may not have much choice when selecting a vet. You may want to consider a newer vet. A vet who is new to the field may be a wise choice because she may be more up-to-date on the latest developments in exotic pet care. If you find someone who seems qualified, make an appointment and bring in your pet. You need to feel comfortable with the way the vet handles your pet and that the vet is capable and confident, with a herp bedside manner that impresses you.

The vet needs to clearly communicate with you about what she is doing. You want to feel included in the process so ask questions if you don't understand something. The best vets take time to answer your questions about feeding, housing, and care, and probably keep some of their own exotic pets at home. Note that some exotic pet vets treat birds and small animals as well as reptiles, amphibians, and other exotics.

What to expect during the first exam

You may be a little hesitant to take a tiny tree frog or a little lizard to the vet. You're probably wondering: Do I really need to pay for an office visit? Even if your new exotic seems healthy, this initial vet visit is vital.

The vet's practiced eye may recognize problems you don't know how to spot. If your adopted exotic is suffering from a nutritional deficiency, a parasite like mites or ticks, or any other health problem, your vet can tell you exactly what to do. But even if the final pronouncement is that you have a healthy pet, this information is valuable and gives the vet a point of reference and comparison, if anything goes wrong with your pet in the future.

At the first vet visit, your vet gives your exotic pet a thorough once-over, examining him for any signs of disease, injury, and pests such as mites. The vet will probably weigh your pet and record that weight, as a baseline for future visits. Unless you have a concern or the vet detects a problem, your vet probably won't need to do any tests.

Be sure to ask your vet about any questions or concerns you may have and inquire about what you need to do in case of an emergency. Is the vet on-call 24/7? Is an associated emergency clinic available for you to use if your animal needs help in the middle of the night? Write down this information and post it at home where you can quickly find it.

Recognizing special health problems adopted exotics may have

Every exotic pet has certain health problems that it can potentially develop, but adopted exotics tend to have a few in particular. These problems are the kind your adopted reptile can have and that the vet should check for during your first vet visit. If you suspect any of these problems or notice something like mites or ticks, be sure to mention it to your vet on that first vet visit:

✔ **Malnutrition:** Malnutrition is probably the number one health problem common to exotics abandoned to shelters, rescue groups, and pet stores. Exotic pets have very specific needs that often aren't met, and the stress shows in their bodies.

One of the most common nutrition-related disorders in exotics is metabolic bone disease, which reptiles and amphibians can get. A lack of calcium and generally poor nutrition usually cause metabolic bone disease, which often is caused by insufficient light resulting in insufficient calcium metabolism. Signs of calcium deficiency include malformed jaws, weakness and muscle tremors, humped spines, and weakened or broken bones. You can reverse a calcium deficiency with full-spectrum light, calcium supplements, and sufficient nutrition to strengthen bones, but some of the malformations probably will remain permanent, even if the animal survives.

Malnutrition can also cause the following:

- Spindly leg syndrome in amphibians

- Tremors and seizures caused by a thiamine deficiency in reptiles or amphibians

- Vitamin A deficiency resulting in puffy swollen eyes, common in turtles

- Basic dehydration causing a dry shriveled, sunken-eyed look and eventually an inability to drink water or eat food

✔ **Mites:** Many adopted reptiles have mites. If you have other reptiles at home when you adopt your new snake, keep them separated for at least a month to ensure everyone is mite-free. Consider mites the reptile's equivalent of a dog having fleas — these little critters multiply fast and can also transmit diseases. For more on how to get rid of mites, see the section on grooming later in this chapter.

✔ **Constipation and diarrhea:** These symptoms can result from intestinal blockage from eating something foreign or too large. Signs include bloating and going several weeks without defecating after eating. Stress, a change in water, parasites, or other health problems can cause diarrhea. Talk to your vet if you notice any symptoms.

✔ **Mouth rot:** When an exotic pet injures his mouth, he can develop an abscess that can turn into mouth rot. Signs are crusty dried pus around the mouth, mouth bleeding, and whitish areas. The animal may need antibiotics. Talk with your vet if you notice mouth rot.

✔ **Bacterial and fungal infections:** Amphibians can develop bacterial and fungal skin infections because of dirty conditions. Red leg and softshell turtle fungal infections cause skin lesions and discoloration, and mold actually grows on the skin, and pieces of skin fall off. These conditions require immediate treatment.

✔ **Signs of abuse:** Some adopted pets have been abused; cigarette burns on large snakes, dehydrated lizards, and reptiles with tails or limbs missing are all too common. People sometimes fear what they don't understand or know, and exotics have often borne the brunt of human ignorance. If your animal has an injury caused by abuse, it must be treated by a vet.

Noticing when your exotic is sick and needs a vet

You also want to have a vet (and an initial vet visit for your exotic pet under your belt) so that when emergency strikes, you already know where to take your pet. If your exotic pet exhibits any of the following signs, immediately call the vet or, when noted, rush your pet to an emergency clinic without hesitation:

✔ **Breathing problems:** If your exotic pet demonstrates noisy breathing, difficulty breathing, prolonged panting, wheezing, bubbles in the nostrils, or his mouth hangs open, call your vet right away. Breathing problems can be caused by something as simple as incorrect lighting, temperature, or humidity, but the result can be serious, and you need to get immediate advice from your vet about what to do. Your vet may recommend that you bring in your pet, or may recommend trying some things at home first, but don't wait around to see whether the problem resolves itself when breathing is at risk.

✔ **Damaged body parts:** A broken tail, a dangling toe, a crackled shell, or any part of your exotic pet's body that doesn't look normal needs immediate veterinary attention. Your pet also needs immediate veterinary attention for bites from other animals — other pets or a live mouse or rat intended as food — burns from heating elements or lights, and any kind of wound or swelling body part, including those that appear without cause. Take your pet to the vet or emergency clinic.

✔ **Looking up:** Snakes, particularly boas, can get a virus that affects their nervous system and causes them to raise their heads as if looking upward. Sometimes called Stargazer's disease, this condition is an incurable and contagious disease, so don't wait around if your snake can't seem to stop looking up. Call the vet.

✔ **Refusal to eat:** Some exotics don't eat very often, and larger snakes can go several months without eating. Ask the shelter when the snake had its last meal, and what it was. If it was a big meal, then don't worry too much until it has been eight weeks or longer. Then, mention this problem to your vet and tell your vet what the last meal consisted of. All reptiles need to eat on a regular schedule, and lizards shouldn't go more than two or three days without eating, turtles or tropical amphibians for more than a week, or nontropical frogs or salamanders for more than two weeks. Exotics generally won't want to eat when they are getting ready to shed, and if it's winter, ask the vet whether your pet is hibernating. Even when considering all these things, if it still seems your pet has gone too long without a meal, give your vet a call.

✔ **Unresponsiveness:** If your animal seems unconscious — limp, pale, or for any reason different than when he's normally sleeping — immediately call your vet or go to the emergency clinic. Dehydration, starvation, malnutrition, incorrect temperature, or a serious health condition can all cause unresponsiveness.

✔ **Weight loss:** Exotics grow; they don't shrink. If your pet seems to be losing weight, call your vet. If your exotic looks skinnier than usual, emaciated, or if you can see his bones or his skin looks shriveled, be sure he has plenty of water, and give your vet a call.

Identifying reasons not to be alarmed

If you notice your exotic pet demonstrating the following conditions, don't worry. The following behaviors are all perfectly natural for exotics:

✔ **Hiding:** Exotics like to spend most of their time buried under *substrate* (bedding or litter on the bottom of the cage) or hiding in little caves or shelters. They demonstrate this behavior in the wild to protect themselves from predators and to remain unseen to potential prey. This behavior is natural, so don't spend time worrying about how to get your snake, lizard, or amphibian out and on display every minute of the day. When you dangle food, he'll probably come out and have a look around.

- ✔ **Shedding:** Reptiles and amphibians shed their skins as they grow. Before they shed, their eyes get cloudy, and they lose interest in food. Snakes may rub their snouts on rough surfaces to help break the old skin so they can wiggle out of it. After they shed, they're often hungry and look their shiny bright-eyed best. Some reptiles and amphibians eat their shed skin, which also is normal.

- ✔ **Sneezing:** Iguanas sneeze frequently to clear salt out of their bodies. This symptom is normal, but breathing difficulties, spasms, gagging, or other respiratory issues are not normal for any exotic.

Exotics and kids: What you must know

Kids think exotic pets are cool, but they don't always understand how to handle these pets correctly and safely, nor do they always have the self-control to be gentle or supervise the animal while he's out of his cage. Never let kids handle exotic pets without direct supervision by a responsible adult.

Remember that all reptiles carry salmonella bacteria in their intestines and shed them in their waste, so anything that has touched reptile waste and goes into a human mouth can cause salmonella infection. Salmonella infection in humans can cause severe abdominal cramps, diarrhea, and fever. Therefore, don't forget these salmonella safety tips:

- ✔ Always wash your hands with hot soapy water after handling a reptile, cleaning its cage or cage parts like food and water bowls, or cleaning up or touching anything the reptile has touched.

- ✔ Never allow kids to handle reptiles unsupervised or to pass reptiles around to their friends. After children have touched reptiles, make sure they wash thoroughly with soap. If you aren't sure whether your child can obey these rules, don't keep the reptile in his or her room. Supervision is the key to safety.

  According to the Centers for Disease Control (CDC), no child younger than 5 should handle a reptile, and no household with a child younger than a year old should even own a reptile. That same rule also applies for households with people who have compromised immune systems.

- ✔ Never let reptiles roam free in the kitchen or the bathroom, where people often eat or touch their faces. Don't keep caged reptiles in these rooms, either. Use a large bucket or portable washtub in a separate room or outside to clean reptile cages and equipment — don't clean them in the kitchen or bathroom.

- ✔ No matter how cute your reptile may be, don't kiss him! Don't eat or don't even drink a beverage while handling your reptile.

Exotic Meals: Feeding Your Exotic Pet

Everybody loves a good meal, and one of the best ways to encourage good health in your exotic pet is to make sure he has the right nutrition. In this section, you'll get a quick primer on the basic nutritional needs of popular exotic pets. Start here, but also talk to your vet and other hobbyists about the latest research in exotic nutrition.

Snacks for snakes

Snakes are carnivorous. In other words, they need meat, in the form of mice or rats of varying sizes. Some snakes need or will happily eat other kinds of meat, such as lizards or frogs, small birds, other snakes, or insects. Some hobbyists recommend feeding snakes in an enclosure that's different from where they live so they don't associate hands coming to pick them up as prey and so they know that food only comes when they're in that special container. Any clean container works, even a new sterilized garbage pail or bucket. Just don't leave your snake in there unsupervised without a ventilated lid tightly attached.

Never leave your snake alone unsupervised with a live rodent. Although you might think watching your snake eat a mouse or a rat is fun, feeding live food to a snake can sometimes result in injury to the snake when the rodent defends itself. A bite or scratch can get infected. Many hobbyists recommend acclimating snakes to eat freshly killed or frozen thawed rodents, an economical and convenient alternative, by warming up the killed animals and using long-handled tongs to make them twitch enticingly.

Some snakes eat killed food easily as long as it's warm. You can warm up thawed rodents under a heat lamp or put them in a sealed plastic bag and float them in hot water for a few minutes. *Note:* Never microwave a dead rodent, because it will likely explode and can burn your snake internally. If your snake doesn't take to the boring limp bait, hold the dead rodent in a long pair of tongs and give it a few wiggles, or dangle it temptingly over the snake. Many snakes soon figure out to take this prey. Be very careful doing this, because many snakes have a vigorous feeding response, and you don't want your fingers to get in the way of those powerful jaws.

Ball pythons can be very picky eaters and tend to stick with what they know, so you may have trouble convincing a ball python accustomed to live food that a dead mouse is a worthy meal. If your ball python suddenly stops eating altogether (ball pythons are notorious for going on hunger strikes), talk to your vet about what to do.

Never handle snakes for at least a few days after feeding. The stress can cause them to vomit their meal before it is digested.

Lizard lunch

Lizards need a varied diet, but what that diet consists of depends on the lizard. A few general caveats apply:

- ✔ Never feed spinach to a lizard (or any reptile) because it binds valuable calcium, making it unavailable.

- ✔ Iceberg lettuce is nutritionally void and not worth feeding.

- ✔ Some people like to catch wild bugs to feed their bug-eating lizards, but don't do this if the bugs have been exposed to insecticides, herbicides, or any other chemical toxins, such as people might use on their lawns in neighborhoods.

- ✔ A few insects are downright poisonous to lizards, so never feed your reptile fireflies, bees, centipedes, roly-polies (pill bugs), butterflies, wild maggots or houseflies, or any kind of ants, just to be on the safe side.

Specific environments and diets for the most popular lizards include the following:

- ✔ **Iguanas** need a correct diet to be healthy. They're entirely herbivorous and they need no animal products whatsoever, including insects. Instead, iguanas need a daily dose of freshly chopped leafy greens, fruits, and vegetables. The best choices are grated carrots, squash, zucchini, berries, tropical fruits, such as mango, papaya, and kiwi, and some flowers including hibiscus, nasturtium, and dandelion.

  Limit cruciferous vegetables, such as broccoli, cabbage, Brussels sprouts, and cauliflower, which can contribute to thyroid problems. Bananas are okay in small amounts, as a treat. Always have fresh pure water in a bowl and spray down the cage and the iguana daily with a mister. Change their food daily to keep it from getting moldy and attracting bugs.

- ✔ **Anoles** eat a wide variety of insects in the wild, but to be safe and ensure chemical-free meals, purchase live insects for your anoles to chase around the cage. They like a real smorgasbord, so look on the Internet or ask if you can special-order a variety of insects from the pet store. Anoles don't do well if they just get crickets or mealworms. Be sure to review the information at the beginning of this section on which insects *not* to feed a lizard.

- ✔ **Leopard geckos** can thrive on a diet of crickets and mealworms dusted with a calcium supplement.

- ✔ **Bearded dragons** eat insects, such as crickets, mealworms, and clean roaches, and a daily dose of chopped greens — collards, turnips, dandelions — and other vegetation including hibiscus blossoms, apples, berries, and squash.

Turtle tidbits

The most common pet turtles are land-dwelling box turtles and water-dwelling sliders. Here is what to feed them:

- **Box turtles** are omnivorous and benefit from a mixed salad of dark leafy greens, fresh chopped vegetables, fruits, flowers, and bugs like crickets and mealworms, prepared fresh daily. They can also eat high-quality canned dog food, but only as a small part of their diets. Adult turtles also need calcium and vitamin supplements every week. Baby turtles need supplements about three times per week. Vary the turtle's diet every day so he's constantly getting different healthy foods — that's the best way to keep him healthy.

    Box turtles also tend to hibernate from fall to spring, burying themselves in their substrate and not moving. Stop feeding your box turtle in the fall and give him plenty of water to bathe in so he can purge his body of digesting food before hibernation. If you're worried about hibernation, talk to your vet about what to expect. It isn't necessary to hibernate a turtle, but if you do it, be sure the turtle is at a nice heavy weight. Because the temperature must be decreased and your turtle won't be eating for awhile, a vet visit is important before attempting to let your turtle hibernate. Or just don't allow the turtle to hibernate, making sure the turtle gets enough daylight so he doesn't go into hibernation on his own.

- **Sliders** and other aquatic turtles need bugs and tadpoles to munch on as well as aquatic plant matter when they are young. Older sliders become more vegetarian in their tastes and needs, eating mostly aquatic plants, lettuce, apples, berries, leafy greens (not spinach), and commercially prepared high-quality aquatic turtle food. You can even throw in a few tiny pieces of puppy chow for these guys, when they're large enough to eat it.

Amphibian appetizers

Beyond their need to stay clammy-cool and slimy-wet, amphibians also need proper diets:

- **Small frogs** generally eat small insects like crickets.
- **Large frogs** sometimes eat smaller frogs, large insects, and even small rodents.
- **Salamanders and newts** generally eat a variety of insects, worms, and small fish.

Arachnids and other "bug" basics

You might be surprised at what arachnids and other bugs eat:

- ✔ **Tarantulas** eat mostly insects — crickets and mealworms. Larger tarantulas enjoy the occasional pinkie mouse. (*Pinkie* mice are baby mice that don't have fur yet.)

- ✔ **Giant centipedes and scorpions** also eat crickets, mealworms, and pinkie mice.

- ✔ **Giant hissing cockroaches** prefer to eat chopped fresh vegetables and fruit, and the occasional piece of dry dog food.

Hungry hermit crabs

Feed hermit crabs a high-quality commercial diet supplemented with leafy greens, broccoli, carrots, fresh fruit, little bits of fish and meat, nuts, seeds, and sheets of seaweed, called *nori*. Crabs are omnivorous, and a fresh varied diet helps them thrive.

Herp Hygiene and Grooming

You don't groom an exotic pet the same way you groom most other pets. You don't brush and comb them, spray them with conditioner, tease out their tangles or even brush their teeth. But exotic pets need good grooming, too. It's just that for these guys, good grooming is all about cleanliness.

Reptiles, amphibians, arachnids, and all other exotic pets need scrupulously clean environments, and they need to be kept clean themselves, too. No, you don't need to give your snake a shower or your tarantula a bath, but animals that shed their skins do need moisture. Snakes and lizards sometimes enjoy long soaks in buckets of lukewarm water, and amphibians need constant access to fresh water. Hermit crabs soak in it, and even spiders need light misting within their enclosures to stay hydrated and healthy.

Exotics don't normally get fleas, but one common grooming-related problem they do have is mites. Mites can be a big problem with adopted exotics, particularly reptiles. How can you tell whether your exotic has mites? You can see the little critters if you look closely. They look like tiny brown or black bugs crawling on and under your pet's scales. In snakes, they sometimes collect around the eyes, or you may see them floating in the water. In severe cases, you may also see signs of skin damage such as ulcers, sores, or just a dull appearance to the skin. The animal may rub against rocks or bedding because mite infestations itch.

If your exotic has mites, follow these steps to get rid of them.

1. **Soak your reptile in warm water to drown the mites.**

   While your reptile is soaking, completely clean your reptile's tank. Throw away all litter, scrub everything with hot soapy water, and rinse well. You can let your reptile soak unattended as long as you're sure he can't get out and other pets can't get to him. Some people use a large bucket and put a screen over the top with a weight to prevent escape but allow for ventilation.

2. **Pick off as many mites as you can, and use a cotton swab to gently remove mites on your reptile's face.**

   Some people also suggest coating the reptile in olive oil, but that can get pretty messy.

3. **If necessary, use an appropriate insecticide product.**

   Ask your vet about the best mite treatment to use and attack those little critters aggressively until they're gone. Be careful with insecticides, however. Many are toxic to certain reptiles, so ask your vet before choosing and using one. Some people recommend keeping a flea collar made for a dog or cat outside the tank, but don't put it inside, because this insecticide can be too toxic for your pet.

Some reptiles can also get ticks, which need to be plucked off carefully — use rubber gloves or tweezers — and flushed down the toilet.

Tarantulas can get mites, too, which is problematic because both mites and tarantulas are arachnids, and any mite insecticide also would kill a tarantula. Never use any insecticide on a tarantula! Instead, carefully remove as many mites as possible using a cotton swab dipped in petroleum jelly, then move the spider to a fresh clean cage. Repeat daily for a week or two. Watch for a molt and remove the freshly molted bug immediately. A mite problem on a tarantula can be dealt with, but it takes much dedication and vigilance, and mites cause many people to lose their spiders.

Chapter 23

Snake Charming and Herp Handling: How to Train Your Exotic Pet

In This Chapter

▶ Training and taming your exotic pet

▶ Picking up reptiles, amphibians, tarantulas, and other exotics in the safest way

▶ Knowing what to do if a herp bites

Can you really train a snake? A spider? A hermit crab? Well . . . sort of. Adopted exotics often don't trust humans, and for good reason. Although you probably can't get your iguana to do back flips or even coax your snake to rise up cobra-style from a big basket while you play a flute, you may be able to accustom your herp to handling, and you may even get your pet to actually enjoy the occasional scale stroking or shoulder taxi. However, if you adopt an exotic pet, please do so with the recognition that your pet may never be comfortable being handled, and you really can't do much about it.

If you want to try and tame your herp, just remember that training herps and other exotics requires a certain amount of common sense, caution, and restraint. These animals aren't like fuzzy kittens and wiggly puppies that just can't wait to crawl into your arms for a snuggle. Handling an exotic pet the same way you handle a domesticated mammal can injure, traumatize, and even kill your poor creature.

This chapter tells you what you need to know about how much and in what way you can and should handle your exotic pet, so everybody remains safe, sound, and comfortable in each other's company, and it provides you with vital information in case your exotic herp bites you.

Exploring the Possibilities and Limits of Exotic Taming and Training

Taming an exotic seems relatively straightforward, and you usually don't think of exotic pets as experiencing complex behavior problems. In fact, exotic behavioral consulting isn't a big field, because these wild creatures aren't really amenable to the kind of advanced behavior training domesticated animals respond to. They're wild, and their behavior is centered on survival. An experienced herp hobbyist recognizes that. This wild spirit is a central part of what has mystified and fascinated humans about reptiles, amphibians, and other creepy-crawlies for thousands of years.

Many pet owners are programmed to think that pets need human touch to thrive. However, your exotic pet can live happily for the rest of his natural born life if you never, ever touched him. Unlike mammals, especially the domesticated ones, that love to be touched and even need to be touched for health and happiness, reptiles, amphibians, arachnids, and other exotics are neither mammalian nor domesticated.

In fact, your exotic's little brain registers being touched, at an instinctual level, as step one in a process that inevitably ends in a fight to eat or be eaten. That doesn't make it easy to start off on the right foot when you're trying to get in touch, literally, with your new exotic.

The good news for you is that many exotics can discover that touch by humans doesn't inevitably end in being served up for lunch. Although not everyone agrees that exotic pets can be exactly trained, many do agree that exotics can, to some extent, be *tamed*.

How to recognize a tamed exotic

You just adopted an exotic pet from a shelter or rescue. You think it is perhaps the coolest looking pet you ever saw. But how can you tell whether your new pet is tamed?

A tame exotic doesn't freak out and experience unhealthy levels of stress in the presence of humans. Some even become quite receptive to human handling and will crawl onto your hand to be stroked or carried around. But if your exotic pet scrambles around, quivers, hides, hisses, or tries to bite whenever you come near, he probably isn't tame. Because stress is unhealthy for pets, keeping an untamed exotic can actually be an unpleasant experience for everyone — your pet will become stressed every time you walk into the room, and you, in turn, will be stressed knowing your pet isn't thriving. No, your iguana, ball python, tarantula, or hermit crab is never, by any stretch of the imagination, going to behave like a dog, a cat, or even a hamster. But you may be able to tame your exotic animal to tolerate your presence in the room without cowering in fear or gearing up to attack.

How to tame your exotic

If your adopted exotic isn't tame, you may wonder what you can do about it. This section helps you get started taming your new pet. First, assess what you want out of taming, and what you think is possible with your individual exotic. Do you want to be able to hold your pet every day and have him enjoy it? With an exotic that is already used to humans, this task may be relatively easy to do. If your exotic is already an adult and scared stiff whenever you look at him cross-eyed, your dreams of a python scarf or iguana on a leash may not be realistic.

Or maybe you don't mind so much if you don't hold your exotic often, but you don't want him to suffer from stress whenever you have to handle him once in awhile, such as when you have to take him out of his enclosure to clean it. This goal is realistic and important.

 Taming an exotic is simply a matter of handling the animal frequently without scaring him. Just remember before handling your pet that some adopted exotics may have already experienced trauma associated with the presence of and handling by humans, and the simple fact is that many exotic pets won't ever be very tame. If your herp associates being touched with fear, he probably will try to defend himself or at least hide from you. But if you always move slowly, pick him up gently, and avoid waving him around in the air or passing him around the room at a party, he can discover that you aren't anything to fear. He can also discover that your hand isn't food. He may get used to the smell of humans and eventually (probably) tolerate the occasional handling.

 Stress isn't good for exotics, so if you can at least tame them enough so they relax in your presence, you're doing them a great service. Exotics still can be healthy, interesting pets even if you don't touch them all the time. Simply make your presence known, feed them regularly, keep their cages clean, give them enough space to move around, and spend time near them. For the ones that do accept it, or are only a little bit nervous about it, handle them for brief periods every day. The longer they live in your presence without harm or fear, the tamer they'll become. Just don't force anything. Enjoy your herp for what he is and what he can do, and if nothing else, you can let him live out the rest of his life free from abuse and neglect.

 Avoid handling some exotics, such as venomous herps and spiders, very large snakes, or individuals that tend to be nippy. Children, amateur hobbyists, or anyone who feels uncertain definitely needs to avoid handling these kinds of exotics, because they generally aren't good candidates for adoption anyway, unless you're an experienced herp hobbyist.

Handling Your Exotic Pet

Check out the following sections for a rundown on the various types of exotics and how well they respond to handling, with tips on how to get your exotic used to this essentially mammalian form of intraspecies bonding.

Always wash your hands before and after picking up your exotic pet. You have bacteria on your hands, and you don't want to pass it along to your animal. If you have food on your hands, you can smell like food and accidentally confuse your near-sighted exotic, who may try to take a bite. A perfectly honest mistake, mind you. You also don't want to pass on any of your exotic's germs to anyone else, or take on any of your pet's germs yourself.

Snake couture

Why do people hold — or wear — their snakes? Is it for show? To shock people? Is it to fulfill some basic human need for touch? Feeling that muscular coil curl around your wrist and giving a little squeeze is definitely an interesting experience, and if you've never worn a 12-foot Burmese python around your shoulders or wrapped around your waist, you're missing out on one of the weirder experiences life has to offer (see Figure 23-1).

But think about it . . . snakes don't hug each other or ride around on each other's backs. They may even think you're just as curious as you think they are, and larger snakes like pythons and boas, being generally mellow sorts, are fairly adaptable and often are open to handling. However, face it. Don't ever think for a moment that your snake requires this kind of interaction. It's really just for your own sake.

Figure 23-1:
Some snakes don't mind coiling around you or taking a ride out in public, but don't pass the snake around or lose track of him. Be a responsible pet owner.

Because you sometimes need to remove your snake from his enclosure to clean it, however, and because you may want to get a better look at him, you need to know the right way to handle your snake and to identify when your snake doesn't want to be held.

If your snake feels frightened, threatened, or particularly hungry, or if he is getting ready to shed his skin and can't see very well (eye caps also are shed so the snake's vision gets blurry just before it sheds), he may rear back, or even hiss at you. He doesn't want to be held. Seriously, come back later. Or give him some lunch first.

You can't always tell when a snake is ready to strike, but when they strike, they move quickly. Sometimes they simply curl their heads back slightly toward their bodies so they have a length to use in springing forward, but they rarely open their mouths or look ready to sink their teeth into you, like you may see cobras doing in action movies. Do, however, remember that when a snake has its head and the first part of its body extended in a straight line, it is not able to strike, but a snake with its head retracted and waiting can strike at any moment if he feels the urge.

Remember these points when helping your snake get used to being picked up:

- ✔ **Move slowly and be respectful.** Although people who are frightened of snakes — and many are for some reason — think it may sound absurd that they can actually be the scary ones, snakes do get scared whenever they're suddenly picked up and flailed around.

- ✔ **Use a hook.** Some snakes are nervous or nippy with human hands but easily accept being scooped up by a metal snake hook (see Figure 23-2). They are available from pet stores that specialize in reptile supplies, or look for them on the Internet at Web sites such as www.tongs.com. After the snake is used to the hook, you can transfer him from the hook to your hands.

- ✔ **Pick up the snake by placing one hand around the snake behind the head and then supporting the heaviest part of the snake's body.** Don't be alarmed when your snake curls around your arm or hand. He's holding on and doesn't want you to drop him. Put him where he needs to go or admire his beauty for a moment. Move slowly so you don't startle the snake.

- ✔ **Slowly put him back down.** Place him in his cage slowly, head first or all at once. Pick him up every few days, and your snake may become accustomed to the procedure, even if he doesn't particularly enjoy it. Some don't mind at all, particularly the mellow ball python and small corn snakes.

Don't handle large aggressive snakes, venomous snakes, or giant snakes more than 8 feet long if you're alone. If these guys decide to argue about the merits of snake handling, you don't want to lose that argument.

Figure 23-2:
A snake
hook is a
handy tool
for moving a
snake with-
out actually
touching
the snake.

Lizard love

Some lizards seem to think that humans are fairly interesting and come to you while in their enclosures to look at you, even jumping against the glass or climbing the screen as if desperate for interaction. Some iguanas can be socialized to the extent that they actually seem to enjoy being with people, being handled and petted, and getting attention from humans. They even seek it out. Other smaller lizards may lose all fear of you as they seek you out in the hopes of food or an interesting show of expressions.

Every individual is different, and only you can test your own pet's limits and tolerances. Whatever they are, be patient, be flexible, and continue to work with your pet, remembering that not all exotics can be tamed, but all exotics deserve a healthy life.

Many iguanas, in particular, are waiting for second homes and have reached adulthood without ever being tamed. They may never be comfortable being touched or held, and can bite, scratch, and whip you with their tails out of fear. These iguanas need patience and the willingness to let them climb around in a large enclosure without constant human harassment.

If your lizard scrambles madly around the tank to get away from you, or hisses at you and tries to whip you with his tail, assume that he isn't in the mood to be handled. Iguanas that hiss, flare their *dewlaps* (the flap of skin on the throat of some lizards), or try to bite don't want to be held or bothered.

Talk to experienced iguana keepers about the best way to begin handling these large wild reptiles if you're determined to tame yours to minimize his stress. Brief daily handling is the trick, but doing so can be dangerous without someone with experience guiding you. For more information on how to tame your iguana, check out *Iguanas For Dummies* by Melissa Kaplan (Wiley).

Younger lizards are easier to sell on the whole handling concept. To pick up a small iguana or other lizard like an anole, gecko, chameleon, water dragon, or bearded dragon, gently scoop him up and hold him firmly but loosely around the body. If he is wiggly, put your other hand loosely around his neck. For very small lizards, cup your fingers into a cage. For larger lizards, scoop them up with one hand and use the other hand for support under the chest, just behind the front legs.

Some lizards have defense mechanisms to escape when they're afraid — anoles can drop their tails and geckos can split their own skin open. When handling these little guys, be careful. If your lizard drops his tail or splits his skin, put him immediately back into his enclosure. If you still need to move him, coax him into a container. Don't worry, his skin will heal and his tail will grow back — this can take a few weeks or months depending on the animal and the extent of the damage — even if it doesn't look exactly the same. But it is a shame to damage your pet and scare him to the extent that this happens.

Iguanas, tokay geckos, monitor lizards, tegus, and other large lizards can be dangerous, so don't handle them — or adopt them at all! — unless you're confident in your abilities. They have sharp claws and teeth, and strong jaws, and iguanas have long tails that can painfully whip you.

Turtle touch

Turtles don't necessarily like to be picked up, but many of them don't necessarily mind it, either. If you need to move your turtle, gently grasp the sides of his shell with one or both hands and lift slowly. To put him down, lower him down slowly and when his feet touch the ground, let go of the shell.

Turtles live up to their reputation as slow movers, and because they can't really get to you while you're holding their shells, nor would they usually try, they aren't as dangerous as some of the larger lizards or a large snake in a bad mood. Still, if a turtle pulls his head and limbs inside his shell, he is trying to tell you, in his best Greta Garbo impression that he wants to be alone and that this is not the time to harass him, get him to eat a piece of lettuce, or pass him around to your friends. Put him into his enclosure and let him be.

An annoyed turtle can also bite, but turtle bites are more likely when they mistake your fingers for food. Aquatic turtles may mistake your hand for a tasty fish when in the water but wouldn't make the same mistake when on land. A land tortoise may nip your finger by mistake when you hand him a tasty bit of fruit. Turtles can be a bit near-sighted, but they are not generally aggressive.

Snapping turtles and soft-shelled turtles are another story, however. These guys can deliver nasty bites and should not be handled by amateur hobbyists. In fact, they don't make good adopted pets unless you're experienced at keeping herps.

To discover more about turtles, check out *Turtles & Tortoises For Dummies* by Liz Palika (Wiley).

Touchy toads and feely frogs

Washing your hands before you pick up any amphibian is particularly important because their porous skin is so susceptible to contamination. Use cold water and leave your hands wet — amphibians like cool temperatures and hot hands can be very uncomfortable for them. Dry hands can scratch their delicate skin resulting in an infection.

Frogs can be jumpy and hard to hold onto, so scoop them up carefully around the waist, if you must. But take a hint: If a frog is jumping away from you, that means he is not eager for any cuddling. In general, frogs don't want to be and shouldn't be handled. Try especially hard never to touch small delicate frogs like dart frogs, only because you can injure them. Poison dart frogs are poisonous in the wild but in captivity, they lose their poisonous coating after a few weeks, so you don't have to worry that your frog will slay you. Still, their delicacy makes them unsuitable for any kind of handling. Instead, guide them into a small container and move them that way. Remember to keep them in a moist environment when you're cleaning their cages. You can grasp salamanders and newts around the waist to move them. In general, amphibians aren't aggressive and don't bite, but you don't want to hurt them or scare them, so remember to move slowly and be gentle. Don't handle them more than you have to.

Tarantula taming

What can be more startling than having a giant spider creeping up your arm? Some people really groove on these guys and think a tame tarantula is an incredibly interesting pet. The mellower and more popular pet spiders — most notably the Chilean Rose Hair — usually are easy to handle if you move very slowly and handle them gently.

To pick up your tarantula, follow these steps:

1. **Coax a spider onto your hand by tapping it gently from behind.**

   Use a pen (see Figure 23-3) or a soft spidery paintbrush to urge your tarantula forward — the feel of the brush is similar to the feel of another spider and less startling to a tarantula.

2. **Lift your hand gently.**

   Or, if your spider is very tame, you can pick him up gently by the body, behind the front legs, as shown in the second part of Figure 23-3.

3. **Hold him loosely in an open palm.**

Figure 23-3:
Carefully coax a tarantula into your hand to pick him up (left). Or pick him up gently by the *carapace*, the spider's body (right).

Tarantulas look large, but they're fragile, so stay close to the floor or a tabletop. A drop to the floor can injure or kill a tarantula. Move slowly and keep your other hand handy if your spider wants to play musical palms, or you want to encourage him *not* to explore the nice dark space down the front of your shirt.

4. **To set him down, place him gently into his enclosure with all eight legs on the ground.**

You can easily tell when your tarantula doesn't want to be held or bothered. Tarantulas rear up with their front legs as if getting ready to strike. Don't pick up your new tarantula until you're sure that he is docile.

As for other nonherp exotics, unless you're an experienced hobbyist, don't try to pick up any scorpion or centipede because they are venomous. Scorpions brandish their stingers in a menacing fashion. They mean business. Centipedes may not reveal their displeasure until it is too late. You can pick up your hissing cockroach gently if you must, and he may not care, or he may hiss at you, but he won't bite.

Hermit crab handling

Hermit crabs are social guys and do best in groups of three. Unlike some of the other exotic pets, they find interaction interesting, but you need to handle them gently and carefully. They can be seriously injured or killed if you drop them, so sit on the floor when holding them.

Pick them up by holding their shells, and then set them gently on your open palm. Let them crawl around your hand for a few minutes every day, and they'll soon get used to you. Keep a close eye on them, because they may scoot right out of your hand. If your hermit crab hides in his shell or pinches you, take a hint. He isn't in the mood for socializing.

Dealing with a Herp Bite

So you touched your herp even though he gave you signals that he wanted to be left alone, and he bit you. Well . . . welcome to the club. Exotic pet hobbyists with years of experience all have their bite stories to tell. Whether you get a snake stuck to the end of your finger or a mad iguana mauls your arm, you probably discovered what *not* to do next time. In the meantime, animal bites can range from the incidental to the get-to-the-emergency-room-right-now. Here's what to do if it happens to you:

1. **Don't panic.**

   Easier said than done of course, but panicking only makes you feel worse, and if the animal is still hanging on, it may make him hang on tighter. If the animal doesn't let go, try to relax. Put the animal on the ground and don't hold on to him. If you relax, he'll relax his grip and let go, but it might take a few minutes, so calm down and try to relax. Bigger snakes are more likely to take several minutes to let go, because they usually bite accidentally when confusing you for food. It takes a while for the snake to figure out that it has gotten hold of the wrong thing. Don't struggle or pull, not only because it will encourage more pressure (for constrictors), but also because you can dislodge teeth, even leaving them in your skin.

2. **When the snake lets go, put him into his cage and securely fasten the top. Stay calm.**

3. **Wash the bite thoroughly with soap and water.**

4. **Apply pressure to a bleeding wound and call the doctor.**

   If you don't think the bite is serious enough for the doctor, put antibiotic cream on it and watch for signs of infection, such as red streaks, swelling, or discharge.

   If the bite is very bad or is on your face, have someone take you to the emergency room. Be sure the animal is securely locked in his tank before you leave the house.

5. **After you have taken care of your own wound, keep an eye on your animal to make sure he didn't get broken teeth or a mouth wound from biting you.**

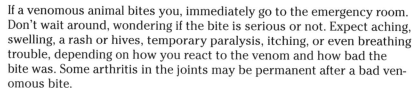

If a venomous animal bites you, immediately go to the emergency room. Don't wait around, wondering if the bite is serious or not. Expect aching, swelling, a rash or hives, temporary paralysis, itching, or even breathing trouble, depending on how you react to the venom and how bad the bite was. Some arthritis in the joints may be permanent after a bad venomous bite.

Part VII
The Part of Tens

The 5th Wave   By Rich Tennant

"You know, you're never going to get that dog to do its business in your remote control dump truck."

In this part . . .

These three chapters give you some helpful lists you can use again and again. If you aren't sure whether you need to spay or neuter your pet, are curious about some of the most wonderful favors you can do for your adopted pet, or if you need some ideas about how best to support the cause of animal sheltering, read these lists and refer to them often.

Chapter 24

Ten Great Reasons to Spay or Neuter Your Adopted Pet

In This Chapter

▶ Benefiting from inexpensive spaying or neutering surgery for an adopted pet

▶ Maintaining health, good behavior by spaying or neutering your adopted pet

▶ Controlling the pet population through spaying or neutering

You know you should do it but for some reason you just haven't spayed or neutered your new pet. Here are ten reasons why you shouldn't delay.

You Can Do It on the Cheap

Animal shelters and rescue groups often offer coupons for discounted or free spay/neuter surgery from a shelter-associated vet.

Spaying/Neutering Makes Pets Healthier

Spay/neuter reduces the risks of many kinds of common cancers in pets.

Spaying/Neutering Keeps Pets Home

Dogs and cats on the make tend to escape in search of a mate. Spay/neuter surgery relieves them of the urge so they stay happily at home.

So What If Your Pet Is a Purebred?

Shelters are full of unwanted purebreds. Purebred status is no reason to contribute to the problem of pet overpopulation.

Spaying/Neutering Improves Behavior

Whether Chief keeps courting the innocent legs of your guests or Tiger insists on tomcatting, spaying or neutering your pet will make him calmer and more receptive to training and handling. The same idea applies to ferrets and rabbits, too.

If They Never Do It, They Never Miss It

If pets never experiences the joys of copulation, they won't keep trying to replicate the experience.

Reproduction Is Risky

Pregnancy and birth are fraught with dangers for the mother and can be traumatic for the babies. Many don't make it or require emergency vet care.

Your Pet Won't Miss the "Family Jewels"

Your dog may lick himself in that special place, but he won't care what exactly he is or isn't licking.

Eight Million Pets and Counting

The Humane Society of the United States estimates that up to 8 million dogs and cats enter animal shelters every year. Half are euthanized. On behalf of all shelter workers, rescue workers, pet foster parents, and anyone else who ever witnessed firsthand the tragedy of pet overpopulation in its many forms, I implore you: Spay or neuter your beloved pet.

Chapter 25

Ten Favors You Can Do for Your Adopted Pet

In This Chapter

▶ Providing your pet with a permanent home and a good diet

▶ Attending to your pet's needs for shelter, exercise, and attention

▶ Establishing your pet's physical and mental health in your home

All pets need things from their owners, but adopted pets need some special favors. No matter what kind of pet you adopt, this chapter lists ten favors your adopted pet needs from you.

A Forever Home

A pet that has been passed from home to home probably has learned not to depend on humans, and that can lead to health and behavior problems. Make your pet feel like he's in a permanent home and he'll likely settle down into a grateful, loving, well-behaved animal friend.

The Right Diet . . . at Last

If your adopted pet is too thin, too fat, or suffers from physical problems related to malnutrition, find the best diet for your pet and watch his health and behavior improve.

Indoor Shelter

With few exceptions, domesticated pets *should* live inside, with time to play, supervised, outside. Give your animal the shelter she deserves to keep her safe and out of the elements.

Exercise, Exercise, Exercise

Animals that don't get enough exercise can become overweight, destructive, or exhibit other behavioral problems. Exercise can solve a multitude of problems often attributed to supposedly incorrigible adopted pets.

Attention

All animals need it. Even for animals that don't necessarily like or need handling, like reptiles and amphibians, attention is important for taming them.

Physical Touch . . . or Not . . .

Many adopted animals crave physical touch, while other animals, like reptiles, amphibians, and spiders, can do without it. Whatever your adopted pet's need for or reluctance to physical touch, respect that need, and you'll gain your pet's trust.

Mental Challenges for Better Behavior

Animals without mental engagement can develop serious behavioral problems. No matter what kind of pet you have, give it something to do so it can exercise its mind *and* body.

Family Member Status

Your adopted pet thinks of you as part of his family, so please consider him a part of yours rather than an expendable possession.

Grooming and Good Housekeeping

Good grooming and good housekeeping of your pet's enclosure are crucial to good health and good behavior. Give them that gift, and they'll reward you by being extra clean, soft, and sweet-smelling when you play with them.

Regular Vet Care

Many adopted pets may never have seen a vet in their lives, but veterinary care is one of the greatest things you can do for your adopted pet. Even for the smallest or most exotic pets, regular vet care is worth every penny.

Chapter 26

Ten Ways to Support Your Local Shelter or Rescue Group

*A*dopting a pet is a great way to support your local shelter and rescue organizations, but maybe the experience has prompted your desire to do more. Here are ten great ways to help.

Volunteering

Most animal shelters need help. Stop by yours and ask what you can do.

Donating Money or Talent

Most shelters and rescue groups are underfunded and can really use your donations. If you're handy, ask about building or painting projects. If you're a writer or computer whiz, ask about designing a newsletter or brochure. If your kids want to get involved, help them set up a lemonade stand or have a bake sale, advertising that all proceeds go to the local shelter.

Fostering a Pet

Work with a local rescue group as a foster pet parent, taking in pets and helping them adjust to life with a family before they find their forever homes.

Dropping Off Food and Supplies

The next time you go to the grocery or pet store, pick up some extra food, litter, toys, or grooming tools and drop them off at the shelter.

Giving Gifts in Others' Names

Make a donation to a shelter or rescue group in a friend or family member's name. Most animal lovers would be thrilled with such a meaningful gift.

Referring Your Friends

Share your great experiences and encourage your interested friends to consider the pet adoption option.

Staying Informed

Stay informed about what's going on in the area of pet welfare. These sites can help: www.aspca.org (The American Society for the Prevention of Cruelty to Animals); www.hsus.org (The Humane Society of the United States); www.adoa.org (The American Dog Owner's Association, Inc.); www.altpet.net (National Alternative Pet Association).

Spreading the Word

Speak up! Get involved with publicity or PR for your shelter or rescue group, or with a local pet club to raise awareness.

Starting a Rescue

If you think you have the business sense and objectivity to do the job right, check out these resources on starting a pet rescue: ASPCA (www.aspca.org/site/PageServer?pagename=startshelter); Pet Rescue.com (www.petrescue.com/library/start-rescue.htm); Cyber-Pet (www.cyberpet.com/dogs/articles/rescue/startrescue.htm).

Adopting Another Pet

I'd never recommend exceeding your capacity for pets, but if you can fit another pet into your home and heart, I hope you'll return to the shelter.

Index

Numerics

1-800-Save-A-Pet (Web site), 29, 211

• A •

AAV (Association of Avian Veterinarians), 270, 271
Adamson, Eve (*Labrador Retrievers For Dummies*), 2
adult cats, adopting, 139–140
adult dogs, adopting, 53–54
Advantage, 97
African grey parrots, 253
alcohol, 278
altpet.net (Web site), 40
Amazon parrots, 253, 278
American Dog Owner's Association, Inc. (Web site), 346
American Ferret Association (Web site), 40, 211
American Kennel Club (Web site), 39, 67, 116
American Pet Product Manufacturer's Association, 18, 137
American shorthair (cat breed), 149–150
American Society for the Prevention of Cruelty to Animals (ASPCA), 29, 256, 346
amphibians. *See also specific species*
  choosing, 304
  feeding, 326
  handling, 336
  heat, light, bedding, and water, 312
anapsid.org (Web site), 40, 317
anesthesia, 56, 108
Animal Behavior Society (Web site), 134, 195
animal control agencies, 24
Animal Poison Control Center, ASPCA, 75, 99, 152, 171

animal shelters
  adoption process, 30–34
  basics, 21
  birds, 256
  cat temperament testing/information, 143, 145–146
  checking out the facility, 30–31
  cons, 27
  description, 23–24
  finding, 28–29
  funding of, 24, 25
  no-kill, 21, 26
  pet examination at, 31–32
  pros, 26–27
  recommendations, 29
  rescue groups, cooperation with, 24
  spaying/neutering pets, 94
  success of, 25
  supporting local, 345–346
  temperament testing, 58–59
  types, 24–26
  volunteering, 30, 345
anoles, 325, 335
antifreeze, 75
anxiety, 130–131, 133
arachnids. *See also* tarantulas
  adoption considerations, 20–21, 305–306
  feeding, 327
  housing, 311
  life span, 11
ARAV (Association of Reptilian and Amphibian Veterinarians), 319
ASPCA (American Society for the Prevention of Cruelty to Animals), 29, 256, 346
ASPCA Animal Poison Control Center, 75, 99, 152, 171
aspergillosis, 273
Association of Avian Veterinarians (AAV), 270, 271
Association of Pet Dog Trainers (Web site), 115

Association of Reptilian and Amphibian Veterinarians (ARAV), 319
attack behaviors in cats, 189–191
Avian Rescue (Web site), 40, 257
Avian Web (Web site), 40

• *B* •

bacterial infections, 272–273, 321
bark collar, 126
barking, 126
Bartlett, Patricia (*Reptiles & Amphibians For Dummies*), 2, 299, 304
bathing
  birds, 265, 280
  cats, 181–182
  dogs, 107
  small animals, 229–230
beak trimming, 280
bearded dragons, 325
bedding
  for birds, 265
  for reptiles, 312
  for small animals, 218
begging, by dogs, 129–130
behaviorist
  avian, 288
  dog, 134
  feline, 191, 194–195
Bird Adoption.org (Web site), 257
bird behavior
  by adolescents, 293
  aggression, 286–287
  behavior consultant, 288
  biting, 286–287
  bonding, 288–289
  chewing, 287
  fear and anxiety, 283–284
  feather picking, 273, 287–288
  mating season, 293–294
  noise, 285–286
  socialization, 288, 290
  solving problems, 282–288
  training, 289–293
  understanding, 281–282
bird diet
  balanced diet, 275–276
  best foods, 276–277
  converting to proper, 279–280

feeding frequency, 279
fresh food, 276
pelleted, 276
seed, 276
species-specific, 278
worst foods, 277–278
bird health
  bacterial infections, 272–273
  bumblefoot, 273
  diet, 275–280
  egg binding, 274
  feather picking, 273–274
  fungal infections, 273, 279
  gout, 273
  injuries, 272
  obesity, 273
  parasites, 272
  respiratory distress from environmental causes, 274
  veterinarian, choosing, 270–271
  veterinary visit, first, 271–272
  viral infections, 273
Bird Placement Program (Web site), 40, 257
bird species
  African grey, 253
  Amazon parrots, 253, 278
  blue-and-gold macaws, 252, 278
  blue-throated macaws, 278
  budgies, 278
  choosing, 250–251
  cockatiels, 255–256, 278
  cockatoos, 252, 278
  conures, 254
  doves, 255, 278
  eclectus parrots, 255
  fighting, 250
  green-winged macaws, 253, 278
  health and temperament, 251
  hyacinth macaws, 253, 278
  lories, 254, 278
  lorikeets, 278
  lovebirds, 254
  macaws, 252–253, 278
  military macaws, 253, 278
  parakeets, 255–256
  pigeons, 255, 278
  Quaker parakeets, 254
  species-specific diets, 278

bird supplies
  bedding, 265
  cage, 262–263, 264
  cage cover, 264
  cement perch, 265
  climbing devices, 264
  cuttlebone, 265
  food, 263
  nail trimmers, 265
  perch cleaner, 264
  perches, 263
  toys, 264
  travel carrier, 264
birdbath, 265, 280
bird-proofing your home, 259–261
birdrescue.com (Web site), 257
birds
  adoption considerations, general, 20
  bathing, 265
  bird-proofing your home, 259–261
  biting, 248, 252–256, 266, 286–287
  breeding prevention, 274–275
  cat introduction to, 162
  difficulties of, 247–249
  dog introduction to, 88
  feeding, 275–280
  finding for adoption, 256–257
  first-year costs, 13–14
  free-flying, 261–262
  grooming, 265, 280
  introducing to children, 267–268
  introducing to family, 267
  introducing to new home, 266–267
  introducing to other pets, 268
  life span, 11
  location, 293
  needs of adopted bird, 249–250
  nesting by, 275, 293–294
  rescue groups, 40
  signs of good health, 251
  supplies, 262–265
  transporting, 264, 266, 272
  understanding adopted bird, 248–249
  vocalizations, 247–248, 252–255, 285–286
  wing clipping, 261–262
bite inhibition, 129
biting
  by birds, 248, 252–256, 266, 286–287
  by cats, 189–191

  dealing with herp bites, 338
  by dogs, 129
  by small animals, 232–233
  by spiders, 305, 306
  by turtles, 335
bleeding, uncontrolled, 171
blue-and-gold macaws, 252, 278
blue-throated macaws, 278
boas, 300
body evaluation test, 103–104, 177
bonding, by birds, 288–289
Bordatella, 115
bowls, food and water, 77, 154, 218
breathing problems, in exotics, 321
breeders, 39
brushes, 77
brushing
  cats, 179
  dogs, 106
budgies, 278
bugs, 305–306, 311, 327
bumblefoot, 207, 273

caffeine, 175, 278
cage
  bird, 249–250, 261, 262–263, 264
  exotics, 309–311, 315
  small animal, 216–218
  travel, 264, 266, 315
cage cover, 264
calcium deficiency, 320
calicivirus, 168
Canine Good Citizen test, 115, 116
carrier, 153–154, 264, 272
cat behavior
  attack, 189–191
  climbing, 188–189
  escaping/wandering, 192
  evolution of, 141
  hunting, 185–186
  hyperactivity, 194
  interactions with other pets, 193–194
  redirecting, 188
  scratching and clawing, 186–188
  shyness and hiding, 191–192
  talking, 193

cat breeds
American shorthair, 149–150
Himalayan, 148
Maine coon, 150
mixed-breed cats, 146–147
Persians, 148–149
Siamese, 149
cat food
avoiding harmful foods, 174–175
choosing, 154, 173–174
dry, 174
free feeding, 175–176
meal feeding, 176
organic, 174
prescription, 173
price as indicator of quality, 174
raw diets, 174
switching, 175
cat grooming
bathing, 181–182
brushing, 179
combing, 179
drying, 182
as health-care checkup, 178–179
mats, 179
nail clipping, 179–181
shaving, 179
cat supplies
bed, 155–156, 157
bling-bling, 158
bowls, food and water, 154
carrier, 153–154
clothing, 158
grooming, 156–157
high-tech, 158
litter boxes and fillers, 154–155
scratching post, 156
toys, 157
trees, 156, 158, 189
catnip, 188
cat-proofing your home, 151–153
cats
acclimating to your home, 158–159
adjustment problems, 163
adoption considerations, general, 19
adult cat adoption, 139–140
annual exam, 172
attack behaviors, 189–191
behaviorist, animal, 194–195
birds and, 268
body evaluation test, 177
breeds, 146–150
catnip effect on, 188
cat-proofing your home, 151–153
climbing, 188–189
coat, 142
curiosity, 143
deworming, 168
emergencies, 171–172
escaping/wandering, 192
eyes, 142
feeding, 154, 172–178
feline immunodeficiency virus (FIV), 171
feline leukemia (FeLV), 170–171
feral, 138, 140–141
first-year costs, 13–14
giving run-of-the-house, 163
grooming, 178–182
healthcare, 165–172
hunting, 185–186
hyperactive, 194
interactions with other pets, 193–194
introducing to family, 159–160
introducing to other cats and dogs,
87–88, 160–162
introducing to small animals, birds, and
fish, 162
kitten adoption, 138–139
life span, 11
litter box location, 158–159
litter-box training, 183–185
long-haired, 147
mixed-breed, 146–147
parasites, 142, 169
personality, 143–145
pest control, 169
rescue groups, 39
scratching and clawing, 186–188
sex, choosing, 140
short-haired, 146–147
shyness and hiding, 191–192
signs of health, 141–143
sleeping arrangements, 155–156
spaying and neutering, 167–168
stray, 138, 140–141
supplies, 153–158
talking, 193
temperament testing, 143–146

toys, 190
training, 195–196
transporting, 153–154
urinary blockage, 172
vaccination, 168–169
veterinarian, choosing, 166
weight, 176–178
Cats For Dummies (Spadafori and Pion), 2
cavies. *See* guinea pigs
cavyrescue.com (Web site), 40, 211
cement perch, 265, 280
centipedes, giant, 305, 306, 312–313, 327
chew toys, 78, 249, 264
chewing
   by birds, 287–288
   destructive, 127–128
   by small animals, 234
children
   age, 202
   birds and, 267–268
   dog introduction to, 84
   exotics and, 315, 323
   introducing cat to, 159–160
   maturity level, 202
   responsibility, 202
   small animals and, 201–202, 220
Chinchilla Rescue (Web site), 211
chinchillas
   anesthesia sensitivity, 226
   basic facts, 209
   breeding prevention, 226
   dust bath, 225, 230
   enclosures, 217
   feeding, 229
   handling, 240
   health problems, 225
chlamydiosis, 273
chocolate, 75, 175, 278
choking hazards, 74
clawing behavior in cats, 186–188
clicker training, 118, 196, 289
climbing behavior in cats, 188–189
clothing, for cats, 158
coat conditioner, 79
cockatiels, 255–256, 278
cockatoos, 252, 278
cockroaches, 305, 306, 312–313, 327
collar, 77, 156

Colorado Herpetological Society
   (Web site), 317
colubrids, 301
combing
   cats, 179
   dogs, 106–107
Come cue, 119, 241
companion dogs, 67–68
complaints, from neighbors, 12
Congo African grey parrots, 253
constrictors, 300
contract, rescue, 47–48
conures, 254
corn snakes, 301
cost
   affording a pet, 13–14
   first-year, 13–14
   rescue group adoption fee, 48
crabs. *See* hermit crabs
crate, 77, 82–83
crate training, 112–113
crepuscular behavior, 235
curiosity, of cats, 143
cuttlebone, 265
Cyber-Pet (Web site), 346
cysts, 57

• D •

day-care centers, doggy, 113
declawing, 187
Delta Society (Web site), 116
den, dog, 81–83, 88–89
dental care, dog, 108
dewlaps, 334
deworming, 95
digging
   by dogs, 130–131
   by small animals, 234
dog behavior
   aggression, 131
   bad habits, breaking, 123–124
   barking, 126
   begging, 129–130
   chewing, 127–128
   digging, 130
   jumping up, 127
   in mistreated dogs, 133–134
   nipping and biting, 129

dog behavior *(continued)*
  praising good behavior, 124
  professional help, 134
  redirecting, 124
  separation anxiety, 130–131
  supervision, 124
  wandering, 125–126
dog breeds
  guardian, 68–69
  herding, 61, 72
  hounds, 61, 70–71
  northern, 61, 70
  sporting, 60, 69
  temperament, 59–61
  terriers, 61, 71
  toy, 61
  working, 60
dog food/feeding
  bad nutritional habits, 101
  BARF diet, 104
  choosing right food, 100–101
  homemade, 104
  transition, 101
  when to feed, 102
Dog Health and Nutrition For Dummies
  (Wiley), 100
dog trainers, 29
dog training
  basic training cues, 118–123
  buckle collars, 116
  Canine Good Citizen certification,
    115, 116
  classes, 114–116
  clicker training, 116–117, 118
  Come cue, 119
  crate, 112–113
  Down cue, 121–122
  Heel cue, 122–123
  housetraining, 110–114
  reward, 118–119
  Sit cue, 120
  socialization strategies, 116–117
  Stay cue, 121
  trainers, locating, 115
dogs
  adjustment problems, 89–90
  adoption considerations, general, 18–19
  adult dogs, 53–54

aggression, 131–132
bad habits, breaking, 123–124
behavior problems, managing, 125–130
birds and, 268
body evaluation test, 103–104
den, 81–83, 88–89
deworming, 95
downtime, 88–89
ears, 56
equipment/accessories, 76–79
eyes, 55–56
feeding, 99–102
first-year costs, 13–14
grooming, 79, 105–108
healthcare, 92–99
healthy signs of, 55–58
housetraining, 77, 80–81, 110–114
hybrid vigor, 65
introducing to adults, 83–84
introducing to cats, 87–88, 160–161
introducing to children, 84
introducing to other dogs, 85–87
introducing to small animals, 88
life span, 10–11
mistreated dog, managing, 133–134
mixed breeds, 64–66
nose, 56
parasites, 56–58, 93, 95–97
personality types, 63–64
potty spot, 80–81
puppies, adopting, 51–52
puppy-proofing your home, 73–76
purebred, 25
purebred dog breeds, 66–72
rescue groups, 39
separation anxiety, 130–131
sex, choosing, 54
skin and coat, 56–57
sleeping arrangements, 89
socialization, 85
spaying/neutering, 94
symptoms of illness, 98–99
teeth, 56, 108
temperament, 58–64
toys, 78, 79
training, 114–123
traveling with, 117
vaccinations, 94–95, 115–116

weight, 102–105
welcoming home, 80–89
dogs, purebred
adopting, 66–72
at animal shelters, 25
companion dogs, 67–68
guardian breeds, 68–69
health of, 65
herding, 72
information of, 67
northern, 70
rescue groups, 66
scenthounds, 71
sighthounds, 70
sporting, 69
terrier, 71
doves, 255, 278
Down training cue, 121–122
dust baths, for chinchillas, 225

• E •

ear infections, 56
ear mites, 56
eclectus parrots, 255
ectropion, 56
egg binding, 274
electrocution hazards, 74
enclosure. *See also* cage
exotic, 309–311
small animal, 215–218
entropion, 56
euthanasia, 21, 141
exercise equipment, for small animals, 218
exercise pen, 82
exotic pet health
abuse, signs of, 321
bacterial and fungal infections, 321
constipation and diarrhea, 321
environment, importance of, 318
feeding, 321–323, 324–327
malnutrition, 320
mites, 321
mouth rot, 321
signs of poor health, 321–323
veterinary care, 317, 318–320
exotic pet supplies
enclosures, 309–311
light, heat, bedding, and water, 311–313

outdoor housing, 314
supply list, 313
exotic pets. *See also specific species*
adoption considerations, general, 20–21
bites, dealing with, 338
bugs, 305–306
children and, 323
constrictors, 300
enclosures, 217, 311
escaped, locating, 309
feeding, 324–327
finding, 306
first-year costs, 13–14
frogs, 304
green iguanas, 301–302
handling, 332–337
hermit crabs, 305
herp-proofing your home, 307–308
hygiene and grooming, 327–328
introducing to other pets, 316
introducing to your home, 315–316
life span, 11
lizards, 303–304
newts, 304
picking a pet, 299–306
questions to ask yourself before
adoption, 298–299
rescue groups, 40
salamanders, 304
snakes, 300–301
supplies, 309–314
tamed, how to recognize, 330–331
taming, 330, 331
training, 329–331
transporting, 314–315
turtles, 302–303
eyelids, dog, 56
eyes, examining, 55–56, 142

• F •

fatty acids, 173, 227
favors you can do for your adopted pet,
343–344
fear, in cats, 191–192
feather picking, 273, 287–288
feathers, trimming, 262, 280
Fédération Cynologique Internationale
(Web site), 67

feline immunodeficiency virus (FIV), 141, 171
feline leukemia virus (FeLV), 141, 168, 170–171
Feline Rescue Network (Web site), 39
feline viral rhinotracheitis, 168
FeLV (feline leukemia virus), 141, 168, 170–171
fences, for dogs, 125–126
feral (wild) cats, 137, 140–141
Ferret Central (Web site), 40
ferrets
    attention requirements, 203
    biting behavior, 232–233
    boredom, 235
    cost, 204
    deafness, 204, 224
    enclosures, 216
    feeding, 227
    grooming, 229
    hand-taming, 239
    health problems, 224
    housing, 203
    introducing to new home, 220
    litter box, 219, 234
    litter-box training, 237–238
    neutering, 234
    odor, 204
    rescue groups, 40
    scruffing, 233
    sounds and behavior, understanding, 241–242
    spaying and neutering, 225
    special considerations, 204
    tattoo, 204
    tendency for trouble, 203
    time commitment, 203
Ferrets For Dummies (Schilling)
fish, cat introduction to, 162
FIV (feline immunodeficiency virus), 141, 171
Flash and Thelma Memorial Hedgehog Rescue (Web site), 211
flea comb, 156–157
fleas, 56, 57, 96–97, 142, 169
food/feeding. *See specific pet types*
Foster Parrots (Web site), 257
fostering, 37, 46, 345

frogs
    adoption considerations, 304
    feeding, 326
    handling, 336
    housing, 311, 312
Frontline, 97
fungal infections, 273, 321
FVRCP vaccinations, 168–169

• *G* •

garter snakes, 301
gerbils
    basic facts, 207
    behavior, 244
    breeding prevention, 226
    enclosures, 217
    feeding, 228
    grooming, 230
    hand-taming, 239
    health problems, 225
gout, 273
green iguanas. *See* iguanas
green-winged macaws, 253, 278
grooming
    birds, 265, 280
    disguised as a checkup, 105–106
    dogs, 79, 105–108
    exotics, 327–328
    products, 79
    small animals, 229–230
grooming supplies, for cats, 156–157
guardian breeds, 68–69
guinea pigs
    attention requirements, 205
    care and maintenance requirements, 205–206
    feeding, 228
    grooming, 229
    hand-taming, 239
    health problems, 224
    housing, 205, 216–217
    rescue groups, 40
    sounds and behavior, understanding, 243–244
    tendency for trouble, 206
    vocalization, 205

• H •

hairballs, in rabbits, 224, 229
hamsters
  basic facts, 207
  behavior, 244
  biting behavior, 233
  breeding prevention, 226
  enclosures, 217
  feeding, 228
  grooming, 230
  hand-taming, 239
  health problems, 225
hand-taming pocket pets, 239
harness, cat, 156, 158
heartworm, 93, 95–96
heatstroke, 117, 224
hedgehogs
  basic facts, 210
  enclosures, 217
  feeding, 228
  grooming, 230
  health problems, 225
  hibernation, 225
Heel training cue, 122
herding breeds, 61, 72
hermit crabs
  adoption considerations, 305
  feeding, 327
  handling, 337
  housing, 311, 313
Hermit Crabs For Dummies (Wilkins), 305
Herp Vet Connection (Web site), 319
herp-proofing your home, 307–308
herps. *See also* exotic pets
  bites, dealing with, 338
  enclosures, 309–311
  escaped, locating, 309
  hygiene and grooming, 327–328
  light, heat, bedding, and water, 311–312
  outdoor housing, 314
hibernation, hedgehog, 225
hiding
  by cats, 191–192
  by exotics, 322
  by small animals, 233
Himalayan (cat breed), 148
hot spots, 56, 57
hounds, 61, 70–71

House Rabbit Society (Web site), 40, 208, 211, 222
house visit, by rescue group, 44–45
houseplants, toxic, 152, 274
housetraining, dog
  associating word with, 111
  basics, 110–111
  choosing a potty spot, 80–81
  crate training, 112–113
  doggy day-care centers, 113
  lapses in, 110
  leash, use of, 110
  mistakes, dealing with, 113–114
  pet sitters, 113
  praise and reward, 110, 111
  punishment, 113–114
  schedule training, 113
  signs to look for, 110
  timing of, 111, 113
housing restrictions, 12–13
humane societies, 21, 24
Humane Society of the United States (HSUS), 21, 29, 66, 346
hunting behavior in cats, 185–186
hyacinth macaws, 253, 278
hyperactivity, 62–63, 194
hypothyroidism, 57

• I •

icons, used in book, 6
identification tags, 76–77, 156, 192
iguanas
  adoption considerations, 301–302
  feeding, 325
  handling, 334–335
  housing, 310, 311, 314
  sneezing, 323
Iguanas For Dummies (Kaplan), 334
insects, 305–306
intelligence, of small animals, 244
interview, rescue group, 42–44

• J •

jumping up, by dogs, 127

• K •

Kaplan, Melissa (*Iguanas For Dummies*), 334
kennel, 34, 48, 77, 82
kennel cough, 115
king snakes, 301
kittens. *See also* cats
    adoption of, 138–139
    cat-proofing your home, 151–153
    energy level of, 194
    litter box choice for, 154
    litter choice for, 155
    litter-box training, 183–185
    vaccination schedule, 168–169

• L •

Labrador Retrievers For Dummies (Walton and Adamson), 2
landlords, 12
laws, regarding pets, 12
leash, 77, 78, 158
leash-training cats, 192
leopard geckos, 303, 325
Leopard Geckos For Dummies (Palika), 303
life span chart, 10–11
litter, 155
litter box
    cats, 158–159, 183–185
    dog, 79
    ferrets, 219, 234, 237–238
    placement of, 158–159
    rabbits, 219, 234, 238–239
litter boxes and filler, 154–155
lizards
    adoption considerations, general, 20–21, 303–304
    feeding, 325
    handling, 334–335
    housing, 311, 312
    life span, 11
lories, 254, 278
lorikeets, 278
lovebirds, 254

• M •

macaws, 252–253, 278
Maine coon (cat breed), 150
malnutrition
    in dogs, 102
    in exotics, 320
mange mites, 56, 57, 97
metabolic bone disease, 320
mice
    basic facts, 208
    behavior, 244
    breeding prevention, 226
    enclosures, 217
    feeding, 228
    grooming, 230
    hand-taming, 239
    health problems, 225
microchip, 34, 76–77, 156
military macaws, 253, 278
mites
    in birds, 272
    ear, 56
    in exotics, 321, 327–328
    mange, 56, 57, 97
Moluccan cockatoos, 252
mosquitoes, 169
Moustaki, Nikki (*Parrots For Dummies*), 2, 250, 274, 293
mouth rot, 321

• N •

nail clipper, 77, 157, 180, 265
nail trimming
    birds, 280
    cats, 179–181
    dogs, 107–108
    ferret, 229
    rabbit, 230
names, pet, 10
National Alternative Pet Association (Web site), 346
National Animal Poison Control Center, 274, 308
neighbors, complaints from, 12
nesting, by birds, 293–294

Netpets Dog Rescue Groups (Web site), 39
neutering
    cat, 167–168
    discounts on, 168
    dogs, 94
    effect on aggression, 234
    ferret, 204, 225, 234
    rabbit, 225, 234
    reasons for, 341–342
    small animals, 225–226
newts, 304, 311, 312, 326
niacin, 173
nipping, by dogs, 129
nocturnal behavior, 199, 235
no-kill animal shelters, 21, 26
northern breeds, 61, 70
nutritional deficiencies, 173, 176

• *O* •

obedience classes, 114–116
obesity
    in birds, 273
    in cats, 175, 176–177
odor remover, 114
1-800-Save-A-Pet (Web site), 29, 211
onions, 75, 277

• *P* •

Pacheco's disease, 273
Palika, Liz
    Leopard Geckos For Dummies, 303
    Turtles & Tortoises For Dummies, 303, 336
panleukopenia, 168
parakeets, 255–256
parasites
    in birds, 272
    in cats, 142, 169
    in dogs, 56–57, 93
parrot fever, 273
parrots. *See also* birds
    African grey, 253
    Amazon, 253
    cockatoos, 252
    eclectus, 255
    macaws, 252–253

Parrots For Dummies (Moustaki), 2, 250, 274, 293
Pavia, Audrey *(Rabbits For Dummies),* 2
perch cleaner, 264
perches, 263
Perfect Pet Profile Quiz, 15–18
Persian (cat breed), 148–149
personality, cat, 143–145
pest control products, 169
Pet Profile Quiz, Perfect, 15–18
Pet Rescue.com (Web site), 346
pet sitters, 113
pet stores, 29, 306
Petfinder (Web site), 29, 39, 211, 256
Pets 911 (Web site), 29, 39, 211, 256
pheromones, 186–187
pigeons, 255, 278
Pion, Paul D. *(Cats For Dummies),* 2
plants, toxic, 152, 274
poisoning
    birds, 274
    cats, 152, 172
    dogs, 75
    herps, 308
    signs of, 152
polyomavirus, 273
pouncing behavior in cats, 189–191
ProCare Dental Gel, 108
psittacosis, 273
psitticine beak and feather disease, 273
punishment, 113–114, 289
puppies. *See also* dogs
    chew toys, 78
    choosing for adoption, 51–52
    den use, 82
    feeding, 100
    housetraining, 110–114
    puppy-proofing home, 74–76
    training classes for, 115
puppy vaccination schedule, 95
pythons, 300, 324

• *Q* •

Quaker parakeets, 254
quiz, Perfect Pet Profile, 15–18

• R •

rabbit.org (Web site), 40, 211
rabbits
  antibiotic sensitivity, 224
  basic facts, 205
  biting behavior, 233
  boredom, 235
  digging behavior, 234
  feeding, 228
  grooming, 229–230
  hand-taming, 239
  health problems, 224
  hutches and cages, 216
  introducing to new home, 220
  litter box, 219, 234, 238–239
  neutering, 234
  rescue groups, 40
  sounds and behavior, understanding, 242
  spaying and neutering, 225
  urine, 224
  wild, 208
Rabbits For Dummies (Pavia), 2
rabies vaccination, 94, 115, 168
ramps and stairs, for dogs, 79
Rat and Mouse Club Rescue (Web site), 40
Rat Rescue Association (Web site), 211
rat snakes, 301
RatRights (Web site), 40
rats
  attention requirements, 206
  behavior, 243
  biting behavior, 233
  enclosures, 216
  feeding, 228
  grooming, 230
  hand-taming, 239
  health problems, 225
  housing, 207
  tendency for trouble, 207
raw diets, 174
readiness for adoption, assessing
  affording a pet, 13–14
  creative-specific factors, 18–21
  housing restrictions, 12–13
  responsibility, 10
  special-needs pet, 22
  time commitment, 10–11

redirecting bad behavior, 124
Remember icon, 6
reptiles. *See also* exotic pets; *specific types*
  adoption considerations, general, 20–21
  enclosures, 310–311
  iguanas, 301–302
  life span, 11
  light, heat, bedding, and water, 311–312
  lizards, 303–304
  mites, 327–328
  rescue groups, 40
  turtles, 302–303
Reptiles & Amphibians For Dummies
    (Bartlett), 2, 299, 304
rescue contract, 47–48
rescue groups
  animal shelters, cooperation with, 24
  basics, 22
  birds, 256–257
  cat temperament testing/information,
    145–146
  cons, 38
  contacting, 41
  description, 35–36
  fees, 48
  finding, 38–40
  fostering, 37, 46
  house visit, 44–45
  interview, 42–44
  pet examination, 45–46
  pros, 36–37
  purebred, 66
  questions asked by, 42–44
  questions to ask, 41
  recommendations, 39, 46, 3937
  references, checking, 41–42
  rescue contract, 47–48
  screening process, 40–46
  starting, 346
  supporting local, 345–346
  Web sites, 39–40
Rescue Network (Web site), 40
respiratory infection, 56
retrovirus, 170
Rodent Club (Web site), 40
rodents. *See* small animals; *specific
    species*
ruffrider.com (Web site), 34, 48

• S •

salamanders, 304, 311. 312, 326
sandpaper perches, 280
sarcoma, vaccination-site, 169
scarlet macaws, 253
scenthounds, 71
schedule training, 113
Schilling, Kim (*Ferrets For* Dummies)
scorpions, 305, 306, 312–313, 327
scratching behavior in cats, 186–188,
    189–191
scratching posts, 156
screening process, rescue groups, 40–46
seat belt, dog, 77, 117
seed, 276
seizure, 99, 171
self-mutilation, by birds, 273–274, 287
separation anxiety, by dogs, 130
sexual behaviors, in small animals, 232
shampoo, 77, 79, 181
shedding, 323
shelters, for small animals, 219
shock collars, 126
shyness
    in cats, 191–192
    in dogs, 62
Siamese (cat breed), 149
sighthounds, 70
Sit training cue, 120
small animals. *See also specific types*
    adjustment problems, 220
    adoption considerations, general, 19–20
    appeal of, 200
    bedding, 218
    breeding, preventing, 225–226
    cat introduction to, 162
    children and, 201–202, 220
    chinchillas, 209
    choosing right type, 203–211
    considerations for adoption, 199–202
    critter-proofing your home, 214
    dog introduction to, 88
    enclosures, 215–218
    feeding, 227–229
    ferrets, 203–204
    finding adoptable, 210–211
    first-year costs, 13–14
    food, 218

free-roaming, 214–215
gerbils, 207
grooming, 229–230
guinea pigs, 205–206
hamsters, 207
handling, limits of, 219
hand-taming, 239
health problems, 222–223, 223–225
hedgehogs, 210
hunting by cats, 186
intelligence, 244
introducing to new home, 219–220
life span, 11
litter-box training, 237–239
mouse, 208
preparing home for, 213–215
rabbits, 205, 208
rats, 206–207
rescue groups, 40
signs of illness, 226–227
sounds and movements, interpreting,
    241–244
supplies, 215–219
training, 236–241
veterinarian, finding, 222–223
when to avoid, 201
small animals behavior
    accepting unchangeable, 235
    age of adopted animal, effect of, 231–232
    aggression, 233–234
    biting, 232–233
    chewing and digging, 234
    elimination, 234
    excess energy, 234
    hiding, 233
    physical problems and, 236
    sexual, 232
    sounds and movements, interpreting,
        241–244
snakes. *See also* exotic pets
    adoption considerations, general, 20–21
    constrictors, 300
    enclosures, 310–311
    feeding, 324
    handling, 332–334
    life span, 11
    small species, 301
    Stargazer's disease, 322

socialization
  bird, 288–289, 290
  dog, 85, 116–117
soft paws (claw covers), 188
Southern California Rabbit and Small
    Animal Rescue Association
    (Web site), 211
Spadafori, Gina *(Cats For Dummies)*, 2
spaying
  cat, 167–168
  discounts on, 168
  dogs, 94
  ferrets, 225
  rabbits, 225
  reasons for, 341–342
  small animals, 225–226
special-needs pet, 22, 31, 141
spiders, 305–306, 312–313, 326, 336.
    See also tarantulas
sporting breeds, 60, 69
spot-on treatment, 97
stain removal, 114
Stargazer's disease, 322
Stay training cue, 121
Step-up (training cue), 291–292
strangulation hazards, 74
stray cats, 137, 140–141
submissive urination, 46
sulfur-crested cockatoos, 252

• T •

tarantulas
  adoption considerations, 305–306
  feeding, 327
  mites, 328
  taming, 336–337
tartar, 56, 108
taurine, 173
tear stains, 55, 107
teeth
  cleaning, 108
  dog, 56
  overgrown or misaligned, 223, 224
  small animal, 223, 224

temperament
  assessing at animal shelter, 31
  birds, 251
  cat, 143–146
  dog's, 58–64
temperament, dog
  bad, 59
  basics, 62–63
  breeds and, 59–61
  chill-outers, 63
  go-getters, 63
  health problems and, 58
  personality types, 63–64
  testing, 58–64
  wait-and-seers, 64
  warning signs, 62–63
terriers, 61, 71, 88
theobromine, 175
Therapy Dogs International (Web site), 116
ticks, 56, 57, 96–97, 169, 328
Timneh African grey parrots, 253
Tip icon, 6
titer tests, 94
toads, handling, 336
toxins, cat-specific, 152
toy breeds, 61
toys
  bird, 264
  for birds, 249
  for cats, 157
  dog, 78, 79
trainer, dog, 29, 115, 134
training, bird
  cage-free manners, 292–293
  clicker training, 289
  description, 289
  hand-training, 290–291
  shoulder behavior, 292
  socialization, 290
  step-up cue, 291–292
training, cat
  clicker training, 196
  leash-training, 192
  litter-box, 183–185
  obedience, 195–196

training, dog
  basic training cues, 118–123
  buckle collars, 116
  Canine Good Citizen certification, 115, 116
  classes, 114–116
  clicker training, 116–117, 118
  Come cue, 119
  crate, 112–113
  Down cue, 121–122
  Heel cue, 122–123
  housetraining, 110–114
  reward, 118–119
  Sit cue, 120
  socialization strategies, 116–117
  Stay cue, 121
  trainers, locating, 115
training, exotics, 329–331
training, small animals
  come on cue, 241
  description, 236–237
  hand-taming, 239–240
  litter-box training ferrets, 237–238
  litter-box training rabbits, 238–239
transporting
  birds, 264, 266, 272
  exotics, 314–315
  pets, general, 34, 48, 117
trash, 74–75
traveling with your pet, 153
tumors, 57
tunnels, for small animals, 219
turtles
  adoption considerations, 302–303
  biting, 335
  feeding, 326
  handling, 335
  housing, 311, 314
Turtles & Tortoises For Dummies (Palika), 303, 336

umbrella cockatoos, 252
United Kennel Club (Web site), 67
urinary blockage, 172

• V •

vaccinations
  cat, 168–169
  dog, 94–95, 115–116
  sarcoma from, 169
vegetarian diet, 173
veterinarian
  animal shelter recommendations from, 29
  annual exam for cats, 172
  annual exam for dogs, 99
  avian, 262, 270–272
  choosing for cat, 166
  choosing for dog, 92
  deworming cats, 168
  emergency availability, 171, 320
  examination by prior to adoption, 31, 55
  exotic pets, 317, 318–320
  first exam for cat, 166–169
  first exam for dog, 93
  preparing dog for visit, 93
  rescue group recommendations, 39
  separation anxiety treatment, 131
  for small animals, 221–223
  spaying/neutering cats, 167–168
  vaccinations for cats, 168–169
vinegar, white, 114
viral infections, in birds, 273
vitamin A, 173, 273, 320
vitamin C, 228
vocalization
  bird, 247–248, 252–255, 285–286
  cat, 193
  ferret, 241
  guinea pig, 243
  rabbit, 242
volunteering, 30, 37, 345

• W •

Walton, Joel (*Labrador Retrievers For Dummies*), 2
Warning! icon, 6
water bottle, 218

Web sites
  altpet.net, 40
  American Dog Owner's Association,
    Inc., 346
  American Ferret Association, 40, 211
  American Kennel Club, 39, 67, 116
  American Society for the Prevention
    of Cruelty to Animals (ASPCA),
    29, 256, 346
  anapsid.org, 40, 317
  Animal Behavior Society, 134, 195
  animal shelters, 28–29
  ASPCA Animal Poison Control Center, 75
  Association of Avian Veterinarians
    (AAV), 271
  Association of Pet Dog Trainers, 115
  Association of Reptilian and Amphibian
    Veterinarians (ARAV), 319
  Avian Rescue, 40, 257
  Avian Web, 40
  Bird Adoption.org, 257
  Bird Placement Program, 40, 257
  birdrescue.com, 257
  cavyrescue.com, 40, 211
  Chinchilla Rescue, 211
  Colorado Herpetological Society, 317
  Cyber-Pet, 346
  Delta Society, 116
  Fédération Cynologique Internationale, 67
  Feline Rescue Network, 39
  Ferret Central, 40
  Flash and Thelma Memorial Hedgehog
    Rescue, 211
  Foster Parrots, 257
  Herp Vet Connection, 319

  House Rabbit Society, 40, 208, 211, 222
  Humane Society of the United States
    (HSUS), 29, 346
  National Alternative Pet Association, 346
  Netpets Dog Rescue Groups, 39
  1-800-Save-A-Pet, 29, 211
  Pet Rescue.com, 346
  Petfinder, 29, 211, 256
  Pets 911, 29, 39, 211, 256
  rabbit.org, 40, 211
  Rat and Mouse Club Rescue, 40
  Rat Rescue Association, 211
  RatRights, 40
  rescue groups, 39–40
  Rescue Network, 40
  Rodent Club, 40
  ruffrider.com, 34, 48
  Southern California Rabbit and Small
    Animal Rescue Association, 211
  Therapy Dogs International, 116
  United Kennel Club, 67
  World Animal Net, 29
Wiley Publishing, Inc. *(Dog Health and
    Nutrition For Dummies)*, 100
Wilkins, Kelli A. *(Hermit Crabs For
    Dummies)*, 305
wing clipping, 261–262
working breeds, 60
World Animal Net (Web site), 29
worms, parasitic, 58, 93, 95, 272

yeast infections, in birds, 273, 279

BUSINESS, CAREERS & PERSONAL FINANCE

0-7645-5307-0

0-7645-5331-3 *†

Also available:
- Accounting For Dummies †
  0-7645-5314-3
- Business Plans Kit For Dummies †
  0-7645-5365-8
- Cover Letters For Dummies
  0-7645-5224-4
- Frugal Living For Dummies
  0-7645-5403-4
- Leadership For Dummies
  0-7645-5176-0
- Managing For Dummies
  0-7645-1771-6

- Marketing For Dummies
  0-7645-5600-2
- Personal Finance For Dummies *
  0-7645-2590-5
- Project Management For Dummies
  0-7645-5283-X
- Resumes For Dummies †
  0-7645-5471-9
- Selling For Dummies
  0-7645-5363-1
- Small Business Kit For Dummies *†
  0-7645-5093-4

HOME & BUSINESS COMPUTER BASICS

0-7645-4074-2

0-7645-3758-X

Also available:
- ACT! 6 For Dummies
  0-7645-2645-6
- iLife '04 All-in-One Desk Reference
  For Dummies
  0-7645-7347-0
- iPAQ For Dummies
  0-7645-6769-1
- Mac OS X Panther Timesaving
  Techniques For Dummies
  0-7645-5812-9
- Macs For Dummies
  0-7645-5656-8

- Microsoft Money 2004 For Dummies
  0-7645-4195-1
- Office 2003 All-in-One Desk Reference
  For Dummies
  0-7645-3883-7
- Outlook 2003 For Dummies
  0-7645-3759-8
- PCs For Dummies
  0-7645-4074-2
- TiVo For Dummies
  0-7645-6923-6
- Upgrading and Fixing PCs For Dummies
  0-7645-1665-5
- Windows XP Timesaving Techniques
  For Dummies
  0-7645-3748-2

FOOD, HOME, GARDEN, HOBBIES, MUSIC & PETS

0-7645-5295-3

0-7645-5232-5

Also available:
- Bass Guitar For Dummies
  0-7645-2487-9
- Diabetes Cookbook For Dummies
  0-7645-5230-9
- Gardening For Dummies *
  0-7645-5130-2
- Guitar For Dummies
  0-7645-5106-X
- Holiday Decorating For Dummies
  0-7645-2570-0
- Home Improvement All-in-One
  For Dummies
  0-7645-5680-0

- Knitting For Dummies
  0-7645-5395-X
- Piano For Dummies
  0-7645-5105-1
- Puppies For Dummies
  0-7645-5255-4
- Scrapbooking For Dummies
  0-7645-7208-3
- Senior Dogs For Dummies
  0-7645-5818-8
- Singing For Dummies
  0-7645-2475-5
- 30-Minute Meals For Dummies
  0-7645-2589-1

INTERNET & DIGITAL MEDIA

0-7645-1664-7

0-7645-6924-4

Also available:
- 2005 Online Shopping Directory
  For Dummies
  0-7645-7495-7
- CD & DVD Recording For Dummies
  0-7645-5956-7
- eBay For Dummies
  0-7645-5654-1
- Fighting Spam For Dummies
  0-7645-5965-6
- Genealogy Online For Dummies
  0-7645-5964-8
- Google For Dummies
  0-7645-4420-9

- Home Recording For Musicians
  For Dummies
  0-7645-1634-5
- The Internet For Dummies
  0-7645-4173-0
- iPod & iTunes For Dummies
  0-7645-7772-7
- Preventing Identity Theft For Dummies
  0-7645-7336-5
- Pro Tools All-in-One Desk Reference
  For Dummies
  0-7645-5714-9
- Roxio Easy Media Creator For Dummies
  0-7645-7131-1

* Separate Canadian edition also available
† Separate U.K. edition also available

SPORTS, FITNESS, PARENTING, RELIGION & SPIRITUALITY

0-7645-5146-9

0-7645-5418-2

Also available:

- Adoption For Dummies
  0-7645-5488-3
- Basketball For Dummies
  0-7645-5248-1
- The Bible For Dummies
  0-7645-5296-1
- Buddhism For Dummies
  0-7645-5359-3
- Catholicism For Dummies
  0-7645-5391-7
- Hockey For Dummies
  0-7645-5228-7

- Judaism For Dummies
  0-7645-5299-6
- Martial Arts For Dummies
  0-7645-5358-5
- Pilates For Dummies
  0-7645-5397-6
- Religion For Dummies
  0-7645-5264-3
- Teaching Kids to Read For Dummies
  0-7645-4043-2
- Weight Training For Dummies
  0-7645-5168-X
- Yoga For Dummies
  0-7645-5117-5

TRAVEL

0-7645-5438-7

0-7645-5453-0

Also available:

- Alaska For Dummies
  0-7645-1761-9
- Arizona For Dummies
  0-7645-6938-4
- Cancún and the Yucatán For Dummies
  0-7645-2437-2
- Cruise Vacations For Dummies
  0-7645-6941-4
- Europe For Dummies
  0-7645-5456-5
- Ireland For Dummies
  0-7645-5455-7

- Las Vegas For Dummies
  0-7645-5448-4
- London For Dummies
  0-7645-4277-X
- New York City For Dummies
  0-7645-6945-7
- Paris For Dummies
  0-7645-5494-8
- RV Vacations For Dummies
  0-7645-5443-3
- Walt Disney World & Orlando For Dummies
  0-7645-6943-0

GRAPHICS, DESIGN & WEB DEVELOPMENT

0-7645-4345-8

0-7645-5589-8

Also available:

- Adobe Acrobat 6 PDF For Dummies
  0-7645-3760-1
- Building a Web Site For Dummies
  0-7645-7144-3
- Dreamweaver MX 2004 For Dummies
  0-7645-4342-3
- FrontPage 2003 For Dummies
  0-7645-3882-9
- HTML 4 For Dummies
  0-7645-1995-6
- Illustrator CS For Dummies
  0-7645-4084-X

- Macromedia Flash MX 2004 For Dummies
  0-7645-4358-X
- Photoshop 7 All-in-One Desk Reference For Dummies
  0-7645-1667-1
- Photoshop CS Timesaving Techniques For Dummies
  0-7645-6782-9
- PHP 5 For Dummies
  0-7645-4166-8
- PowerPoint 2003 For Dummies
  0-7645-3908-6
- QuarkXPress 6 For Dummies
  0-7645-2593-X

NETWORKING, SECURITY, PROGRAMMING & DATABASES

0-7645-6852-3

0-7645-5784-X

Also available:

- A+ Certification For Dummies
  0-7645-4187-0
- Access 2003 All-in-One Desk Reference For Dummies
  0-7645-3988-4
- Beginning Programming For Dummies
  0-7645-4997-9
- C For Dummies
  0-7645-7068-4
- Firewalls For Dummies
  0-7645-4048-3
- Home Networking For Dummies
  0-7645-42796

- Network Security For Dummies
  0-7645-1679-5
- Networking For Dummies
  0-7645-1677-9
- TCP/IP For Dummies
  0-7645-1760-0
- VBA For Dummies
  0-7645-3989-2
- Wireless All In-One Desk Reference For Dummies
  0-7645-7496-5
- Wireless Home Networking For Dummies
  0-7645-3910-8